Y0-BYE-964

# REASONS FOR ACTION

What are our reasons for acting? Morality purports to give us these reasons, and so do norms of prudence and the laws of society. The theory of practical reason assesses the authority of these potentially competing claims, and for this reason philosophers with a wide range of interests have converged on the topic of reasons for action. This volume contains eleven new essays on practical reason by leading and emerging philosophers. Topics include the differences between practical and theoretical rationality, practical conditionals and the wide-scope "ought," the explanation of action, the sources of reasons, and the relationship between morality and reasons for action. The volume will be essential reading for all philosophers interested in ethics and practical reason.

DAVID SOBEL is Robert R. Chambers Distinguished Professor of Philosophy at the University of Nebraska–Lincoln.

STEVEN WALL is Associate Professor in the Department of Philosophy, University of Connecticut.

# REASONS FOR ACTION

Edited by

DAVID SOBEL
*University of Nebraska*
and
STEVEN WALL
*University of Connecticut*

CAMBRIDGE UNIVERSITY PRESS
Cambridge, New York, Melbourne, Madrid, Cape Town, Singapore, São Paulo, Delhi

Cambridge University Press
The Edinburgh Building, Cambridge CB2 8RU, UK

Published in the United States of America by Cambridge University Press, New York

www.cambridge.org
Information on this title: www.cambridge.org/9780521877466



First published 2009

Printed in the United Kingdom at the University Press, Cambridge

*A catalogue record for this publication is available from the British Library*

*Library of Congress Cataloging-in-Publication Data*

Reasons for action / edited by David Sobel and Steven Wall.
p. cm.
Includes bibliographical references and index.
ISBN 978-0-521-87746-6 (hardback)
1. Practical reason. 2. Ethics. I. Sobel, David. II. Wall, Steven, 1967–

BC177.R3447 2009
170′.42–dc22

2008054457

ISBN 978-0-521-87746-6 hardback

# *Contents*

# *Notes on the contributors*

**Michael E. Bratman**
Durfee Professor in the School of Humanities and Sciences and Professor of Philosophy, Stanford University

**Ruth Chang**
Associate Professor of Philosophy, Rutgers University

**Philip Clark**
Associate Professor of Philosophy, University of Toronto

**Justin D'Arms**
Professor of Philosophy, Ohio State University

**Stephen Darwall**
Professor of Philosophy, Yale University

**James Dreier**
Professor of Philosophy, Brown University

**Daniel Jacobson**
Associate Professor of Philosophy, Bowling Green State University

**Peter Railton**
John Stephenson Perrin Professor, Department of Philosophy, University of Michigan

**Joseph Raz**
Professor, Columbia University School of Law and Research Professor, Oxford University

**Michael Ridge**
Professor of Moral Philosophy, University of Edinburgh

**Michael Smith**
Professor of Philosophy, Princeton University

**David Sobel**
Robert R. Chambers Professor of Philosophy, University of Nebraska–Lincoln

**Steven Wall**
Associate Professor of Philosophy, University of Connecticut

**Gary Watson**
Professor of Philosophy, University of California, Riverside

# *Acknowledgments*

Most of the essays assembled in this volume were presented at the conference on Practical Reason at Bowling Green State University in 2006. We are very grateful to the Department of Philosophy at Bowling Green and to the Social Philosophy and Policy Center for generous funding which was necessary for making this conference and the resulting volume actual. We are also grateful to the contributors for being willing to join in this project, being so easy to work with, and for producing such excellent essays. Finally we are grateful to all those that helped us run the conference and produce the volume, especially Margy DeLuca, Nicholas Maloberti, Fred Miller, Ian Young, the philosophy graduate students at Bowling Green, Ralph Wedgwood, and Hilary Gaskin.

CHAPTER I

# *Introduction*

*David Sobel and Steven Wall*

Philosophical reflection on practical reason and practical rationality is expanding in all directions. The work being done under these headings has become so broad and diverse that it is difficult to say much useful about the whole area. We will not try. Rather we shall pick a few points of entry into the discussions and try to situate some of the chapters in this volume within these frameworks.

## PRACTICAL AND THEORETICAL RATIONALITY

Normative reasons are facts that count in favor of doing some action, believing some claim, or having some attitude or emotion. Rationality refers to a capacity to recognize and respond appropriately to these facts (or one's take on these facts). There can be more or less demanding standards of rationality. On a common view, a person acts rationally if she does something that, were her beliefs true, she would have sufficient reason to do. On this view, what it is rational for a person to do depends on her beliefs.[1] This brings out an important dependence of practical rationality on theoretical rationality.

It is natural to wonder how significant are the differences between practical and theoretical rationality. Recently, some philosophers have argued that the differences are not as significant as they first appear. The demands of practical rationality, they argue, can be explained in terms of the requirements of theoretical rationality.[2] A less radical view of this kind holds that certain important requirements of practical rationality can be explained in terms of the requirements of theoretical rationality, even if all of the demands of practical rationality cannot be so explained.

[1] Parfit (1997): 99. But seemingly in some cases the irrationality of the belief can affect the rationality of the action based on the belief.

[2] See, for example, Velleman (2000).

For example, a number of philosophers have recently argued that the instrumental rationality (IR) requirement, which certainly looks to be a requirement of practical rationality, is in fact best understood as a requirement of theoretical rationality.[3]

In his contribution to this volume, Michael Bratman (chapter 2) challenges this latter view, which he refers to as "cognitivism about instrumental rationality." The cognitivist about instrumental rationality seeks to show that the requirement of instrumental rationality – the requirement that if I intend an end, believe that a necessary means to the end is M, and believe that M requires that I intend M, then, barring no change to these beliefs, I must either intend M or give up the end – is an instance of the belief-closure requirement on theoretical reason. The belief-closure requirement holds that if I believe an end, and believe that the end will occur only if M, then, barring a change in either of these two beliefs, I must believe M. In response, Bratman presents a number of examples in which an agent satisfies the belief-closure requirement, but fails to satisfy the instrumental rationality requirement. These examples suggest that the instrumental rationality requirement demands more than consistency between beliefs. Bratman concludes that it is best understood as an internal norm that applies to planning agents, a norm that agents need to be guided by if they are to successfully coordinate and control action.

Means-end and belief-closure requirements are demands of rationality. An adequate understanding of the differences between theoretical rationality and practical rationality plainly requires an understanding of the nature and differences between reasons for action and reasons for belief. Joseph Raz discusses some of these differences in his contribution to this volume (chapter 3). Reasons for belief, in one sense, can be practical reasons. Suppose one will be given a large sum of money if one believes that the Red Sox will win the next World Series. Then one will have a practical reason to acquire this belief. But reasons for belief, on a more standard understanding, refer to considerations that are truth-related. If some consideration counts in favor of the truth of a belief, then it is a reason for that belief. Raz refers to these truth-related reasons for belief as epistemic reasons. He then discusses the differences between reasons for action and epistemic reasons, perhaps the most basic of which is that epistemic reasons, unlike reasons for action, are not related to values. As

[3] See Harman (1976); Wallace (2001); Setiya (2007).

Raz explains, it is not the case that having true beliefs is always of value or that having false beliefs is always of disvalue. Much of Raz's essay is concerned with exploring the implications of the idea that epistemic reasons are not value-related. They form part of a class of reasons which Raz terms "adaptive." These are reasons to have attitudes that are appropriate in the sense that they track how things are.

The distinction between practical and adaptive reasons, Raz claims, has important consequences. It shows that normativity cannot be explained by value. Adaptive reasons for an attitude are normative reasons, but they are unrelated to value. It also illuminates the contrast between practical and epistemic reasons. A practical reason to have a belief is not a reason that can be followed. It is, in Raz's terms, a non-standard reason. By contrast, an epistemic reason is an adaptive reason and one that can be followed. A so-called conflict between a practical reason to believe p and an epistemic reason to believe not p is not a genuine conflict. The two kinds of reason do not compete. If an agent follows the reasons that apply to her in this kind of case, then the epistemic reason will win out. But it does not prevail because it overrides or cancels the opposing practical reason.

## THE GROUNDS OF PRACTICAL REASON

Practical reasons for actions are facts that count in favor of these actions. But what, if anything, grounds these facts? A central debate in discussions of practical reason is over what makes it the case that a person has reason to do one thing and not another. We will discuss the answer to this question that is offered by subjectivism, Kantian rationalism, neo-Aristotelianism, non-metaphysical, non-reductive normative realism, non-cognitivism, and error theory. We will then situate the views of some of the contributors to this volume with respect to these positions. The positions we outline below are not by any means exhaustive. But they do sketch a map of much of the most densely occupied territory.

Subjective accounts of practical reasons are worth keeping distinct from both internalism and Kantian accounts. The thesis Stephen Darwall has labeled "existence internalism" insists on a necessary condition for a consideration to provide an agent with a reason.[4] Bernard Williams' version of internalism held that one only has a reason to ο if one could

[4] Darwall (1983): 55.

arrive at a pro-attitude or motivation to o via sound deliberation.[5] Since internalism specifies a necessary precondition, rather than a constitutive condition, it is compatible with the thought that the relevant desire or motivation merely tracks independently grounded facts about our reasons. Subjectivism claims that the relevant sort of rationally contingent desires grounds the correctness of claims in a normative domain. The vast majority of the most influential versions of subjectivism have held that it is an agent's radically informed desires, and not other sorts of desires, that determine that agent's reasons. Similar subjectivist accounts of well-being have also found favor.

Like subjectivists, Kantian rationalist accounts of practical reason claim that a privileged kind of non-truth-assessable attitude grounds one's reasons. Kantians unite with subjectivists in rejecting the thought that a response-independent reality grounds reasons and embrace the thought that agents confer value via their coherent attitudes. But on the Kantian view, ideal rationality significantly constrains what is desired or willed in the authoritative way and this will make the grounding desires or willings unresponsive, or only derivitatively responsive, to the contingent motivational sets of the agent. Rather the authoritative attitude will be determined by what an ideally rational and coherent agent necessarily wants. Michael Smith's admirably clear Kantian account of reasons for action, for example, maintains that convergence in the desires of all possible ideally rational agents is a prerequisite for anyone having reasons to do anything.[6] Perhaps the clearest way to see the contrast between Kantian and subjectivist accounts is in what each says about immoral ends. Kantian accounts paradigmatically maintain that desires for immoral options necessarily contain hidden contradictions or incoherencies and would not exist in ideally rational agents. Subjectivists maintain that desires for immoral options at best contingently contain self-contradictions or incoherencies and thus allow that some possible agents have good reason to behave immorally. Subjectivists and Kantians maintain that there are truths about our reasons, but that these truths are fundamentally unlike the sort that exists on the theoretical side where there are pre-existing facts and these facts – barring special cases such as theoretical facts about an agent's psychology – are not made true by facts about what goes on in any actual or hypothetical person's mind.[7]

[5] Williams (1981).
[6] Smith (1994).
[7] See Korsgaard (1996b).

Neo-Aristotelian accounts diverge from Kantian accounts by allowing that our reasons, even our moral reasons, are generated by contingent features of agency. However these views also diverge from subjectivism as they maintain that the contingent features of agency that ground (at least an important class of) reasons are not the agent's desires but rather her species membership or life-form. Such views derive inspiration from Aristotle's function argument which held that we should look to the nature of the kind of thing we are assessing to understand how it ought to be.[8]

Non-reductive normative realists, on the other hand, maintain that there are *sui generis* normative facts which set standards for what we ought to want and do in something like the way facts about the external world determine what we ought to believe. This view need not accept the Platonist claim that such *sui generis* facts exist in some non-spatiotemporal realm.[9] Yet, just as facts about the properties of flowers are not made true by anyone thinking something, so facts about our reasons have the same sort of independence from our take on the situation.[10] Such a view need not deny that some of our reasons for action have subjective conditions.[11] The view is non-reductive in that it maintains that the normative is not reducible to non-normative facts. T.M. Scanlon writes that "the judgment that such a proposition would, if it were true . . ., . . . be a *good* reason for some action or belief contains an element of normative force which resists identification with any proposition about the natural world."[12]

Contemporary expressivism has its origin in emotivism. As originally developed, emotivism was a thesis about morality, not all of the normative. Emotivists combined two conceptually distinct thoughts: (1) that moral claims are not truth-apt and (2) that moral claims give vent to a non-cognitive attitude. Some of the pressures towards emotivism seem limited to the moral case while other such pressures press outward to encompass the whole of the normative. Contemporary expressivists have tended to expand the thesis to include the whole of the normative.[13] And they have found claim (1) above more negotiable so long as it is conceded that a normative claim is primarily to be understood to be expressing a conative attitude. Realists, too, have found that (1) and (2) above need not

[8] See Foot (2001): 2–3. See also Hursthouse (1999); Thompson (1995).

[9] The label for this position we take from Parfit (2001): 17–39. See also Parfit (forthcoming).

[10] Shafer-Landau (2003).

[11] See Scanlon (1998, 2002).

[12] Scanlon (1998): 57.

[13] See, among others, Gibbard (1990).

form a bundle and have argued that their position is compatible with (2) above suitably understood.[14]

Error theorists, such as J.L. Mackie who first introduced the view, remind us that it is one thing to understand the central presuppositions of a discourse – what would have to be true for that discourse to be in good order – and another thing to vindicate those presuppositions.[15] Error theorists argue that nothing can live up to the strong presuppositions involved in moral discourse. For example, if it were thought that to live up to the term "morality" something had to move all rational agents regardless of their desires, and one held that what rationally moves one is a function of one's rationally contingent desires, then one might conclude that moral claims are an attempt to describe the way the world is, but systematically fail to do so accurately. So nothing can meet the high standards that would have to be met for something to be a genuine moral requirement. Positive moral claims are truth-apt, but they are never true. Positive moral assertions, according to error theorists, are all false. Some motivations for error theory would limit the thesis, as Mackie did, to moral discourse. Others suggest that extending the view to cover the whole of normative reasons discourse is a live possibility. Again think of Smith, who maintains that if there is not convergence in the desires ideally rational agents would have, as he allows may be the case, all positive normative reasons claims would be false.

Philip Clark (chapter 10) aims to highlight the force of Mackie's original argument for being an error theorist about morality and to demonstrate that this argument is immune to prevalent objections to it. For example, many have thought that Mackie's argument must controversially assume judgment internalism about moral judgments. Clark argues that Mackie's case can be re-stated without this assumption and still remain quite forceful. Clark argues that Mackie could accept the possibility of amoralists – those who make sincere moral judgments but are not moved by them, thus rejecting judgment internalism. Mackie's good point would then be that moralists – those who think that morality does necessarily provide reasons regardless of one's desires – have a false view. And this view is false for the reason Mackie originally outlined, namely that there are no objective values that we all ought to promote regardless of our desires. So, Clark argues, if Mackie has made a good case against objective values, his error theory about the moral point of view is

[14] See, for example, Copp (2001).
[15] Mackie (1977).

in good order without needing the strong assumption of judgment internalism.

Michael Ridge's essay (chapter 11) is an instance of the recent trend of expressivists pressing outward the scope of their thesis beyond the moral. His chapter also follows the recent pattern of realists and expressivists attempting to help themselves to their opponent's good points while still maintaining the boundaries of their respective positions enough so that the positions remain importantly distinct. Ridge hopes to show how the expressivist can continue to say that normative claims centrally express a conative attitude of approval or disapproval, but also express a belief. Ridge hopes to show how these thoughts can peacefully co-exist in a way that vindicates expressivism over realism without marrying the fortunes of expressivism to deflationism about truth. Ridge finds that differentiating senses of what counts as a belief helps us see how this fancy trick can be pulled off.

Ruth Chang's essay (chapter 12) explores the prospects for maintaining that there are fundamentally different sources of our reasons. She maintains that none of the traditional accounts of reason offers a story which can plausibly account for all of our reasons. Chang maintains that, take what fundamental account of reasons you like, when reasons of that type run out we are frequently capable of giving ourselves voluntarist reasons to choose one of the options that our fundamental reasons did not rule out. So subjectivism or non-reductive normative realism might provide the truth of our "given" reasons with which our voluntarist reasons cannot compete. But, she argues, we can best understand several features of our reasons if we accept that we have the power to create reasons when our given reasons run out.

## PRACTICAL REASON AND MORALITY

We have been discussing the nature of practical reason in general. Several contributors to this volume address one particularly important class of practical reasons; namely, those that concern morality. Many have held that moral reasons for action are especially stringent. Moral reasons override or defeat opposing reasons for action. Others have held that moral reasons for action are incomparable with other kinds of practical reasons, such as those that concern what would best advance a person's own interests. Both of these views assume that moral reasons for action form a distinct category of reasons for action.

There are, to be sure, different ways of classifying certain reasons for action as moral reasons. These classifications depend on the context or purposes of the classifier. But the above views suggest that there is a deeper, and philosophically more important, divide between moral and non-moral reasons for action. It is an important question in the theory of practical reason whether there is any such divide; and, if there is, what best accounts for it.

Stephen Darwall argues that there is a distinctive kind of reason for acting, a kind he refers to as second-personal, that is an essential component of fundamental moral concepts, such as moral rights, moral responsibility, and moral obligation. Second-personal reasons for action, unlike other kinds of practical reasons, are conceptually linked to authoritative claims and demands. These are claims and demands that can be addressed to those to whom they apply. The appeal to second-personal reasons for acting, then, might provide a way to account for the distinctiveness of moral reasons. Of course, as Darwall allows, there can be agent-neutral reasons to bring about good states of affairs. These reasons are not second-personal. But agent-neutral reasons, if Darwall is right, cannot give rise to moral demands. Or, to put the point more precisely, agent-neutral reasons can give rise to moral demands only by also being considerations that persons can authoritatively demand that one another observe.

A natural challenge to Darwall's view holds that the authority to make claims and demands on others can be fully explained without recourse to second-personal reasons. Suppose, for example, that it is possible to explain adequately how one person could have practical authority with respect to another person without invoking second-personal reasons. This would show that the second-personal character of authority is not fundamental. It also would suggest that second-personal reasons for acting are not essential to fundamental moral concepts like authority and obligation. By so doing, it would cast doubt on the idea that second-personal reasons for action can account for the distinctive nature of moral reasons.

In his contribution to this volume, Darwall (chapter 7) attempts to turn back this challenge, focusing specifically on Raz's account of practical authority. Darwall argues that Raz's normal justification thesis either must presuppose the second-personal authority to make demands and claims on others or be understood to be not a thesis on authority at all, but rather one about preemptive reasons for action. Either way it cannot explain second-personal authority by appeal to reasons that are not second-personal.

Darwall's second-personal authority is not something that persons must earn. It is a kind of standing to make claims on others, a standing that each person has in virtue of being a person. As such, it is associated with the Kantian idea of dignity. The standing to make claims on others can explain how persons, through the exercise of their will, can change their normative standing. As Gary Watson explains in his contribution to this volume (chapter 8), the fact that persons can change the normative requirements that they are under by acts of will is initially puzzling. Normative reasons are supposed to guide the will. But how can they do this if they can be created and rescinded at will? (One might wonder if such a question could be pressed against Chang's voluntarist reasons.) Watson discusses promissory obligations in particular. If A makes a promise to B, and if B accepts the promissory offer then, by the joint exercise of their wills, the two parties will have changed the normative requirements that they are under. The possibility of this kind of normative power, Watson argues, is bound up with the moral standing that persons have, a moral standing that includes the idea that persons have the power to determine what others may permissibly do to them.

Watson argues that if the normative power to make promises is grounded in the moral standing that persons have, then this moral standing constrains the kinds of binding promises that persons can make. In particular, persons have no authority to make promises that are immoral. For this reason, an immoral promise cannot give rise to a reason to comply with it. But it does not follow that an immoral promise has no normative consequences. If one party promises to do something that it would be impermissible for him to do, then another party might innocently accept the promissory offer. She might not know, for example, that the promisor is promising to do something that he is morally forbidden to do. Here, Watson argues that the promisor cannot have a reason to carry out the promise, but he may have a reason to compensate or make amends to the other party.

## FURTHER THEMES

We now review a range of further topics addressed by contributors to this volume. Normative reasons for action contrast with explanatory reasons for action. The former refer to considerations or facts that count in favor of an action, whereas the latter refer to considerations that explain why an action is performed. On the standard Humean account of action explanation, an action is a bodily movement that is caused in the right way by an agent's desire and means-end belief. Thus, on this standard model, there are two psychological elements that figure in action explanation; namely a desire for some end and a means-end belief related to that end. Michael Smith challenges the standard model in his contribution to this volume (chapter 4). Following the lead of Carl Hempel, and taking issue with Donald Davidson, Smith argues that a third psychological element is necessary for an adequate explanation of an action. The third element is the agent's exercise of the rational capacities that he in fact possesses.

A key claim in Smith's argument is that an agent's capacity to be instrumentally rational is a matter of degree. A fully spelled-out account of action explanation must cite the exercise of the specific capacity that the agent possesses. In this way, Smith counters Davidson's argument that there is no need to posit a third psychological element because the exercise of a minimum capacity for instrumental rationality is entailed by the fact that an agent's desire and means-end belief cause his body to move in the right way. Hence, on Davidson's view, the exercise of this capacity is not an additional element in the explanation of action. However, as Smith points out, it is a fallacy to infer from the fact that a minimum capacity for instrumental rationality is necessary if an agent's desires and beliefs are to cause his body to move in the right way (Davidson's point) to the conclusion that this minimum capacity is the specific capacity that the agent actually possessed and exercised when he acted.

Action explanations seek to identify the elements that make an action an action. But if Smith is right that one of the elements is the possession and exercise of a capacity for instrumental rationality on the part of the agent, then it becomes possible to identify standards of excellence that are internal to action. Reference to these standards, while not necessary for providing an account of what makes an action an action, can be appealed to in explaining the actions of rational agents. They also can explain the sense in which an agent's action is better in the sense that it results from "a better specimen of one of its constitutive causes." As Smith leaves the matter, it is an open question how far one can go in providing explanations of actions in terms of the agent's being rational. Such explanations might include, in addition to the capacity to be fully instrumentally rational, the capacity to revise desires for ends in a rational manner. If so, Smith's argument would show that there is much less of a divide than it is commonly thought between reasons that figure in the explanation of actions by rational agents and normative reasons for action.

In their contribution to this volume (chapter 9), D'Arms and Jacobson consider the role of regret in practical reasoning. Regret has two aspects, they suggest: a hedonic aspect, given by the painfulness of the feeling; and an intentional aspect, which involves seeing something (primarily an act of the agent's) as a mistake. While the former aspect informs practical rationality by supplying hedonic reasons for action, the latter, they argue, is an important source of intuitions about how we ought to make decisions – in other words, about good principles of practical reasoning for human beings. They make use of the debate over the Allais problem for decision theory to explicate the distinction between these aspects of regret, and to explain the relationship between regret, rationality, and good practical reasoning.

One of their central conclusions is that philosophers who have advanced arguments from regret to reconcile the apparently paradoxical Allais preferences with orthodox decision theory have focused on the wrong aspect of regret, its hedonic aspect. Such arguments therefore do not provide a sufficiently robust defense of those preferences to resolve their problematic status. Nevertheless, D'Arms and Jacobson suggest that the Allais preferences (and some analogous phenomena more widespread in human psychology) reveal something important about practical reasoning. While decision theorists have tended to suggest that rationality requires that we obey certain local rules, such as the "sure-thing principle," in practical deliberation, this conclusion cannot be secured by formal arguments alone. What is to be counted as good practical reasoning must depend in part on widespread and predictable human propensities, whether or not these propensities are themselves rationally defective. D'Arms and Jacobson argue that this point suffices at least to show that certain practical policies that are inculcated in normal reasoners by our tendencies to regret – such as taking the certainty of a prospective payoff, or the singularity of an opportunity, to be an additional reason to prefer it – cannot be ruled out as bad reasoning simply because they violate the formal canons of practical rationality embraced by decision theory. They conclude that human propensities to regret illuminate grounds for denying that good reasoning, in the human context, must involve policing one's actions by such decision theoretic canons.

James Dreier's essay (chapter 6) discusses practical conditionals of the form "if you want X, then you ought to Y." Some think such conditionals capture an important truth of instrumental rationality. Such a conditional claim would seem to have us think that the person who wants to kill people in a messy way ought to get a chainsaw (or some such implement).[16]

[16] Darwall (1983).

Partly in reaction to this, some writers have suggested that such conditionals are best seen as taking "wide-scope."[17] The truth in such cases, according to this view, is that one Ought: either stop wanting X or start doing Y. One who thought that surely one ought not to Y, the thought goes, would likely think one ought to stop wanting X, and so could still accept the conditional understood in the wide-scope way.

Dreier argues that wide-scoping is implausible because it does not capture what we confidently assert when we use practical conditionals. He argues that if wide-scoping were the correct account of conditional requirements, we should expect wide-scoping to seem plausible when it comes to conditional permissions as well. But, he argues, wide-scoping is not plausible in this context. Further, Dreier argues, wide-scoping practical conditional requirements fails Ramsey's plausible test for the acceptability of practical conditionals. Dreier goes on to suggest tentatively a new direction for understanding practical conditionals which he argues has more promise.

Peter Railton's wide-ranging essay (chapter 5) marshals psychological findings and reflection on ordinary unself-conscious activity to argue that views of practical rationality which give pride of place to premeditated self-conscious decisions as the paradigm of rational activity are missing much that must be in place for successful agency. One of his arguments concludes that "*all* action – including in particular paradigmatic premeditated intentional action – has *and must have* unpremeditated action at its source and core . . . Most of the reasons for which we act, and that give us the name of rational beings, are not made effective by 'choosing one's reasons'." Railton argues that views which insist that we are only fully or paradigmatically autonomous when we self-consciously pick up the reins and act on a consideration that we have explicitly taken to provide us a reason face a regress problem. If consciously choosing X as my reason is to be fully autonomous, I must do it for a reason that I consciously choose, and so on. If this were what it took to be fully autonomous, we could never manage it. But we can sometimes manage to be autonomous, so views that champion this requirement must be mistaken, Railton argues.

[17] See Broome (2007).

CHAPTER 2

# *Intention, belief, and instrumental rationality**

*Michael E. Bratman*

## I TWO APPROACHES TO INSTRUMENTAL RATIONALITY

Suppose I intend end E, believe that a necessary means to E is M, and believe that M requires that I intend M. My attitudes concerning E and M engage a basic requirement of practical rationality, a requirement that, barring a change in my cited beliefs, I either intend M or give up intending E.[1] Call this the *Instrumental Rationality* requirement – for short, the *IR* requirement.[2]

* This essay is a sequel to my "Intention, Belief, Practical, Theoretical," in Simon Robertson, ed., *Spheres of Reason* (Oxford: Oxford University Press, forthcoming). Some of the ideas developed here are also in that earlier essay, but I hope in this present chapter to go somewhat beyond that earlier work. I do, however, see my overall argument in favor of (to use terminology to be introduced in the main text) the practical commitment view, in contrast with cognitivism, as drawing on both of these essays (as well as on the basic account presented in my *Intention, Plans, and Practical Reason* [Cambridge, MA: Harvard University Press, 1987; reissued by CSLI Publications, 1999]). The present essay was motivated in part by Kieran Setiya's "Cognitivism about Instrumental Reason: Response to Bratman" (2005), which constituted his very thoughtful and helpful comments on "Intention, Belief, Practical, Theoretical," at the Conference on Practical Reason, University of Maryland, April 2005. My present chapter has also benefited from conversation with John Perry, Jennifer Morton, and Sarah Paul, detailed comments from Gideon Yaffe and John Broome on earlier drafts, and very helpful comments from George Wilson and from the editors of this volume.

1 Concerning the need for the belief that M requires that I intend M, see Robert Binkley, "A Theory of Practical Reason," *The Philosophical Review*, 74 (1965): 423–448, at 443. The language of "requirement" comes from John Broome; see "Normative Requirements," *Ratio*, 12 (1999): 398–419.

2 In other work I have focused on what I have called a requirement of means-end coherence of one's intentions and plans. I see IR as a central aspect of that requirement, though the requirement of means-end coherence goes beyond IR, strictly speaking, in requiring that an agent fill in her plans with one or another sufficient means when what is needed is that the agent settle on some such means or other. And the requirement of means-end coherence allows for delay in filling in plans with means when there remains sufficient time. (For some of these complexities see *Intention, Plans, and Practical Reason*: 31–35.) But IR is at the heart of the requirement of means-end coherence, and it will simplify my discussion here to focus on it. Note that both IR and the requirement of means-end coherence specifically concern means-end rationality with respect to *intended* ends; there remain further issues about means-end rationality concerning things one wants, prefers, or values.

Suppose now that I believe that E, and I also believe that E will only occur if M. My beliefs engage a basic demand of theoretical rationality, a demand that, roughly, either there be a change in at least one of these two beliefs or I believe M. Call this the *Belief-Closure* requirement – for short, the *BC* requirement. BC, note, is not a consistency demand on my beliefs: failure to add the further belief that M need not involve inconsistency in the way that adding a belief that not-M would. Nevertheless, something like BC seems a basic rationality constraint on belief.[3]

Both IR and BC express constraints on the coherence of the agent's relevant attitudes; and these constraints are aspects of the normal rational functioning, in the psychic economy of believing-and-intending agents, of the cited attitudes. The intentions and beliefs of such agents will tend to be responsive to these constraints. But the requirements differ in important ways. IR is engaged only if I intend E; whereas BC is engaged if I believe E, whether or not I intend E. And a central way of meeting the demands of IR involves intending M; whereas a corresponding way of meeting the demands of BC involves, rather, believing M. Further, if we ask why these principles – IR and BC – are, indeed, aspects of the rational functioning of the cited attitudes, we arrive, I believe, at importantly different answers. Roughly: In the case of BC we will appeal, I think, to something like a general need for coherence of one's beliefs if one is to understand the world. In the case of IR we will appeal, I think, to something like a general need to intend necessary means if one is to be an effective agent and if one is to have a practical standpoint that has the kind of efficacy characteristic of self-government.[4]

These last claims about what lies behind IR, on the one hand, and BC, on the other, are, of course, sketchy; and I cannot pursue these matters in detail here. I do think, though, that there is here a general and plausible idea. This is the idea that these stories will differ, and that one will cite

[3] There are important issues, in understanding BC, about what Gilbert Harman calls "clutter avoidance": as Harman emphasizes, we do not suppose one must add *all* beliefs entailed by other beliefs one already has. See Gilbert Harman, *Change in View* (Cambridge, MA: MIT Press, 1986): 12. These issues do not arise in the same way for IR. Given that the agent believes that intending M is itself necessary for E, forming that intention will not be mere "clutter." I return to this matter briefly below in n. 21.

[4] That is, the concerns and commitments that constitute the practical standpoint with which one identifies need to be ones that are effectively in control of one's intentional conduct, if one is to be self-governing. One aspect of such effective control will be conforming, in general, to IR when one's beliefs about what is required are accurate and when the intended ends are elements in, or in other ways endorsed by, the practical standpoint with which one identifies. I try to deepen this connection between central norms on intention and self-government in "Intention, Belief, Practical, Theoretical."

basic theoretical concerns – with understanding, for example – and the other will cite basic practical concerns – with effective agency and self-governance, for example. When we put this very general idea together with our initial observations about the differences between IR and BC – the focus on intention, in the one case, and belief in the other – we are led to the view that these are importantly different demands of rationality – in one case practical, in the other case theoretical – though these demands will, of course, significantly interact in many cases.

There are, however, philosophical pressures that have led a number of philosophers to draw principles along the lines of IR and BC much more closely together. Their idea, roughly, is to see IR, or something close to it, as, at bottom, a special case of the theoretical requirement expressed in BC, or something close to it, together perhaps with some further principle of theoretical rationality. There are different versions of this idea, as we shall see. But what they share is the idea that IR is, at bottom, a theoretical demand on beliefs. This is *cognitivism* about instrumental rationality.[5]

Cognitivism about instrumental rationality identifies what had seemed to be a basic element of practical rationality with theoretical rationality. It need not, however, say that all demands of practical reason are, at bottom, demands of theoretical reason.[6] So, for example, I see John Broome, Wayne Davis, Gilbert Harman, Kieran Setiya, J. David Velleman, and R. Jay Wallace as, in different ways, cognitivists about instrumental rationality;[7] but whereas Velleman is, quite broadly, a cognitivist about practical reason – he sees practical reason as grounded in a theoretical

[5] More precisely, this is cognitivism about that aspect of instrumental rationality that IR, and closely related principles, aims to capture. For this use of the term "cognitivism" (in contrast with its standard use in meta-ethics) see my "Cognitivism about Practical Reason," as reprinted in my *Faces of Intention* (New York: Cambridge University Press, 1999), and my "Intention, Belief, Practical, Theoretical." Kieran Setiya also uses this term in this way in "Cognitivism about Instrumental Reason," *Ethics*, 117 (2007): 649–673.

[6] Setiya makes this point in "Cognitivism about Instrumental Reason: Response to Bratman."

[7] See John Broome, "The Unity of Reasoning?," in Jens Timmerman, John Skorupski, and Simon Robertson, eds., *Spheres of Reason* (Oxford : Oxford University Press, forthcoming); Wayne Davis, "A Causal Theory of Intending," *American Philosophical Quarterly*, 21 (1984): 43–54; Gilbert Harman, "Practical Reasoning," reprinted in Gilbert Harman, *Reasoning, Meaning, and Mind* (Oxford: Oxford University Press, 1999): 46–74; Setiya, "Cognitivism about Instrumental Reason"; J. David Velleman, *Practical Reflection* (Princeton, NJ: Princeton University Press, 1989), *The Possibility of Practical Reason* (Oxford: Oxford University Press, 2000), and "What Good is a Will?," in Anton Leist and Holger Baumann, eds., *Action in Context* (Berlin and New York: de Gruyter and Mouton, 2007); R. Jay Wallace, "Normativity, Commitment, and Instrumental Reason," *Philosophers' Imprint*, 1 (3) (2001). Setiya's cognitivism about instrumental rationality goes directly by way of his version of BC. My strategy in this essay of focusing on the role of BC in such cognitivism follows Setiya in this respect.

concern with self-knowledge and self-understanding – the cognitivism defended by the others is more limited: it extends at least to IR but does not purport to extend to all of practical reason. I do think that it would be difficult to be a cognitivist about IR but not about certain other rationality requirements on intention. This is clearest with respect to the consistency requirement on intentions. This is the requirement that one's overall set of intentions be consistent as well as consistent with one's beliefs: one needs to be able to put one's various intentions together – to agglomerate them – into an overall plan that is internally consistent and consistent with one's beliefs.[8] A marriage of cognitivism about IR with a rejection of cognitivism about these consistency demands is likely to be unstable, since the alternative story about the consistency demands will threaten to spill over to a story about IR. It is a hard question what a cognitivist about IR should say about norms of cross-temporal stability of intention. In any case, my primary focus here will be on cognitivism about IR.

Here is one way to look at it. Suppose you now prefer A at some later time to its envisaged alternatives. This is not yet to intend A. After all, while you do now prefer A you may still see the issue as not yet settled and be engaged right now in further deliberation about whether to A. Now suppose that this further deliberation does issue in an intention to A. In what, precisely, does this transition from a preference to an intention consist? In particular, in now intending to A you come to be under the rational pressure of IR: you now need, roughly, to intend known necessary means, or give up your intention to A. In contrast, the mere preference for A did not, by itself, engage IR. What about the transition from preference to intention explains why IR is newly engaged?[9]

A cognitivist about IR will see the transition from preference to intention as at least in part a matter of belief. And a cognitivist about

[8] Note that this demand for consistency is not just that each intention have a consistent content; it includes, as well, the demand that one be able to agglomerate one's various intentions into an overall intention that has a consistent content. I will sometimes emphasize this way in which this demand for consistency involves an implicit agglomerativity demand; but sometimes, for ease of exposition, I will simply speak of consistency, leaving the idea of agglomeration implicit. As this formulation of the consistency demand suggests, there are puzzles here that parallel puzzles about consistency of belief and the "preface paradox"; but I put these aside here.

[9] Cf. R. Jay Wallace: "there must be something about the attitude of intending to do *x* that goes beyond the attitude of desiring that one do *x*, in a way that brings a distinctively rational requirement into play" ("Normativity, Commitment, and Instrumental Reason": 18). (Though note that I allude to preference whereas Wallace appeals to desire.) As my remarks below indicate, though, I think we need to be careful here, since the step from preference to an attitude that engages something like IR might be only a step to a "settled objective" and not a step all the way to intention, strictly speaking.

IR will appeal to the belief aspect of this transition to explain why IR is newly engaged. In contrast, on the view I would like to defend – and the view suggested by our preliminary remarks about the differences between IR and BC – the step from preference to intention is a practical step, a step to a distinctive kind of practical commitment that is not itself a belief. And it is that, not belief, that is at the heart of the new applicability of IR. So we can contrast cognitivism with such a *practical commitment* view of instrumental rationality.

A basic idea that underlies the kind of practical commitment view I would want to defend is that intentions are elements of a planning system, one that has fundamental roles in the coordination and control of action. Planning agents like us normally need to intend means if we are to achieve our intended ends. We are not gods who can simply and effectively will "let there be E!" (If I were simply to will "let there be light!" it would not work: I need to flip the switch.) And insofar as one fails to intend means intending which is necessary for intended ends, this planning system will fail to be effective.[10] Further, insofar as one's intentions are inconsistent with each other and/or with one's beliefs, this planning system will fail in its coordinating role, a role that is at the heart of the cross-temporal effectiveness of that system. So, in general, conformity to norms of consistency and means-end rationality are – at least for non-divine planning agents with reliable beliefs about the world – conditions for the successful operation of this system of coordinated control. Further, a full-blown planning agent will not just happen to conform to such norms: she will think in ways that are at least implicitly guided by these norms; and this will be part of the explanation of the successful functioning of her planning agency. In particular, she will be responsive in her thinking to the need to intend means intending which is needed for her intended ends; and she will be responsive in her thinking to a demand for consistency of intentions and beliefs. Norms of means-end rationality and consistency will be, for her, internal norms.[11] Her intention in favor of E is a practical commitment in part in the sense that it engages these internal norms.

There is a complexity here, however. IR is tied to the normal, successful functioning of the planning system as a system that effectively controls action in pursuit of intended ends. A norm of consistency of intention is

[10] Here I am in agreement with Joseph Raz, "The Myth of Instrumental Rationality," *Journal of Ethics and Social Philosophy*, 1 (1), www.jesp.org, (2005): 17.

[11] For this terminology see *Intention, Plans, and Practical Reason*: 109.

tied to the normal, successful functioning of the planning system as a coordinating system. Intentions are elements of a planning system whose central roles are those of effective coordinating control. However, we are also capable of commitments to ends that we do not treat as subject in precisely the same way to the sorts of coordinating pressures that impose a demand for agglomeration and consistency. I might try to get into Harvard Law, and try to get into Stanford Law, while knowing that these law schools coordinate admissions and so that, while I have a shot at getting into each, it is not possible to get into both.[12] As I see it, I do not, strictly speaking, intend to get into Harvard Law, or intend to get into Stanford Law. This is because if I intended one I would, by the symmetry of the case, intend the other; so I would thereby have intentions that violate rational demands for agglomeration and consistency. Nevertheless, I do have getting into Harvard Law as what Hugh McCann calls a "settled objective";[13] and similarly concerning getting into Stanford Law.

Such examples seem to show that, while each settled objective needs to be internally consistent, not all settled objectives engage agglomeration and consistency demands in precisely the way characteristic of intention. In some cases a settled objective is not embedded in the standard intention-like way within the overall coordinating role of one's planning system, though the pursuit of the settled objective does impose more localized coordination pressures. (I need, for example, first to get the Harvard application, then fill it out; if I try to proceed in the reverse order it won't work. And I need to ensure that my plan for filling out the application meshes with my other plans for the day.) The conclusion I draw is that not all settled objectives are intentions, strictly speaking[14] (though they may be associated with intentions – say, to get into some law school or other, or intentions about means to the objective). Nevertheless, settled objectives do engage a requirement that is something like IR: after all, in the envisaged case, I am under rational pressure to settle on means to get into Harvard Law, pressure I would not be under if I merely desired to get into that school. Rational pressures of means-end rationality can be engaged even if one's attitude does not engage pressures of agglomeration and consistency in precisely the way characteristic of intention.

[12] This example is modeled on the video games example I discuss in *Intention, Plans, and Practical Reason*: chapter 8.

[13] Hugh McCann, "Settled Objectives and Rational Constraints," *American Philosophical Quarterly*, 28 (1991): 25–36.

[14] It is in this conclusion that I disagree with McCann, though I will not here try to respond to his arguments against this conclusion.

Now, it seems that certain non-planning agents can still have settled objectives. Perhaps a squirrel can have getting the nuts as a settled objective even though it does not have sufficient structure in its thinking about the future to be a planning agent.[15] However, when a planning agent like us has certain settled objectives that are not, strictly speaking, intentions, pressures of means-end rationality engaged by such settled objectives will normally be met by forming *intentions* about means. Even if my commitment to getting into Harvard Law is a settled objective but not an intention, my sub-plans for pursuing this end will normally be intended, strictly speaking. This is because those sub-plans still need to mesh with my sub-plans for getting into Stanford Law. After all, the plan is for one and the same agent – namely, me – to carry out both sub-plans even though they are in pursuit of objectives that are, given the special features of the case, not co-possible.[16]

An implication of these reflections on settled objectives is that the two different norms on intention highlighted here – IR and a norm of consistency – have a slightly different status. A norm of means-end rationality that is similar to IR will be engaged by settled objectives, whereas the cited norm of agglomeration and consistency will not be engaged in the same way by settled objectives as by intentions, strictly speaking. But, having noted this complexity, I will focus primarily on the account of IR for intentions, since it is here that cognitivism about instrumental rationality has its best chance.

As I have said, I envisage an account of IR that ties it to the proper functioning of the planning system as a system of coordinated, effective control. And in other work I have also emphasized an even broader significance of this planning system in our lives as an element in both our self-governance and in our sociality.[17] By itself, however, this picture of our planning agency, and of the central roles in it of norms of agglomeration, consistency and means-end rationality, does not show that cognitivism is false. A cognitivist can agree with all this and then argue

[15] So the step from such a non-planning agent with settled objectives to a full-blown planning agent would be an important step in a Gricean "creature construction" model of agency. See Paul Grice, "Method in Philosophical Psychology (From the Banal to the Bizarre)," (Presidential Address), *Proceedings and Addresses of the American Philosophical Association* (1974–5): 23–53, and Bratman, "Valuing and the Will," reprinted in *Structures of Agency: Essays* (New York: Oxford University Press, 2007).

[16] In this last sentence I have benefited from discussions with Luca Ferrero and Michael Nelson. And see *Intention, Plans, and Practical Reason*: 137–138 (though there I proceed in the language of "guiding desire" rather than McCann's language of "settled objective").

[17] "Intention, Belief, Practical, Theoretical."

that these norms turn out, on examination, to derive from theoretical norms on associated beliefs. What these appeals to the proper functioning of the planning system do indicate, though, is that there is an initial plausibility to the idea that these norms are practical norms grounded in the practical roles of the planning system of coordinated control. If we are to be led to cognitivism we need some further arguments, ones that go beyond noting that we do, indeed, appeal to and depend on these norms insofar as we are planning agents. We need arguments for thinking that we should see these norms as, at bottom, theoretical; and we need a defense of the idea that theoretical norms really can do the requisite work. So let's see.

## 2 HARMAN'S BASIC IDEA

We can begin with what I will call *Harman's basic idea*, since it derives from his ground-breaking 1976 paper "Practical Reasoning" (though the way I will present it here goes a bit beyond that paper). Harman, like many cognitivists about IR,[18] supposes that intending E necessarily involves believing E. Further,

> since intention involves belief, theoretical and practical reasoning overlap.
>
> In theoretical reasoning, one seeks to increase the coherence of one's overall view of the world . . . Since intention involves belief, and theoretical and practical reasoning overlap, coherence must be relevant to any sort of reasoning about the future, theoretical or practical . . .
>
> The thesis that intention involves belief associates practical reasoning about means and ends with theoretical reasoning. It brings these two sorts of reasoning under a single principle.[19]

[18] There are important qualifications. Wallace endorses only a weak belief condition: intending to *A* requires believing *A* is possible. (As I note in "Intention, Belief, Practical, Theoretical," this weak belief condition does not on its own explain the rational agglomerativity of intention.) Broome says only that if you believe you intend *A* then you believe *A*. I will return to this view of Broome below. In his 1976 paper Harman *identifies* intention with a kind of belief that one will *A*; whereas in a later paper ("Willing and Intending," in Richard Grandy and Richard Warner, eds., *Philosophical Grounds of Rationality*, Oxford: Oxford University Press, 1986: 363–380) Harman only says that intending *A* requires believing *A*. The argument for cognitivism I am now sketching is neutral as between these two ways of understanding the connection between intending *A* and believing *A* – though below (pp. 28–29), the purported identification will matter.

[19] *Reasoning, Meaning, and Mind*: 49–50. In the original essay, Harman had said that "[I]n theoretical reasoning, one seeks to increase the explanatory coherence of one's overall view of the world." In this more recent version of his essay he appeals broadly to coherence, where explanatory coherence is one kind of coherence (though the appeal specifically to *explanatory* coherence remains: 56 and 63).

Given the emphasis on the claim "that intention involves belief," it seems that the "single principle" to which Harman alludes is a principle of coherence on one's beliefs. It is because "intention involves belief" that this principle of coherence on belief extends to one's intentions. And – though at this point I go beyond what Harman says – it seems plausible to see something like BC as an aspect of belief coherence that is importantly relevant in this way to IR. A violation of BC would normally be a form of belief incoherence,[20] and it is this form of incoherence that may seem to be at stake in violations of IR. After all, if I intend E (and so believe E) and believe M is a necessary means to E, BC requires that, if I do not change those two attitudes, I believe that M. If I also believe that M will obtain only if I intend M,[21] BC requires, if I do not change those two attitudes, that I believe I intend M. And it can seem that to believe I intend M I need actually to intend M (though this is a matter to which I will return). So the demand to satisfy BC – a demand that seems to be a central element in the requirement for belief coherence – seems to issue in a demand to satisfy IR. And that is cognitivism about IR.

As I am understanding it, then, Harman's basic idea is that we arrive at cognitivism about instrumental rationality in two steps: we begin by noting that intention involves corresponding belief; we then reflect on the nature of the theoretical pressures on those involved beliefs – where, as I have developed this idea here, these pressures include BC. And now I want to point to two problems for this route to cognitivism about IR.[22] The first concerns the idea that intention involves corresponding belief. Suppose, to take an example I have discussed elsewhere, I intend to stop at the bookstore on the way home.[23] Still, I know that I am forgetful; so I am not confident that I will stop – after all, once I get on my bicycle I do have a tendency just to pedal on home. About this case I am inclined to say: I intend to stop, but I do not believe I will stop (though I do not believe

[20] Putting to one side issues of "clutter avoidance." See n. 21.

[21] Setiya argues that a cognitivist may appeal to something like this belief to block, for such cases, Harman's worries about "clutter avoidance." ("Cognitivism about Instrumental Reason.") In order to give the cognitivist a sympathetic hearing, I am following Setiya here.

[22] I also believe a third problem looms, a problem concerning the distinction between intending X and merely expecting that X will be a result of something one intends. See "Intention, Belief, Practical, Theoretical"; and for a discussion of this problem as it arises for Velleman's theory, see "Cognitivism about Practical Reason," reprinted in *Faces of Intention*. I put this potential third problem to one side here. My own discussion of this distinction is in *Intention, Plans, and Practical Reason*: chapter 10.

[23] *Intention, Plans, and Practical Reason*: 37, and "Practical Reasoning and Acceptance in a Context," in *Faces of Intention*: 31–32. My use of this example in the present context benefited from discussion with John Perry.

I will not stop).[24] Many think, though, that it is a misuse of the word "intend" to say that I intend to stop but do not believe I will. Concerning this issue about the word "intend" there seems not to be a consensus one way or the other.[25] What matters for our present discussion, though, is not primarily what we would say using this word, but whether my attitude toward stopping, however labeled, engages the basic demand at the bottom of IR. And it seems to me that it does.

My attitude toward stopping is not a mere preference to stop: I have, rather, settled on stopping. If there were two routes home, only one of which went by the bookstore, my commitment to stopping at the bookstore would require that I take the route that goes by the bookstore. It would also require that I not settle also on another alternative known by me to be inconsistent with my stopping.[26] So my attitude toward stopping engages demands of consistency and means-end rationality that are characteristic of intention. And it does this even in the absence of a belief that I will stop. This suggests that we should seek an account of, in particular, IR that applies to my commitment to stopping at the bookstore, whether or not I also believe I will stop, contrary to Harman's basic idea.

My second reason for being skeptical about Harman's basic idea can allow, for the sake of argument, that if you intend A you believe A. What this second reason for skepticism involves is the idea that you can misidentify what you intend: you can falsely believe you have a certain intention. The mind, after all, is not an open book, even to the person

[24] As I note in "Practical Reasoning and Acceptance in a Context": 32, I may nevertheless accept, in the context of relevant deliberation, that I would stop if I were to decide to stop. As I explain in that essay, acceptance in a context is not the same as belief. Wallace also alludes to something like this idea in "Postscript" to "Normativity, Commitment, and Instrumental Reason," in *Normativity and the Will: Selected Essays on Moral Psychology and Practical Reason* (Oxford: Oxford University Press, 2006): 116. But Wallace seems to suppose that such acceptance is itself a kind of belief, whereas I would balk at this. These observations about acceptance in a context do raise the question of whether there is available to us a kind of cogitivism that goes by way of acceptance in a context, rather than belief. I have my doubts that what will emerge is really a kind of cognitivism, since the connection between intending and accepting in a context seems itself to be grounded in practical rationality; but I cannot pursue these matters here. Both Facundo Alonso and Olivier Roy have been pursuing this and related issues in unpublished work.

[25] For a lively sense of the disagreement here, see Paul Grice, "Intention and Uncertainty," *Proceedings of the British Academy*, 57 (1971): 263–279; Donald Davidson "Intending," reprinted in *Essays on Actions and Events*, 2nd edn. (Oxford: Oxford University Press, 2001): 83–102; Gilbert Harman, "Willing and Intending."

[26] So my commitment to stopping is not a mere "settled objective," in the sense in which my commitment to the end of getting into Harvard Law, in the example described earlier, is. In contrast with such mere settled objectives, my commitment to stopping at the bookstore not only requires settling on means, it also needs to be consistent with my other intentions.

whose mind it is. However we understand our special first-person access to our minds in general and, more specifically, to our intentions, it does not ensure incorrigibility about our own intentions.

In particular, there can be cases in which one believes one intends a means but does not intend that means. Perhaps I get confused and believe I intend to go shopping next Tuesday, though in fact I do not intend this but intend, rather, to go shopping next Thursday.[27] So there can be cases in which one intends E, believes that E requires both M and one's intending M, believes both M and that one intends M, but still does not, in fact, intend M. Though one believes one intends M one is mistaken about this. One's beliefs satisfy BC; but this does not ensure satisfaction of IR since, in the case envisaged, one does not in fact intend M. So it seems that we should reject cognitivism about IR.

These, anyway, are two concerns about Harman's basic route to cognitivism. In each case there are complexities we need to examine; and I will proceed to some of these complexities below. This will put me in a position to reflect on several related ideas that others have offered in defense of a version of cognitivism about IR. But first I want to note, and try to defuse, a line of argument that can seem to make cognitivism attractive.

## 3 CONSTITUTIVE AIM: VELLEMAN

Belief aims at truth. Or so it seems plausible to say.[28] Let me note three aspects of this idea. The first is that beliefs are embedded in a psychic economy that tends, in belief-formation, to track the truth, though of course it can on occasion fail. An attitude embedded in a psychic economy that, in its formation of that attitude, tracked instead the pleasant-to-think-of, would be a candidate for fantasy, not for belief. A second and closely related aspect of this idea is that, as Bernard Williams puts it, "truth and falsehood are a dimension of an assessment of beliefs."[29] Beliefs are criticizable if they are false, if they fail to track what – given the kind of attitudes they are – they tend to track. And, third, part of the explanation

[27] For this example, see my "Intention, Belief, Practical, Theoretical." I first discussed this objection to Harman's cognitivism in "Intention and Means-End Reasoning," *The Philosophical Review*, 90 (1981): 252–265, at 255–256, n. 4.

[28] A classic discussion of this idea is Bernard Williams, "Deciding to Believe," in *Problems of the Self* (Cambridge: Cambridge University Press, 1973): 136–151.

[29] *Problems of the Self*: 137.

of how, for agents like us, beliefs track the truth will appeal to an internal norm that assesses beliefs in terms of their truth.[30]

That said, it is a hard question precisely how these three aspects of the truth-directedness of belief are related. So, for example, at one point J. David Velleman thought that the second, normative aspect derived from the first, descriptive aspect.[31] In later work with Nishi Shah, however, Velleman has come to a more complex view of the relation between these two aspects.[32] These are difficult issues, and I will not try to sort them out here. It suffices for my purposes here simply to include all three, inter-related aspects in the idea that belief aims at truth.[33] Following Velleman, we can express this idea by saying that a "constitutive aim" of belief is truth.[34] And it seems plausible to say that demands on belief of consistency and coherence are closely related to this purported truth-aim.

So far, all this is neutral with respect to cognitivism. But one might think that the availability of such a story about various normative demands on belief supports the idea that these very same demands account for the cited normative demands on intention. Or at least this may seem plausible given the assumption that to intend A is, at least in part, to believe A. After all, if belief aims at truth there is, on this assumption, a story about the demand for consistency of intention: consistency is needed for the associated beliefs all to achieve their constitutive aim. Granted, even given the assumed connection between intention and belief, cognitivism about IR is more delicate, since failure of one's associated beliefs to conform to BC does not ensure that any of

[30] Something like this seems implicit in Williams' remarks about the underlying problem with believing at will. See *Problems of the Self*: 148.

[31] In "Introduction" to *The Possibility of Practical Reason*, Velleman claimed that "belief aims at the truth in the normative sense only because it aims at the truth descriptively" (2000: 17). Velleman discusses these matters further in "On the Aim of Belief," in *The Possibility of Practical Reason*. His most recent discussion is in Nishi Shah and J. David Velleman, "Doxastic Deliberation," *The Philosophical Review*, 114 (2005): 497–534.

[32] "There is both a descriptive and a normative component to belief's truth-directedness." "Doxastic Deliberation": 530, n. 10. See also Nishi Shah, "How Truth governs Belief", *The Philosophical Review*, 112(4) (2003): 447–482. Shah and Velleman, in this joint work, are concerned with the issue of how "to explain the fact that the deliberative question *whether to believe that p* is transparent to the question *whether p*" ("Doxastic Deliberation": 497). I do not try to address this issue here.

[33] As does Williams, who also includes the further idea that in *saying* one believes p one is *claiming* that p is true. "Deciding to Believe": 137.

[34] For the language of "the constitutive aim of belief," see "Introduction": 16. Since Shah and Velleman say that "there is both a descriptive and a normative component to belief's truth-directedness," I am assuming that talk of constitutive aim carries over to include, in this new work, both the descriptive and the normative component, even though the latter is no longer seen as derivable from the former.

them are false (though it does ensure that if one's actual beliefs do achieve their constitutive aim then one's set of beliefs do not maximally achieve this aim – since the failure of closure would be a failure to add a true belief). Still, there may seem to be some close connection between the truth-aim of belief and BC.[35] So if we could see IR as grounded in BC, we would then have the beginnings of an account of IR that grounds it in the purported constitutive aim of belief. So there may seem to be philosophical pressure in favor of cognitivism.[36]

I think, however, that it is important to see that if we are attracted to this idea that norms on belief are tied to its constitutive aim of truth, then we can argue, in parallel fashion, that norms on intention are tied to the (or anyway, a) constitutive aim of intention. And this parallel argument is independent of cognitivism. So appeal to constitutive aims of relevant attitudes does not, on its own, provide support for cognitivism.

In particular, if we are attracted to the appeal to constitutive aims of attitudes we can interpret the planning model of intention as articulating a constitutive aim of intention, namely: coordinated, effective control of action. Each intention aims at its realization in coordination with one's overall system of intentions. Coordination involves consistency among one's intentions, given one's beliefs; effective control requires that one intend means intending which one knows to be needed to achieve intended ends. So it is plausible that we can see norms of consistency and means-end rationality – norms characteristic of intention – as related to the (or, an) aim of intention in a way that parallels the relation between analogous norms on belief and the truth-aim of belief.

We can put the idea this way: The planning theory of intention articulates characteristic roles of intention in coordination and effective agency: intentions are embedded in a planning system that tracks coordination and effective control and systematically adjusts, when need be, in their direction. The planning theory sees the achievement of coordinated effectiveness as, to return to Williams' remark, "a dimension of an assessment" of intentions.[37] And the planning theory supposes that the explanation of how plans support coordination and effectiveness will involve associated internal norms. So the planning theory provides

35 It may be that we should here appeal instead to a concern with understanding; but I put this complexity to one side here.

36 An argument broadly in this spirit is in J. David Velleman, "What Good is a Will?." I discuss this essay in "Intention, Belief, Practical, Theoretical," where I also develop further the ideas to follow about the aim of intention.

37 Though, of course, not all failures of coordination or effectiveness will be cases of irrationality.

resources that parallel the trio of ideas I have included within talk of the aim of belief. So we seem to have as much reason to appeal to an aim of intention as we do to an aim of belief – though, of course, the aims are different.

This does not require that it is essential to *agency*, quite generally, that one be a planning agent, one who forms intentions that have – or so we are now supposing – the constitutive aim of coordinated, effective control of action. Planning agency is a distinctive form of agency, one that contributes substantially to the pursuit of complex, temporally extended aims, to structures of self-governance, and – though I have not emphasized this here – to forms of sociality.[38] There can be agents who are not planning agents,[39] and these agents can even act intentionally in an attenuated sense that doesn't bring with it planning structures. But if you are, as we are, a planning agent[40] your intentions and plans have – we are now assuming – characteristic aims, aims associated with norms of consistency and means-end rationality. And this does not require cognitivism about IR.

This possibility of appealing to an aim of intention, in contrast with the aim of belief, tends to be obscured from within Velleman's cognitivist theory because, when he turns from belief to intention, he turns not to a distinctive aim of intention (other than – since intention is, on Velleman's view, a kind of belief – the aim of belief) but to a purported aim of, most generally, agency.[41] His central idea is that agency itself has an intellectual constitutive aim – namely self-knowledge and self-understanding. And this leads to Velleman's overall cognitivism about practical reason. But we can seek a practical parallel to the appeal to the aim of belief, without appeal to a purported aim of agency. We can talk, rather, of the aim of intention. And the planning theory gives us a plausible way to do that, a way that avoids cognitivism.

38 Concerning this connection to forms of sociality, see essays 5–8 in *Faces of Intention*.

39 This is implicit in the general strategy of Gricean "creature construction" in the philosophy of action (see above, n. 15). In unpublished work, Jennifer Morton pursues further implications of, as she puts it, the "varieties of agency."

40 I discuss the question, why (continue to) be a planning agent?, in "Intention, Belief, Practical, Theoretical," where I emphasize the roles of planning agency in cross-temporally effective agency, in self-governance, and in our sociality. In these ways there are distinctively practical pressures in the direction of a kind of planning agency within which intentions have (or so we are now supposing) the cited constitutive aims. Note that this does not entail that we actually have a choice about whether to be planning agents. Nor does it rule out the possibility of cases in which things go better if one's planning system does not on that occasion function properly.

41 See *The Possibility of Practical Reason*.

Now, one might think that we need to appeal to cognitivism to explain the special nature of the demand expressed in IR. In particular, we need to explain why violations of IR are a kind of *incoherence*.[42] The cognitivist will say that this is because the demand expressed in IR just is the demand for a kind of belief coherence. And the cognitivist sees this demand of coherence on belief as tied to the very nature of belief – where this includes the way it must be embedded in a system that tracks truth. But we can say something similar about intention without being cognitivists. We can say that the demand of coherence on intention (taken together with belief) is tied to the very nature of intention – where this includes the way it must be embedded in a planning system that tracks coordinated and effective control of action. And we can say this while acknowledging that not all agents are planning agents.[43]

## 4 MISTAKES ABOUT ONE'S OWN INTENTIONS: HARMAN AND SETIYA

Let me turn now to the complexities I promised concerning my two objections to Harman's basic idea. Begin with the second objection[44]: I might falsely believe I intend a certain means intending which is, I know, needed for my intended end. In such a case I might satisfy BC but not IR. So IR is not grounded in BC. Or so I have averred. What might a cognitivist say in reply?

Well, a cognitivist might argue that such a false belief about one's own intention ineluctably violates a further basic theoretical demand on one's beliefs. So the theoretical demands on one's beliefs – where these theoretical demands include those necessarily violated by one's false belief about one's intention – really do, taken together, fully account for the rational force of IR. So my appeal to the apparent possibility of false belief about one's own intentions does not work as an objection to cognitivism about IR, so long as that cognitivism is allowed to appeal not only to BC but also to broad theoretical constraints against false belief about one's own intentions.[45]

[42] Setiya raises this issue in his comments on my "Intention, Belief, Practical, Theoretical."

[43] In this last sentence I am in disagreement with Setiya.

[44] I discuss the first objection in the context of my discussion, in the next section, of the views of John Broome.

[45] Wallace offers a version of this reply. I discuss it in "Intention, Belief, Practical, Theoretical." Here I focus on versions of this reply due to Gilbert Harman and to Kieran Setiya.

For this to work there must be a form of theoretical irrationality – and not just fallibility – whenever one misidentifies what one intends. What could that be?

One idea here – once suggested by Harman[46] – is that in falsely believing I intend M I falsely believe I *believe* M. And a false belief about what one believes involves a set of beliefs that are incoherent. After all (though here I go beyond Harman's explicit remarks), if I believe I believe p I should be willing to use p as a premise in my ordinary reasoning; but if I do not believe p I should not.[47] And the claim is that this incoherence within one's beliefs is ineluctably triggered by a false belief about what one intends.

But why say that in falsely believing I intend M I falsely believe I *believe* M? Well, as noted, cognitivist theories see intention as at least involving corresponding belief; and some see intention as itself a special kind of belief. So perhaps it will seem that, on such assumptions about the connection between intention and belief, when I falsely believe I intend M I do falsely believe I believe M. But, on reflection, we can see that this need not be so.

Suppose we say only that to intend A is, in part, to believe A, though it also involves other elements as well – perhaps intention involves both such a belief and, as well, a preference for A.[48] Well, then, I might falsely believe I intend M and yet still in fact believe M; it is just that, as a matter of fact, I do not satisfy the further condition for intending M – in the example, a preference for M. I believe I intend M but I do not intend M – though I do believe M I do not, unbeknownst to me, satisfy the further condition for intending M. So it is not true in this case that in falsely believing I intend M I falsely believe I believe M.

Now suppose we identify intending with believing. Well, we cannot plausibly say that intending to M is simply believing one will M. If we identify intending with believing it must be with a special kind of

[46] In a footnote to his 1980 APA comments on "Intention and Means-End Reasoning," Harman wrote:

> In "Practical Reasoning" I assumed that to intend to do *B* is to have a certain sort of self-referential belief. So in this case [that is, the case of falsely believing one intends the necessary means] one believes one believes something which in fact one does not believe, and this might count as a kind of incoherence in one's beliefs.

I also discuss this suggestion of Harman in "Intention, Belief, Practical, Theoretical."

[47] Here I put to one side complexities involved in the possibility of acceptance in a context that is not belief.

[48] See Davis, "A Causal Theory of Intending."

believing. To intend M is, in this special way, to believe M. Harman's 1976 theory has this form: to intend M is to believe you will M by way of this very belief, where this belief is a conclusion of practical reasoning. Intentions are reflexive beliefs[49] that are, as well, the output of practical reasoning. Well, then, I might believe I intend M and, indeed, reflexively believe M, and yet not actually intend M. This could happen if my reflexive belief that M is not, in fact, the conclusion of practical reasoning. So I might falsely believe I intend M even though I do in fact reflexively believe M.

Indeed, Harman himself provides an example (one he attributes to Derek Parfit) in which one's reflexive belief is not a conclusion of practical reasoning, and so is not an intention. An insomniac might believe that he will stay awake because of his very belief that he will; yet he does not intend to stay awake. On Harman's 1976 theory, the insomniac's reflexive belief is not an intention because it is not a conclusion of practical reasoning.

Suppose now that the insomniac somehow mistakenly thinks his reflexive belief is the conclusion of practical reasoning – reasoning that is concerned, perhaps, with his desire to stay awake in order to write his paper for a conference on practical reason. He thereby mistakenly thinks he intends to stay awake. His belief that he intends to stay awake is false, though he does (reflexively) believe that he will stay awake. So, again, it is not true in such a case that in falsely believing one intends x one falsely believes one believes x.

I conclude that if misidentification of one's own intentions is always a form of theoretical irrationality, it will need to be for a reason different from that alluded to by Harman. And, indeed, Kieran Setiya has sketched a different argument for thinking there will always be a form of theoretical irrationality.[50]

Setiya begins with a theory of intention that is close to Harman's 1976 view: to intend to A is to have a self-referential belief that one will A by way of this very belief, where this belief is itself motivating.[51] Setiya thinks that if this is what intention is, then false belief about what one intends is

[49] That is, intentions are beliefs whose contents have the form: I will M in part because of this very belief.

[50] An initial formulation was in his comments on "Intention, Belief, Practical, Theoretical"; a more detailed version is in "Cognitivism about Instrumental Reason."

[51] In saying that the belief itself is motivating, Setiya may be going beyond what Harman claims in his 1976 paper, though Harman does sketch a similar view in his 1986 essay "Willing and Intending."

always a form of theoretical incoherence in which one violates "the epistemic 'should'."

In defense of this last claim, Setiya begins with an idea he derives from work of Richard Moran: "In the epistemic sense of 'should', one should never make an inference" – where Setiya is focusing on non-deductive inference "on the basis of evidence" – that is of a kind that "could never be both sound and ampliative."[52] But, given Setiya's theory of intention,

> An inference to the conclusion that I intend to x, from *any* premise, will instantiate a pattern that cannot be both sound and ampliative. For suppose that I infer that I intend to x on the ground that *p*. If the conclusion is false, the inference is unsound. But if the conclusion is true, the self-reference of intention ensures that the inference is redundant. If I intend to x, I already believe that I am going to x because I so intend . . .
>
> It follows . . . that there is something incoherent about the belief that I intend to x, unless it is constituted by the intention to x. It is an inherently defective belief.[53]

Is it really true, on Setiya's theory of intention, that "If I intend to x, I already believe that I am going to x because I so intend"? If this were true it would be surprising, since it seems at least *possible* to have intentions one does not believe one has (which is not yet the possibility of mistakenly believing one has an intention one does not have). So if Setiya is accurately representing an implication of his theory we should be wary of that theory. The theory combines the idea that (a) intention is a kind of belief, with the idea that (b) intention involves reflexivity. Each of these ideas has a certain plausibility, though I myself would want to resist at least (a). And – it is important to note – these ideas are independent: one could accept (a) without (b), and vice versa.[54] But, if Setiya is accurately representing an implication of his theory, then what has happened is that when we put these two ideas together we get a surprising conclusion that one *never* intends something without believing that one so intends. By my lights, this should lead us to go back and re-examine the proposed merger of (a) and (b).

But perhaps Setiya is not accurately representing an implication of his theory. To be sure, on the theory, if I intend x then I believe I will x because of this very *belief*. But not all such reflexive beliefs – even true

52 "Cognitivism About Instrumental Reason": 670. Setiya is here extending talk of soundness to non-deductive inference.

53 "Cognitivism about Instrumental Reason": 671 (I have changed the action variable).

54 John Searle, for example, accepts (b) but not (a). See *Intentionality: An Essay in the Philosophy of Mind* (Cambridge: Cambridge University Press, 1983): chapter 3.

ones – are intentions; that is the lesson we learn from Parfit's insomniac case. So perhaps, even on Setiya's theory, I can in fact intend x without believing I *intend* x, though in intending x I reflexively believe I believe x, and this reflexive belief is, in fact, my intention. If so, I might newly come to believe, on the basis of evidence, that I do indeed intend x and do not merely reflexively believe I will x. If I do in fact intend x then the reasoning that leads me to this new belief about my intention could be both sound and ampliative. So it would not violate Setiya's epistemic prohibition of inference that is of a kind that "could never be both *sound* and *ampliative*." If I do not in fact intend x then I will have a false belief about what I intend even though the reasoning leading to that false belief is of a kind that *could* be both sound and ampliative (though, of course, it is not in this case).

My conclusion, then, is that Setiya has not convincingly shown that a false belief about one's own intentions ineluctably violates an epistemic "should." If we interpret his theory of intention in a way that does seem to show this, the theory is problematic; if we interpret the theory in a less problematic way, it does not show this.

## 5 BROOME ON PRACTICAL REASONING

Both of my objections to Harman's basic idea interact with recent work by John Broome on practical reasoning, work that leads Broome to a version of cognitivism about IR. Broome's views are complex; but for present purposes we can understand the relevant aspects of his view in terms of the following claims[55]:

(1) Intention is not belief.
(2) It is not in general true that if you intend E you believe E.

This last is because (and here Broome and I agree)

(3) You can sometimes intend E but fail to believe you intend E; and in such cases you may well not believe E.
(4) But, if you do believe you intend E then you will believe E.
(5) And for your intention to E to enter into practical reasoning about means to E, you need to believe you intend E.
(6) So when your intention to E enters into your practical reasoning about means to E, you believe E.

[55] In this discussion I focus on Broome's "The Unity of Reasoning?." I quote from the manuscript of August 2008.

(7) And it is this belief that E that provides the premise for your reasoning, namely: E.
(8) If you also believe that E only if M, and if these beliefs do not change, BC requires that you believe M; and that is where your reasoning can lead.
(9) But if in the "background" you believe that M will obtain only if you intend M, then if you do arrive at the belief that M this will normally be by way of intending M. In satisfying BC in this way you will satisfy IR.

This, then, is Broome's broadly cognitivist picture of reasoning from intended ends to intended means. Broome wants to acknowledge, though, that it remains possible to intend E, believe that this requires both M and that you intend M, but falsely believe that you intend M. Broome grants that in such a case you fail to satisfy IR, though you may well satisfy BC. But, says Broome,

(10) In such a case "your false belief blocks any reasoning that can bring you to satisfy" IR.[56] So,
(11) Insofar as IR is a rational demand *that can be satisfied by reasoning* it is demand that derives from BC. Insofar as IR seems to impose demands that go beyond what is imposed by BC, these are not demands that can be satisfied by reasoning.

In this sense, it is BC that is fundamental for a theory of practical reasoning from ends to means.

Let me focus here on two ideas. The first is that my intention to E enters into my means-end reasoning by providing the believed premise that I will E. I will believe this premise since, for my intention to enter into my reasoning I need to believe I so intend; and if I believe I intend E then I believe E. The second idea is that a false belief that I intend M blocks the possibility of arriving at an actual intention to M by way of practical reasoning that begins with my intention to E. The first idea is that the relevant practical reasoning that can lead me to satisfy IR is theoretical reasoning concerning the contents of my associated beliefs. The second idea is that insofar as IR may seem – in cases of false belief about what one intends – to impose a rational demand that goes beyond what such theoretical reasoning can satisfy, it imposes a rational demand that no reasoning can satisfy. Taken together, these ideas amount to a kind of cognitivism about IR. And I think that both of my reasons for

[56] "The Unity of Reasoning?": msp. 17.

objecting to Harman's basic idea also suggest challenges to this form of cognitivism.

Broome supposes, in claim (5), that my intention to E can enter into my practical reasoning only if I believe I so intend. This seems delicate. On the one hand, it seems that we do not suppose that the belief that p can enter into theoretical reasoning only if one has the second-order belief that one believes p. It seems, for example, that a child might reason theoretically without having the concept of belief, and so without having a belief that she believes.[57] (Though perhaps, if her reasoning is *conscious*, she needs some higher-order thought that is in fact about her belief.[58]) So why should we think that intention is different from belief in this respect? On the other hand, a reasoning system needs to keep track of whether an attitude involved in reasoning is a belief or an intention. And one way to do this is to have second-order beliefs – or perhaps some other sort of higher-order thought – about which attitude is in fact involved.

Since I do not want to try to sort out this matter here, I will proceed by bracketing this complication and simply granting claim (5) for present purposes. Note though that Broome also needs claim (4), the claim that if you believe you intend E then you believe E. Claim (4) assumes that the only breakdowns between intending E and believing E occur when you fail to believe you intend E. But there is reason to be skeptical about this assumption: that is the point of the example of my commitment to stopping at the bookstore while being aware of my absent-mindedness, an example I offered as part of my first objection to Harman's basic idea.

Broome notes the possibility of such examples, and he acknowledges that we sometimes call the agent's attitude towards his action in such examples "intention." Broome says that in the case of such a non-confident intention one would normally express one's intention not by saying (or thinking) that one will so act (as one would, according to Broome, in the normal case of intention) but, rather, by saying (or thinking) that one intends so to act. And Broome acknowledges that such a non-confident intention in favor of E will not provide, as a premise for one's practical reasoning, the believed proposition E. Since Broome's story of the role of an intention to E in providing a premise for such practical reasoning is that it provides the believed proposition that E, he must grant – as he does – that his story of

[57] Example courtesy of John Broome, in correspondence.

[58] See David Rosenthal, "A Theory of Consciousness," in Ned Block, Owen Flanagan, and Guven Guzeldere, eds., *The Nature of Consciousness: Philosophical Debates* (Cambridge, MA: MIT Press, 1997): 729–753.

practical reasoning from ends to means does not apply to the case of a non-confident intention in favor of E: such non-confident intentions are "beyond the scope" of his account.[59]

But even if my intention to stop at the bookstore is non-confident it involves a distinctive kind of practical commitment that goes beyond mere preference: I have, in some practical sense, settled on stopping there. This returns us to the basic question of whether it is this practical step that newly engages a requirement like IR, or whether the relevant requirement of instrumental rationality is only engaged once one actually believes one will do as one intends. If we say the former – that even non-confident intention engages a requirement along the lines of IR – then we should worry that Broome's account of practical reasoning from ends to means is inappropriately limited in scope. Broome identifies such practical reasoning with a form of theoretical reasoning that is commonly – though, it seems, not necessarily – associated with practical reasoning from ends to means. And that identification seems problematic.

What about Broome's claim (10), the claim that in a case in which you knowingly intend E and know that this requires your intending M, but you falsely believe you intend M, "your false belief blocks any reasoning that can bring you to satisfy" IR? Broome's view here is that

> [t]here is simply no way you can reason your way to an actual intention, past your belief that you have an intention.[60]

This leads to Broome's idea that insofar as IR goes beyond what is required by BC – since IR requires that you actually intend M in cases in which BC is satisfied by your false belief that you so intend – it does not require something you can achieve by reasoning. This is Broome's strategy for responding to the issues raised by my second objection to Harman's basic idea. What to say?

Well, consider reasoning in which one aims to *reconfirm* what one in fact already believes. I believe I locked the door when I left home earlier today. But I find myself engaged in reasoning that aims at reconfirmation:

> Susan was there. She would have seen whether I locked it. If she had seen that I had failed to lock it she would have said something. She didn't say something. So, I locked it.

Granted, in many such cases I suspend my belief that I locked it, once I embark on the reasoning. But I don't see that this is necessary. A concern

[59] "The Unity of Reasoning?": msp. 13.
[60] "The Unity of Reasoning?": msp. 16.

with reconfirmation need not begin with doubt about what is to be reconfirmed; it might be focused, rather, on articulating the precise grounds for one's belief.

Suppose now that I didn't really believe I had locked the door, though I somehow believed I believed that. It seems that I could engage in the cited reasoning – reasoning that I mistakenly thought of as merely reconfirming my belief – but which, in fact, leads to my newly believing I locked the door. As a matter of fact, this reasoning finally fully convinces me that I locked the door. My earlier false belief that I already believed I locked the door need not block this.

Return now to the case of a false belief about what one intends. Suppose I intend E (and I know this), I know that E requires M by way of intending M, I do not in fact intend M, but I falsely believe I intend M. Though I satisfy BC (in the relevant respect) I am in violation of IR, though I do not know that I am. Suppose I aim to go through the practical reasoning in favor of intending M as a way of articulating the rational support for the intention in favor of M that I falsely believe I already have. (Perhaps, for example, M is my engaging in unpleasant physical therapy, and I seek to reconfirm the grounds for doing this unpleasant thing as a means to my intended end of recovery from my accident.) It seems I can go through the relevant means-end reasoning and thereby in fact be led newly to intend M, though by my own (false) lights my intention to M is not new and this reasoning merely reconfirms an intention I already have. My earlier false belief that I already intend M need not block this way of newly coming into conformity with IR by way of reasoning. So – though I grant that such cases are unusual – I do not think we should accept Broome's claims that "[t]here is simply no way you can reason your way to an actual intention, past your belief that you have an intention" and that "your false belief blocks any reasoning that can bring you to satisfy" IR. So we need a version of IR that goes beyond BC in order to understand how reasoning your way to an intention in favor of necessary means despite a prior false belief that you already so intend can newly bring you into conformity with a requirement of instrumental rationality. And that means that we should not be cognitivists about IR.

## 6 CONCLUSION

What conclusion should we draw from these reflections? Well, cognitivism seems beset by difficulties associated with the possibility of mistaken beliefs about what one intends; and many versions of cognitivism do not sufficiently come to terms with the way in which non-confident intentions seem to engage a basic demand of instrumental rationality even in the absence of a belief in success. Further, it seems plausible that we do not need cognitivism to see the relevant norms as tied to a constitutive aim of intention, or thereby to explain their special nature. So, though there remain important unresolved problems that arise for both cognitivism and for the practical commitment view, the weight of these reflections seems so far to argue in favor of the practical commitment view as a better model of this fundamental aspect of reason.[61]

[61] As noted, I am including in these reflections the arguments in both this present essay and in "Intention, Belief, Practical, Theoretical." Let me note, however, an issue I have not tried to address in either of these essays. One might conjecture that cognitivism about IR is needed in order to avoid the kind of unacceptable bootstrapping described in "Intention and Means-End Reasoning" and in *Intention, Plans, and Practical Reason*: 24–27. The idea, in a nutshell, is that it is only by seeing IR as, at bottom, a theoretical requirement on belief rather than a requirement of practical rationality on intention, that we can avoid seeing intending *E* as always providing a kind of practical reason for *M* that constitutes unacceptable bootstrapping. Setiya develops an idea along these lines in "Cognitivism about Instrumental Reason." I hope to address this issue on another occasion.

CHAPTER 3

# *Reasons: practical and adaptive**

*Joseph Raz*

I will consider some of the differences between epistemic reasons and reasons for action, and use these differences to illuminate a major division between types of normative reasons,[1] which I will call 'adaptive' and 'practical' reasons. A few clarifications of some aspects of the concept of epistemic reasons will lead to a distinction between standard and non-standard reasons (section 1). Some differences between epistemic and practical reasons will be described and explained in section 2, paving the way to generalising the contrast and explaining the difference between adaptive and practical reasons (section 3). Sections 4 and 5 further explain and defend the views of the preceding sections. My ultimate goal is an explanation of normativity. But the present essay does more to explain a difficulty such an explanation faces than to resolve it.

## 1 STANDARD AND NON-STANDARD REASONS

Reasons for action, I will assume, are facts which constitute a case for (or against) the performance of an action. Epistemic reasons are reasons for believing in a proposition through being facts which are part of a case for (belief in) its truth (call such considerations 'truth-related'). These

* The first draft of this essay was presented at a conference on practical reason at Bowling Green, April 7–9, 2006. Parts of it were presented on various subsequent occasions. I am grateful for comments given me at the conference, and by others, including Stephen Everson, Ulrike Heuer, Mark Kalderon, David Owens, Anthony Price, Peter Railton and Kieran Setiya.

[1] On the difference between, and the relations of normative and explanatory reasons, see Joseph Raz, 'Reasons: Normative and Explanatory', in C. Sandis, ed., *New Essays on the Explanation of Action* (Basingstoke: Palgrave, 2008). I will generally use 'reasons' to refer to normative reasons, adding the adjective only occasionally to underline the point. Reasons are inherently relational. 'P is a reason' means that there is someone and some action or belief so that P is a reason for that person to have that belief or to perform that action. The same is true of evidence: 'E is evidence for P' means that there is someone such that at a particular time E is for that person a reason to believe that P.

maxims (as I shall call them) have proved controversial. Confining myself to the epistemic maxim, two clarifications and one argument may help.

The first clarification concerns the question of what determines whether available epistemic reasons are sufficient to warrant belief. It is not my view that only truth-related considerations figure among those determining the sufficiency of the case. However, the factors or principles which determine whether the case for the truth of a proposition is adequate to warrant belief are not themselves reasons for belief. Therefore, the maxim is not affected by this point.[2]

The second clarification concerns arguments that simplicity, elegance, explanatory power, or other such considerations govern rational belief or theory acceptance. The maxim is consistent with such views, so long as theory acceptance is understood for what it is: acceptance of theories, not belief in them. The maxim is about reasons for belief only. It denies that the simplicity of a proposition or a theory is always a reason to believe it. But such considerations may be relevant to acceptance of propositions. As Ulrike Heuer suggested to me, accepting a proposition is conducting oneself in accord with, and because of, the belief that there is sufficient reason to act on the assumption that the proposition is true: acceptance of the proposition that P entails belief, but not belief that P. Rather it entails belief that it is justified to act as if P. Thus acceptance combines epistemic and practical reasons, though its target is action rather than belief. Acceptance dominates many areas of practical thought. The whole system of law enforcement via courts and tribunals is based on acceptance of presumptions, like the presumption of innocence, and on accepting verdicts based on evidence presented in court, while ignoring all other evidence. Juries and judges are not required to believe that the accused is guilty or innocent. They are required only to accept and pronounce verdicts which are correct according to the evidence before them. Often other people who do not believe that the verdict is correct have compelling reasons to conduct themselves as if it were correct, that is to accept its content.

My one argument in support of the maxim is directed against the suggestion that since believing something can have benefits or disadvantages independently of the truth of what is believed there can be epistemic reasons which are not part of the case for its truth. For example, should an evil demon credibly threaten to punish me unless I believe something, would that not be a reason to believe that something? Perhaps it is. I will

[2] See for example Sarah Stroud, 'Epistemic Partiality in Friendship', *Ethics*, 116 (2006): 498–524, at 498, in support of the relevance of non-truth-related considerations.

return to that question in section 3. For the moment let us accept a terminological convention and continue to call the truth-related reasons for belief epistemic reasons. The others are practical reasons, perhaps they are practical reasons for belief. There are fundamental differences between truth-related and non-truth-related reasons for belief which show that the latter are practical.

Among others, truth-related considerations differ from other alleged reasons for belief in two important respects. First, one who believes that there is a conclusive case for the truth of a proposition cannot but believe that proposition (pathological cases[3] apart). There is no gap, no extra step in reasoning, between believing that the case for the truth of the proposition is conclusive and believing the proposition. Similarly, there is no gap between believing that the case for the truth of a proposition is inadequate and withholding belief in it.[4] More directly and more generally (and again excepting pathologies), reasoning from (what we treat as) reasons for belief to a conclusion (from: 'the door is open' to 'therefore anyone could have walked in') we acquire the belief as we arrive at the conclusion. As we conclude that therefore anyone could have walked in, we come to believe that anyone could have walked in. By way of contrast, one cannot similarly reason from a non-truth-related reason for having a belief to having that belief. I cannot believe that Bush is a good president because I believe that I would get a plum job offer if I did so believe. All that is conceptually possible for us to conclude is that we should believe that Bush is a good president. But that is a different conclusion. It, too, is a belief, but a different one. Of course if we should believe that Bush is a good president then we have reason to bring it about that we so believe.

[3] Pathological cases are ones where some of the conditions which constitute belief are met while others are not. There are many possible pathologies. One simple one is when one manifests all the criteria for such a belief, except in a particular context, say when thinking about one's relations with one's parents, when the belief sort of disappears.

[4] These claims require a more elaborate, qualified and subtle formulation than I can give them. For an argument for a position a good deal stronger than the two claims I make here see Jonathan Adler, *Belief's Own Ethics* (Cambridge, MA: MIT Press, 2002). For various discussions of non-truth-related reasons see Gilbert Harman, 'Rationality', reprinted in Gilbert Harman, *Reasoning, Meaning and Mind* (Oxford: Oxford University Press, 1999); D.N. Osherson *et al.*, eds., *Thinking: An Invitation to Cognitive Science*, vol. 3 (Cambridge, MA: MIT Press, 2nd edn. 1995–8); Derek Parfit, 'Rationality and Reasons,' in Dan Egonsson *et al.*, eds., *Exploring Practical Philosophy* (Burlington, VT: Ashgate, 2001); Jonas Olson, 'Buck-Passing and the Wrong Kind of Reasons,' *The Philosophical Quarterly*, 54 (2004): 295–300; Justin D'Arms and Daniel Jacobson, 'Sentiment and Value,' *Ethics*, 110 (2000): 722–748; Wlodek Rabinowitz and Toni Rønnow-Rasmussen, 'The Strike of the Demon: On Fitting Pro-Attitudes and Value,' *Ethics*, 114: (2004): 191, 391–423; Pamela Hieronymi, 'The Wrong Kind of Reason,' *The Journal of Philosophy*, 102 (2005): 435–457, at 437.

Needless to say, belief in the advantages I will enjoy if I believe that Bush is a good president can cause me to deceive myself into believing that there are adequate truth-related reasons to believe that Bush is a good president. But that does not undermine the contrast between truth-related and other considerations to which I pointed.[5]

Second, think of the distinction, familiar from practical reasons, between conforming with reasons and following them. A reason to Φ is conformed with when one Φs, and is followed when one Φs for that reason. In some cases conforming requires following: some reasons are reasons not merely to perform an action, but to perform it for a reason (this is normally the case when the reason is to perform the action intentionally), and some reasons require performing it for that very same reason (one's love may be a reason to perform actions out of love). Often, however, reasons are reasons to perform the action, regardless of the reason why. I sometimes find myself in my office at a time I promised to be there, even though I forgot about the promise. Still, I did all I promised to do. I conformed to the reason my promise is. Applying an intuitively analogous distinction to theoretical reasons, we see that in coming to believe what one has non-truth-related reasons to believe one conforms to those reasons, but one cannot come to that belief by following them. One cannot come to believe a proposition for the reason that there are non-truth-related normative reasons for having that belief. That cannot be one's reason for holding that belief. By way of contrast, one can come to have a belief by following truth-related reasons for it. One can have the belief for which they are reasons, and one can have it for those reasons.[6]

These considerations, especially the second one, suggest a distinction between standard and non-standard reasons for action, belief, intention, emotion, or whatever. Standard reasons are those which we can follow directly, that is have the attitude, or perform the action, for that reason. Non-standard reasons for an action or an attitude are such that one can conform to them, but not follow them directly.

The importance of the distinction is shown by its relevance to many other issues. Not least that having a belief for adequate truth-related

[5] This failure of the simple route to belief is (a generalised form of) Williams' condition that one reaches the belief 'because in some way he is considering the matter aright': Bernard Williams, *Moral Luck* (Cambridge: Cambridge University Press, 1981): 109. See also section 4 of my 'Reasons: Normative and Explanatory', and S. Darwall in *The Second-person Standpoint* (Cambridge, MA: Harvard University Press, 2006): 66.

[6] The same points are at the core of Nishi Shah's 'A New Argument for Evidentialism', *The Philosophical Quarterly*, 56 (2006): 481–498.

reasons is rational, and having it for non-truth-related reasons (i.e. when one's (belief in) non-truth-related reasons to believe is – part of – the explanation of why one believes), even if useful and desirable, is irrational. This vindicates a familiar thought: epistemic reasons can warrant belief. Non-truth-related reasons cannot. So while it may be best (because it is advantageous, or conducive to the common good, etc.) to believe that, e.g., one's loved ones are in perfect health, or that one will win a competition, the factors which make it so are not epistemic reasons for that belief. They are non-standard practical reasons for having the belief.

## 2 EPISTEMIC REASONS AND REASONS FOR ACTION: SOME DIFFERENCES

It is time to turn to the difference between reasons for action and epistemic reasons. I will focus on evidence-based reasons. Here are some others: that today is Friday the 17th is reason to believe that Sunday will be the 19th. That the visitor I expect is a bachelor is reason to believe that he is male. That citizens have a right to vote in elections and that you are a citizen, is reason to believe that you have a right to vote. Logical, conceptual, norm-based, expert-based, testimonial and other epistemic reasons differ from evidence in important respects. The crucial differences, the first two below, apply to all of them, and that makes it unnecessary to discuss them separately.

### *(a) The First Two: Pluralism and Value*

Two fundamental differences between epistemic and practical reasons[7] follow from the maxims. Epistemic reasons are governed by one concern: determination whether the belief for which they are reasons is or is not true. Reasons for a single action may, and typically are, governed by many concerns. A single action can serve or disserve a number of intrinsic values: it may be an act of friendship and of justice. Moreover, even when the reasons for an action derive from a single value the action may serve independent concerns: a single act can advance the welfare of several individuals, when the interest of each of them is a reason, an independent reason, to perform it.[8]

[7] As indicated at the outset I will argue that reasons for action are but one kind of practical reasons. However, to expedite expression I will refer to them using the generic category, 'practical reasons' rather than the less flexible in use 'reasons for action'. What I say is meant to be true of all practical reasons.

[8] See my 'Personal Practical Conflicts', in Peter Baumann and Monica Betzler, eds., *Practical Conflicts: New Philosophical Essays* (Cambridge: Cambridge University Press, 2004): 172.

To the extent that reasons for action represent independent concerns, we have reason to satisfy all of them. When reasons deriving from independent concerns conflict it is impossible to do so. In that case whatever we do some of the concerns which generate reasons for us will remain unsatisfied (by our actions at the time).

Hence when (independent) reasons for action conflict, even when it is clear which action is supported by the better reason, there is some loss, consisting in the fact that even when we successfully do our best there are concerns that we have reason to meet or satisfy which were left unsatisfied. Typically, concerns which remain unsatisfied provide reason for some action in the future, to satisfy them, or if impossible (or unjustified because of further conflicts) to do the second best, to come as close to satisfying them as possible (which is what compensation often is). If I have reason to have a relaxed weekend by the seaside and a stronger conflicting reason to work in the office to meet an urgent deadline, then I should work in the office and find a way of taking half a day off on Monday to get at least some holiday.

There is no close analogue of the need to satisfy independent concerns and therefore no close analogue of reasons for compensatory actions in epistemic reasons. Epistemic reasons can conflict, but all of them are about the truth of the propositions for or against belief in which they are reasons. The weaker reasons are just less reliable guides to one and the same end. There is no loss in dismissing a less reliable clue. This is a fundamental difference between epistemic and practical reasons. Noting this difference, Susan Hurley[9] compared reasons for belief to rules of thumb, useful when useful, but happily replaced when better ones are available. She used this difference between practical and epistemic reasons to explain the absence of epistemic akrasia.

To put it in my own terms: because there is no possibility that the lesser reason for belief serves a concern which is not served better by the better reason there is no possibility of preferring to follow what one takes to be the lesser reason rather than the better one. The possibility of akrasia depends on the fact that belief that a practical reason is defeated by a better conflicting reason is consistent with belief that it serves a concern which the better reason does not, and which can motivate one to follow it.

[9] Susan Hurley, *Natural Reasons* (Oxford: Oxford University Press, 1989): 130–135. The argument is not conclusive, but the case for epistemic akrasia is not the current subject. The disanalogy Hurley points to is real enough.

So far, I argued that practical reasons serve many concerns and epistemic ones can serve only one. It is tempting to explain this by saying that practical reasons derive from many values, whereas epistemic reasons derive from one value only, presumably the value of having true beliefs, or two, the values of having true beliefs and of not having false ones. I think that there is some, though only some, truth in the first half of that proposition: the value of actions constitutes reasons for them and as actions can have many distinct evaluative properties there are many concerns those reasons express. But reasons for belief are not similarly connected to values, not even to a single value.

First, the diversity of concerns manifested in practical reasons is not entirely due to the diversity of values. Diverse values do generate diverse concerns, but so do other factors: for example, being a medically qualified caretaker of sheltered accommodation for disabled people I have a reason to help anyone there who needs insulin injections. There are several such people. So I have a reason to help each of them. Each of these reasons represents an independent concern, and they can conflict with each other, even though they all derive from the same value.

Second, epistemic reasons do not derive from the value of having that belief in the way that reasons for an action derive from the value of that action. It is not the case that there is always value in having a true belief, whatever it is. Nor is it the case that it is always a disvalue to have a false belief. If that is so, and since there can always be reasons for believing at least any true proposition, it follows that reasons for belief are not provided by values in the way that reasons for action are.

To maintain that reasons for belief do not derive from the value of having true beliefs one need not deny that often having true beliefs is instrumentally valuable, nor that there are some types of beliefs such that having true, or warranted true beliefs of those kinds is intrinsically valuable. The point is about epistemic reasons. Whether or not there are adequate reasons to believe in a proposition is a question unrelated to the value of having that belief. It is not the case that there are reasons for belief only when there is value in the belief. That is all that is required to show that reasons for a belief do not derive from the value of the belief in the way that reasons for an action derive from the value of the action.[10]

[10] The same goes for knowledge. There is no value in having knowledge as such, and reasons which underwrite knowledge do not depend on the value of having that knowledge. For a survey of recent writings on the value of knowledge, see David Prichard, 'Recent Work on Epistemic Value', *American Philosophical Quarterly*, 44 (2007): 85–110.

To argue to the contrary, one needs to establish that if we have a belief it is better that it be true than false, or that it be warranted than unwarranted, or some variants of these. In considering such claims we have to dismiss as irrelevant two slightly different views. First, that on balance given that true beliefs are less likely to mislead than false ones, it is (instrumentally) better that one's beliefs be true. Whatever the truth of the generalisation it does not warrant the conclusion that regarding any one of one's beliefs it is better that it be true than false. Second, while the fact that one's beliefs are warranted is evidence that one is functioning rationally, it does not follow, even assuming that it is good to function rationally, that it is better to have warranted than unwarranted beliefs (only that it is a byproduct of something good). Given these points it is hard to see what is meant by affirming the value of having true beliefs other than that true beliefs are correct, that is true.

Imagine the contrary, that is imagine that in all cases, if we have a belief about a certain matter then it is better to have a true rather than a false belief, just because it is true. Consider an example: a month ahead of time I believe that Red Rod will win the Derby or that the Social-Democrats will win the elections in Denmark. There may be ways to increase the likelihood that my belief is true. Perhaps I could give valuable advice to Red Rod's jockey, or lend my expertise to the Social-Democrats. Is the fact that that will make it more likely that my beliefs are true a reason to do so? If there is value in one's beliefs being true as such then there should be no difference between making reality conform to the belief and making the belief conform to how things are.

### *(b) Third Difference: Presumptive Sufficiency*

The value-independent character of epistemic reasons has important implications which will occupy much of the rest of this essay. Here I will argue that it is responsible for another difference between epistemic and practical reasons. Practical reasons are presumptively sufficient. Epistemic reasons are not necessarily so. To see this, we need to recall that often what appear to be references to several reasons may be references to one and the same reason. That my mother is in hospital, that there is a rail strike today, that she forgot her slippers at home may all be cited by me as my reason for heading towards the bus stop. But clearly they all refer to one reason. Facts which are part of a reason are commonly stated as a way of referring to the (complete) reason of which they are a part.

A (complete) reason to $\Phi$ at a particular time is *presumptively sufficient* because if there is no other reason either for or against so acting then (a) $\Phi$-ing at that time is justified, and (b) if the agent rationally believes that the reason applies, and that there is no other, then his failing to try to $\Phi$ is akratic.[11]

Things are different with epistemic reasons.[12] Even if at a particular time there is only one reason for the agent to believe that a particular proposition is true, and no reason against that belief, coming to have that belief on the strength of that reason may be unjustified and irrational, and failing to do so may be justified and rational. Even a good and undefeated epistemic reason may be insufficient to warrant belief. It may support it, but not be sufficient to warrant it.[13]

One may object that it is possible to define epistemic reasons as reasons which warrant belief, thus eliminating the difference between the two kinds of reason. Such a move is, however, too artificial to make any difference. We can identify practical reasons independently of whether they are presumptively sufficient, simply by identifying their normative force. We then show by example or argument that they are presumptively sufficient. If one insists on defining complete epistemic reasons as those which are presumptively sufficient to warrant belief it would follow that there are good, independent epistemic reasons, which are not complete reasons. They nevertheless have normative force and that would be enough to establish the difference between practical and epistemic reasons, as there are no practical reasons with normative force which are not sufficient to warrant action.

This contrast between epistemic and practical reasons is made possible by an important difference between belief and action. We can suspend belief, but not suspend action. Suspending belief means believing neither the proposition nor its contradictory. But there is no third option between doing an action and not doing it. If not performing an action is the contradictory of performing it then suspension of action, that is neither

[11] Michael Stocker and Jonathan Dancy are among writers who reject the second feature. I find their views difficult to sustain, but we need not consider them here. The first feature is sufficient to establish the difference between practical and epistemic reasons. See, e.g., Michael Stocker, 'Raz on the Intelligibility of Bad Acts', in R. Jay Wallace, Philip Pettit, Samuel Scheffler and Michael Smith, eds., *Reason and Value: Themes from the Moral Philosophy of Joseph Raz* (Oxford: Oxford University Press, 2004), and Jonathan Dancy, 'Enticing Reasons', in the same (2004) work.

[12] See Joseph Raz, *Engaging Reason* (Oxford: Oxford University Press, 1999); and David Owens, 'Epistemic Akrasia', *The Monist*, 85 (2002): 381.

[13] For a contrary view, see Donald Davidson, 'How is Weakness of the Will Possible?', in J. Feinberg, ed., *Moral Concepts* (Oxford: Oxford University Press, 1970), reprinted in Donald Davidson, *Essays on Actions and Events* (Oxford: Oxford University Press, 1980): 21.

performing it nor not performing it, is not possible. But while this difference between action and belief makes room for the possibility of undefeated epistemic reasons which do not warrant beliefs, it does not in itself explain the difference. The explanation for this lies in the first two differences. Given that epistemic reasons are governed by a single concern they have, as we saw, the character of clues, and like clues they may be both good clues and insufficient to enable one rationally to form a view about the solution. Analogously, evidence may be good evidence but insufficient to warrant belief. On the other hand, a practical reason exists only if there is some good or some point in performing the action for which it is a reason. This is what it is to be a reason, to be a fact which confers value or point on the action. Hence, a single reason is sufficient to give point or value to the action, and absent any other reason it is sufficient to justify it.

## 3 GENERALISING THE CONTRAST: PRACTICAL AND ADAPTIVE REASONS

Reasons (taken together) determine the ways people should relate to the world, in their beliefs, emotions, actions and the like. But epistemic and practical reasons do so in fundamentally different ways. Briefly stated, the basic difference between practical and epistemic reasons is that practical reasons, taken together, determine what and how, in light of the value of things, we should change or preserve in ourselves or the world. Epistemic reasons do not. They determine the way our beliefs should adjust to track how things are.

There are other normative reasons. Do they divide into two classes of which reasons for action and epistemic reasons are examples? For lack of appropriate terminology I will use 'practical reasons' to designate the class of which reasons for action are an instance, and 'adaptive reasons' to designate the class to which epistemic reasons belong. Reasons which are value-related are practical reasons, even if they are reasons for having a belief, or an emotion. Reasons are adaptive if they mark the appropriateness of an attitude in the agent independently of the value of having that attitude, its appropriateness to the way things are. Are there other instances of these types?

### *(a) The Case of Emotions*

Standard reasons for belief are adaptive, while non-standard reasons for belief are practical. How about reasons for or against having an emotion?

I will just introduce the topic, which is too large to deal with here. The role of reasons in our emotional life is very different from their role in our beliefs. I will mention only two differences. First, reasons allow much greater latitude regarding whether an emotion is required. For the most part even when appropriate there is nothing amiss in not having it. Fear is appropriate when facing great danger, but only exceptionally would its absence when in danger be against reason. Nor is its appropriate degree strictly regulated by reason. Second, emotions do not necessarily respond to reasons with the immediacy which characterises belief's relationship to reasons. When convinced that a belief is not supported by reasons we lose the belief, but typically realising that we were mistaken to think that there were reasons for an emotion does not instantly kill off the emotion. A period of adjustment is usually needed. These and other differences notwithstanding, emotions, like beliefs, are subject to at least two kinds of reasons. For we can usefully distinguish between affect-justifying reasons for emotions and practical reasons for having an emotions, which are not affect-justifying reasons.

Affect-justifying reasons are part of a case for the emotion being an appropriate response to how things are. Affect-justifying reasons are reasons awareness of which could rationally induce, as well as (other things being equal) establish the rationality of, having an emotion. Having been insulted is an affect-justifying reason for resentment. The fact that anger with one's competitor may, in the circumstances, improve one's chances of winning the competition is not an affect-justifying reason. Absent any other reason for anger, it will be irrational to be angry for that reason.[14] But that anger will help one win the competition is a practical reason (not necessarily a sufficient one) for experiencing that emotion.

Affect-justifying reasons are adaptive. We can test their independence of value as before: given that I am afraid of the journey (for no reason), do I have any reason at all to make my journey dangerous and make my fear appropriate? Given that I am jealous of Abe, do I have any reason to induce Abe to do something which will give me reason to be jealous of him? Only in jokes. The same applies to other emotions: we have adaptive

[14] Judgements of irrationality are notoriously tricky to analyse. One complication regarding the rationality of the emotions results from the fact that we may have (sometimes conflicting) affect-justifying and practical reasons for them. Anger with my competitor, deliberately induced to help me win the competition, may, in so far as it was so induced, not be irrational, while being irrational in so far as my competitor did nothing to merit that anger. Perhaps the best way to sort out this apparent conflict is to say that my inducing the anger was not irrational, even though being angry is irrational.

reasons that they be appropriate given how things stand. But it is not the case that when we have an emotion there is always value in its being appropriate. Sometimes this is so, but sometimes the reverse is the case.

To be sure, the very meaning of 'appropriate to the way things are' when applied to emotions, is problematic in ways in which the appropriateness to the way things are of true beliefs is not. Possibly the concept is incoherent. Possibly emotions are appropriate only in the case that beliefs, which are part of what makes them the kind of emotions they are, are true. This may be related to the fact that some emotions appear not to have appropriate reasons. A murderous rage, for example, appears never to be appropriate, perhaps because there is no belief which one must have to have the emotion. This would explain why it is not irrational to feel murderous rage. It is just immoral. Generally speaking, an emotion is irrational if one experiences it without there being an adaptive reason for having it. But this is so only if there can be adaptive reasons for it. Where none can exist neither experiencing nor not experiencing the emotion can be rational or irrational, though there can be practical reasons for or against having it. This is not the place to consider these vexed matters. For our purposes suffice it to establish that affect-justifying reasons are not value-related.

This would explain why there can be adaptive reasons for having emotions which it is always wrong to have. For example, some people believe that there is never a good reason to be envious. They must refer to practical reasons, for surely there are adaptive reasons for envy. If you envy someone his victory then you have no reason to envy him if he did not in fact win, if you are mistaken about his victory. If you continue to envy him after your mistake has been corrected, you are irrational. If he was victorious then you may have an emotion which it is bad or wrong to have, but you are not irrational.

So far so similar to beliefs – affect-justifying reasons are the standard reasons for emotions, and they are adaptive. There are, however, also non-standard reasons for emotions, which are practical reasons. Arguably, however, matters are much more complex. As I have already mentioned, given the circumstances reasons for emotions may require an emotion. Not having the emotion in such circumstances may show a deficiency in the people concerned. But we are unlikely to take them to be factors which contribute to a judgement that the person lacking the emotion is irrational. Furthermore, at least sometimes the deficiency may be a moral deficiency. Think, e.g., of people who do not feel compassion when it is appropriate, and 'required', as it were, to feel compassion. We are likely to think of this as a moral blemish, but not as a case of irrationality, not even if the person believes that compassion is required. Why not? Does it mean that the reason for the emotion is a moral, therefore a practical reason? That would show that there are standard practical reasons for emotions. But it would not explain why flouting them is not irrational, even if one is aware that one is flouting them.

But perhaps even though the emotion is a moral emotion, and its inappropriate absence or presence is a moral defect, the reason for the emotion is an adaptive reason. We can compare these cases to the moral deficiency betrayed by one's beliefs, which does not show that the reasons for the beliefs are themselves practical reasons. That would explain why the deficiency does not affect judgement of rationality (the reasons are adaptive, and we assume permissive in the cases under consideration) while also explaining how emotions can contribute to the evaluation of the morality of one's life or character.

### *(b) Actions*

There seem to be no adaptive reasons for actions, no sense of a reason for action which is unrelated to its value. Does the fact that all reasons for action are practical reasons mean that there are no non-standard reasons for action? Or does it mean that they require some alternative explanation? I think that the latter is the case.

The case for there being non-standard reasons for action arises out of the familiar case of actions which have a certain value only if they are not performed in order to realise that value. Some may say that where the value of an action cannot be realised if it is done in order to realise it then that value does not provide a reason for the action which would have it. The alternative is to take it as providing a reason to perform the action but not for that reason. In other words, the value of the action is a reason which is conformed with only if it is not followed. Performance of the act which manifests the value need not be coincidental. We may create some other reasons (e.g. by an appropriate bet, or by habituation to follow an appropriate rule) for performing the action.[15] (Such manipulation is not always possible, but then not always can we conform to reasons which apply to us.) This suggests that even such values provide reasons for the actions which have them.

[15] We may want to distinguish two senses of following a reason: (1) one follows a reason to Φ which applies to one if, for that reason, one does something to facilitate one's Φ-ing, and (2) one follows a reason to Φ if one Φs for that reason. Where an action has value only if performed not in order to realise that value it can be followed in sense (1), but not in sense (2) which is the standard sense of the expression (and to which I referred earlier as 'directly following').

These will be, though, non-standard reasons for action. The value of the action cannot be the reason for which the action is done: we cannot successfully perform the action we have reason to perform for that reason (because the action we have reason to perform is 'to perform a specific act but not for that reason'). But the reason is a reason to get ourselves to perform the action. So it seems that there are both standard and non-standard reasons for action, both kinds being practical reasons.

### *(c) Intentions*

Intentions present complications of their own. Reasons for action are either reasons for intentional actions, or for actions which need not be intentional. Put another way, practical reasons may be conformed to either only by an intentional action, or by actions which need not be intentional. Either way they are also reasons for intending the action, because performing it intentionally is a way of performing it.[16] If the reason is to perform an intentional action then having the intention is necessary for conforming with the reason. But even if the action need not be intentional intending it is the normal way to secure its performance, and therefore an undefeated reason for the action is also a reason for intending it.

Reasons to Φ are standard reasons for intending to Φ. But there can be others. There can be reasons to intend an action which are independent of whether there is reason for the action. I will call them independent reasons (for intentions). For example, it may be a good thing to reassure some people that I will perform an action, say, in a year's time. This may be so even though there is no reason to perform the action.[17] If I now intend to perform the action they will be reassured. So I have a reason to intend to perform an action which I do not have, and I know that I do not have, adequate reason to perform. A few months down the line that reason may disappear (e.g. it may become clear that the action will be performed anyway, if not by this agent then by another). In fact the agent never performs the action. Nevertheless he had a reason to intend it at the time.[18]

[16] Reasons to perform an action unintentionally are the sole exception to the above.

[17] The Toxin Puzzle (Gregory Kavka, 'The Toxin Puzzle', *Analysis*, 43 (1983): 33) raises the question whether when we believe that there is reason against an act we can still respond to a reason for having the intention. The phenomenon here discussed is wider, in not relying on a belief that there are reasons against the act.

[18] Sometimes there may be reasons against having intentions when there is no reason for the action. I will disregard such cases.

Just as a reason to perform an action is also a reason to intend the action so, at least in many cases, an independent reason to intend an action is, *ipso facto*, a reason to perform the action so intended. Sometimes this will be so because it is impossible to intend to Φ without Φ-ing, as is the case when the intention is the one embedded in the action (the intentionality which makes an intentional action intentional) or, more generally, when performing the action will make it easier to have the intention to perform it we may have a reason to perform the action to facilitate having the intention.

The question is: is it possible to intend to perform an action, which we do not believe that we have any (other) reason to perform, for an independent reason for that intention? We can manipulate ourselves to have such an intention, for example by inducing in ourselves false beliefs about the case for the action, and we can come to have such beliefs through self-deception. We may even be able to create reasons to perform the action (e.g. promise to do so), thus making it possible to intend to perform it. Such cases do not show that it is possible to intend to perform an action for an independent reason. If they are the only ways in which we can follow independent reasons for having an intention then such reasons are non-standard. Like other non-standard reasons they are practical reasons. If so then as with reasons for action, both standard and non-standard reasons for having intentions are practical reasons.

To examine the matter, suppose that one has an intention which one has only independent reasons to have. Regarding beliefs, emotions and actions, if they need to be supported by what the agents take to be adequate reasons to be rational then they are irrational if agents believe that they are supported only by non-standard reasons. Emotions and beliefs are irrational in these circumstances because the reasons needed to make them rational are adaptive reasons, and the agents believe that they are supported only by practical reasons. Actions are irrational in these circumstances because while they are supported, as they should be, by practical reasons, these reasons are as the agents know followed in a self-defeating way. Non-standard reasons for intentions are practical. So the question turns on whether directly following them is impossible or self-defeating.

Here is an example: suppose that you offer me something worth having (which there is no reason why I should not wish to receive from you) if I intend to move my hand, resting on the sofa, 5 inches to the left. You do not care whether or not I actually move my hand, and there are no other reasons I am or can become aware of which bear on either action or intention. I ask myself: should I form that intention, and of course that immediately raises in my mind the question about the action: should I move my hand? Yes I say, for if I do, I will be doing so intentionally, thus earning the offer. My deliberation relies on the fact that in the circumstances acting is a way of having the intention, hence the reason for the intention becomes a reason for the action. This kind of independent reason for an intention is therefore a standard reason for it.

Now suppose that your offer is on condition that I intend now to move my hand tomorrow (and that we know that there will be no other reason regarding the intention or the action tomorrow). You care neither whether I move my hand tomorrow nor whether I maintain my intention to move it for more than a few minutes. The difference being that in this case once I now intend to move my hand tomorrow I no longer have reason either to maintain the intention or to perform the action. I have already met the condition of the offer. The question is: can I form an intention now when I now believe that I will not have reason to maintain it or to act on it? If an intention presupposes belief that there is reason to perform the action one intends then I cannot form such an intention for the independent reason, for I do not now believe that there will be a reason to perform the action tomorrow.[19] In conclusion, independent reasons to form future-directed intentions can be followed only indirectly, by making ourselves form them, but we cannot form future-directed intentions for independent reasons. Therefore independent reasons for future-directed intentions are non-standard reasons. But, both reasons for the (to be intended) action, and independent reasons for having the intention embedded in an intentional action are standard reasons for intentions.

## 4 STANDARD AND NON-STANDARD REASONS: AGAIN

The distinction between practical and adaptive reasons, as drawn here, depends on the prior distinction between standard and non-standard reasons. I identify non-standard reasons as reasons for some action or attitude which cannot be (directly) followed (call this 'The Condition'). In discussion, Kieran Setiya raised an objection, whose exploration will help clarify the nature of the distinction.

[19] A similar conclusion is arrived at by Nishi Shah, in 'How Action Governs Intention', (*Philosophers' Imprint*, 8 (2008): 1–19, http://hdl.handle.net/2007/spo.3521354.0008.005) who writes 'The constitutive norm for intention is this: intending to *A* is correct only if *A*-ing is the thing to do.' However, he disregards the possibility that independent reasons to intend to *A* provide reasons to *A*.

Can the standard/non-standard distinction rest on The can-be-directly-followed Condition? Is it not the case that anything which anyone takes to be a reason can be followed by that person? Is that not what we mean when saying that it is taken to be a reason? How can one take something to be a reason without following it as a reason?

Suppose that one replies that The Condition applies only to ('real') reasons. It is not a test by which to determine what is taken to be a reason and is not. There are independent ways of establishing whether a fact is a reason for someone to do something or to have some attitude. Allowing this point does not altogether resolve the difficulty. Suppose that a certain fact is a reason. For example, imagine that someone promises Jake a large sum of money if he believes that P. By all accounts this is a reason to have that belief. I claim that it is a non-standard reason for it cannot be followed. But suppose that Jake does not think that. Suppose that he is philosophically minded (it is possible to develop the example so as to get rid of this assumption) and believes that the promise is an ordinary, standard, reason for believing that P, and that as a result he comes to believe that P. Of course, I will say that he has not followed the reason that the promise gave him, that he deceives himself into believing that he followed the reason and that it is a standard reason for belief. Perhaps. But that cannot be established by The Condition. I am presupposing that he did not follow the reason because I take it not to be standard. But I have to establish that he did not follow the reason first. I have to establish this independently of assuming that the reason is not standard, for only this way would The following-a-reason Condition establish which reasons are standard.

Could one reply that The Condition is about following-reasons-without-being-guilty-of-conceptual-confusions, whereas Jake is conceptually confused and only because of that can he follow the reason directly? But that reply concedes too much. It seems to me that the more accurate reply is that, just as in the case of 'following' something which is no reason at all, Jake merely thinks that he is following the reason, whereas in fact he does not. He is self-deceived.

That establishes that the question of whether one follows a reason is not purely a matter of how the agent understands his situation. To follow a reason he must behave in a way which is possible given the nature of that reason. That I am thirsty is a reason for me to drink the water in front of me. But it is not a reason to call my mother. Suppose that I say (bizarrely, but bizarre things happen) that my reason for calling my mother was that I was thirsty. Barring some complicated story to make the claim true, I am

(a) confused, either conceptually, or about the nature of telephone calls, or about thirst, and (b) I did not follow that reason, I merely thought that I did. That much follows from the kind of reason that thirst is.

Two questions loom: first, does the nature of a reason also determine what it is a standard reason for (as I shall argue later, any non-standard reason for one thing is a standard reason for another)? Second, is the claim that the nature of a reason determines what it is a reason for consistent with taking the possibility of following a reason as a mark of being a standard reason? The doubt embodied in the first question is that the non-standard reasons for belief, emotions, intentions, actions, etc. are reasons for belief, emotions, intentions, actions, etc. The distinction between standard and non-standard reasons depends, if you like, on more subtle factors. But are they part of the nature of the reasons?

Both questions can be answered in one by examining the factors which make it impossible to follow reasons, thus rendering them indirect. I can make no claim that the analysis of this essay is exhaustive, but let me briefly recap the factors here explained, starting from the case of non-standard reasons for action and intentions. Here, two kinds of factor may make a reason non-standard. First, if following it is self-defeating. Second, in the case of intentions, if the formation of the intention is impossible, as it violates some necessary condition for having an intention. These conditions are met when the reason for the action is a reason for an action not performed for that reason, and when the reason for the intention does not provide a reason for the action (not even as a way of having or of facilitating the having of the intention). The existence or absence of these conditions does not presuppose any claim about the impossibility of following reasons which meet them. They are part of, or derive from, the character of those reasons, and the claim that reasons which meet the conditions cannot be followed results directly from them.[20]

[20] Setiya offers the following example: 'If you offer me a lot of money to intend to buy an apple tomorrow, it seems that I can follow that reason, deciding to buy an apple and doing so (so long as I think it is sufficiently likely that I will buy the apple tomorrow).' That seems to me to be mistaken. Whatever happens today, come tomorrow I will not buy the apple. I would not be able to think of a single reason to do so. (There is no problem if I can now think of a reason, independently of the offer, to buy an apple tomorrow – but that is irrelevant to our case.) So I will not buy the apple. If I know that now (as I can do) then I know that buying the apple will not help me in forming the intention now to buy it tomorrow. So I have no reason to buy the apple, and your offer does not constitute one. Hence the offer, though it is a reason for having the intention, is not one which can be followed. Of course, people form intentions when they should know that that is silly so often that we think that we could do so in this case as well. And indeed if we are confused or mistaken we will succeed. But, when we do so we merely think that we follow the reason (if we do). We do not in fact do so.

Turn now to adaptive reasons for belief and emotions. Here the case is different. The reasons which are in fact non-standard do not comply with the maxims governing such reasons: they are not part of a case for the beliefs or emotions being appropriate (not part of the case for the truth of the belief, and whatever substitutes for truth in the case of various emotions).[21] That, too, is part of the nature of the reasons. The question is: why does that show that the reasons cannot be followed? Here we need to rely on the various points made in drawing the distinction in section 1 (the case of emotions is analogous, but their discussion here is too sketchy to allow one to do more than to rely on the analogy based on their character as adaptive reasons). Perhaps most importantly the fact that non-epistemic reasons cannot serve to warrant belief shows that they cannot be followed. Ultimately, however, the explanation of the force of this point depends on understanding the normativity of reasons, their hold on us, a matter I deal with elsewhere.

## 5 SPECIAL PRACTICAL REASONS FOR BELIEFS AND EMOTIONS?

There is one last question to consider: we saw that there are standard and non-standard reasons for actions and standard and non-standard reasons for having intentions. The question is are the practical reasons for having beliefs or emotions distinct types of practical reasons, on a par with reasons for actions and for intentions, or are they simply reasons for actions (and for intentions)? Surface appearances suggest that practical reasons for having beliefs and emotions are just that. They suggest that it distorts things to regard them as reasons for action. Perhaps they yield instrumental reasons for action, as the way of bringing it about that we conform to the primary reasons to have those beliefs and emotions. But it would merely distort things to deny that there are practical reasons for beliefs and for emotions.

But this argument from surface appearances is suspect. Consider: we have reasons to have efficient transport systems, and good housing. Does it mean that there are distinct transport and housing types of practical reasons? In a way there are, but that is simply to classify practical reasons by the subject matter they relate to. That is not the sense in which epistemic reasons differ from reasons for emotions, or reasons for actions differ from reasons for intentions. These distinctions are based on the

[21] Non-standard reasons for actions and intentions do conform to the maxims governing actions and intentions in being part of the case for the value or point of the actions or intentions.

thought that reasons are normative and we respond to them through recognising them as such. Our beliefs respond to reasons: as we recognise epistemic reasons our beliefs change in line with them. With due modifications the same is true of emotions, and of intentions. The basic classification of reasons is a classification of standard reasons, because the fact that they can be followed is what makes reasons into reasons.

We also respond to non-standard reasons for beliefs and emotions, but we do so directly by performing actions and only indirectly by changing our beliefs and emotions. Non-standard reasons for belief are like reasons for having good houses, they are reasons for actions which will have those results. The result is that all non-standard reasons are practical reasons. All non-standard reasons for one thing are standard reasons for another: a non-standard reason to believe that P is a standard reason to bring it about that I believe that P.[22] A non-standard reason to Φ is a standard reason to bring it about that I Φ.

This conclusion helps with some of the points raised in the discussion of the emotions above. For example, if one has an emotion which is not supported by adaptive reasons (where adaptive reasons are possible) it is an irrational emotion to have in the circumstances. But if one has an emotion in defiance of decisive practical reasons against having it one is morally or otherwise deficient, but not irrational. Why not? Is not defiance of (what are taken to be) valid reasons irrational? It is, but since the reasons are not *really* reasons for the emotions, since they are reasons for action to bring it about that one has the emotions, the irrationality is in the failure to try to prevent or suppress the emotions. If one tries and fails one is not irrational at all, but one is still morally or otherwise deficient.

Does that argument prove too much? Does it not show that there are no reasons for actions, only reasons for intending, for we can only respond to reasons to act by intending to act, just as we can only respond to non-standard reasons for belief, or to reasons for having good housing, by acting? We know, of course, that reasons for action are primary, for standard reasons for intentions are reasons for the intended actions. But does not that simply undermine the argument I used in the previous paragraph? To think so is to misconceive the relations of intention and action, imagining that when acting intentionally one acts by forming an intention which causes one to act. In fact, the intention of an intentional action is not a mental event separate from the action but an aspect of the

[22] It is also, and this is true of practical reasons generally, a standard reason to believe that there is a reason to bring about that I believe that P.

action, the way it is performed. One responds to a (perceived) adequate reason to act by acting (intentionally). Sometimes we respond now to (as we see it) an adequate reason to act in the future by forming now an intention to act in the future. Future-directed intentions are separate from the actions. The reasons for them, though normally deriving from the reasons for the actions, are a distinctive kind of reasons simply in virtue of the fact that we respond to them directly by forming the intentions. But reasons for action do not require future-directed intentions. We can respond to them by acting.[23]

## 6 CONCLUSION

The distinction between adaptive and practical reasons has important consequences. For example, we may well say that practical and adaptive reasons do not conflict. While we may have epistemic reasons for a particular belief and a practical reason not to have it the two conflict neither in the way that two epistemic nor in the way that two practical reasons conflict. The outcome of 'conflict' between adaptive and practical reasons is not, as in genuine conflict between practical reasons or between epistemic ones, that the better reason prevails. They are not in competition, and reasons of neither kind can be better than reasons of the other. Rather, adaptive reasons, being the standard reasons for belief or for having emotions, prevail. Practical reasons, being non-standard, can 'win' only by stealth.[24] There is much here which remains to be explored, not least being the question: in what sense are reasons of the two types reasons in the same sense? This is due to their being normative in the same sense. These are matters for another occasion.[25] In this essay I merely tried to help to sort out the terrain, to show that normativity is not to be explained by value, and to endorse one implication of Bernard Williams' work, namely that the key to normativity is in the concept of following a reason.

[23] Scanlon's discussion of the same issue is similar in some respects, but he mistakenly concludes that 'judgement-sensitive attitudes constitute the class of things for which reasons in the standard normative sense can sensibly be asked for or offered' (*What We Owe to Each Other*, Cambridge, MA: Harvard University Press, 1998: 21). The mistake leading to this conclusion is his view that 'actions are the kind of things for which normative reasons can be given only insofar as they are intentional, that is are the expression of judgement-sensitive attitudes'. That is at best ambiguous. Of course we respond to reasons intentionally. But it does not follow that reasons are always for intentional actions, that they can be conformed with only by intentional actions. There are plenty of reasons which are conformed with by actions, intentional or otherwise.

[24] Note though that standard and non-standard reasons for action, both being practical, do conflict in a straightforward way. And the same is true of reasons for intentions.

[25] See my 'Reason, Reasons and Normativity', unpublished.

CHAPTER 4

# *The explanatory role of being rational**

*Michael Smith*

Humeans hold that actions are movements of an agent's body that are suitably caused by a desire that things be a certain way and a belief on the agent's behalf that something she can just do, namely perform a movement of her body of the kind to be explained, has some suitable chance of making things that way (Davidson 1963). Movements of the body that are caused in some other way are not actions, but are rather things that merely happen to agents.

Actions can, of course, be explained in other ways. Perhaps every action can be explained by neural activity, or by goings on at the sub-atomic level, and presumably many actions can be explained by the states of the world that make the beliefs that figure in Humean explanations true: that is, the states that make those beliefs knowledge. But Humeans insist that belief-desire explanations are distinctive because their availability is what makes our bodily movements into *actions* (Davidson 1971a). A belief-desire explanation of a bodily movement is thus, as we might put it, a *constitutive* explanation of an action (Smith 1998). Other explanations of actions may be available, but they are all non-constitutive: their availability is not what makes our bodily movements into actions.

We can represent the Humean's view as in figure 1.

Humeans may seem to hold that the constitutive explanation of an action has *four* basic elements: two psychological (a desire for an end and a means-end belief), one non-psychological (a bodily movement), and a relation that holds between them (a causal relation of the right kind). The main task of this essay is, however, to argue that this appearance is misleading. Humeans decompose actions into *five* basic elements, not four, as they posit *three* psychological elements, not two. An additional

* Many thanks to David Sobel and Steven Wall for their helpful comments on a draft of this chapter.

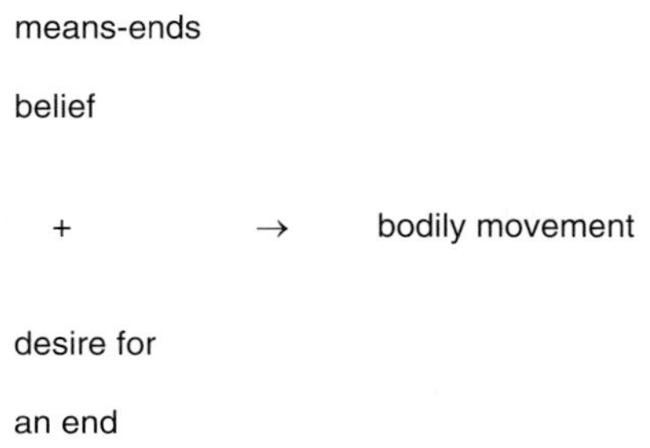

means-ends

belief

\+ → bodily movement

desire for

an end

Figure 1. Humean account of the constitutive explanation of an action

psychological element – the agent's possession and exercise of his rational capacities – is represented by the "→" sign.

So, at any rate, I shall argue (section 1). But once we acknowledge that an agent's possession and exercise of his rational capacities is part of the constitutive explanation of an action, a further question naturally suggests itself. To what extent can an agent's possession and exercise of his rational capacities be a part of a *non-constitutive* explanation of an action? As we shall see, the Humean's concession that an agent's possession and exercise of his rational capacities is part of the constitutive explanation of an action makes possible an answer to this question that is radically at odds with Hume's own strictures (section 2).

## 1 HEMPEL VS DAVIDSON ON THE EXPLANATION OF ACTION

The idea that explanations of actions require an extra psychological element beyond desire and belief is not original to me. The idea emerged many years ago as a point of disagreement between two Humeans, Carl Hempel and Donald Davidson, over the proper form of a fully spelled-out action explanation (Hempel 1961, Davidson 1976).

According to Hempel, explanations of action must conform to the following schema:

A was in a situation of type C
A was a rational agent
In a situation of type C any rational agent will do x
———
Therefore A did x

(Hempel 1961: 291)

a schema which he fills out as follows:

When we call someone a rational agent, we assert by implication that he will behave in certain characteristic ways if he finds himself in certain kinds of situations; but . . . those situations cannot be described simply in terms of certain environmental conditions and external stimuli; for characteristically they include the agent's having certain objectives and entertaining certain relevant beliefs. (Hempel 1961: 292–293)

We attribute certain desires and beliefs to an agent (this is what is captured in the first claim of the schema), and we also make the substantive claim that the agent is rational and hence will respond in certain characteristic ways to those desires and beliefs (this is what is said in the second claim of the schema). Given that actions are among the characteristic responses that rational agents have to their desires and beliefs (this is what is said in the third claim of the schema), it follows that we are thereby in a position to derive a conclusion about how the agent in question will act.

There are various questions we might ask about Hempel's schema. In particular, we might ask how plausible it is to suppose, as Hempel does, that there are strict empirical generalizations of the kind he imagines there to be (see again the third claim of the schema), generalizations which in turn allow us to explain actions not just causally, but in terms of Hempel's own deductive–nomological model. For present purposes, however, we can be more relaxed about these empirical generalizations. What is to be at issue here is not the plausibility of fashioning such claims so that we can fit action explanations into Hempel's deductive nomological model, but rather his suggestion that an agent's being rational is a distinct psychological element in any such explanation.

Hempel puts the crucial point this way:

[I]nformation to the effect that agent A was in a situation of kind C, and that in such a situation the rational thing to do is x, affords grounds for believing that it would have been *rational for A to do x*; but not for believing that A did *in fact* do x. To justify this latter belief, we clearly need a further explanatory assumption, namely that – at least at the time in question – A was a *rational agent* and thus was *disposed* to do whatever was rational under the circumstances. (Hempel 1961: 290)

We need such a further explanatory assumption, according to Hempel, because

there are various kinds of circumstances in which we might well leave our belief- and goal-attributions unchanged and abandon instead the assumption of rationality. First of all, in deciding upon his action, a person may well overlook certain relevant items of information which he clearly knows or at least believes to be true and which, if properly taken into account, would have called for a different course of action. Second, the agent may overlook certain items in the total goal he is clearly seeking to attain, and may thus decide upon an action that is not rational as judged by his objectives and beliefs. Thirdly, even if the agent were to take into account all aspects of his total goal as well as all the relevant information at his disposal, and even if he should go through deliberate "calculation of means to be adopted toward his chosen end". . . the result may still fail to be a rational decision because of some logical flaw in his calculation. It is quite clear that there could be strong evidence, in certain cases, that an agent had actually fallen short of rationality in one of the ways here suggested; and indeed, if his decision had been made under pressure of time or under emotional strain, fatigue, or other disturbing influences, such deviations from rationality would be regarded as quite likely. (Hempel 1961: 297)

Though rational agents respond in characteristic ways to their desires and beliefs, Hempel's idea thus seems to be that it is possible, and perhaps even likely, when agents are under certain sorts of pressure – "emotional strain, fatigue, or other disturbing influences" – that they do not respond in one of these ways. In such cases they will not be rational and so we won't be able to explain their doing what they do in the way characteristic of action.

Let's apply Hempel's ideas to a very simplified case. Imagine an agent, John, who has a non-instrumental desire to get healthier and the belief that something he can just do, namely flex his biceps, would make him healthier. Imagine further that, as a result, John flexes his biceps. If Hempel is right then the fully spelled-out explanation of his action must contain at least the following three elements:

(1) John desires to get healthier
(2) John believes that he can get healthier by flexing his biceps
(3) John is instrumentally rational
∴ (4) John flexes his biceps

(3) is necessary, Hempel seems to be saying, because John may have a non-instrumental desire to get healthier and a belief that he can get healthier by flexing his biceps but, because he is instrumentally irrational, not form the instrumental desire to flex his biceps, and so not flex his biceps.

I take it that this possibility is either part of what Hempel had in mind, or is in any event a natural extension of what he had in mind, when he said that when an agent is set to act we need to allow for the possibility of a "logical flaw in his calculation." Since, in the circumstances, there is no way that John will flex his biceps if he doesn't have the instrumental desire to do so, it follows that if flexing his biceps is something that John is to do then he must have more than the non-instrumental desire and means-end belief mentioned in (1) and (2). He must put these together in the way in which someone who is instrumentally rational would and actually desire the means. This is what (3) guarantees. Absent his putting them together he will not be instrumentally rational and so we won't be able to explain his doing anything in the way characteristic of action because he won't act.

Note, however, that we require a particular interpretation of (3) in order to secure this result. The claim that John is instrumentally rational is ambiguous between two readings. I will call the first of these the "pure-capacity" reading and the second the "capacity-plus-exercise" reading. On the pure-capacity reading, all that (3) says is that John *has the capacity* to be instrumentally rational in the circumstances. So understood, (3) is true even when John fails to exercise that capacity in the circumstances. This is plainly too weak to guarantee the truth of (4). For the truth of (4) requires at the very least that John has an instrumental desire to flex his muscles, something he won't have if he doesn't exercise his capacity. What Hempel must have had in mind, then, is a stronger reading of (3) than the pure-capacity reading.

On the alternative capacity-plus-exercise reading, (3) says that John *has and exercises the capacity* to be instrumentally rational. In so doing, it thereby guarantees that John has the instrumental desire to flex his biceps, because an exercise of a capacity for instrumental rationality, in the presence of a relevant non-instrumental desire and a means-end belief, is all it takes to bring an instrumental desire into existence. Indeed, we might well think that what it is for John's instrumental desire to flex his biceps to come into existence isn't for a separate entity above and beyond his non-instrumental desire and means-end belief to come into existence – an instrumental desire isn't like a new baby that is born to its non-instrumental desire and means-end belief parents – but is rather simply for John's non-instrumental desire and means-end belief to be brought together by the exercise of his capacity to be instrumentally rational in the circumstances (Smith 2004). So understood – perhaps together with some further plausible assumptions as well – (1)–(3) do indeed seem to entail (4).

My suggestion that there is an extra psychological element in a Humean constitutive explanation of an action can now be stated rather simply. Every constitutive explanation of an action, I want to suggest, comprises three basic psychological elements: a desire, a means-end belief, and the agent's exercise of her capacity to be instrumentally rational. This is what the "+" in figure 1 represents. What makes a bodily movement into an action is the fact that these three elements combine to cause the bodily movement in the right way. In order to reach this conclusion, however, we must first address some problems with Hempel's own view. To anticipate, though the worries with Hempel's view are well founded, they point the way to a more nuanced view, where the more nuanced view is the one just stated: constitutive explanations of actions comprise three basic psychological elements: desire, means-end belief, and agents' exercise of their capacity to be instrumentally rational.

The problems with Hempel's own view are well brought out by Davidson in his commentary on "Rational Action." Davidson baulks at the suggestion that we need to make the substantive empirical assumption that an agent is rational – an assumption like the one we just made with respect to John's being instrumentally rational – and cite that fact about him as part of the explanation we give of any action:

> Hempel says rationality is a kind of character trait: some people have it and some don't, and it may come and go in the same individual. No doubt some people are more rational than others, and all of us have our bad moments. And perhaps we can propose some fairly objective criteria for testing when someone has the trait; if so, knowing whether someone is rational at a given time may help us to explain, and even predict, his behaviour, given his beliefs and desires. But reference to such a trait does not seem to me to provide the generality for reason explanations Hempel wants. For in the sense in which rationality is a trait that comes and goes, it can't be an assumption needed for every reason explanation. People who don't have the trait are still agents, have reasons and motives, and act on them. Their reasons are no doubt bad ones. But until we can say what their reasons are – that is, explain or characterize their actions in terms of their motives – we are in no position to say the reasons are bad. So being in a position to call a person rational, irrational, or nonrational in this sense presupposes that we have already found it possible to give reason explanations of his actions . . . What is needed, if reason explanations are to be based on laws, is not a test of when a person is rational, but of when a person's reasons – his desires and beliefs – will result, in the right way, in an action. At this point the assumption of rationality seems in danger of losing empirical content. (Davidson 1976: 266–267)

We can discern several points here, points that it would be best to state and evaluate separately.

The first is that agents can only be assessed as being more or less rational against a background assumption that they have desires and beliefs and act, and hence against a background assumption of being rational. The idea here is, of course, the familiar Davidsonian one that being at least minimally rational is a precondition of a creature's having desires and beliefs at all (Davidson 1970a, 1971b). Let's concede that this is so. Does that concession undermine the plausibility of the claim that every action explanation requires the substantive assumption that an agent is rational? Well, if when we say that an agent is rational all we mean is that she is minimally rational, in the familiar Davidsonian sense, then there would be nothing substantive added by the assumption of rationality, given that the agents in question are already being said to have certain desires and beliefs. In terms of Hempel's original schema, the second claim ("A was a rational agent") would follow *a priori* from the first ("A was in a situation of type C"). An agent's being minimally rational is, after all, a precondition of her having desires and beliefs. But being minimally rational plainly isn't what the assumption of instrumental rationality discussed earlier amounts to. It amounts rather to ruling out the possibility that an agent may desire some end and have a relevant means-end belief, but not desire the means. This kind of rationality is distinct from the minimal rationality that is required for a creature to have desires and beliefs at all, for, assuming that the creature has desires and beliefs, it simply amounts to the requirement that the desires and means-end beliefs are put together in such a way as to make it true that the agent has an instrumental desire. The first point that we can discern in the passage from Davidson is thus correct, but irrelevant.

The second point is, however, far more telling. Consider a case in which there is, as Hempel puts it, "strong evidence . . . that an agent ha[s] actually fallen short of rationality in one of the ways here suggested": A case in which an agent's decision is "made under pressure of time or under emotional strain, fatigue, or other disturbing influences," pressure of a kind that makes "deviations from rationality . . . quite likely." Suppose, for example, that John desires to get healthier and believes that he can get healthier by flexing his muscles – a regime of exercise is just what's needed – but fatigue makes him instrumentally irrational. He doesn't form an instrumental desire to flex his muscles. Instead, let's suppose, he relaxes and watches TV. The trouble is that, if this is what John does, *he still acts*. His relaxing on the couch and watching TV is an action, not something that merely happens to him. And, of course, to the extent that he acts, he also forms some instrumental desire: in this case, the instrumental desire to relax on the couch and watch TV. But if this is right then, in whatever sense it is true that John exhibits instrumental irrationality in such a case, it cannot be required that his being instrumentally rational, *in that very respect*, is an essential element of every action explanation. We will return to this point presently.

The third point builds on the second. Conceding now that agents do indeed display a kind of instrumental rationality every time they act, it focuses more squarely on whether being instrumentally rational in that sense could be a part of the explanation of every action. Davidson's suggestion is that it could not. For, his idea seems to be, being instrumentally rational in that sense is not conceptually distinct from the thing that it would have to explain, which is the agent's desires and means-end beliefs causing action in the right way. An agent's having and exercising his capacity to be instrumentally rational in the circumstances just is a matter of his acting on his desires and means-end beliefs in those circumstances, or so Davidson suggests. His having and exercising that capacity thus cannot be a distinct element in the explanation. (In terms of figure 1, the element that I think is represented by "+" is, Davidson seems to think, already represented by the "→".)

There are two responses we might make to this third point. The first is that, since an agent's possession of an instrumental desire would appear to be one state of an agent, and the bodily movement that that instrumental desire may or may not cause is a distinct event, so, on the face of it at least, Davidson seems quite wrong to suppose that the agent's possession and exercise of the capacity to be instrumentally rational is not logically distinct from his desires and means-end beliefs causing his bodily movement in the right way. An agent's possession and exercise of his capacity to be instrumentally rational guarantees that his desires and means-end beliefs are put together in such a way as to make it true that he has the instrumental desire. It does not guarantee that that instrumental desire, in turn, causes a bodily movement.

In fact, however, this first response fails to appreciate the full force of Davidson's objection. In order to see why, we need to remember why Davidson introduced the idea that desires and beliefs must cause bodily movements *in the right way* for those bodily movements to count as actions. The problem, as he saw things, was that reflection on a range of examples shows that though causation by a desire and belief is a necessary condition for a bodily movement's being an action, it isn't clear what you need to add in order to provide a necessary and sufficient condition – or rather, it isn't clear what you need to add beyond the uninformative further requirement that the desire and belief must cause the bodily movement in the right way. The examples he had in mind were all cases of *internal wayward causal chains* (Davidson 1973). This is important, as the solution to the problem of internal wayward causal chains turns out to be very close to the issue at hand: very close to settling whether or not an agent's being rational is, or is not, conceptually distinct from his acting at all.

Imagine an actor playing a role that calls for her to shake as if extremely nervous. We can readily suppose that, despite the fact that she wants to play her role and believes that she can do so by shaking, once she gets on stage her desire and belief so unnerve her that she is overcome and rendered totally incapable of action. Instead of playing her role as required, she just stands there, shaking nervously. What examples like this suggest is that it is insufficient for an agent's bodily movements to be actions that she has relevant desires and beliefs that cause those movements. An agent may well have desires and beliefs that cause such movements, and yet, because they cause those movements in the wrong way, the movements aren't actions. In order to give necessary and sufficient conditions for an agent's bodily movements to be actions we therefore need to rule out the possibility of such wayward causal chains. In this particular case, we would need to rule out the possibility of the agent's desires and beliefs causing her to shake via causing her to become nervous.

Though Davidson is pessimistic about the possibility of doing this in anything other than the uninformative way – desires and beliefs must cause the bodily movements in the right way – others think it is plain what is needed (Peacocke 1979). The crucial feature in all such cases, they say, is that the match between what the agent does and the content of her desires and beliefs is entirely fluky. In the case just described, for example, it is entirely fluky that the actor wanted to make just the movements that her nerves subsequently caused. In order to state a sufficient condition for an agent's bodily movements being actions, we must therefore ensure that her movements are especially sensitive to the content of her desires and beliefs, as opposed to being sensitive to the operation of wayward factors like nerves. The movement of an agent's body is an action, the suggestion goes, only if, in addition to the other conditions, over a range of desires and beliefs that the agent might have had that differ ever so slightly in their content, she would still have performed an appropriate bodily movement. Suppose she had desired to act nervously and believed that she could do so making her teeth chatter. Then she would have made her teeth chatter. Or suppose she had desired to act nervously and believed that she could do so by walking around wringing her hands. Then she would have walked around wringing her hands. And so on. This further condition of non-flukiness is clearly violated in cases of internal wayward causal chains because, even if the actor had had such ever-so-slightly different desires and beliefs, her nerves would still have caused her to shake when she went on stage.

Whether or not this further requirement turns the necessary condition into a necessary and sufficient condition is a moot point (see Sehon 2005). But, for present purposes, that's not what's important. What's important is rather that everyone seems agreed that there is indeed some such requirement on the relationship between an agent's bodily movements and her desires and beliefs for those bodily movements to count as actions. But consider now the requirement itself. What does it amount to? It amounts to nothing less than the requirement that the agent has and exercises the capacity to be instrumentally rational *in a very local domain*. For a desire and belief to cause a bodily movement in the right way for that bodily movement to count as an action, is, *inter alia*, for the agent to have and exercise her capacity to be instrumentally rational in those circumstances. In the example just discussed, she mustn't just have the instrumental desire to shake, but must also be such that she would have had the instrumental desire to wring her hands if she had believed that wringing her hands was a way of acting nervous; that she would have had the instrumental desire to make her teeth chatter if she had believed that making her teeth chatter was a way of acting nervous; and so on. The requirement that desires and beliefs cause actions in the right way thus does indeed seem to entail that the agent has and exercises the capacity to be instrumentally rational, at least in a very local domain. So far, then, the main thrust of Davidson's third point would appear on the mark.

What I want to argue now, however, is that the capacity to be instrumentally rational whose exercise plays an explanatory role in the production of action need not be the exercise of the very localized capacity to be instrumentally rational that Davidson has in mind. In order to see that this is so, however, we will need to consider the various ways in which an agent's being more fully instrumentally rational in the circumstances in which he acts may and may not manifest itself, and how this differs from the manifestation conditions of the very localized capacity that Davidson has in mind. So let's begin by imagining a very simple example. Suppose that John has a non-instrumental desire to get healthier and that he believes there are two ways in which he could bring this about. He believes that his getting healthier would result from flexing his biceps or from flexing his triceps, but he does not believe that he could flex his biceps and his triceps at the same time. If John were fully instrumentally rational, what would he desire in this case?

The answer is that if John were fully instrumentally rational then he would put his non-instrumental desire to get healthier together with each of these beliefs. This is because his non-instrumental desire is already targeted, so to speak, on each of these ways the world could be. He desires the realization of the possibility that he is healthy, and he believes that this possibility partitions into two sub-possibilities: The possibility that he flexes his biceps and the possibility that he flexes his triceps. Putting at least one of his means-end beliefs together with his non-instrumental desire would allow him to be instrumentally rational to a certain degree – that would amount to a very local exercise of his capacity to be instrumentally rational – but he would be more instrumentally rational if he were to put his non-instrumental desire together with both his means-end beliefs. He would be more instrumentally rational because doing so prepares him for action in a modally strong sense: he is actually such that, had he believed himself unable to (say) flex his biceps, he would still have desired to flex his triceps, and vice versa. If, as seems plausible, being fully instrumentally rational is a matter of maximal preparedness to act in this modally strong sense, then being fully instrumentally rational would seem to require him to have both an instrumental desire to flex his biceps and an instrumental desire to flex his triceps.

Moreover, sticking with this case, being fully instrumentally rational would seem to have implications for the strengths of John's instrumental desires. If, for example, he is equally confident about the two causal claims just made – equally confident that flexing his biceps will cause him to get healthier and that flexing his triceps will cause him to get healthier – then, if he were fully instrumentally rational, he would be indifferent between the two options: his instrumental desires would be equally strong. But if he is more confident of one than the other, then it seems that, in order to satisfy all of the demands of instrumental rationality, his instrumental desire for the one about which he is more confident would have to be stronger. The effect of decreased confidence should be to dilute desire for that option. This, too, manifests itself modally. If John is fully instrumentally rational then he is actually such that he instrumentally desires more that about which he is more confident, but had he believed that to be impossible, he would have instrumentally desired that about which he is less confident. So even though agents might be instrumentally rational to the extent that their non-instrumental desires are suitably related to two means-end beliefs they have, they might still fail to meet instrumental rationality's further demand on the strengths of their two instrumental desires.

Instrumental rationality would seem to make other more global demands on agent's instrumental desires, as well. Suppose this time that John has two desires, a non-instrumental desire to get healthier and a non-instrumental desire for knowledge, and that he believes all of the following: that flexing his biceps causes health, that reading causes knowledge, and that he cannot flex his biceps and read at the same time. Finally, just to keep things simple, suppose he is equally confident about each of these things and that he has no further desires or beliefs. If John were fully instrumentally rational, then the considerations adduced above would seem to apply equally to the two non-instrumental desires. Instrumental rationality requires that his two non-instrumental desires be suitably related to each of his means-end beliefs. If he were instrumentally rational then he would have both an instrumental desire to flex his biceps and an instrumental desire to read.

Moreover it once again seems that, though he might be instrumentally rational in this local sense, he might fail to meet a further demand that instrumental rationality makes on the strengths of these instrumental desires. If his non-instrumental desires for health and knowledge are equally strong then it seems that, if he were instrumentally rational, he would be indifferent between the two options: his instrumental desires to flex his biceps and to read would be equally strong. But if one of his non-instrumental desires is stronger than the other then it seems that, in order to satisfy the more global demands of instrumental rationality, his instrumental desire for the one which leads to the outcome that he desires more strongly would have to be stronger. The effect of having one desire greater than another in the face of equal confidence about the ways in which those desires can be satisfied should be to intensify the desire for the means to that which one desires more.

There are also cases that contain elements of both those discussed thus far. Suppose that John has a stronger non-instrumental desire to get healthier and a weaker non-instrumental desire for knowledge, and that he believes that flexing his biceps causes health, that reading causes knowledge, and that he cannot exercise and read at the same time, but that he is more confident of the connection between reading and knowledge than he is about the connection between flexing his biceps and health. What does instrumental rationality require in that case? Once again, it seems that if John were fully instrumentally rational then he would have instrumental desires both to exercise and to read, where the strengths of these instrumental desires would depend on the strengths of his two non-instrumental desires and the levels of confidence associated with his two means-end beliefs. Indeed, if his confidence is greater enough, then instrumental rationality may even require that the instrumental desire to read is stronger than the instrumental desire to flex his biceps, notwithstanding the fact that the non-instrumental desire for knowledge that partially constitutes it is weaker than the non-instrumental desire for health which partially constitutes the instrumental desire to flex his biceps.

Let's now return to Davidson's suggestion that there is nothing for an agent's being locally instrumentally rational in the circumstances to amount to beyond the fact that his desires and means-end beliefs issue in action. We can now see that, even when an agent's desires and means-end beliefs do issue in action, and hence the agent is instrumentally rational to some extent – the agent has and exercises his capacity for instrumental rationality in the very localized domain entailed by causation in the right way – there are at least two quite distinct ways the agent might be counterfactually. These two possibilities turn on the *extent* to which the agent is instrumentally rational in the circumstances.

Sticking with our very simple example, suppose that John has an intrinsic desire to get healthier and that he believes both that he could get healthy by flexing his biceps and by flexing his triceps, but that he is more confident of the former than the latter and hence, because he is instrumentally rational to a certain extent and has no other desires and means-end beliefs, he has a stronger instrumental desire to flex his biceps and so flexes his biceps. From this description of the case we cannot tell how strong John's instrumental desire to flex his biceps is. We know that it is stronger than his instrumental desire to flex his triceps, but that doesn't entail it is as strong as it should be, if he were fully instrumentally rational, for that requires that the strength of his instrumental desire to flex his biceps reflects the strength of both his non-instrumental desire to get healthier and his confidence that flexing his biceps will lead to his getting healthier. So far, all we know is that it reflects his degrees of confidence. What does this further difference consist in?

The answer is that it consists in facts about what (say) John would have done if he had also had a weaker non-instrumental desire for knowledge, but had had the same level of confidence that reading a book would provide him with knowledge as that flexing his biceps would make him healthy. One answer to this counterfactual question is that, since John's instrumental desire to flex his biceps would have been stronger than his instrumental desire to read a book, he would still have flexed his biceps. Another is that, since his instrumental desire to flex his biceps would have been weaker than his instrumental desire to read a book, he would have read a book. If the answer is the first then, in the actual circumstances, it follows that John is instrumentally rational to a greater extent than he is if the answer is the second. For in that case the strength of his instrumental desire to flex his biceps reflects not just his confidence levels about the effect of flexing his biceps and triceps on his health, but also the strength of his non-instrumental desire to get healthier.

We are now in a position to see why Davidson is quite wrong to suggest that, since being instrumentally rational in a very local domain is entailed by an agent's desires and means-end beliefs causing his bodily movement in the right way, it follows that his being instrumentally rational cannot be a part of the explanation of his action. Different agents possess the capacity to be instrumentally rational to very different extents, and the extent to which they possess this capacity, and whether or not they exercise their capacity to whatever extent they have it, fixes not just what actually happens when they act – fixes not just that they do exercise their capacity to be instrumentally rational in the very local domain – but also what they would do in various counterfactual circumstances, circumstances in which they have very different non-instrumental desires, or in which their beliefs about their options are very different. It is thus an agent's possession and exercise of his capacity to be instrumentally rational *to the specific extent that he has it and exercises it* that figures in the explanation of his actions. To be sure, some agents may be so minimally instrumentally rational that, when they act, they thereby exercise all of the capacity to be instrumentally rational that they have. This is, if you like, the limit case of an agent. But not all agents are the limit case of an agent. Some are far more instrumentally rational than that and, when they act, they exercise their far more extensive capacity to be instrumentally rational. This more extensive capacity is what's involved in the explanation of their actions. This is evident from the very different counterfactuals that are true of them.

What is thus true, of course – and perhaps this is what misled Davidson – is that the *minimum required* for a bodily movement to be an action is that the agent possesses and exercises the very local capacity for instrumental rationality required for his desires and beliefs to cause his bodily movement in the right way. But it would be a fallacy to move from this to the conclusion that it is an agent's possession and exercise of the minimal capacity that figures in the explanation of his actions. It would be a fallacy on a par with supposing that, just because all that is strictly necessary for an agent to intentionally flip the switch (say) is that he has a very specific desire concerning the outcome of his flipping the switch, so the only desires that are ever part of the explanation of any agent's flippings of switches are desires with very specific contents.

Let me summarise. Hempel claimed, and Davidson denied, that an agent's being rational is a part of the explanation of every action. Davidson's argument against Hempel in effect takes the form of a dilemma. On the first horn, Hempel is committed to the conclusion that agents who are irrational never act. But that's plainly not true, even by Hempel's own lights. On the other horn, Hempel is claiming that the minimal exercise of instrumental rationality that is necessary whenever agents act on their desires and beliefs is itself a part of the explanation of those actions. But, while it is true that every agent who acts must possess and exercise the capacity for instrumental rationality in that very local domain, since this is entailed by the fact that their non-instrumental desires and means-end beliefs cause their bodily movements in the right way, it cannot be a separate causal element in that explanation. It simply falls out of the account we give of what it is for desires and beliefs to cause actions in the right way.

Against this, I have argued that though a minimal exercise of instrumental rationality is indeed necessary whenever an agent acts, it does not follow from this that what agents exercise, when they act, is a minimal capacity to be instrumentally rational. Agents are instrumentally rational to different degrees and they exercise whatever capacities they have to different degrees. This is why very different counterfactuals are true of agents depending, first, on the extent to which they are instrumentally rational, and second, on whether their being instrumentally rational to that extent is or is not a part of the explanation of their bodily movements. This, it seems to me, is the crucial insight that we discover when we think through Davidson's disagreements with Hempel about the explanatory role of being rational. Hempel is essentially right. The Humean account of a constitutive explanation of an action posits three distinctive psychological elements, not two. Actions are bodily movements that are caused in the right way by desires, beliefs, and exercises of the capacity, which agents may have to a greater or a lesser extent, to be instrumentally rational.

## 2 ARE THERE ANY DISTINCTIVE NON-CONSTITUTIVE EXPLANATIONS OF ACTION?

Once we acknowledge that an agent's possession and exercise of his capacity to be instrumentally rational is part of the constitutive explanation of an action, a further question naturally suggests itself. To what extent can an agent's possession and exercise of his rational capacities be a part of a distinctive *non-constitutive* explanation?

Non-constitutive explanations, remember, are simply those explanations of actions which, even when available, are not explanations whose availability is what makes actions actions. Not all non-constitutive explanations are on a par, however, for, given the nature of the constitutive explanation of an action, the availability of certain non-constitutive explanations will be a mark of excellence in action, where the standard of excellence is internal to action itself. One such non-constitutive explanation is implicit in what's been said already. For when an agent does what he does not just because he is instrumentally rational to the extent that he is, but because, as it happens, the extent to which he is instrumentally rational is *fully*, then his action, though no more or less an action than it would have been if he had acted but been less than fully instrumentally rational, is better in a distinctive sense. It is better in the sense that it is the product of a better specimen of one of its constitutive causes.

What I want to argue now is that an agent's being fully rational – not just fully instrumentally rational, but fully rational both instrumentally and in such other departments of rationality as there are as well – can also figure in a non-constitutive explanation of his action. If this is right then it follows that the availability of an explanation of this kind will be the mark of an even better kind of action. For such an action will be the product of perhaps the very best specimen of one of its constitutive causes. In order to see that this is so, however, we must first remind ourselves about the argument that Hempel gave in favor of his schema for the explanation of action.

Hempel's argument, you'll recall, was that absent the assumption that an agent is rational there is no reason to expect him to respond in the way a rational agent would to the fact that he has certain desires and means-end beliefs. But note that a parallel line of argument shows that constitutive explanations of *rational beliefs* – these are explanations of beliefs in virtue of which they count as *rational beliefs* – must conform to a very similar schema:

A was in a situation of type D
A was a rational subject
In a situation of type D any rational subject will believe that p
______
Therefore A rationally believed that p

Imagine that A is in some type-D situation that makes the third premise of the schema come out true. At the most general level, perhaps we can describe this as a situation in which a conclusive reason to believe that p is available, where a conclusive reason to believe that p may be some set of further facts – some facts that q and r – that bear evidentially on whether p. Absent the explicit assumption that A is a rational subject – this is the second premise in the schema – the most that we can derive from the fact that he was in a type-D situation, and that in such a situation any rational subject will believe that p, is that the rational thing for A to believe in that situation is p. In order to derive the conclusion that A in fact rationally believes that p we must add the further substantive claim that he is rational. By parity of reasoning from the case of action explanation, then, it follows that when subjects form rational beliefs, their being rational – that is to say, their possession and exercise of the capacity to revise their beliefs in a rational manner – plays a crucial causal role. And this in turn suggests that a further distinctive non-constitutive explanation of action is possible.

Imagine that some agent desires to (say) illuminate a room and that there is available a conclusive reason to believe that moving his finger against a switch will achieve that result. Imagine further that the agent forms the belief that moving his finger against a switch will illuminate the room precisely because of the availability of this conclusive reason – in other words, suppose he possesses and exercises the capacity to revise his beliefs in a rational manner – and that his desire and belief causes his finger to move against the switch in the right way. In that case we can explain his finger movement by citing not just his desire and belief – this is all that is required for a constitutive explanation of his action – but also by citing his desire and the fact that he *rationally believes* that moving his finger against the switch will illuminate the room. To be sure, this isn't a constitutive explanation. An agent's finger movement against a switch may be an action whether the belief that causes it is rational or irrational. But it is an explanation that may sometimes be available none the less.

We can represent this kind of non-constitutive explanation of an action in terms of a modified version of figure 1 (figure 2).

The "⇒" in figure 2, like the "+", represents the agent's possession and exercise of a rational capacity. The only difference is that whereas the "+" represents the possession and exercise of the capacity to be instrumentally rational, the "⇒" represents the possession and exercise of the capacity to revise his beliefs in a rational manner. The "⇒" and the "+" thus represent the operation of different departments of rationality.

The non-constitutive explanation represented in figure 2 is distinctive for much the same reason as a non-constitutive explanation of action in

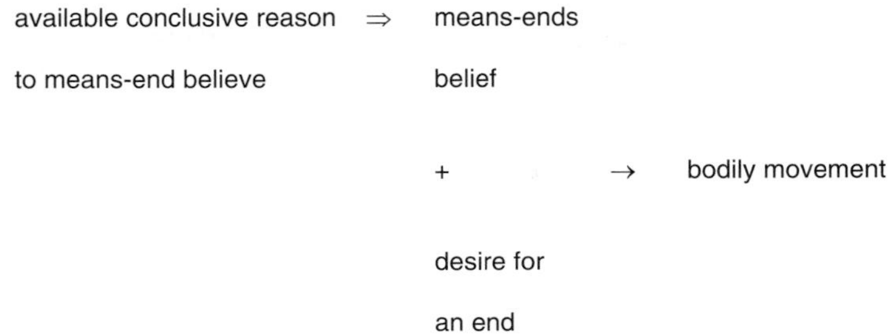


Figure 2. A Humean account of a distinctive non-constitutive explanation of action

terms of the agent's being fully instrumentally rational is distinctive. It is distinctive because an action so explained is the product of a better specimen of one of its constitutive causes. An action caused not just by the agent's possession and exercise of the capacity to be instrumentally rational, but also by his possession and exercise of the capacity to revise his beliefs in a rational manner, is an action that is caused by an even better specimen of the underlying psychological state of being rational in all of its departments than is an action that cannot be so explained. The agent of such an action is, after all, more fully rational. This is what's reflected by the availability of the distinctive non-constitutive explanation represented in figure 2.

At the beginning of this section I said that my aim is to argue that an agent's being fully rational – not just fully instrumentally rational, but fully rational both instrumentally and in such other departments of rationality as there are as well – can also figure in a distinctive non-constitutive explanation of his action. Is that argument now complete? In other words, is the non-constitutive explanation represented in figure 2 the only such distinctive non-constitutive explanation of an action that there can be? The issue that we must address in providing an answer to this question literally leaps off the page when we look at figure 2. What about the desire for an end? Is it too susceptible to explanation in much the same way as the means-end belief?

Hume would of course insist that it is not. As he puts it:

> 'tis not contrary to reason to prefer the destruction of the whole world to the scratching of my finger. 'Tis not contrary to reason for me to chuse my total ruin, to prevent the least uneasiness of an Indian or person wholly unknown to me. 'Tis as little contrary to reason to prefer even my own acknowledg'd lesser good to my greater, and have a more ardent affection for the former than the latter . . .

In short, a passion must be accompany'd with some false judgement, in order to its being unreasonable; and even then 'tis not the passion, properly speaking, which is unreasonable, but the judgement. (Hume 1978: 416)

In other words, as Hume sees things the only kind of irrational desire is an irrational *instrumental* desire, where, as we have seen, an instrumental desire is simply a non-instrumental desire and means-end belief that have been brought together by an agent's exercise of his capacity to be instrumentally rational. The irrationality of an instrumental desire, according to Hume, resides in the irrationality of the means-end belief that partially constitutes it. He thus draws the radical conclusion that there is no such thing as a rational non-instrumental desire. Desires for ends cannot be either rational or irrational.

Hume seems to think that this radical conclusion follows from the fact that, whereas beliefs can be true or false – true beliefs are those whose contents represent the world as being the way it is, false beliefs are those whose contents fail to so represent the world – a desire "is an original existence . . . and contains not any representative quality" (Hume 1978: 415). Desires for ends can be satisfied or unsatisfied, but not true or false. But it is hard to see why Hume should think that the conclusion follows from the premise. What is the connection supposed to be between a psychological state that can be true or false and a psychological state that can be rational or irrational? This question is somewhat urgent because, on the face of it, notwithstanding the fact that desires for ends cannot be true or false, it seems that a parallel line of argument to those already discussed in the case of action and rational belief would suffice to show that there are constitutive explanations of *rational desires for ends*. These are explanations of desires for ends in virtue of which, and contrary to Hume, they count as *rational* desires for ends.

The parallel line of argument I have in mind appeals to the following Hempelian schema:

A was in a situation of type E
A was a rational subject
In a situation of type E any rational agent will desire the end that q
_______________________________________________
Therefore A rationally desired the end that q

The crucial premise in this schema is of course the third. What exactly is a type-E situation? Borrowing from the Hempelian schema in the case of rational belief, we might suppose that a type-E situation is one in which a conclusive reason to desire the end that q is available. Here is where

Hume would presumably dig in his heels. For, he might ask, what is it for there to be a conclusive reason to desire the end that q? We understand what conclusive reasons *to believe* are because reasons to believe are simply considerations that bear on the truth of the thing believed. But what are we to make of reasons *to desire some end*?

The trouble is, however, that there is an obvious answer to this question. To be sure, a reason *to believe* is a consideration that bears on the truth of the thing believed, but that's simply because what such a reason is is a reason *to believe*. Desires for ends cannot be true or false, rather they can be satisfied or unsatisfied. It therefore follows that reasons *to desire ends*, if such there be, will be considerations that bear not on truth or falsehood, but rather on the satisfaction of the desired ends. Thus, just as the question we must ask ourselves in figuring out what reasons there are to believe what we believe is whether there are considerations that bear on how we currently take it that things are, so the question that we ask ourselves in figuring out whether there are reasons to desire what we desire is whether there are considerations that bear on how we currently take it that things are to be. The mere fact that a reason to believe is a consideration that bears on the truth of the thing believed thus has no bearing on whether there is anything else for a reason to be except a consideration that bears on the truth of the thing for which it is a reason.

Hume's argument also seems, to me at least, to be somewhat disingenuous. The first time we all heard about (say) Thomas Nagel's wonderful book *The Possibility of Altruism* (1970), we knew exactly what the point of the book was. It was supposed to lay out a number of considerations that provide reasons for desiring the end that people not suffer excruciating pain. The considerations were things like: that we each take ourselves to have a reason not to suffer excruciating pains when we have them; that the reason-giving feature of the pains that we suffer when we have them seem to be internal to the excruciating pains themselves, having to do with their intrinsic nature, not with the fact that the pains are present to us; that it follows from this that the intrinsic nature of our own future excruciating pains are reason-giving; and that it follows from this that the intrinsic nature of other people's pains are reason-giving, too. Whether we found Nagel's argument convincing once we read and thought about it is unimportant. What's important is rather that we immediately understood what his argument was supposed to be an argument for. Moreover I assume that when Hume wrote, he too had read books that attempted to do what Nagel attempts to do, and that he too understood what it was that they were attempting to do.

In terms of the Hempelian schema, what Nagel's book purports to provide is an elaborate specification of a type-E situation: a range of considerations which are such that any rational person who appreciates them will end up desiring the end that people not suffer excruciating pain. But of course, as the Hempelian schema makes plain, even if Nagel is right and an agent A is in such a type-E situation, absent the additional premise that A is a rational subject – this is the second premise in the schema – we will be unable to derive the conclusion that A rationally desires the end that people not suffer excruciating pain. Absent this premise, all we can conclude is that the end that people not suffer excruciating pain is the rational thing for the subject to desire as an end in such a type-E situation. By parity of reasoning from the cases of action explanation and rational belief explanation, then, we are forced to conclude that, if indeed it is possible for subjects to form rational desires for ends, as Nagel's book argues that it is, then their being rational – that is to say, their possession and exercise of the capacity to revise their desires in a rational manner – must play a crucial explanatory role.

This suggests that there may therefore be a distinctive anti-Humean kind of non-constitutive explanation of an action, a kind we can represent in terms of the following modified version of figure 2 (figure 3).

The "⇛" in figure 3, like the "⇒", represents the agent's possession and exercise of a rational capacity. The difference between the "⇛" and the "⇒" is simply that, whereas the "⇒" represents the possession and exercise of the capacity to revise *beliefs* in a rational manner, the "⇛" represents the capacity to revise *desires for ends* in a rational manner. The "⇛", the "⇒", and the "+" each represent the operation of different departments of rationality.

What figure 3 suggests is that we might explain (say) an agent's performing some bodily movement that he believes will cause the relief of some other person's excruciating pain by citing the fact that he *rationally desires* the end that people not suffer excruciating pain. Such would be the case if (say) Nagel were right and the agent in question came to desire the end that people not suffer after being convinced by what he says in *The Possibility of Altruism*. To be sure, such an explanation is non-constitutive. A bodily movement performed by an agent who desires the end that people not suffer excruciating pain and believes that that bodily movement will relieve someone else's excruciating pain may be an action whether the desire is rational or irrational. But, if Nagel is right, it is an explanation that may sometimes be available none the less.

Note that the non-constitutive explanation represented in figure 3, if such there be, is distinctive in that an action that can be so explained is the

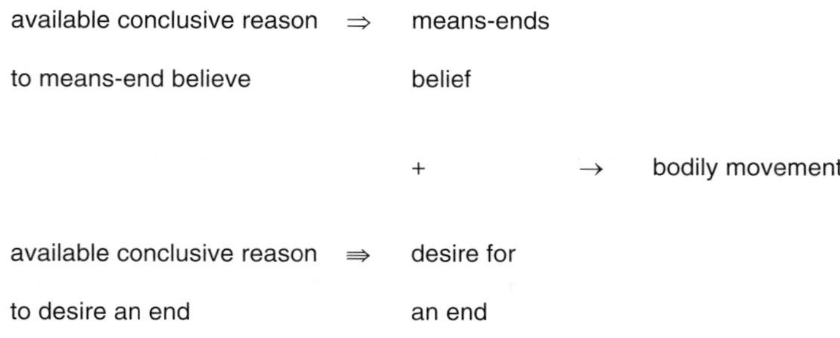


Figure 3. An Anti-Humean account of a distinctive non-constitutive explanation of action

product of an even better specimen of one of its constitutive causes than one that cannot be so explained. An action caused not just by the agent's possession and exercise of the capacity to be instrumentally rational and his possession and exercise of the capacity to revise his beliefs in a rational manner – this is what is represented in figure 2 – but also by his possession and exercise of the capacity to revise his desires for ends in a rational manner, as in figure 3, is an action that is caused by an *even better* specimen of the psychological state of being rational in all of its departments. The agent of such an action is more fully rational: indeed, it seems that he may be as fully rational as he can be, as there doesn't seem to be anything that is a further candidate for rational explanation.

Of course, nothing that I have said shows that Nagel is right, or that anyone else arguing for a similar conclusion is right, and hence nothing that I have said shows that there are non-constitutive explanations of the distinctive kind represented in figure 3. What I have been concerned to show is simply that we can make sense of their possibility: the mere fact that beliefs can be true or false, whereas desires for ends cannot, goes no way towards showing that such explanations do not exist. The discussion has, however, been instructive, because it suggests how we might make progress on the more substantive issue of whether any such non-constitutive explanations do exist. What the discussion suggests is that believers and disbelievers in the possibility of non-constitutive explanations of the distinctive kind represented in figure 3 should focus their attention on the crucial third premise of the final Hempelian schema: the claim that there is some type of situation, E, such that, in a situation of that type any fully rational agent will desire the end that q. What the believers desperately need to provide are concrete examples of Es and qs that make this claim seem credible, examples that make it clear that it is *rationality* that is at issue, not some other form of evaluation. And what the disbelievers need to provide, if they want to argue against the very possibility of such explanations, is some argument, radically different from Hume's own, for supposing that the search for such examples is quixotic.

Speaking for myself, I am not sure that either side enters this debate with the upper hand. The substantive issue about the rational status of non-instrumental desires that divides those who follow Hume from those who oppose him seems to me to be wide open (though contrast the optimistic argument in Smith 1994, chapter 6, with the more pessimistic line of argument in Smith 2006). And this in turn means that it is wide open what exactly the scope is for providing non-constitutive explanations of actions in terms of agents' being rational.

CHAPTER 5

# *Practical competence and fluent agency**

*Peter Railton*

## INTRODUCTION

My first attempts to drive a car were torture – for myself, my older brother (who unwisely had agreed to help teach me), and the family car. The car had a manual transmission and clutch, and we bucked and lurched around town. Each intersection, even each gear shift, posed a challenge that demanded my full attention – if only I could have given it. Instead, my mind was churning with embarrassment at my incompetence, driven to fever pitch by the chorus of horns that greeted me each time I stalled in traffic. I could barely follow the simplest directions from my brother, and his occasional attempts to calm things down with conversation fell on deaf ears. Despite himself, he groaned quietly as I ground the gears and lugged the engine.

Like everyone, I eventually I got the hang of driving – the way we eventually get the hang of talking, eating without a bib, telling a joke without ruining it, finding our way in a strange city, or politely discouraging an over-eager salesman. What had changed about me as a driver? Not my *rationality*. It was not irrational of me to drive when I was so annoyingly clumsy at it – I had to learn, and there was no other way. My driving was incompetent, but not really dangerous. True, I was responding badly to the available reasons. So I was not a good *detector of* or *responder to* reasons. But not out of irrationality. Believe me, I was squeezing whatever I could out of reason alone.

What changed was my *competence* or *fluency* as a driver. As I gradually acquired the component skills and gained confidence in my ability,

* I would like to express my appreciation to the editors of this volume, David Sobel and Steven Wall, as well as to those who attended the 2006 Bowling Green conference on Practical Reason, for helpful comments and criticisms. As always, I owe a special debt to my colleagues Elizabeth Anderson and Allan Gibbard, and also to my former colleagues Stephen Darwall and David Velleman. Richard Nisbett helped introduce me to recent work in cognitive social psychology.

I became able to drive in traffic without causing bottlenecks and precipitating a barrage of honking. Once skilled enough and sufficiently confident in myself and my skills, I could delegate the task of driving largely to an acquired *habitus*, permitting me to focus on other things while I drove – following complex directions, say, or having an intense conversation with a companion. Skilled driving is not, however, like being on "autopilot" or following a set, mechanized routine. Each drive is different in a variety of ways from the drive before it, and so each presents the driver with somewhat different conditions – somewhat different reasons – to respond to. Moreover, competent drivers do not all drive alike, nor do they drive the same way each time. You can come to know a fair amount about someone or her mood from the way he or she drives. Fluency permits one's driving to be self-expressive, for better or worse.

Which brings me to the fact that although driving fluency permits better responsiveness to reasons and greater self-expression, it does not guarantee that one's driving will be rational. If anything, fluency can put one at risk of much more dangerous and irrational driving. When I first began to drive, there was no risk of my threading my way through heavy traffic at excessive speed, or driving when three sheets to the wind.

## MISSING PIECES

In philosophy, we find debates between internalists and externalists in virtually every domain, and along a multiplicity of dimensions. Some philosophers, for example, insist that the theory of practical reason should take as its starting point the standpoint of an agent facing a conscious choice. Such *first-personal approaches* require us to focus on whether the agent makes appropriate use of information and motives actually available to her in the situation. This represents one form of "internalism" about practical reasons.[1] Primacy is given to the subjective "ought," in terms of which any putatively objective practical "ought" will be analyzed. In a competing camp we find philosophers who approach the analysis of rational action from a standpoint "external" to the agent's own perspective – the *third-personal standpoint* of explanation. For such theorists, the essential

[1] Note that this sort of internalism is distinct from the sort in play in debates over whether motivation is in some sense "internal" to the content of normative judgment (i.e. so-called *judgment internalism*), or a necessary condition for the existence of *bona fide* practical reasons (i.e. so-called *existence internalism*). Here there is a closer anology with the way the internalism/externalism issue is drawn in epistemology.

thing is to understand the causal structure of intentional action, emphasizing the variety of mechanisms by means of which behavior is responsive to reasons. Primacy is accorded to the objective "ought," in terms of which any subjective "ought" will be analyzed.

Relatedly, there is a debate about the role of autonomous agency in practical rationality. For some, the very paradigm of practical rationality occurs when an agent deliberates and consciously exerts choice, reflecting upon her reasons, deciding upon their relevance and weight, and making them effective by means of the directed exercise of her will. Contrast approaches that focus in the first instance on the various processes by which our thoughts, feelings, and actions may track, or fail to track, available reasons. For example, individuals engaged in an intense conversation can be observed to mimic one another's posture, gestures, facial expressions, eye movements, and voice. All this coordination occurs without conscious thought. Normal babies manifest this sort of mimicry from their earliest days, and developmental problems will face those whose show no sign of it. Even in adulthood, such mimicry plays a fundamental role in establishing and sustaining our mutual understanding in social settings. Each of us therefore typically has reason to reciprocate to some degree the movements, gestures, voice, etc. of our conversational partners – failure to do so may impede effective interaction and contribute to misunderstanding. Moreover, failure to notice when the other has stopped mimicking can lead one to fail to see that something has gone awry in the conversation or that one has overstayed one's welcome. Virtually everyone in society becomes proficient at producing and interpreting "body language," but vanishingly few are ever aware of doing so. To those philosophers who stress autonomy and deliberate choice in their conception of practical rationality, this sort of acquired, intelligent, reason-responsive conduct is not genuinely rational, because it involves no conscious agency. The reasons to which the individual is responding are seen as *acting on* her, rather than the other way around. To those philosophers who stress the tracking of reasons, however, the notion of a form of agency in which the individual can distance herself from "empirical determination" is suspect on psychological and philosophical grounds – it smacks of a revival of "rational homuncularism" or "agent causation."

My primary sympathy lies with the second group of philosophers in each pair, above, but there is too much to be said for the other side for me to think that either one gives a full solution to the puzzle of practical reason. Perhaps we philosophers are fighting over how to fit together the pieces of a jigsaw puzzle when several pieces are missing. Neither side can assemble the puzzle satisfactorily until those pieces are brought to the table. *Agent-competence* and *practical intelligence* are two of those pieces. At any rate, that is what I will argue.

## AGENT-COMPETENCE

By "agent-competence" I have in mind something analogous to two more familiar competencies: linguistic competence and social competence. Despite many differences in the language and culture into which they are born, and despite wide variation in their personal history, virtually all children acquire linguistic competence in a mother tongue. Such competence goes beyond the ability to distinguish grammatical from ungrammatical sentences, and includes a capacity to understand and produce entirely novel sentences, and to use language successfully for meaningful communication. Indeed, by young adulthood, virtually all children have become fluent speakers – able to express complex, conditional thoughts, and capable of producing and understanding sentences at the speed of thought.

That all of this takes place in almost all children and without special training has led linguists to posit a native grammatical capacity, which equips children with a special aptitude for acquiring vocabulary and a tacit knowledge of the syntactic and semantic rules of their language, even though the evidence they will have received from the speech of others is often fragmentary and imperfect. Further evidence of this native capacity comes from the stagewise pattern of linguistic development in infants, and the fact that disease, injury, and birth defects tend to cause discrete, systematic deficits in linguistic abilities, deficits that often are unrelated to general intelligence, and which typically can be overcome, if at all, only with great difficulty. In light of the limited range of formal variation among natural languages and the rapidity with which humans raised in one culture can learn the languages of another, it is supposed that this native capacity has a universal form. The diversity of natural languages arises from separate lexical traditions and grammatical variation along a finite number of parameters.[2]

[2] For two views, see M.D. Hauser, N. Chomsky, and W.T. Fitch, "The Faculty of Language: What Is It, Who Has It, and How Did It Evolve?," *Science*, 298 (2002): 1569–1579 and R. Jackendoff, *Foundations of Language: Brain, Meaning, Grammar, and Evolution* (Oxford: Oxford University Press, 2002).

It is also reasonable to suppose that children have a native capacity for sociability, and, with maturity, for fluent social competence. Newborns typically spontaneously form deep bonds with parents or care-givers, and quickly respond reciprocally to signs of others' pleasure or distress. They track whether others are focusing on them, and learn how to attract and hold attention. These are things that normally need not be, and probably could not be, taught. Perceptual discrimination of intentional vs non-intentional movements and entities appears very early, and without special training. Under ordinary conditions, this social orientation and aptitude leads to development of a sense of self vs others, as well as a greater capacity to understand the thoughts and feelings of others, and to respond appropriately. As in the case of language, we see here a pattern of regular, stagewise, nearly universal acquisition of capacities that together yield a distinctive kind of competence. In most individuals, the end result is a form of fluent sociability in familiar settings. Like language, too, we can observe some global similarities in basic social forms, as well as inter-cultural intelligibility and individual facility in adapting to the norms and customs of other societies.[3] We also find that persistent deficits in sociability tend to appear in distinctive patterns, often linked to particular diseases, dysfunctions, injuries, childhood trauma, or birth defects.

Linguistic and social competence are usually called *tacit* competencies since individuals typically lack direct insight into the rules, norms, conventions, etc. they follow as they speak and act. To be sure, individuals do have many "intuitions" – intuitions about the meanings of words, about which sentences are grammatical, about what polite conversation requires, about who is dominant in a given group, or about which behavior is "properly" masculine or feminine. These intuitions, articulate or otherwise, reflect the individual's internalization of local rules, norms, and conventions. The smooth operation of these competencies does not require conscious attention – individuals are guided by an intuitive sense of what is appropriate or anomalous, and of course sheer *habitus* does much of the work in regulating behavior. In acquiring a second language or learning the tacit norms of an organization or society, it is the mark of the transition from plodding competence to genuine fluency that one no longer need mentally "look up" rules or principles in order to speak grammatically or to act *comme il faut*. Fluency is by no means a matter

[3] For some sample overviews, see A.P. Fiske, *Structures of Social Life: The Four Elementary Forms of Human Relationships* (New York: Free Press, 1991). Relatedly, see D. Goleman, *Emotional Intelligence* (New York: Bantam, 1995) and *Social Intelligence* (New York: Bantam, 2006).

of sheer "mechanization" or "routinization" alone. Rather, greater fluency typically makes speech or behavior less mechanical, more personally expressive, and more open to innovation. Indeed, highly fluent individuals have a good sense of when it is appropriate to bend or break the rules.

Linguistic and social competence, and, more generally, the capacity to acquire the values and ways of life of the community into which one is born, are so central to human life that we can expect natural selection to have equipped us with the wherewithal for the reliable acquisition and fluent deployment of these interlocking skills. Each competence is, moreover, sufficiently integrated functionally to warrant speaking of them as *psychological natural kinds*. (Some psychologists speak of these competencies as involving "modules," though that is a much more controversial claim.)

My speculative hypothesis is that the capacity to *act intentionally* and *interpret the actions of others* is likewise an essential competency. Let me dub the cluster of abilities that creates the ability to exercise effective intentional agency and interpretation *practical competence*. This is, I believe, like *intentional action* itself, a psychological natural kind, functionally integrated and bound to have been evolutionarily shaped and favored.

The first component of practical competence is what I will call *agent-competence*. Roughly, this is a set of skills akin to the skills that equip someone to be an effective administrator, *inter alia*: an ability to focus attention selectively, but also to be somewhat mindful of several things at once; an ability to set goals and make plans, but also to revisit and revise them in light of experience; an ability to interpret situations and form a view about what's at stake and which actions are in the offing; an ability vividly to imagine alternatives and identify necessary means toward them as well as their remoter consequences; an ability to deliberate and decide among options; an ability to adjust means to ends; an ability to maintain morale and generate motivation in the face of difficulty; and so on.

Many of the elements in this list might be thought to be part of practical rationality. How is agent-competence different from practical reason itself? Practical reason, we might say, represents a distinctive way of *deploying* one's agent-competencies, just as rational driving is a distinctive way of deploying one's driving competence and rational discourse and social conduct are distinctive ways of deploying one's linguistic and social competences. Developmentally, agent-competencies emerge over time, and are important *precursors* to, and *conditions* for, mature practical rationality. However, although they play an important role in enabling the exercise of effective rationality, their successful development, even to the point of fluency, is no guarantee of rational conduct. Highly effective administrators have, for example, been keenly involved in carrying out some of the most senseless or horrible economic, military, and political strategies.

Garden-variety irrational actions – those stemming from weakness of the will, failure to consider alternatives or remoter consequences, indecision or irresoluteness, failure to adjust means to ends, etc. – typically involve some measure of failure in agent-competence. But even in our irrational moments, we typically retain a sufficiently high level of agent-competence to give our actions some efficacy. A warehouse employee with a prior record of arrest for shop-lifting understands that he *must not* pilfer – management is keeping an eye on him, and a second arrest on his record would ruin his hopes for a decent job. He knows that he can't blow this chance. Yet when a shipment of sleek, new iPods comes in, temptation sets in. While stocking the shelves, he stacks cartons high enough to block the hidden camera as he bends down to open a fresh box of iPods, and deftly palms one and slides it under his shirt. His theft, if successful, will net him one rather expensive and useful gadget; but if detected, it will cost him his job and much more. Were he fully rational, he wouldn't risk it. But he isn't fully rational – temptation gets the better of him. Still, his irrational theft is enacted very competently. He does not attempt to steal something of very low value or impossible to conceal, and he accurately envisages how he might be detected and acts accordingly. He goes through with it with the required feigned nonchalance, and continues about his task as if nothing had happened. All of this is his agent-competence at work – even in the name of an aim a rational person in his shoes would have rejected outright. Sheer competency cannot save us from ourselves.

We might contrast this employee's behavior with that of a young child stealing from the change bowl. After spotting the change bowl on a low shelf, he may approach it hesitantly, conspicuously looking around to see if he is being watched, pausing with his hand poised over the change bowl still trying to make up his mind and momentarily stymied by the unanticipated problem of deciding which coins to take. He then grabs a handful of coins noisily, still looking around nervously, and darts out of the room in a state of high nervous agitation and with a very guilty look on his face. A parent or friend encountering him in the next room would sense at once that something was up. His pilfering would be as incompetent as my early driving.

At bottom, the child and the adult succumbed to remarkably similar psychic forces. Each knew better than to steal in the circumstances, and each was swayed by the presence of a highly salient stimulus. In that sense, the adult behaved "like a child." Yet in another sense, the adult's behavior was not childish at all, and deserves higher marks for execution. We would, in effect, see a *double* lack of mature agency in an adult who, in attempting to pilfer the iPod, went about it just like the young child.

It might seem that we prefer personalities, even among adults, inimical to skillful wrongdoing. Good people, one might think, will by nature make bad thieves. After all, accomplished thieves seem disturbingly cold-blooded and indifferent to the harm they cause others, especially to those most vulnerable individuals who often are their targets. Perhaps skill at theft deserves nothing but contempt? This pious thought is not sustainable. There will be cases in which we need to steal for a good cause – to filch food from the rations stored in a municipal warehouse in wartime in order to provision the Resistance, say. In such circumstances, we may especially *admire* someone who, even though brought up never to steal and hating the thought of putting her fellow employees at risk, nonetheless has the self-mastery, *sang froid*, and shrewdness to carry out the theft with the fluency needed for success. This is no time to be weak-kneed, or paralyzed by conventionality. Yet admirable as such self-mastery, *sang froid*, and deftness may be, I doubt we see them as part of practical rationality. We do not, for example, lower our opinion of the practical rationality of otherwise estimable agents who simply could not pull off this off.

Agent-competence lends structure and meaning to behavior, permitting us to see the intentions of the agent behind it – even when the intentions are irrational or malevolent. Trying to understand the concern behind the flailing and wailing of an overwrought child is difficult precisely because the child is failing to manifest agent-competency – rather like the case of trying to interpret the speech of a highly agitated individual lacking basic competence in our language. Figuring out what is bothering an overwrought child often requires finding some way to bring into play the competencies he *does* possess, even when distraught. "Can you *point* to what's bothering you?," the nurse asks in a reassuring tone.

## PRACTICAL INTELLIGENCE

The second component of practical competence, and the second piece of the puzzle of practical rationality that I would like to bring to the table, is what I will call *practical intelligence*. One credible way of characterizing "general intelligence" is *problem-solving ability*, and we can think of practical intelligence as the ability to solve a range of problems specific to the exercise of agency. Practical intelligence will often be needed in order to possess or exercise practical competencies.

A paradigmatic example is possession of the ability to contend with the problem of impulsivity in the face of temptation, as in the example above. What equips us for it? In a classic series of experiences, Walter Mischel tested the ability of four-year-olds to resist eating a marshmallow placed before them, on the strength of a promise that if they could refrain from eating it for the next quarter-hour, they would receive a second marshmallow. This sounds like a job for practical reason and "will power," but the four-year-olds who resisted impulse successfully relied less on iron logic and steely resolve than on indirect strategies of distraction or disengagement – pretending the marshmallow was something else, placing their head down on the table to hide their eyes, concentrating on other things, trying to fall asleep. The central importance of this capacity to find a way of *working around* or *working with* impulse – since it is a motivational state one cannot cancel at will or refute by argument – became manifest when the same individuals were studied again in grade school and then, still later, in high school. Those unable to work around or with their temptation, who ate the first marshmallow soon after the test began, were found to have had more problems with social adjustment, behavior control, peer relationships, and schoolwork.[4]

Importantly, the skill in question is not sheer "self-denial" or "self-mastery," though it is a skill that may facilitate denying oneself and mastering one's feelings when this serves a purpose. Just as those who immediately indulged themselves had greater subsequent problems in life, so did those who stoically soldiered on in self-denial, resisting the second marshmallow once it was produced and failing to reward themselves by eating the marshmallows, once there was nothing to gain from further delay.

Moreover, the skill involved does not appear to be excellence in practical reasoning. True, those who managed to fend off impulse, and to enjoy the reward of success once achieved, were more responsive to available reasons than the others. But the explanation does not appear

[4] Y. Shoda, W. Mischel, and P.K. Peake, "Predicting Adolescent Cognitive and Self-Regulatory Competencies from Preschool Delay of Gratification," *Developmental Psychology*, 26 (1990): 978–986.

to lie in their reasoning ability or recognition of what was required or prudent in the situation. All the children liked marshmallows, and all preferred two over one. All understood the point of the game and the advantages of waiting. In that sense, the children all saw the same reasons to consume the first marshmallow and the same, stronger, reasons to delay. The differences among the groups appear to have arisen from a bundle of non-deliberative cognitive, imaginative, and affective abilities. It was possession of this bundle, it appears, that proved so valuable in so many areas of their lives as they grew older and faced new problems.

Research on *moral* development also suggests that reasoning capacity and grasp of principles may be less central than a capacity for empathy and emotional engagement. Children's behavior in actual choices, for example, was better predicted by these affective capacities than by the complexity of their moral reasoning or ability to enunciate principles.[5] Similarly, among a group of Polish policemen ordered by Nazi occupiers to execute civilians at point-blank range, those who succeeded in non-compliance were those who seem empathetically to have mirrored the fear and panic of their victims and experienced a visceral revulsion at shooting. By contrast, few cited moral principles or religious convictions to explain their conduct.[6]

These characteristics – empathy and visceral resistance – are in some sense pre-moral or proto-moral, rather than "moralized" or "judgmental." Empathy, for example, can operate contra-judgmentally. It will induce alarm and distress in response to the terror seen in others' faces even when those exhibiting terror are judged to be one's enemies or to deserve punishment. Similar characteristics, and similar neurological structures – a similar chemistry of "bonding," "cooperativeness," and "inhibition toward harming con-specifics who signal helplessness" – can be found in social

[5] See J. Metcalf and W. Mischel, "A Hot/Cool System Analysis of the Delay of Gratification," *Psychological Review*, 106 (1999): 3–19; M.L. Hoffman, "Development of Prosocial Motivation: Empathy and Guilt," in N. Eisenberg, ed., *The Development of Prosocial Behavior* (New York: Academic Press, 1982); J. Haidt, "The Emotional Dog and Its Rational Tail: A Social Intuitionist Approach to Moral Judgment," *Psychological Review* 108, (2001): 814–834; A. Damasio, *Descartes' Error* (New York: Putnam, 1994); and C.D. Batson *et al.*, "Value Judgments: Testing the Somatic-Marker Hypothesis Using False Physiological Feedback," *Personality and Social Psychology Bulletin*, 25, (1999): 1021–1032. One interesting qualification: moral reasoning ability was more strongly linked with successful inhibition of delinquent behavior than successful initiation of helping behavior. See S.J. Thoma *et al.*, "Does Moral Judgment Development Reduce to Political Attitudes or Verbal Ability?," *Educational Psychology Review*, 11 (1999): 325–341.

[6] For discussion, see R.F. Baumeister, *Evil: Inside Human Violence and Cruelty* (New York: W.H. Freeman, 1997): 209–210. Baumeister's analysis is based upon the research of Christopher Browning, *Ordinary Men: Reserve Police Battalion 101 and the Final Solution in Poland* (New York: HarperCollins, 1992).

animals, who presumably lack a capacity for practical reason. So, too, do we find in social animals and humans alike neural processes that replicate the behavior of others, and brain systems for the empathic emotional "simulation" of the states of others on a substrate of the individual's own affective system. Humans may differ from animals less in their capacity for such responses and feelings, than in their ability to mobilize or (regrettably often) *de*-mobilize these responses in the name of abstract ideals or conceptions of "sameness" vs "otherness," or "superiority" vs "inferiority" – and, of course, in the magnitude of the harm they can do when some of these systems are absent or deficient.[7]

The affective and emotive systems that appear to play a pivotal role in our thought and conduct are informed about the world directly from the senses, not only through conscious experience, but also via dedicated, fast pathways unmediated by higher-order cognitive interpretation. Typically, they come into play even before cognitive judgments are formed, and they characteristically prime and color such judgment. Individuals who suffer from impairments in these affective and emotive systems, or in the pathways by which they send signals to higher-order cognition, appear to have greater difficulty forming accurate judgments of the risks they face, and to show lesser ability to track their own risk judgments effectively in the choices they make. Moreover, they more likely to experience difficulties in social relations, or to exhibit asocial or sociopathic behavior.[8]

This *primacy of affect* is a fundamental and pervasive feature of our psyche. It probably is no exaggeration to say that the bulk of our everyday mental activity – perception, attention, memory, learning, inference, association, intention-formation – is affect-mediated.[9] The role of affect in shaping subsequent judgment and behavior is sometimes called the "automatic evaluation process," and the picture of the psyche that emerges is known as a "dual-process" model, in which separable and interacting affective cognitive processes run simultaneously in the mind.[10] Information

[7] Practical reason *can* play an important role here, for example, by alerting us to these risks, and by challenging conceptions of "otherness" or otherwise encouraging the development of empathic responses. In this way, humans can be "argued into" sending aid to the other side of the globe, or passing and enforcing laws to ban violence or discrimination. No animals have yet shown these abilities. At the same time, no animals have ever shown violence toward con-specifics on the human scale.

[8] See Damasio, *Descartes' Error*, esp. chapter 3. The implications of this for "judgment internalism" are briefly discussed below.

[9] The seminal work is R. Zajonc, "Feeling and Thinking: Preferences Need No Inference," *American Psychologist*, 35 (1980): 151–175. For more discussion, see Haidt, "The Emotional Dog."

[10] For discussion, see J.A. Bargh and T.L. Chartrand, "The Unbearable Automaticity of Being," *American Psychologist*, 54 (1999): 462–479.

arriving directly from the senses is compared with expectations and immediately coded in the brain as favorable, neutral, or unfavorable. Because the coding is affective, it not only frames judgment, but also sets in motion motivation and emotion.[11] Thus a judgment and a corresponding emotive or motivational response will tend to co-occur, not because either one constitutes the other, but because they are, in part, effects of a common cause. The first stages of these processes occur with remarkable speed, at a level unavailable to conscious introspection. From the standpoint of our self-awareness, the flow from perception to intuitive judgment is "seamless" – we see a dangerous condition *as* dangerous, immediately feeling the peril it poses and preparing for action.

Moral judgment may be an example of just this phenomenon. The psychologist Jonathan Haidt has studied human moral judgment by presenting subjects with hypothetical scenarios and recording their reactions. He finds that subjects presented with a moral scenario involving incest, for example, have a quick affective response, pro or con, which precedes and appears to prime conscious judgment. Because the origin and occurrence of this intuitive affective response is not introspectively available, subjects asked to explain *why* they judged the scenario as they did must improvise a plausible rationale. Of course, they do not sense that they are constructing a rationale *post hoc* – it seems to them that they are giving their actual reasons, and they do tend to cite considerations of a kind that *would*, if present in the scenario, explain their judgment. However, the scenario has been carefully designed so that most of the considerations it initially occurs to people to cite are not in fact present. Thus, the scenario stipulates that the incestuous act took place between mature adults who cared for each other, acting fully voluntarily and without coercion, avoiding the possibility of conception, and suffering no subsequent psychological trauma. When the disparity between the scenario actually presented and the rationale they provide for their judgment is pointed out to subjects, they tend *not* to withdraw or reconsider their initial judgment.[12] This firmness of judgment in the absence of a rationale would make sense if the explicit judgment and the *post hoc* rationalization have a common cause, namely, the intuitive affective

[11] Fiske introduced the term "category-based affect" to describe this phenomenon. See S.T. Fiske, "Schema-Triggered Affect," in M.S. Clark and S.T. Fiske, eds., *Affect and Cognition* (San Diego: Academic Press, 1982).

[12] Haidt, "The Emotional Dog."

response. Since the intuitive response never depended causally upon the rationale, it is unaffected by its collapse.

The primacy of affect over reasoning in giving rise to judgment makes sense.[13] We are after all the products of millions of years in which progenitors less well endowed with higher-order cognitive resources were selected for their ability to rapidly and reliably discriminate the propitious or beneficial from the risky or harmful. Studies of primate neurology support the hypothesis that the brain makes a fast "triage" of incoming information, as positive, neutral, or negative, priming the animal's responses accordingly. At the same time, the brain updates prior expectations according as the new information is better than, worse than, or the same as expected. In this way the "triage" process is constantly *learning* rather than operating with a fixed standard. In effect, it learns from experience how to do its triage more accurately and guide the organism toward its goals more reliably.[14] Humans appear to have retained this "automatic evaluation system," the power of which is increased by the range and complexity of the expectations we can form and the goals we can pursue. Those with highly developed practical skills – in sports, seamanship, teaching, etc. – appear to draw upon this evaluation system, as refined by experience, in forming a quick intuitive "sense" of what is happening in a given situation, and how to respond appropriately.

## AFFECTIVE REGULATION: IT'S NOT JUST FOR HUMEANS ANY MORE

The pervasive regulatory role of affect in our mental life is, of course, a favorite theme of Humeans, but the phenomenon did not altogether escape the founders of other traditions in the theory of practical reason. Kant located the will in the "faculty of desire," rather than some separate, higher faculty.[15] Moreover, he characterized the empirical psychology of a virtuous agent who respects the moral law in affective terms – our respect for the moral law is "the moral feeling," not a pure cognition.[16] Our sense of the

[13] Haidt found an exception to this pattern in the case of moral judgments when subjects are presented with a classic "moral dilemma," which makes reasoning salient. This phenomenon is discussed further, below. See Haidt, "The Emotional Dog" and S. Murphy, J. Haidt, and F. Bjorklund, "Moral Dumbfounding: When Intuition Finds No Reason" (pre-print).

[14] See W. Shultz, P. Dayan, and R.P. Montague, "A Neural Substrate of Prediction and Reward," *Science*, 275 (1997): 1593–1599.

[15] I. Kant, *The Metaphysics of Morals*, trans. M.J. Gregor (Cambridge: Cambridge University Press, 1966): 6:213.

[16] *The Metaphysics of Morals*: 6:402.

beautiful or sublime in both morality and nature is immediate, and "not brought to concepts," even though it guides our respect, strikes down our self-conceit, and produces our appreciation and awe.[17]

Aristotle, for his part, stressed that virtue is not a matter of conscientiousness and rational application of principle alone – for such is the nature of mere continence – but of right feeling and finding happiness in the right things. Affect, he thought, had the fundamental regulatory role in our psyche:

> [A]nd to a greater or lesser extent, we regulate our actions by pleasure and pain. Our whole inquiry, then, must be concerned with them, because whether we feel enjoyment and pain in a good or bad way has great influence on our actions.[18]

The phenomenon of regulation by affect (one example of which is Aristotle's treatment of pleasure and pain as "regulators") is exemplified at its most basic by classical conditioning. Teaching animals – whether rats in a cage or elephants at the circus – invariably involves the carefully regulated use of reward and punishment, in effect redeploying the animal's internal affect-governed regulation process on behalf of an agenda set externally by the trainer.

This mention of the training of animals will surely prompt thoughts that an account of psychology assigning a central role to affect regulation "reduces us to mere animals." But this would be "reducing" only if the things in which humans find intrinsic reward were animalistic. They are not. Humans find reward in pleasant experience, to be sure, but also in such things as successful pursuit of abstract ideals, excellence in the exercise of skills and capacities, discovery and the creation of knowledge, friendship, humor, self-expression, aesthetic appreciation, romantic love, and commitment to kith and kin. Human affect regulation can be as diverse and conceptually rich as our desires and passions themselves.

## PRACTICAL COMPETENCE

Human affect regulation is part of what some psychologists have come to call our "emotional intelligence." This intelligence includes a sense of one's own feelings and wants as they occur, an ability to sense and anticipate the thoughts and feelings of others, an ability to motivate oneself on behalf of a goal, an ability to control impulse and modulate

[17] I. Kant, *The Critique of Judgment*, trans. W.S. Pluhar (Indianapolis, IN: Hackett, 1987): 266.

[18] Aristotle, *Nichomachean Ethics*, trans. R. Crisp (Cambridge: Cambridge University Press, 2000): 1105a3–5.

or channel one's emotional responses, and an ability to form bonds with others and manage emotion within a relationship.[19] Evidence ranging from health indicators to measures of financial success and personal achievement and life-satisfaction supports the view that this sort of intelligence may be more important for one's well-being, effectiveness, and overall life prospects than cognitive intelligence.[20] It is readily seen that this sort of intelligence would be an important part of our intelligence *as agents*–that is, of our practical intelligence.

Practical intelligence is largely a matter of *know-how* rather than *knowledge-that* or formal reasoning – knowing how to hold off impulse, how to sustain one's motivation and protect one's morale, how to plan, how to play one's part in a conversation, how to reciprocate affection, how to acknowledge and learn from one's mistakes, how to apply the information one has, and so on. Moreover, it often involves something like "opponent processing." Alongside knowing how to plan and stick to a plan is knowing how to avoid crippling rigidity by remaining open to challenge, change, unanticipated experience, and emergent opportunities. Alongside knowing how to hold off impulse is knowing how to escape untempered asceticism, rewarding oneself effectively and enjoying life's pleasures. Alongside knowing how to face up to one's mistakes and limitations is knowing how move on and not be too hard on oneself. Most such know-how cannot be codified as rules. It is acquired, if at all, through experience and emulation, and it manifests itself in our lives through the fluent and effective exercise of competencies.

Taking together agent-competence and the practical intelligence, then, we arrive at what might be called *practical competence*.

## PRACTICAL COMPETENCE AND AUTOMATICITY

Fluencies such as skilled driving, speaking one's native tongue, or adapting rapidly to the mood or manners of a group are often called "automatisms" by psychologists, but this term may misleadingly suggest that the operation of these fluencies is mechanical, unintelligent, or unfeeling. In truth the exercise of these fluencies is, or at any rate can be, extraordinarily well attuned to circumstance and mood. Once we have become fluent, walking upright and speaking a second language are "automatic"

19 See P. Salovey and J.D. Mayer, "Emotional Intelligence," *Imagination, Cognition, and Personality*, 9 (1990): 185–211.

20 For an overview, see Goleman, *Emotional Intelligence*.

behaviors in the psychologists' sense, but we do not walk and talk like robots following set programs. Instead, it is our very fluency that permits these acts to be spontaneous, even creative.

"Automatized" action goes far beyond the reflexive or instinctual. Reflexes – eye blinks, knee jerks, etc. – involve dedicated circuitry that produces fixed behaviors, often without much help from the central nervous system. Instincts – fear of spiders and snakes, mating rituals, homing behavior – typically manifest themselves in stereotyped behavior elicited by a fixed array of stimuli. Reflexes and instincts are also typically resistant to modification through learning. In contrast, most of the fluencies we have been discussing are intelligent and plastic – they involve extensive learning, anticipating novel problems, generating novel solutions, and a capacity for self-revision. For example, "automatic" eye movements acquired through experience and development can be faster and more subtle learners than our "higher" cognitive faculties, often instructing or guiding our more articulate cognition in quite sophisticated ways. In the "false belief task," a child subject is told a story about two girls, Sally and Anne. Sally has placed a piece of candy in a basket and left the room. Anne, in Sally's absence, removes Sally's candy from the basket and places it in a box. The child subject is then asked where Sally will look for her candy upon returning to the room – the basket or the box? Success at this task requires the ability to impute to another a belief about the world that one does not oneself possess, and to use this imputed false belief to predict and explain the other's behavior. Normal children usually do not succeed at this task until age four. But even before children will have mastered the verbal task, while they are still answering, "In the box," their eyes have begun to dart momentarily toward the basket prior to giving their response. This eye movement is nothing the child is aware of, and certainly not voluntary in the usual sense. Yet the eye movement does appear to cue the later emergence of declarative knowledge that Sally will look in the basket, and is absent in children with forms of autism that impede mastery of the false belief task. This absence in turn is correlated with long-term deficits in their ability to understand the feelings and behaviors of others, deficits that even high intelligence does not seem to remedy fully.[21]

[21] See S. Baron-Cohen, *Mindblindness: An Essay on Autism and Theory of Mind* (Cambridge, MA: MIT Press, 1995). "Solving" the false belief task described above of course involves many other skills on the part of the child, including notably the ability to handle complex verbal instructions involving embedded propositional attitude ascriptions. Non-verbal forms of the task have been developed, and some evidence suggests that children understand them at an earlier age. See P. Mitchell, *Introduction to the Theory of Mind: Children, Autism, and Apes* (London: Arnold, 1997).

The amount, variety, and detail of information gathered by our "intuitive" processes often exceed anything conscious deliberation could manage.[22] In one recent study, experimental subjects facing a hypothetical choice with a small number of variables did better (according to their own announced *ex ante* preferences) when they were given peace to concentrate and time to deliberate. But when the number of variables grew, the same individuals made better choices (again, by their own lights) if they were distracted and allowed insufficient time to deliberate, so that they were forced to rely more heavily on intuition or hunch.[23]

The psychologist Jonathan Haidt writes:

> It is now widely accepted in social and cognitive psychology that two processing systems are often at work when a person makes judgments or solves problems. Because these two systems typically run in parallel and are capable of reaching differing conclusions, these models are usually called *dual-process* models.[24]

One of these systems, Haidt notes, is fast, intuitive, effortless, and its operation is typically not available to introspection. The other is consciously aware, slower, more deliberate, and effortful. Each has its strengths and weaknesses, and their operation in tandem is a distinctive feature of our human ability to respond to reasons in thought and action.

As a result, "automatized" behavior can be found across the entire span of human activity. The resulting actions, while not anticipated by conscious intention, may nonetheless be intentional, and done for reasons. The jazz saxophonist's solo riff, the basketball guard's well-timed jump, the experienced driver's smooth downshift, and the wit's lightning riposte aren't *unintentional* or *mindless* behavior, like absent-mindedly tapping one's foot while writing or succumbing without realizing it to the emotional contagion of a crowd. Rather, they are complex, structured, purposeful activities done mindfully but fluently, without deliberation or intention-formation. Yet were we foolish enough to interrupt these individuals in mid-stream, they could typically answer the Anscombean question, "What are you doing?," without any further observation or inference.

The saxophonist's improvisations, the guard's jumping, the timely downshift, and wicked comment are clearly done *for reasons*, and,

[22] For examples, see R.R. Hassin, J.S. Uleman, and J.A. Bargh, *The New Unconscious* (Oxford: Oxford University Press, 2005).

[23] See A. Dijksterhuis *et al.*, "On Making the Right Choice: The Deliberation-without-Attention Effect," *Science*, 311 (2006): 1005–1007.

[24] Haidt, "The Emotional Dog": 819.

moreover, for reasons *as such* (rather than, say, through a deviant causal path). The saxophonist suddenly drops a register from an active, intuitive sense of how the music and mood are developing, the guard jumps how and when he does in order to block a hook shot, the driver shifts down to get more power in a tight curve, and the wit's words fit the occasion only too well. Far from being merely swept along by a causal chain or robotically enacting a habit or routine, the jazz improviser and skilled basketball player, for example, are exercising agency in a pure form, fully deploying their cognitive and creative skills.[25] Of course, these aren't examples *par excellence* of deliberative agency. But why see deliberative agency as the truest form of acting for the sake of reasons? Why not see deliberative agency as one more domain – distinctive and important, but by no means predominant – in which humans can develop greater or lesser skill at responding aptly to reasons? After all, deliberation itself is embedded in a host of reasons-responsive activities on the part of the agent, and can only occur thanks to them. Indeed, even being adept at when to deliberate is just such a non-deliberative skill.

## AUTONOMY AND AUTOMATICITY

But wait. For all its merits as a way of getting things done well in response to reasons, isn't "automatized" action nonetheless not autonomous? After all, by its nature its operation is not under direct management by the conscious self. The jazz improviser, for example, may be at a loss to explain just how it occurred to him to shift suddenly down a register or to slow down the tempo; the guard who has just blocked a shot may be unable to say just how he "decided upon" which player would receive the pass, or why he leapt at just the instant he did, or how he would raise his arm and spread his fingers in order that they meet the ball. Skills fluently exercised are certainly not be robotic, but they do seem to "have a mind of their own," one that does not require intervention by an agent's deliberation, decision, volition, or even approval. The spontaneous working of a skill in action seems in this way to possess a certain self-sufficiency or autonomy *within* the agent, thereby compromising *his* autonomy as an agent.

A compelling case can be made that the purposive operation of one's unself-conscious self is not the exercise of one's own agency. Passing

[25] For a description of such phenomena, and their ties with optimal experience and self-efficacy, see M. Csikszentmihalyi, *Flow: The Psychology of Optimal Experience* (New York: Harper and Row, 1990).

beyond examples like exercising a skill, David Velleman gives the following example, which is worth quoting at length:

> Suppose that I have a long-anticipated meeting with an old friend for the purpose of resolving some minor difference; but that as we talk, his offhand comments provoke me to raise my voice in progressively sharper replies, until we part in anger. Later reflection leads me to realize that accumulated grievances had crystallized in my mind, during the weeks before our meeting, into a resolution to sever our friendship over the matter at hand, and that this resolution is what gave the hurtful edge to my remarks. In short, I may conclude that desires of mine caused a decision, which in turn caused the corresponding behavior; and I may acknowledge that these mental states were thereby exerting their normal motivational force, unabetted by any strange perturbation or compulsion. But do I necessarily think that I made the decision or that I executed it? Surely, I can believe that the decision, though genuinely motivated by my desires, was thereby induced in me but not formed by me; and I can believe that it was genuinely executed in my behavior but executed, again, without my help. Indeed, viewing the decision as directly motivated by my desires, and my behavior as directly governed by the decision, is precisely what leads to the thought that as my words became more shrill, it was my resentment speaking, not me.[26]

Velleman is careful to add that he is not trying to escape responsibility for the blow-up, since he takes himself to be obliged to be "vigilant against unconsidered intentions" and show self-restraint when angered. However, there will be circumstances in which such vigilance and self-restraint are not a practical possibility. We can imagine that things "happened too quickly" when he began talking with his friend. Involuntarily offended by his friend's manner, a wounding remark escapes his lips before he realizes what he is saying. His friend immediately retaliates with a yet more hurtful remark. Escalation and eventual rupture are now inevitable. Despite their good intentions, the meeting appears to have been hijacked by their feelings. Velleman writes, if his behavior:

> could come about *only* in the manner described here – that is, springing directly from intentions that have simply come over me – nothing would owe its occurrence to either my participating or failing to participate in events, and I might bear no responsibility for anything.[27]

We do indeed have an intuition that supports this notion of the self, and that makes his suggestion that "it was my resentment speaking, not me"

[26] J.D. Velleman, "What Happens When Someone Acts?," reprinted in *The Possibility of Practical Reason* (Oxford: Oxford University Press, 2000): 126–127.

[27] Velleman, "What Happens When Someone Acts?": 127n, emphasis added.

plausible. However, I'd like to suggest that this intuition should be taken with a grain of salt.

Let's begin with an account of intentional action that lays out an explicit role for agency. In *Rationality in Action*, John Searle claims:

> Consider any situation of rational decision making and acting and you will see that you have a sense of possibilities open to you . . .[28]

He contrasts such situations with those in which, for example, you are in the grip of anger and have "no sense that you could be doing something else." There is no distance between how you feel and what you do. You have "lost control" and become a channel for your anger. A similar sense that what happens is no longer "up to you" can be experienced by those in the grip of a powerful addiction or compulsion.[29]

So *bona fide* intentional agency combines a sense of open possibilities with the fact that *which* possibility is realized will be determined by your choice. On this account, we can see an essential role for the self, since choice must insert itself wherever there are "gaps" in agency, and Searle mentions three such gaps.

First, there is a gap between the reasons you consider and the decision you actually make – even when the decision is based upon those reasons. Once you have satisfied yourself that you have identified a "rationally sufficient reason," for example, your job as rational agent is not done. This sufficient reason will not enact itself: you must make up your mind and do the deciding about what will be done and why. In so doing, you make it *your reason* – you choose the reason for which you act, good or bad.

Second, there is a gap between your decision and the action itself, since (except in some special cases) decisions in themselves do not ordinarily causally suffice for initiating the action decided upon. Having decided, you typically cannot sit back, put up your feet, and wait for the action to occur. Here, too, as Searle writes, "you actually have to do it." In so doing, you make this *your doing* – the act that you yourself have undertaken, wisely or foolishly.

Third, there is a gap between beginning an action in this way and carrying it through to completion. Since many actions extend over time, this gap is familiar to all of us. Getting yourself off the couch and doing your nightly exercises may be a real feat, but once underway you cannot simply rest on your laurels. You cannot say, "Well, the die is cast – my

[28] J. Searle, *Rationality in Action* (Cambridge, MA: MIT Press, 2001): 15.
[29] Searle, *Rationality in Action*: 15–16.

nightly exercises are underway." Exercising is not like jumping from a building – one cannot start the action and then simply watch events unfold as the causes operate by themselves. The exercising stops the instant you do. Filling this gap – really, these gaps – calls upon your agency once more. Even as your exercises tire you, "you have to make a continuous voluntary effort to keep going with the action."[30] In so doing, you make this *your accomplishment*, for good or ill.

Practical rationality, Searle claims, operates in these gaps. And when it does, it cannot look around for *something* to plug the gap. In that sense, he writes, "Nothing fills the gap." Rather:

> you make up your mind to do something, or you just haul off and do what you are going to do, or you carry out the decision you previously made, or you keep going or fail to keep going . . .[31]

Let us take an example Searle offers of action for a reason:

> Suppose you are asked to justify voting for Clinton; you might do so by appealing to his superior management of the economy. But it may be the case that the actual reason you acted on was that he went to your old college at Oxford, and you thought, "College loyalty comes first." And the remarkable thing about this phenomenon is: in the normal case you know without observation which reason was effective, because you made it effective. That is to say, a reason for action is an effective reason only if you made it effective.[32]

We have already seen what making a reason *your* reason involves:

> The reasons did not operate on you. Rather you *chose* one reason. You made that reason effective by *acting on it*.[33]

By contrast, in Velleman's example involving loss of temper, we might say that the agent did not choose the reasons that led to the irruption, did not choose to start a fight, and did not choose to carry the quarrel to its rupturing conclusion – the reasons for the quarrel and rupture "operated on" the agent, not he on them. The typical case of intentional action, Searle writes, is quite unlike this. Instead: "Deliberation typically leads to intentional action by way of prior intentions."[34]

To be sure, Searle recognizes that not all intentional activity follows this canonical model of deliberation leading to a "choice of one's reasons"

[30] Searle, *Rationality in Action*: 14–15.
[31] Searle, *Rationality in Action*: 17.
[32] Searle, *Rationality in Action*: 16.
[33] Searle, *Rationality in Action*: 16.
[34] Searle, *Rationality in Action*: 47.

and to formation of an intention. Some intentions are not formed consciously, like Velleman's intention to break off the friendship, and "not all" intentional action is premeditated – some is "spontaneous," like rubbing one's head or rising to one's feet to pace when struggling with the wording of an argument.[35]

What I want to argue is that, as far as I can see, far from being typical of intentional action, Searle's model does not fit the vast majority of everyday intentional actions. Such actions are not deliberated or premeditated, but not for that unintentional. Haidt writes:

> The emerging view in social cognition is that *most* of our behaviors and judgments are in fact made automatically (i.e. without intention, effort, or awareness of process).[36]

Whether Haidt is right or wrong is an empirical question, one about which I have no special expertise. Instead, I wish to argue something stronger, namely, that *all* action – including in particular paradigmatic premeditated intentional action – has *and must have* unpremeditated action at its source and core. A corollary: Most of the reasons for which we act, and that give us the name of rational beings, are not made effective by "choosing one's reasons."

One way to see the problem is to consider again what Searle says about "filling gaps" in the enactment of an intention. What he proposes to fill these gaps in action is each itself an action, a *doing* – my "actually deciding," or my "hauling off and doing," or my "making a continuing voluntarily effort" – and, presumably, a doing *for some reason*. But now, if these are to be full-fledged intentional actions of mine, attributable to my agency in virtue of conforming to Searle's model, each must itself have the same three gaps to be filled.

For example, consider the first gap in Searle's example of facing a choice between Clinton and Bush. The first gap to be filled, Searle explains, is that the agent must "choose his reason" for deciding – the reason cannot simply "act upon him." It must truly be *his* reason, made effective by him. In Searle's example, the fact of sharing an *alma mater* with Clinton is the reason the agent chooses to decide for whom to vote. Very well, but if this is to be a *choice* on the part of the agent, not an arbitrary picking or a reason "acting upon him," this selection of alumni

[35] Searle, *Rationality in Action*: 45.
[36] Haidt, "The Emotional Dog": 819.

status (as opposed to myriad other potential reasons) as the ground for his choice must itself be done by the agent for a reason of his own choosing. That is, on Searle's scheme, it would seem that the agent's choice of Clinton could only be autonomous – *his* choice, for *his* reasons – if he were to choose this reason, too. But now we are on our way to a regress – instead of one gap to fill, we have two. And so on.

Of course, the problem faced here isn't peculiar to Searle's three-gap model. It arises for any model of action that seeks to understand the distinctive operation of autonomous or rational agency in terms of some special sort of action on the part of the agent, whether the act is "choosing one's reasons," or "endorsing certain reasons," or "identifying a certain reason," or "throwing one's weight behind one reason rather than another." Since it would appear that these acts would themselves have to be done autonomously, the would-be agent has become *Zeno's deliberator*.

## DELIBERATING WITHOUT REGRESS

In practice, of course, we do somehow manage to deliberate and act intentionally without losing ourselves in regress. How is this possible, consistent with the idea that the act we decide upon, and its reasons, really are our own? We have seen how certain initially plausible "top-down" solutions would generate a regress unless there were some way for an agent to choose, or endorse, or identify with, or throw his weight behind certain reasons autonomously, but *without* an act of deliberate choice. Suppose there were, in other words, ways in which individuals could come to embrace one reason over others autonomously, but not via a further "full fledged" act? Then regress might be avoided. But then, too, the privileged status of deliberate choice as a model for autonomy would have been undermined, and we would have to ask, "If in these cases an act can be autonomous without involving deliberate choice, why not in other cases?"

I have no quarrel with treating deliberate choice as one paradigm in the theory of rational or autonomous action – it is certainly an important phenomenon for any such theory to explain. My argument instead is that it cannot be the fundamental phenomenon, for it is built up from, and at every step involves, the operation of countless non-deliberative processes that are – and must be – quite unlike choice. These processes are not self-aware or reflective, yet they are intelligent and responsive to reasons *qua* reasons. They make us the agents we are, and give our agency its capacity for rational, autonomous self-expression.

To see such processes in operation, we should look first to a different sort of exercise of autonomous agency from paradigm-case reflective choice. We should look to *fluent* agency. To focus on deliberate choice as the core model for what happens when mature individuals act is like focusing on my initial unskilled, very deliberate driving as the core model of what happens when experienced drivers drive, or on the unskilled, very deliberate way beginners attempt to speak or think in a foreign language as the core model of what happens when fluent speakers think or talk in their mother tongue. It is not as if experienced drivers or native speakers do the very same things as the neophyte, only somehow faster and more smoothly. Rather, they do something quite different, and yet equally or more responsive to reasons *qua* reasons, and equally or more self-expressive and autonomous – equally or more *their* actions done for *their* reasons.

For this to be possible, there must exist non-deliberative causal psychic processes "of the right kind" to be aptly responsive to a given consideration as such, and aptly expressive of one's identity or values, even in the face of competing interests. What would this look like? Consider first an experienced driver, Christine, in a desperate hurry to reach town before the bank closes for the weekend, driving a long gravel country road. She is used to this road, and can drive it at speeds up to 50 mph, despite its many curves and potholes. But driving it that fast, as she is now, requires her full attention, not least because of the risk of equally fast cars moving in the other direction, visible only a split second in advance around the many blind curves. She is on the edge of her seat, muscles taught, intensely studying the road surface ahead to spot potholes and tweaking the steering wheel to weave between them. Rounding a curve onto a straight stretch she suddenly spots an on-coming car, moving slowly at a small distance. In an instant she recognizes that the driver is aged, barely able to see over the steering wheel, and plowing along almost in the middle of the road. The road here is wide enough, however, to allow her to speed past with room to spare. But after a fraction-of-a-second's hesitation, she instead pulls her foot off the accelerator and brakes, slowing almost to a standstill. She rolls down her dust-covered window and waves broadly to the other driver. He looks up at her. His face, tense from the strain of driving with poor eyesight, relaxes into a smile of acknowledgment, and Christine drives on. Why did she do this, losing precious time? She did not know the other driver, or expect ever to see him again.

Well, the instant she saw the anxious look on the other driver's face, part of her mind empathetically simulated his anxiety, and how it would rattle him were she to surprise him with her speed, blasting past in a cloud of dust. The negative feeling generated by this rapid, non-conscious simulation caused her a moment's hesitation, and drew her attention from her own driving to the other driver's situation. Once that had occurred, her sympathetic feelings responded, "Slow down, back off, make it easy for him." Why were these particular feelings so readily available, and why did they take the form they did? Over the years, Christine had spent time with many older individuals, and knew from experience how, for them, driving could be anxious, tentative, and frightening. She knew that facial expression and driving posture. So as soon as awareness of the other driver's situation had come to the surface, she paused and let up, checking her initial impulse to blast past. Moreover, Christine is someone given to placing people and their feelings ahead of many other concerns or goals. As soon as the thought of relenting occurred, it immediately fitted her feelings.

It strikes me that she acted fully intentionally – she did not act reflexively or simply "find herself" slowing down and wondering why. Instead, she deftly executed a suite of well-timed, well-aimed, and well-coordinated actions. She knew she was backing off, and could accurately answer as to why she did it. Of course, many components of this suite of behavior were not themselves conscious or intended. Her simulation of the other driver's feelings occurred without her will or awareness; the idea of slowing down came not from reflection, but from emotionally colored, lightning-quick association. Only two alternatives entered her mind – speed around him or slow down. Neither this range of possibilities, nor the reasons associated with them, were chosen by her. Her thoughts occurred in quick succession, and she rejected blasting past as soon as the alternative of "backing off" became available. What favored the second alternative was not a "chosen reason," but its fit with her sense of the other driver's fear and vulnerability. Yet the rejection of the first alternative, and selection of the second, surely was her intelligence and agency at work. And the reason that led her to slow down was surely *her* – non-accidentally reflecting her understanding, sensitivity, and priorities.

Her behavior, as described, is perhaps not much different from Aristotle's notion of how the brave soldier might conduct himself in battle or the brave mariner in a storm at sea – acting with speed and deftness, intelligently rather than mechanically, focusing on the essentials, alive to the state of the world and of the people around him, not locked into a rigid plan, but quickly identifying the most relevant alternative courses of action, seizing upon an appropriate one with a minimum of deliberation, and acting resolutely even when sacrifice is required. According to Aristotle, such an individual is acting in the right way, at the right time, with the right motive, and toward the right end – a model not only of what we have called agent-competence and practical intelligence, but of rational self-mastery and self-direction. We might say that he is an agent *attuned* to the reasons he faces, and *practically so*, since he translates them effectively into action.

I see Christine's less dramatic actions as practically attuned in the same sense, and therefore have no difficulty seeing her action as both rational and autonomous. She mastered both herself and situation, doing so in line with the fundamental springs of her own scheme of values. Despite the lack of reflection or conscious willing, the shaping force for her action came from within, but without self-centeredness. Anyone who knows Christine would agree that, in slowing down and making herself a bit later, she was absolutely being herself.

Why call such action autonomous? After all, it is quite unlike the familiar paradigms of autonomy, in which an agent stands back from her concerns, reflects, and then makes a choice on the basis of a principle she imposes upon herself. My reason is simple. These paradigms themselves are composed of a suite of thoughts and actions, the basic elements of which each must be reasons-responsive but not, on pain of regress, via an exercise of deliberative agency. As we noted earlier, contemporary psychology increasingly points to the role of affect and affective processing in shaping and guiding such coordinated suites of thought and action. The affective system's response – positive or negative – is quick and non-deliberative, but no mere "emotional reflex," the same for everyone. How a situation strikes the individual affectively, and how this shapes her eventual response, reflects her "affective memory" (past experience and learning), and her implicit goals. In Christine, the negative affect generated by her unconscious simulation of the other driver's situation tended to inhibit her current course of action (blasting ahead), refocus attention, and prompt thoughts of less aggressive alternatives. In her case, time was of the essence. But even the most deliberate of decision-making involves affect in essentially similar ways: by furnishing a "sense" of what needs to be considered, of what evidence is credible, of how weighty a given consideration is, of whether I'm satisfied with the alternatives considered, of when I'm ready to decide, of how confident I am of my decision, of how motivated I am in enacting it, of how resolute I am in sticking with it, and so on.[37]

For any decision involving premeditation, then, there must be many unpremeditated, affect- or trust-guided processes underwriting the deliberation and choice, shaping its course, moving it along, giving it force. The self-conscious decider is a captive audience for the considerations that arise in her mind. What these considerations are, as well as how they strike her, will ordinarily not be something she is able to decide. An agent can no more escape such "captivity" to the outputs of her sub-personal self than she can escape epistemic "captivity" to her own sensory and mental experience. Of course, she may be free to ignore any such considerations – but then, where will *that* thought or dismissive impulse have come from? If a deliberated decision is to be autonomous, these non-deliberative elements must be compatible with, even contributory to, autonomy. When they work together in the right way, the result is autonomy – even in the sped-up form found in Christine's case. Of course, each element need not itself be autonomous – the whole is certainly more than the sum of its parts, and human psychology is rife with such emergent phenomena. But I would insist that the true whole in the case of autonomous action is not the suite of self-conscious mental acts upon which we focus when considering paradigm cases, but rather the whole psyche within which these self-conscious acts are embedded, from which they emerge, and to which they are indebted at every step. *Neurath's deliberator*, not Zeno's.

Self-constitution through action makes sense only if there is enough of a self already constituted, with sufficiently definite opinions, aims, and ideals, to guide the further self-constitutional process in a meaningful way. It is really self-*re*constitution. In this reconstructive effort, however, the already-constituted self, unchosen as it might be, is *ipso facto* accorded some normative authority to make choices and act. If this cannot be autonomous action, then I cannot be an autonomous actor. Creating the self to which one aspires must be done with the self one has – the self that has this aspiration as well as many elements that may impede it. For example, I do not identify with the tacit racial prejudices that lie within

[37] Kant himself, aware of the danger of regress, saw the moral law as coming into the reasoning of the agent through an affect, respect:

> Respect (*reverentia*) is, again, something subjective, a feeling of a special kind, not a judgment about an object that it would be a duty to bring about or promote. For, such a duty, regarded as a duty, could be represented to us only through the *respect* we have for it. A duty to have respect would thus amount to being put under obligations to duties (*The Metaphysics of Morals*: 6: 402–403).

me, as they do in most everyone in our country. I wish instead to construct a self unprejudiced in thought and action. But I must recognize that the self with which I am working *is* prejudiced, and I cannot accomplish a rebirth, cleansed of prejudice by endorsing an unprejudiced self-concept. Self-reconstitution is difficult and often only partially successful work. That much self-understanding, at least, and that much willingness to accept that one's acts are the acts of one's "whole" self, like it or not, is essential to winning one's way to autonomy. Deliberation and decision are a small part of our whole intelligent, sensitive, goal-directed psyche. Such rationality and autonomy as we have resides in this whole, not in our self-awareness alone.

## A LIST

Musical improvisation, whole-hearted engagement in a conversation or sport, and exercise of a skilled craft to solve a challenging problem are, I would argue, our paradigms of self-directed activity. We see the individual as agent especially clearly in such cases, for it is here that she has the greatest degree of control, self-expression, and attunement to available reasons. Moreover, we are told, individuals characteristically report such activities as *optimal experience*.[38] Aristotle would explain: These activities show man acting in accord with his nature, making fullest use of his distinctive capacities. Having such experiences requires, I have argued, not just practical reason and will power, but practical competence, even practical fluency. What might a list of practical competencies look like? Here's a start.

Many general-purpose competencies figure among the conditions for practical competence – e.g. perceptual abilities, inferential capacities, multi-tasking capability, reliable memory, vivid imagination, etc. Others are especially relevant to action and emotional response. We've already mentioned (among others):

- the ability to act intentionally without intending to do so
- the ability to detect, without reflecting and deliberating, conditions calling for reflection and deliberation
- a capacity to direct and focus one's attention in response to cues from one's circumstances, including a capacity to modulate one's attention span and redirect attention, without requiring attention to do so
- the ability to work around or with temptations one cannot suppress

[38] See Csikszentmihalyi, *Flow*.

- the ability to reward oneself effectively, accepting life's diverse pleasures – including, say, the pleasure of doing one's duty
- the capacity of one's emotions to attune one to demands of a situation – e.g. to feel an appropriate degree of fear in response to risk
- the ability to "channel" emotions into effective behavior
- the ability to stick with an intention, other things equal, without constantly revisiting it, along with an opposing disposition to lose confidence in intentions that are not working out
- an ability to represent accurately the mental and bodily states of others or of one's hypothetical future self
- a degree of self-confidence, including a defeasible self-trust of one's capacities
- a capacity to be resilient in response to set-backs and not too hard on oneself, with an opposing disposition to accept criticism and the need for change

Here are some others:

- the ability to transfer the motivational interest of an end onto a means, along with a countervailing tendency to lose confidence in ends that come to seem infeasible or to require intuitively unacceptable means
- a degree of self-awareness, and a capacity to self-locate in space and time, sensing oneself as a distinct and continuing being located at a particular causal nexus
- a modulated sense of one's physical and mental state and capacities – e.g. one's alertness, capacity for thought and effort, health, arousal, etc. – that directly enters into the influences on how one thinks and acts without need for conscious attention
- a felt pressure toward consistency in belief and coherence in desire and comportment, along with a countervailing tolerance for some degree of internal conflict and trial-and-error experimentation

And many others. The list is diverse, but functionally integrated by the requirements for fluent intentional action (much as "administrative skills" or "athletic skills" are functionally integrated by the requirements of certain roles or activities).

Chronic failings in practical competencies can be very serious for an agent – often more serious than garden-variety irrationality. Certain familiar psychological disorders can be seen as persistent deficits or hypertrophies of practical competencies: chronic inability to maintain focus on a task (attention deficit disorder), chronic and inflexible inability to redirect attention from a fixed concern (obsession), chronic inability to attach affect to goals or gain reward from accomplishment (depression), chronic inability to regulate motivation by affect or thought (addiction, compulsion), chronic inability to resist temptation (e.g. impulsivity disorder, kleptomania, etc.), chronic inability to sense the emotional states of others non-inferentially (sociopathy, autism), chronic arousal of the self-schema (narcissism), and so on. Of course, there is a qualitative difference between suffering a long-term deficit in practical competency and experiencing such temporary failures as losing one's temper, failing to match means to ends, succumbing to peer pressure or a sales pitch against one's better judgment, giving in to the temptation to overeat, etc. Unlike episodic irrationalities, chronic deficits in practical competence cannot be remedied by calming down, thinking things through more fully before acting, weighing options more carefully, or exerting more "will power."

## SOME BENEFITS

I do not need to shill for the importance of cultivating the capacities I have grouped under "practical competence" – self-help books abound with this sort of thing. Similarly, tracts in analytic psychiatry and cognitive therapy can do much better than I at categorizing and anatomizing failures of these competences and showing the toll they can take on one's personal efficacy and well-being. Research psychologists are amply critical of the partiality and inaccuracy of our first-personal self-narratives and self-knowledge claims, and the mischief that results. These many sources point to the fundamental role of the "larger self" – underneath and around the self-aware deliberative self – in shaping what we think and do, and to the self-deluding character of the thought that we can transcend or master it with a "rational will." Yet although we cannot master this larger self – Who, after all, is supposed to do the mastering? – we can better understand it. And we can use this understanding to help discern and develop the forms of mastery of which we *are* capable.

I suggested at the outset that there might be some benefits in the theory of practical reason to thinking about agency along the lines laid out in this chapter. What might they be?

One benefit could be a rethinking of the "internalism"/"externalism" debate about the content of moral judgments. In the existing debate, all sides accept that there appears to be a non-accidental tie between making a moral judgment, such as "I ought to *X*," and possessing some motivationally-ert pro-attitude toward *X*-ing. Judgment internalists take their cue directly from this datum, and give a non-factualist reading of such judgments according to which expressing such an attitude is their primary function. For them, motivation is internal to the content of moral judgment. Externalists, who insist that moral judgments are factual, functioning primarily to state normative propositions with ordinary truth-conditions, cannot build motivation into their content. Instead, they have been forced to give more indirect explanations of the intimate link between judgment and affect. Often these are criticized as not intimate enough.

The dual-process models characteristic of contemporary cognitive psychology promise a way of explaining the psychological reality of internalist intuitions without abandoning factualist semantics. We have inherited from countless generations before us a remarkably effective sub-personal learning and evaluation system, which triggers a rapid affective response directly to perceptual experience or mental suggestion. This response then primes and cues judgment while simultaneously inducing emotional response and corresponding motivation or act-preparedness. Does this point to judgment internalism, even emotivism?

Not at all. It's worth keeping in mind that the early elicitation of affect is characteristic not only of moral judgments, but also our responses to images of spiders and smiling babies, even to lists of ordinary descriptive terms ("smooth" elicits positive affect, and therefore finds its way into countless advertisements; "jagged" is not, and therefore does not). "Affective coding" is therefore *normal* for judgments, including paradigmatically factual judgments ("The surface is smooth"; "The surface is jagged"). Small wonder that judgments containing moral terms, which have powerful positive and negative affective valence ("good," "kind," and "right" vs "rotten," "cruel," and "wrong"), have a non-accidental association with positive or negative affect and motivation.

This fact helps explain why judgment internalism *seems* so plausible. Subjects shown a drawing depicting a man menacing a child show a negative affective response milliseconds before the sensory signal has reached the higher cortices, where such verbal labels as "wrong," "bad," or "assault" are available and triggered. Thus an "anti-attitude" seems to be *part of the very thoughts* WRONG or BAD or ASSAULT. But seeing a spider image, too, elicits a negative affective response in the first milliseconds, even before the thought SPIDER is cued. Should we say that an anti-attitude is part of the concept SPIDER as well? Or that a pro-attitude is part of the concept BABY? Should we say that these, too, are normative concepts or "action-guiding" concepts? A more promising line would be that because the judgment and the felt pro-attitude have a common cause, stemming from the pre-conscious affect-coding, there will be an appearance that the emotive attitude is "part of the content" of the judgment. The two will be seamlessly co-present in the conscious mind. But once we see that this does nothing to distinguish moral judgments from many prosaically factual judgments, the pressure to adopt internalism with respect to the content of moral judgments is removed.[39]

This conclusion can be strengthened by noting that the dual-process explanation accounts for another intuitive datum. Some moral judgments are situational, stimulated by a concrete, salient description or perception. Here the immediacy of affect is palpable. But there are also highly *theoretical* moral judgments. For example, an advisor to a legislator might be asked to determine what rate of progressivity in income tax is morally appropriate, taking into account trade-offs with economic growth, wage disparities, and effects on human capital accumulation. Or one might attempt to determine just what portion of an individual's income or effort should be devoted to charitable causes, taking into account differences in income and wealth, reasonable social expectations, etc. When one reaches a conclusion in such a judgment there is little or no affective immediacy. They do not appear to have motive force "built into them." More likely, having reached such a judgment, one might have to cultivate some affective confidence in it or internal motivational support for it. For example, would we think a utilitarian insincere who, after performing an elaborate cost-benefit analysis, arrived at a conclusion about optimal tax schedules or charitable giving without himself experiencing any accompanying motivational force? Haidt's work on a dual-process model of moral judgment revealed that the priority of affect in moral judgments of scenarios is largely absent when the scenarios are presented in such a way as to make abstract moral reasoning more salient than a one-off moral judgment.[40] An externalist can give a straightforward explanation of these data: there is no built-in motivational content in moral judgments, rather, the affective pathway to moral judgment is differentially triggered by concrete vs abstract moral judgments. At first blush, judgment internalism, which imputes built-in motivational content in all moral judgments,

[39] At least, this source of pressure is removed. There are others.
[40] Murphy *et al.*, "Moral Dumbfounding."

fits these data less well. So, one benefit of thinking about the puzzles of practical reason in terms of a dual-process model of human psychology could be rethinking whether the intuitive data really support judgment internalism after all.

Moreover, we now are in a position to see a possible second benefit. Recall the contestation, mentioned at the outset, between internal and external perspectives in the theory of action and practical reason – between a first-personal approach "from the inside out" and a third-personal approach "from the outside in." Of course, both sorts of understanding will figure in any complete account. But there is something more to say: the usual way we talk about internal and external is misleading. Given the limited, and sometimes marginal, position of the self-aware, deliberative "self" within the larger selves by means of which we are competent agents and intelligent responders to reasons, we cannot equate a first-personal approach with the standpoint of the portion of the self that happens to be conspicuous in immediate awareness or open to introspection. "I" refers to the larger self as well, and much that is distinctively me and equips me for practical rationality resides in the whole. Thus an approach working "from the inside out" must recognize that the self-conscious agent needs to supplement introspection with an explanatory, third-personal perspective to understand just what he is doing, and why. That is, the true perspective of the self is available only first- *and* third-personally.

A third possible benefit concerns the much-vexed question of the normative status of means-end coherence. We tend to be of two minds about this. On the one hand, it seems to be a mark of practical rationality to identify means appropriate to one's ends, and to be able to transfer motivational force from the ends to the means. On the other hand, when someone has manifestly irrational or horrific ends, or ends that require horrific means, we do not think it would be a mark of rationality for him to seek out and pursue the requisite means. The only rational response to certain ends or means might be to abandon the end altogether. As Hare once wrote,[41] one can be lulled by means-end statements like:

(1) If you want sugar in your coffee, you should use a spoon.
(2) If you want your coffee warm, you should heat the jug.

[41] See R.M. Hare, "Wanting: Some Pitfalls," in R. Binkley, R. Bronaugh, and A. Marras, eds., *Agent, Action, and Reason* (Toronto: University of Toronto Press, 1971): 81–97.

into thinking that these are "hypothetical imperatives" of rationality – that is, that there is a rational principle of the form "If you want *X*, and *Y* is the most effective means to *X* → you should *Y*." But then notice:

(3) If you want to commit murder on a massive scale, you should poison the city water supply.

Suppose that (3) were accepted as a hypothetical imperative of the form "If you want to commit murder on a mass scale, and poisoning the city water supply is the most effective way to do this → you should poison the city water supply." Then if someone *did* want to commit murder on a massive scale, he could perform *modus ponens*, detach the consequent, and claim that rationality commends his poisoning the city water supply. The following is truer to our rational convictions:

(4) If you want to commit murder on a massive scale, you should see a psychiatrist at once.

Note that (4) does not counsel means-end coherence – going to a psychiatrist is certainly not the most efficient way to commit mass murder. Nor need one withdraw (4) if this individual has no other aim that a trip to the psychiatrist would serve. Rationality, we might think, can tell against an entire system of ends, however coherent.

Still, there is an evaluative difference, irrespective of the nature of the end or the means, between an agent who shows ingenuity and success in matching means to ends vs an agent who elects ill-considered and ineffectual means, or who fails out of self-indulgence to follow through. What's wrong with the second agent is that he is manifesting *agent-incompetence*, which is a distinct defect even in those cases, like wanting to commit mass murder, in which defective agency would on the whole be morally fortunate. Just as we don't want to confuse "technical imperatives" like (1)–(3) with rational imperatives, we don't want to confuse *rational criticism* of an agent's ends or means with *technical criticism* of his agent-competence. Even as we are horrified by the countless lives his actions cost, and the wreckage he finally made of the ideals of the Revolution, we cannot but admire the fluent agency and practical intelligence of Napoleon in battle. Mere possession of an aim – a desire, a whim, an obsession, an ambition – may not suffice to make it rational to pursue. But *any* aim suffices to provide an opportunity to manifest fluent agency and practical intelligence. Or fail to.

The most common way by which we competently match means to ends is not via practical reasoning, but via learned *habitus*, trial-and-error, imitation, or "intuition." Entering a room, I flip on the light to see what I'm doing, place one foot in front of the other to move forward, turn my head toward the table, focus my gaze on the unopened letter on the table, extend my arm while opening my fingers in order to grasp and examine it, etc. In this little scene, means are being matched smoothly to ends, but I rather doubt we should see this sort of learned coordination of thought and act as the work of practical rationality. After all, animals perform essentially the same sorts of purposive, non-deliberative, semi-habitual means-ends matching. Your cat, hearing the door open, runs over to rub against your leg and nudge you gently toward the kitchen where the food is kept. A seeing-eye dog leads her master smoothly through a crowded room, successfully tracking the trajectory of dozens of people and deftly guiding her master through the constantly changing gaps between clumps of people. If it seems inappropriate to credit these actions on the part of cats and dogs to practical rationality, then perhaps we should say the same about our own like actions.

Humans, of course, differ from many other animals in their ability to engage in what is identifiably practical reasoning in matching means to ends – for example, when they conceptualize alternative possibilities, assess and compare costs and benefits, and form complex, branching contingency plans. This capacity equips us for the spectacular explosion in the range of possible ends and means that the human race has brought to the world, for better or worse. Perhaps it will even save us from ourselves, and save life on this beleaguered planet from self-destruction, since practical reasoning is the only capacity on earth able to translate a vivid representation of remote future possibilities into an apt plan for action today, and to guide its implementation across the decades to come.

But it does not take practical rationality to be good at matching means to ends. This had better be so – to call upon the deliberative capacities of practical reason is *itself* to match a means to an end, and if *this* required practical deliberation, then . . . , and so on. With lots of experience and a little luck, we can learn to deploy this distinctive means on those occasions that warrant it, and to carry it off reasonably well without overdoing it. That is, we may become practically competent – perhaps even fluent – at practical reason.

CHAPTER 6

# *Practical conditionals**

*James Dreier*

## INTRODUCTION

Sometimes we are under conditional requirements to do things. We can express them like this:

(1) If *p*, then R φ.

The "R" is for "requirement." We often say "ought" instead; at least, in this essay, I shall assume that what we say when we say that we ought to do something is the same as saying that we are *required* to do it. This may be false, but here I will assume it is true. If I'm wrong then what I am saying applies to conditional requirements, but not to conditional *ought*s.

I am most interested in one particular sort of conditional requirement. It is a form that has as its antecedent a goal-directed intentional state of the agent. Some people think this state is a desire, some think it is an intention, some think it is a preference. (I am in the last camp.) For familiarity and convenience I'll speak of desire, though this may not be the most plausible. The kind of requirement has to do with means-ends rationality. An example:

(2) If you want to lose weight, then you ought to avoid cheeseburgers.

I will call this type of conditional requirement an *instrumental requirement*. One might adjust this requirement to add to the antecedent that you *believe* that the only way to lose weight is to avoid cheeseburgers. If you like(!), imagine that this belief is tacitly included.

On one popular account, the instrumental requirement is misleadingly stated. This account says that although the word "ought" is in the

* Thanks to my commentator Mark Schroeder, and to audiences at Bowling Green, Missouri, and Texas for criticisms that helped me improve this chapter, and especially to Dave Sobel and Steven Wall, whose criticisms ought to have made it better than it in fact is.

consequent of (2), and appears to have scope over the consequent only, that appearance is misleading. The scope of the requirement is wide. The scope is over the whole conditional, and not over the consequence alone. John Broome (2004) offers such an account, adding that the conditional is a material conditional. I will call this account "the wide-scope account" and its advocates "wide-scopers."

I think this account is wrong. I'm not confident about what the correct account is, but I think there are good reasons for thinking that "wide-scoping" the requirement is a mistake. In this essay, I'll argue against wide-scoping, and then (more tentatively) set out my alternative.

Let's first see why wide-scoping seems plausible, and why, indeed, any "account" of instrumental requirements is called for in the first place. It seems plausible mainly because the conditional requirements often do not seem to be detachable. Take Steve Darwall's example:

(3) If you want to kill Jones in a particularly violent way you ought to use a cleaver.[1]

This may strike us as true. But suppose Jill does want to kill Jones in a particularly violent way. We are reluctant then to assert the consequent (addressing Jill). That is, we are (to say the least) reluctant to follow *modus ponens* to the conclusion it seems to demand, even when we find the premises quite acceptable and believable. A plausible explanation is that the logical form is as follows:[2]

(4) $\mathcal{O}$(You want to kill your victim in a particularly violent way $\supset$ you use a cleaver.)

If you do not satisfy (4) then you are incoherent and therefore irrational. And you ought not to be irrational.[3] But it doesn't follow that you ought to use a cleaver, even if you do want to kill most violently, because it's quite likely that you ought to stop wanting to kill in a violent

[1] See Darwall (1983): 15. Darwall says "should" rather than "ought." And he helpfully contrasts the example with "If you want to kill your victim in a particularly violent way, you should see a psychiatrist."

[2] I'll use "$\supset$" to express the material conditional, and I'll use "$\mathcal{O}$" and "$\mathcal{P}$" for requirement and permission in formulas. They can be interpreted as propositional functions, taking a proposition to be the new proposition requiring (or permitting) that it be true. The onus of the requirement or permission is on "you" unless otherwise specified.

[3] Maybe; Broome, for one, is now agnostic about whether you ought in general to be rational; see Broome (2005). Suppose it is not true that you ought in general to be rational. Then the requirement is hypothetical. It is not hypothetical in the sense that it applies to all and only those who have a certain desire! It is unclear what hypothesis the requirement of rationality would be conditional on, in this event. But I assume it would be something like the requirements of law, or chess. These requirements tell you what to do, but sometimes you really ought to abide by them and sometimes not.

way. (Not to belabor the obvious, but you ought to stop wanting to kill your victim, period.)

There is also a similar example from the realm of theoretic reasoning:

(5) If you believe that no whales are mammals and that Nanu is a whale, then you ought to believe that Nanu is not a mammal.

which according to wide-scopers has this form:

(6) $\mathcal{O}$(you believe that no whales are mammals and that Nanu is a whale ⊃ you believe that Nanu is not a mammal.)

In each case the result of detaching seems implausible, even though the premises are plausible. It's not true that you ought to believe Nanu isn't a mammal, for you ought to know that whales are mammals. Even if you do believe that no whales are mammals, you oughtn't. You can't make it true that you ought to believe something silly, just by irresponsibly believing something else silly.

But conditionals are for detachment. The point of a conditional is to get us from the antecedent, when we are in possession of it, to the consequent. So if detachment doesn't work, that's a sure sign that something is wrong. The statement we had in mind must not have the logical form that it appears to have. And one undetachable form it could have is the wide-scope form.

Even when the scope of the operator is made explicitly wide, putting the embedded sentence in the form of a conditional, even a material conditional, may make the consequent feel detachable. Indeed, it would be detachable if a certain rule were valid (in the sense of necessarily truth-preserving). The rule says that when you ought to do one of two things, you ought to do each:

(7) $\mathcal{O}(p \vee q)/\mathcal{O}(q)$.

But this rule is not plausible. In chess, when you are in check, you are required to move your king, interpose, or capture the attacking piece. It does not follow that you are required to move your king.

A weaker, and slightly more plausible rule says that $\mathcal{O}(q)$ follows from $\mathcal{O}(p \vee q)$ along with $\neg p$.

Patricia Greenspan (1975) has suggested an even weaker rule that still manages to derive the unpalatable conclusion. It says that when you are required to do (or make true, let's say) a disjunction, and it is not within your power to make one of the disjuncts true, then it does follow that you are required to make the other disjunct true. This is much more plausible. Suppose you are in double check, so that you cannot escape by capturing the opposing piece or interposing. Then you must move your king. It may be that wide-scoping does not prevent detachment, then, since typically it is not in your power to stop wanting an end. I will not pursue this line of argument here.

If wide-scoping does block the Ugly *Modus Ponens* inferences (hereafter *UMPs*), it does so by giving to the English sentences a logical form that they do not wear on their sleeves. Since they are not really conditionals at all (but *oughts* **about** conditionals, so to speak), they are not ripe for detachment. One might ask, how is it that people *say* the English sentence with the wrong logical form? How is it that the wide-scope *ought* proposition is expressed by the consequent-scope *ought* sentence? An initially plausible answer is that English is generally rigged in this misleading way. In section 1 I'll explain briefly the reason for thinking so: there is a similar phenomenon in the domain of alethic modals. Then in section 2 I'll argue against wide-scoping.

My argument will be linguistic: I'll suggest reasons for doubting that the wide-scope logical form could represent *what we mean when we use sentences of instrumental requirement*. This won't directly challenge a view about what instrumental requirements there are, but it does provide an indirect challenge. My evidence has partly to do with parallel constructions. If (deontic and alethic) modals of requirement take wide scope in instrumental conditionals, that has implications for how modals of permission should work; but they don't work that way. Nor do practical conditionals other than the instrumental kind have logical forms with wide-scope modals. Wide-scoping doesn't generalize in any of the ways one would expect if it were the correct strategy for interpreting instrumental requirements.

Then I'll wheel in the famous Ramsey Test.[4] The Ramsey Test tells us which indicative conditionals are acceptable. I'll argue that the wide-scoping view is not consistent with what the Ramsey Test tells us.

Finally, I'll present a different kind of practical conditional that doesn't detach. Though the diagnosis of this failure doesn't transfer back to instrumental requirements, it suggests a strategy, which I'll go on to pursue.

## 1 THE ALETHIC MODAL ANALOGY

We say things like

(8) If the skies are clear, then necessarily it isn't raining.

[4] See Ramsey (1929), esp. 154.

This seems true. But suppose, furthermore, that the skies *are*, in fact, clear. Does it follow that *necessarily it isn't raining*? Well, in fact, it isn't. But this fact doesn't seem to be necessary. If I reasoned my way to the conclusion and reported it to you ("Necessarily it isn't raining") without explaining my reasoning, you would surely think I had made some mistake. It isn't raining, but it might have been. It is possible that right now it should be raining. And so on.[5]

Plausibly what's going on is that (8) really has this form:

(9) $\Box$(the skies are clear $\supset$ it isn't raining.)

rather than

(10) the skies are clear $\supset$ $\Box$ it isn't raining.

The "strong modal" of necessity, like the strong modal of deontic requirement, burrows its way into the consequent, even though in the logical form it belongs outside, with wide-scope over the whole conditional. The necessity belongs to the connection expressed by the whole conditional, and not to the consequent.

In the alethic example, we have an UMP, which we can block, plausibly, by giving the modal wide-scope contrary to its superficial appearance. Maybe English (along with other natural languages) is systematically misleading in placing modals syntactically in the consequent of a conditional when they properly have wide-scope. Then we would have clear support for using the same approach to blocking the UMP for the practical conditionals.

Now, in the next three sections, I'll explain why I think the wide-scoping strategy is wrong.

[5] Boethius discusses the problem:

> For there are two kinds of necessities; one is simple: for instance, a necessary fact, "all men are mortal"; the other is conditional; for instance, if you know that a man is walking, he must be walking: for what each man knows cannot be otherwise than it is known to be; but the conditional one is by no means followed by this simple and direct necessity; for there is no necessity to compel a voluntary walker to proceed, though it is necessary that, if he walks, he should be proceeding.

The English of the last clause ("it is necessary that, if he walks, he should be proceeding") suggests that Boethius adopts a wide-scope analysis. The Latin (I am told) is much more ambiguous:

> Hanc enim necessitatem non propria facit natura sed condicionis adiectio; nulla enim necessitas cogit incedere uoluntate gradientem, *quamuis eum tum cum graditur incedere necessarium sit* (my emphasis).

## 2 THE PROBLEM OF THE DUALS

Suppose wide-scoping gave the correct logical form for the conditionals of alethic and deontic necessity. Then, it seems to me, something similar would be true for the weak modal of possibility. But nothing similar is right for that modal:

(11) If the sky is overcast, then possibly it will rain.

This perfectly plausible English claim cannot have the form

(12) ◇(the sky is overcast ⊃ it will rain.)

It's clear that (12) is much too weak to represent (11). For this is true:

(13) ◇(the sky is clear ⊃ it will rain.)

even though this is not:

(14) If the sky is clear, then possibly it will rain.

(13) is true because the consequent is possible; it is also made true by the antecedent's not being necessary.

Similarly, this instrumental permission:

(15) If you don't care about the mess, then you may use a chainsaw to kill your victim.

can't be rendered:

(16) $\mathcal{P}$(you don't care about the mess ⊃ you use a chainsaw to kill your victim.)

One thing a wide-scoper might say is that the possibility conditionals are negations of certain necessity conditionals. They are related to the necessity conditionals not by replacing the necessity (alethic or deontic) operators with possibility ones, but negating twice, once inside and once outside. To illustrate, the permissive conditional might rather be formulated:

(17) ¬$\mathcal{O}$(you don't care about the mess ⊃ you don't use a chainsaw to kill your victim.)

(18) P¬ (you don't care about the mess ⊃ you don't use a chainsaw to kill your victim.)

(19) $\mathcal{P}$(you don't care about the mess & you use a chainsaw to kill your victim.)

just as the alethic possibility is better thought of like this:

(20) ◇(the sky is clear & it will not rain.)

That's pretty plausible on its face. Mark Schroeder pointed out to me[6] that the move is motivated by considerations quite independent of any attempt to save the wide-scoping theory from objections. For (11) must, since possibility and necessity are duals, be equivalent to:

(21) If the sky is overcast, then it is not the case that necessarily it will not rain.

But now moving the modal outside requires that we move its external negation (but not its internal one) along with it:

(22) $\neg\Box$(If the sky is overcast then it will not rain.)

which is

(23) $\Diamond\neg$(If the sky is overcast then it will not rain.)

and if the conditional is material, that's just

(24) $\Diamond$(The sky is overcast and it will rain.)

To illustrate the same point with a practical conditional: I might say,

(25) If you want to get to Boston quickly, you ought to take 95.

My wife disagrees:

(26) No, even if you want to get there quickly, you can take Route 1.

(I'm using "can" as a deontic permission, as is most natural in ordinary English.)

She is indeed disagreeing. It is a *conditional* disagreement, but it still feels like my wife and I have adopted contrary positions, even though it is only the consequents of (25) and (26) that are contraries. So it seems plausible that we can find the logical form of the instrumental permission by denying the consequent inside any operator, then denying the whole conditional.

In fact, though, I doubt that this wide-scoped conjunction is an adequate representation of the form of permissive conditionals. In the case of the deontic one, it is very doubtful that anyone would endorse the permission of the conjunction, even someone who didn't accept the rule,

(27) $\mathcal{P}$(A & B)/$\mathcal{P}$(B).[7]

[6] In personal correspondence, and subsequently in an unpublished comment on a version of this essay given at the Spring 2006 Kline Workshop at the University of Missouri.

[7] That seems like a very plausible rule, although an example of Frank Jackson's (Jackson and Pargetter 1986) designed for a different purpose may seem to cause some trouble for it. Jackson

"It's just fine to not care about the mess and to use a chainsaw to kill your victim!" Not a likely inference, even if you are skeptical about the very general rule that would allow you to conclude that it's just fine to use a chainsaw to kill your victim.

Likewise, even if I don't think it's possible that George W. Bush should have been the son of Gary Cooper, and I don't think that it is possible that he should have been Cooper's son and that he will some day find out that he is, I do think that if he is the son of Gary Cooper, it's possible he will someday find out. Compare

(28) If George W. Bush is the son of Gary Cooper, it's possible that he will some day find out that he is.

(29) $\Diamond$(George W. Bush is the son of Gary Cooper & he will some day find out that he is.)

(28) it seems to me, is plausible; (29) is extremely implausible.[8]

So conditionals of possibility, whether instrumental permissions or conditional judgments of alethic possibility, do not seem to be related to the *wide-scope* form of conditionals of necessity in any clear way.

This is not a knock-down argument. It *could* be that strong modals burrow from their proper logical position to the syntactically interior position, while weak ones have some very different logical form. But that would be strange. The modals are duals.

## 3 OTHER CONDITIONAL REQUIREMENTS

Consider now other sorts of conditional requirements, in particular other ordinary language conditional *ought*s. I'll choose a kind that seems relatively unproblematic, philosophically speaking: chess *ought*s.

(30) If you are behind in material, you ought to play for a draw.

The *ought* in (30) may be a "prudential" *ought*, but I won't assume so. We can just say that it is a "chess" *ought*.[9] It is a good bit of chess advice (although it is by no means exceptionless). But the *ought* does detach.

notes that when you are asked to referee a paper, you might know from past experience that you will take much too long and delay the process. So, although you ought to agree to referee and do the job on time, you ought not to agree to do it, since you won't in fact do it on time.

[8] I am now in the uncomfortable position of denying what seems to be the received view about conditionals of alethic necessity, while having no viable alternative suggestion. My suspicion is that conditionals like (8) ("If the skies are clear, then necessarily it isn't raining.") are epistemic.

[9] By this I do not mean that "ought" has a special "chess sense." I am going to be careful about postulating extra senses.

If its scope were wide, it would not detach; that's the whole point of wide-scoping.

Intuitions that a certain inference, like the detachment of the chess *ought,* is valid, are not so convincing evidence as intuitive counterexamples are evidence that an inference is *in*valid. Furthermore, it *could* be that some conditional requirement *ought*s are wide-scope while some are consequent-scope. (I could use a genuine requirement of chess, such as "If you are in check then you are required not to castle.")

But there is a pretty good reason to doubt that scope works one way in instrumental requirements and another way in chess requirements. For we can issue (and understand) both requirements in one breath, using just one occurrence of the word "ought."

My coach tells me before the big tournament:

(31) You ought to play for a draw if you are behind in material, to go for the kill if you sense weakness, and to ask the director for a time out if you want a drink.

Could it really be that one *ought* has narrow scope in the first two conditionals conjoined in (31) and wide scope over the last?

## 4 PROBABILITY

Consider the example of Janet and Reggie.

### JANET AND REGGIE

Janet works at Universal Studios, where she knows the parking lot attendant, Reggie. Reggie has seen better days; he drinks too much and he appears disheveled and unkempt. Janet likes Reggie and from time to time imagines giving him advice or help.

Reggie would very much like to make friends with Paris Hilton. He sees her every once in a while as she drops by the Studios, and though she has never so much as noticed him nor has he ever spoken a word to her, he fantasizes about getting chummy with her and hanging out. Janet is aware of Reggie's strong desire to make friends with Paris Hilton.

One day, Janet stops to chat with Reggie in the parking lot. She tells him, "Reggie, if you want to make friends with Paris Hilton, you ought to stop drinking and clean up your act."

Here are two more facts about the situation.

(a) Janet has no idea whether Reggie's odds of befriending Paris Hilton would increase should he stop drinking and clean up his act; she suspects they would not.

(b) On the other hand, she definitely thinks that Reggie ought to stop drinking. And she definitely thinks that Reggie ought *not* to want to make friends with Paris Hilton. (It is both unfitting and pragmatically bad for him to have a desire like that.)

Now let's consider Janet's advice,

(32) If you want to make friends with Paris Hilton, you ought to stop drinking and clean up your act.

Because of (a), Janet does not really have any confidence in (32). It is, frankly, insincere, though she advises Reggie with the best of intentions. (She is hoping to manipulate him.) If you overheard Janet and later asked her, "Do you really believe that?," she'd say she doesn't.

On the other hand, because of (b), Janet is very confident that

(33) $\mathcal{O}$(Reggie does not want to make friends with Paris Hilton $\vee$ Reggie stops drinking and cleans up his act.)

But this means (33) cannot be the analysis of the English (32). If it were, Janet would be exactly as confident in the one as the other.

The example of Janet and Reggie is based on Frank Ramsey's test for acceptability of an indicative conditional. Ramsey thought that the degree of belief in a conditional is our conditional credence of the consequent given the antecedent. We can then test a proposed analysis of a conditional by checking to see whether confidence in the analysans is plausibly the same as confidence in the conditional it is supposed to analyze. Here, it is not.

***

For a number of reasons, then, it seems unlikely, if not impossible, that instrumental requirements, as they are formed in English, have the logical form that wide-scopers say they have.

A wide-scoper might reply that his view is not about what the logical form of English sentences is. Rather, the theory is about what is *true*. The conditionals governed by wide-scope *ought*s, he might say, are true; they are genuine requirements of rationality, whereas their consequent-scope counterparts are not.

This is a fair reply. But what do we have to go on? We know which sentences seem acceptable. And the English conditional requirement sentences do. They still seem perfectly acceptable even once we are shown the wide-scope alternatives (assuming now that the wide-scope conditionals are *alternatives to* and not *analyses of* the English sentences). True, detachment seems to fail for them. But until we have a diagnosis that accounts for the intuitive acceptability of the English conditionals, we do not have a happy theory.

This concludes the negative, critical part of the essay. Nothing in what I've said so far gives any hint of what the proper account of practical conditionals might be. In the remainder I will suggest a positive view. However, I am much less confident that the positive view is right than I am that the wide-scoping view is wrong.

I'll begin by discussing a rather different sort of 'practical conditional' in the example of King Henry V. The main point of the example is to show how *modus ponens* apparently fails for these practical conditionals. I'll then suggest that the explanation for the failure points the way toward a positive account.

## 5 HENRY'S INFERENCE

The example is from Shakespeare's play *King Henry V*.[10] The scene is just before the battle of Agincourt, at which the British know that they are terribly outnumbered. One of Henry's men wishes aloud that just a few thousand knights could join them in the morning. Henry disagrees. His argument: Either we will win tomorrow, or we will lose. If we win, how much better to win having been so hopelessly outnumbered! If we lose, how ignominious it would be to lose with a multitude on our side! Then

[10] It's act IV, scene III.

The example is due to Hugh Mellor, who used it to illustrate a different point in an unpublished lecture that he gave at the Australian Association of Philosophy in the early 1990s.

I should also say that there is a different interpretation of what Henry is saying in the scene, possibly a more plausible one. He may be saying that it is already fated that his side will win, or fated that his side will lose, so that nothing that happens now can affect the chances. For the record, here is a snippet of the text:

*Westmoreland*:

O that we now had here
But one ten thousand of those men in England
That do no work to-day!

*King Henry V*:

What's he that wishes so?
My cousin Westmoreland? No, my fair cousin:
If we are mark'd to die, we are enow
To do our country loss; and if to live,
The fewer men, the greater share of honour.
God's will! I pray thee, wish not one man more.

The men appear satisfied. Henry then asks, "Thou dost not wish more help from England, coz?" And Westmoreland replies, perhaps ironically, "God's will! my liege, would you and I alone,/ Without more help, might fight this battle out."

in either case, it is better that we have few soldiers. What is wrong with Henry's argument?

This table illustrates the example of King Henry.

| | We win | We lose |
|---|---|---|
| We have few | Glory everlasting! | Defeat (but no shame) |
| We have many | Victory (but no glory) | Ignominy |

When I teach my class in Decision Theory, I say what is wrong is that the State (win or lose) depends probabilistically on the Act (whether we have few or many). It is much more likely that we will win given that we have many, than given that we have few.

I am sure that's correct. However, there is a problem that the decision theoretic analysis does not address. We can put the argument as follows:

Either we will win or we will lose.
If we win, it is better to have few.
If we lose, it is better to have few.
So, it is better to have few.

This argument looks valid, but we know it isn't. We do know how to reason properly with information and judgments like Henry's, but that's not the question. The question is why the apparently valid argument is invalid.

I'll make the logic explicit now.

| | Resting on . . . | |
|---|---|---|
| 1 Either we will win or we will lose. | 1 | Assumption |
| 2 If we win, it is better to have few. | 2 | Assumption |
| 3 If we lose, it is better to have few. | 3 | Assumption |
| 4 We will win. | 4 | Assumption |
| 5 It is better to have few. | 2, 4 | 2, 4 *modus ponens* |
| 6 We will lose. | 6 | Assumption |
| 7 It is better to have few. | 3, 6 | 3, 6 *modus ponens* |
| 8 It is better to have few. | 1, 2, 3 | 1, 5, 7 Or-elimination |

The conclusion rests only on the first three assumptions. They all seem pretty plausible.[11] Only two rules are employed. In some contexts

[11] The first assumption is a little leaky, since the battle might have no decisive outcome, but I think this is irrelevant. We could change it to "We will win or we will not win" and change the Or-elimination accordingly, for example.

Or-elimination is suspect, but not here, I take it. There aren't any intuitionistic or relevance worries, and if anyone perversely has some I just stipulate that the connective in line 1 is the classical *vel* that we learned in introductory logic. The premise, surely, is still true.[12]

That leaves *modus ponens. Modus ponens*, it seems, is invalid for the conditionals in the premises. I don't see how this can be denied, so I accept it.

## 6 TOWARD A POSITIVE ACCOUNT

What is really going on, then?

King Henry's conditionals are somehow defective. The problem is not quite that they don't detach. They don't participate unrestrictedly in *modus ponens*, but simple, two-premise arguments strike us as intuitively valid. For example, the embedded arguments seem fine: on the assumption that *if we win it is better to have few*, and the further assumption that *we win*, it seems just fine to conclude that *it is better to have few*. And likewise, on the assumption that *if we lose it is better to have few*, and the further assumption that *we lose*, it seems just fine to conclude that *it is better to have few*. So in either case (if we win or if we lose), it seems, it is better to have few. But we cannot conclude that it is simply better to have few. The conclusion was fine resting on each assumption separately, but it goes bad when the assumptions are put together, disjoined. It's as if in each little argument, the assumption is playing some role that each can play alone but which gets disrupted when they are discharged in favor of their disjunction.

The conditional judgments of goodness are judgments made *from the point of view* of some probability function or other. Which option is better is always relative to one or another assignment of probabilities to states of affairs.[13] And when a judgment of *better than* occurs in a consequent, it is made relative to a conditional probability, or to a probability function conditionalized on the antecedent. Conditionalizing on each disjunct screens off the probabilistic dependence of the outcomes on the acts (here, having more and having fewer). That dependence is alive and influential in the straight judgment that it would be better to have more than few.

Let me admit up front that I don't generally like the idea of a *judgment made from a point of view*. All judgments are made from a point of view.

[12] Again bracketing concerns about messy, victorless outcomes.

[13] Of course, a judgment could be relative to the trivial probability function that assigns 1 to all true propositions; in that case it is odd, but still correct, to think of it as relative to an assignment of probabilities.

And in general it isn't good philosophy to tag judgments or sentences with "from the point of view of . . ." In general, the *point of view* isn't something that gets tagged onto the judgement, the content, but properly belongs to the person making the judgment. So, for instance, it is sloppy and misleading (and suspicious) to say things like, "From Anne's point of view, Hume was a krypto-rationalist," if what we mean is that Anne believes that Hume was a krypto-rationalist. But here we cannot remove the *from X's point of view* in favor of *X believes that.* The point is not that Henry, or Westmoreland, or anybody, *believes* that having fewer men is better. The judgment is correct, on the condition that we (the British) win, and it is correct on the condition that we lose, but it is incorrect if left unconditional. So, awkward and suspicious as it may sound, I think we cannot get rid of the relativization to a point of view.

The important point is that the conditional judgments are judgments relativized to a probability distribution – a *credence* function. Now thinking of the *ought*s in the instrumental requirements as indexed to credences won't help us understand why they seem problematic. When I consider what to say about cleaver murders first conditionalizing my credences on the assumption (pretence, imagining) that you want to kill your victim in a violent way, I don't then comfortably accept the idea that you ought to use a cleaver, not even conditionally or within a pretence. These special practical conditionals, I suggest, are *outliers*, semantically odd, just as wide-scopers say, but not in the way they say. They are rather members of a family of semantically odd conditionals, all of them departing from the core of conditional semantics in a similar way.

A last word about Henry. My view is that the conditionals in Henry's argument *express no proposition at all.* That's a popular view of indicative conditionals nowadays,[14] so it's not as if I were taking a particularly radical stance. It also fits with the decision theoretic view. For this reason, it may seem wrong to say that *modus ponens* fails in the Henry argument: *modus ponens*, one might say, is a rule for propositions. That's fine with me; I am taking *modus ponens* to be a rule for inferring *sentences* from *sentences*, but I don't insist on my own terminology. The point is that we do typically rely on a rule, call it what you will, for reaching sentences as conclusions from premises that are sentences, and that rule is unreliable for the conditional sentences (not conditional propositions) in Henry's argument.

[14] See Edgington (1995), for instance.

## 7 OUTLIER CONDITIONALS

The most famous outlier conditionals are *biscuit conditionals* (Austin 1961):

(34) There are biscuits on the sideboard if you want them.

Though I think these fit my suggestion reasonably well, they aren't as directly relevant as some other outliers, which is a shame because they share with the problematic practical conditionals the feature that their antecedent is a "you want" sentence. So I'll leave them aside.

The first one I want to consider also has an intentional state antecedent:

(35) If you believe Broome, the operator takes wide-scope.

I can assert (35) happily, and (it seems) truthfully, even though I do not believe that the operator takes wide-scope, and I don't believe it would take wide-scope even if Broome convinced you. Nobody takes (35) to assert any sort of dependence of its consequent on its antecedent.

(36) If you believe their dispatcher, the plumbers will be here by noon.

Well, faith moves mountains, but it can't move plumbers. So how do these faith-based conditionals work?

When I decide whether to accept a conditional, I *try on* its antecedent and see whether I accept its consequent. I'm not sure exactly what "trying on" is, but it's something like pretending or imagining. This is how we decide whether to accept conditionals, I think.[15] So when someone tells me, "If you believe Broome, the operator takes wide-scope," I pretend that I believe Broome and ask myself whether, within that pretense, to accept that the conditional has wide-scope. Well, I am pretending to believe Broome, which is pretending to believe what he says, so I am pretending to believe that, among other things, the operator takes wide-scope. There may be a difference between pretending to believe something and pretending that the something is the case (for instance, it seems difficult but maybe possible to pretend that you are walking through a mine field unaware of the dangers), but the difference is awfully subtle and it would be unsurprising if language ran them together.

[15] It fits Dorothy Edgington's account of what "if" means, in Edgington (1995). I find that account very compelling, which is why I think the line of argument in the text might be right.
Jonathan Ichikawa persuaded me that only *some* conditionals fit the "trying on" picture, which I suppose doesn't damage the argument in the text too much, only I wish I could say systematically which conditionals do fit and why.

The second type of outlier I want to look at is the kind I'll call *conditionals of focus.*

(37) If we're only talking about taste, you should order the fried mozzarella sticks.

(38) If you restrict your attention to hitting, the Rangers are the best team.

These generally have practical or evaluative consequents. Again, what someone ought to order and which team is best can't depend on the vicissitudes of the conversations of philosophers, so these must be outliers, too. And again we get the right interpretation by imagining the antecedent (that is, imagining that it is true) and asking whether the consequent is acceptable. If we're only talking about taste, it would be preachy and querulous to point out that the mozzarella sticks are not conducive to cardiovascular health; if I'm restricting my attention to hitting, I won't notice that their ERA is through the roof.

Now both conditionals of focus and faith-based conditionals are essentially second-personal. Actually, their antecedents can be first-person plural, but in that case they are also *about* the person they *address* – the "we" in (37) includes the addressee, for example. So I'll say that they're "second-personal" even though their grammatical subject can be "we."[16] The "trying on" model explains why this is so. I am being told that if *I* (among others maybe) believe Broome, or consider only taste, then such and such. So I imagine or pretend that *I* am believing or focusing, and then I see right through the belief to its contents, or I see the object of the focus instead of the focusing. And then I'll find the consequents acceptable.[17] Contrast

(39) If the Rangers' management is only attending to hitting, then they're the best team.

To the contrary: that's why they're not a top team! When I pretend or imagine that Jon Daniels is only attending to hitting, I don't ignore pitching, so I don't find the consequent acceptable.

## 8 TRYING ON PRACTICAL CONDITIONALS

Second-person instrumental requirement conditionals fit my "trying on" story pretty well. One time my wife said to me,

[16] For that matter, it can be "I," when the speaker addresses herself: "OK, if I'm just paying attention to the artistic merits, I should give her the highest score."

[17] Here think of what Niko Kolodny (2005) says about the "transparency" of requirements of rationality.

(40) If you want to get me really angry, you should keep using that tone of voice.

This turned out to be good advice. (In a way.) First, suppose I try to decide whether to believe (40). I imagine that I want to get my wife really angry, and ask myself whether I accept the judgment, addressed to me, "You should keep using that tone of voice." Knowing how these things go, I do find the judgment very compelling, when I am imagining that I want to get her really angry. Continuing to use the smug, sarcastic tone seems like a very good idea indeed. Now suppose that I am *not* experienced or reflective enough to have any clear sense, independent of my wife's conditional advice, of what sort of effect my tone has. Trying on the antecedent and working out what would make the consequent then seem compelling makes me realize what that effect is (or, strictly speaking, what effect my wife is telling me it has).

The second-person case fits nicely. It presents the advice as it intuitively should be, and it shows how the intuitive information gets conveyed. Unfortunately (for my little story), instrumental requirement conditionals can, plainly, be in the third person.[18]

(41) If Jesse wants to anger the audience, then he ought to say that conceptual analysis is *a posteriori*.

According to my "trying on" picture, then, we should check (41) for acceptability by imagining that *Jesse* wants to anger the audience, and asking ourselves whether he *ought* to say that conceptual analysis is *a posteriori*. And we feel some resistance, I admit. We feel the same resistance that we feel at the UMPs. So it appears my suggestion is wrong.

Now, suppose I actually asserted the (41) to you, and you remarked that he does indeed want to anger the audience. Then you ask me whether he ought to say that conceptual analysis is *a posteriori*. I balk. But then I say, "Well, *if he really does want to anger the audience*, then he ought to say it, yes." And you repeat that indeed he does. So I am *almost* willing to infer the consequent of the instrumental requirement. I am willing to assert it on the very condition you have assured me is true, as long as I repeat that condition and make it clear that I am asserting it on that condition. Why am I reluctant to assert unconditionally that Jesse ought to say that conceptual analysis is *a posteriori*?

[18] It seems significant that philosophers give examples of them in the second person. For example Darwall (1983) and Hare (1971).

Standing by the conditional is, I think, standing by the consequent *ought* from a certain point of view. We assess behavior and states of affairs from our own point of view, of course, but in assessing someone's rationality we want to take special care to incorporate at least much of that person's own standpoint.[19] And by all accounts, conditionals of instrumental requirement are about the *ought* of rationality (that is, they are about what we rationally ought to do). So when we try on the (41), we imagine *ourselves* wanting to anger the audience, and decide whether we then accept that we ought to say something outrageous. And we do. But then when we detach the consequent, we do so with the belief that *Jesse* wants to anger the audience, and when we assess the consequent we find that we still cannot endorse saying such an outrageously false thing about conceptual analysis. The antecedent is no longer hanging around to remind us of the "proper" point of view from which to do the assessment.

I have been speaking of what one *ought to do from a certain point of view*. And as I said, this sort of talk bothers me, and it sounds suspicious. Isn't what we ought to do from somebody's point of view simply what that person believes we ought to do?

To repeat what I said at the end of the section about King Henry: the *from a point of view* can't be eliminated, in our context, in favor of a *so-and-so believes that*. Just as the way in which having few was better than having many, namely from the point of view of assuming that we win, and also from the point of view of assuming that we do not win, was not a matter of somebody or other *believing* that it is better to have few, so the instrumental *ought* is about what is to be done, not according to one person or another, but from the point of view of having a certain aim or want.

Needless to say, this last idea, and indeed my positive story about how instrumental requirements work, are at best suggestive and cry out for a fuller account. I am not very confident, in fact, that they will turn out to be right or helpful. I am much more confident that the wide-scoping theory of instrumental requirements is wrong.

[19] As Don Hubin says, "It is precisely the fact that in making rational evaluations we adopt the agent's normative standpoint that makes the charge of irrationality have special force for the agent. If we are correct and he understands our rational criticism, he is generally motivated to act on our recommendations" (Hubin 1999: 41).

CHAPTER 7

# *Authority and second-personal reasons for acting**

*Stephen Darwall*

In *The Second-Person Standpoint,*[1] I argue that a distinctive kind of reason for acting, a *second-personal reason,* is an ineliminable aspect of many central moral categories, including rights, moral responsibility, moral obligation, respect for and the dignity of persons, and the very concept of moral agent or person itself. Second-personal reasons are distinguished from reasons of other kinds by their conceptual relations to authoritative claims and demands that must be able to be *addressed to* those to whom they apply (second-personally, as it were). I have argued, more specifically, that there are four interdefinable, irreducibly second-personal notions: the authority to make a claim or demand, a valid (authoritative) claim or demand, responsibility *to* someone (with the relevant authority), and a second-personal reason for acting (that is, for complying with an authoritative claim or demand and so discharging the responsibility). Each one of these notions entails the other three, and no proposition that does not already involve one of these four concepts can entail any that does.

Call the authority I am concerned with *practical authority* to distinguish it from various forms of epistemic authority or expertise, including the kind of authority on practical matters a trusted advisor might have. A challenge that can be posed to my irreducibility thesis is that it is possible to establish claims to practical authority by invoking solely non-second-personal reasons. In what follows, I consider Joseph Raz's influential *normal justification thesis,* according to which claims to

* I am indebted to audiences at the Bowling Green Practical Reason conference, Texas Tech University, Vanderbilt University, University of Toronto School of Law, Yale University, The Graduate Center at the City University of New York, University of Chicago, University of California at Irvine, Northwestern University, and Brugge, Belgium, especially, to John Broome, David Copp, James Dreier, Kyla Ebels Duggan, Margaret Gilbert, Aaron James, Shelly Kagan, Richard Kraut, Victoria McGeer, Douglas MacLean, Marina Oshana, Philip Pettit, David Plunkett, Wlodek Rabinowicz, Peter Railton, Arthur Ripstein, T.M. Scanlon, Mark Schroeder, Scott Shapiro, John Skorupski, Wayne Sumner, Candace Vogler, Gary Watson, Susan Wolf, and most especially to David Sobel and Steven Wall.

[1] Darwall (2006).

practical authority can be established by showing that an "alleged subject" is likely to comply better with reasons that apply to him independently already if he accepts the directives of an alleged authority as binding and tries to follow them than he would if he were to act on his own assessment of independent reasons (Raz 1986: 53). I shall argue that the normal justification thesis does not hold for practical authority as I propose to understand it;[2] moreover, that the correct diagnosis of why it doesn't shows that both practical authority and reasons that are conceptually related to it are irreducibly second-personal.

Let me try to get the intuitive idea of a second-personal reason across with an example. Compare, first, two different ways in which you might try to give someone a reason to stop causing you pain, say, to remove his foot from on top of yours.

One would be to get him to have sympathetic concern for you in your plight and to want you to be free of pain. In desiring this, he would see relief of your pain as a better way for the world to be, a possible outcome or state that, as Moore put it, "ought to exist for its own sake" (Moore 1993: 34). And he would most naturally see his desire, not as the source of the reason, but as a kind of access to an *agent-neutral* (and *state-of-the-world-regarding*) reason for removing his foot that is there anyway.[3] The reason would not be essentially *for him* as the agent causing another person pain. It would apparently exist, most fundamentally, for anyone who is in a position to effect the state of relief of your pain, and *therefore* for him, since he is well placed to do so.[4] Finally, in "giving" him the

[2] Or more cautiously, any cases where it may hold will be by virtue of recourse to reasons that are themselves already within the circle of second-personal concepts (i.e. second-personal reasons).

[3] On this point, see Bond (1983); Darwall (1983); Pettit and Smith (1990); Quinn (1991); Hampton (1998); Scanlon (1998): 41–55; Dancy (2000). Agent-neutral reasons contrast with agent-relative reasons, those whose formulation includes an ineliminable reference to the agent for whom they are reasons (like "that it will keep a promise I made," "that it will avoid harm to others (i.e. people other than me," and so on). Agent-neutral reasons can be stated without such a reference: "that it would prevent some pain from occurring to someone (or some being)." On the distinction between agent-relative (also called "subjective" or "agent-centered") and agent-neutral (also called "objective") reasons, principles, values, etc., see Nagel (1970); Scheffler (1982); Parfit (1984); Darwall (1986); Nagel (1986); McNaughton and Rawlings (1991); Ridge (2005).

I argue for the claim that sympathetic concern involves its seeming that there are agent-neutral reasons to further someone's welfare in Darwall (2002): 68–72. I do not deny, of course, that someone who already accepted various agent-relative norms might not be moved through empathy and sympathy, to feel some special responsibility for relieving the pain. My point is that this would not come through sympathy alone.

[4] Roughly speaking, again, a reason is agent-neutral if it can be formulated without essential reference to the agent (as such); otherwise it is agent-relative. It should also be noted that superficially agent-relative reasons may be grounded more deeply in agent-neutral considerations and values, and/or vice versa. For example, rule-utilitarianism holds that rules of right conduct include agent-relative

reason in this way, you might not need to address or relate to him in any way at all. Anything that would get him to see your being in pain as a bad thing, like an unaddressed grimace or whimper, might serve. In no sense, not even epistemic, need he be taking any reason to move his foot on your authority.

Alternatively, you might lay a claim or address a purportedly valid demand. You might say something that asserts or implies your authority *to* claim or demand that he move his foot and that simultaneously expresses this demand. You might demand this as the person whose foot he is stepping on, thereby claiming and exercising what you take to be a right against him. Or you might demand it as a representative of the moral community, whose members understand themselves as holding one another to a (moral) demand not to step on each other's feet. Or you might do both simultaneously. Whichever, the reason you would address would be agent-relative rather than agent-neutral. It would concern, most fundamentally, your addressee's relations to others, viewed from a perspective within those relations, in this case, that his keeping his foot on yours causes another person pain, causes inconvenience, and so on, and that this is something we can and do reasonably demand that people not do. The reason would not be addressed to him as someone who is simply in a position to alter a bad state, whether of someone's being in pain or even of someone's causing another pain. If he could stop, say, two others from causing an identical gratuitous pain by the shocking spectacle of keeping his foot firmly planted on yours, this second, claim-based reason would not recommend that he do so. The reason would be addressed to him as someone who is himself *causing* gratuitous pain to another person, something we persons normally assume we have the authority to demand that we not do to one another.

What is important for our purposes is that someone can sensibly accept this second reason for moving his foot, one embodied in your claim or demand, only if he also accepts your *authority to demand* this of him (second-personally). That is just what it is to accept something *as a valid claim or demand.* And if he accepts that you can demand that he move his foot, he must also accept that you will have grounds for complaint or some other form of accountability-seeking response if he does not. Unlike the first reason, this latter is second-personal in the sense that although the first is conceptually independent of forms of second-personal address

principles, for example, those defining rights of promise and contract, on grounds of overall agent-neutral value.

involved in making claims and holding people responsible, the second is not. A *second-personal reason* is thus one whose validity depends upon presupposed authority and accountability relations between persons and, therefore, on the possibility of the reason's being addressed person-to-person within these relations. Reasons of this kind simply wouldn't exist but for their role in second-personal address and in mediating our relatings to one another. And their second-personal character explains their agent-relativity. As second-personal reasons always derive most fundamentally from agents' *relations* to one another, they are invariably agent-relative at the most fundamental level.[5]

It is important also to see, however, that a norm or reason can be agent-relative without being second-personal; in other words, there might be a reason of yet a *third* kind that is agent-relative, like the second, but not yet a second-personal reason. We can imagine someone who accepts and scrupulously observes a universal norm of foot-avoidance but who also denies, consistently with that, anyone's authority to claim or demand his compliance with this norm, hence denies that he is responsible to anyone for compliance, even to God. Such a person might conceive of the norm as mandatory in the sense of entailing categorical, indeed supremely authoritative, or "silencing," or even "pre-emptive," or "exclusionary" reasons, without accepting that he is accountable to anyone for complying with it.[6] However, he could not then consistently accept that anyone has a *right* to his foot-avoidance, and in respecting the norm of avoiding people's feet he would not be respecting *them* as persons, since he would

[5] The formulation of the reason may not always be agent-relative, however. Suppose, for example, that the best way of grounding the Categorical Imperative (CI) is, as I argue in *The Second-Person Standpoint*, from the second-person standpoint in an equal authority to make claims and demands that persons presuppose when they address one another second-personally (2006: 32–35, 115–118, 239–242, 304–309). It is at least conceivable that what the CI itself requires is a principle of conduct that can be specified agent-neutrally. R.M. Hare, for example, believes that the CI can be seen to entail the sort of universal prescriptivism he favors *and* that this entails a form of act-utilitarianism (an agent-neutral theory). See Hare (1993).

I take the relevance of the arguments of *The Second-Person Standpoint* to the problem of justifying of agent-relative (or "deontological") therefore constraints to be the following. Justification from the second-person point of view can provide a compelling rationale for agent-relative constraints, like the demand not to step on another's feet, since, if I am right, any moral obligation or constraint is irreducibly second-personal, and second-personal reasons are agent-relative in their foundations. It is, however, conceptually consistent with this that moral obligations are agent-neutral in their content, and some presumably are, such as the obligation to help those in need. I am indebted to David Sobel and Steven Wall for pressing me to clarify this point.

[6] A reason "silences" other reasons if it cancels their weight (and thus does not simply outweigh them [McDowell 1979]). A reason is "exclusionary" or "pre-emptive" if it is not to be added to other reasons, but to replace or "exclude" them (Raz 1975, 1986: 46).

not be recognizing any authority anyone might claim as a person to demand anything, in particular, that he avoid their feet (Feinberg 1980; Darwall 2004). Neither, in my view, could he consistently accept that he is *morally obligated* not to step on others' feet since moral obligation is related to moral responsibility conceptually. It is conceptually impossible for one to be morally obligated to do something but not responsible for doing it, neither to the moral community, nor to God, nor to anyone. So someone who thought he was accountable to no one could not think he was morally obligated not to step on others' feet, whatever priority he might give to a norm requiring him not to do so.

There is thus a significant difference between the idea of an authoritative claim or demand, on the one hand, and that of an authoritative or valid norm or normative reason, or even of a normative requirement, on the other. There can be requirements *on* us that no one has any standing *to require of* us. We are under a requirement of reason not to believe propositions that contradict the logical consequences of known premises, for example. But it is only in certain contexts, say, when you and I are trying to work out what to believe together, that we have any standing to demand that one another reason logically, and even here that authority apparently derives from a moral or quasi-moral aspect, namely, our having undertaken a common goal.[7] Requirements of logical reasoning are, in this way, fundamentally different from moral requirements. I follow Mill and a number of contemporary writers in holding that it is part of the very idea of moral obligation that moral requirements are what those to whom we are morally responsible have the authority to demand that we do.[8] Clearly this

[7] Of course, these further constraints are frequently in the background, as they are, for example, whenever we do philosophy, say, right now. Because of the relationship you and I are currently in, each of us *does* have authority to call one another to account for logical errors, a standing that, without some such context, we lack. But however frequently that or some relevantly similar context obtains, the authority comes, not just from the requirement of reason, but from some other presupposed feature of the context.

[8] "We do not call anything wrong, unless we mean to imply that a person ought to be punished in some way or other for doing it; if not by law, by the opinion of his fellow-creatures; if not by opinion, by the reproaches of his own conscience. This seems the real turning point of the distinction between morality and simple expediency. It is a part of the notion of Duty in every one of its forms, that a person may rightfully be compelled to fulfil it. Duty is a thing which may be exacted from a person, as one exacts a debt" (Mill 1998: chapter V). John Skorupski points out that calling an act "morally wrong . . . amounts to blaming the agent" and maintains that the idea of moral wrong can't be understood independently of that of blameworthiness (Skorupski 1999: 29, 142). Allan Gibbard quite explicitly follows Mill's lead in proposing that "what a person does is *morally wrong* if and only if it is rational for him to feel guilty for having done it, and for others to be angry at him for having done it" (Gibbard 1990: 42). And we can find versions of this Millian idea in other writers also (Baier 1966; Brandt 1979; Shafer-Landau 2003).

is no part whatsoever of the concept of a demand of logic or a requirement of reason.[9]

Now, as I've said, I believe that second-personal reasons are related conceptually to, respectively, the authority to make a claim or demand, a valid or authoritative claim or demand, and responsibilty or accountability *to*. To appreciate the second-personal aspect of moral responsibility, consider Strawson's famous critique of "pragmatist" or consequentialist approaches to responsibility in "Freedom and Resentment" (Strawson 1968). Strawson argued influentially that social desirability cannot provide a justification of "the right *sort*" for practices of moral responsibility "as we understand them" (1968: 74): When we seek to hold people accountable, what matters is not whether some sanction is desirable, either in a particular case or in general, but whether their actions are culpable and whether we have any authority to demand their acceptance of a sanction. Desirability is a reason of the wrong kind to warrant the attitudes and actions in which holding someone responsible consists *in their own terms*.

Strawson's point is an instance of the *wrong kind of reason problem*. For example, there might be pragmatic reasons to believe (or perhaps just to want to believe) some proposition, but that doesn't make that proposition *credible*. It doesn't justify believing it in terms of reasons and standards that distinctively apply to belief. Similarly, as D'Arms and Jacobson have pointed out, it is a "moralistic fallacy" to conclude from the fact that being amused by a certain joke is morally objectionable that the joke is therefore not itself funny (D'Arms and Jacobson 2000a).[10]

To be a reason of the right kind, a consideration must justify the relevant attitude in its own terms. It must be a fact about or feature of some object, appropriate consideration of which could provide someone's reason for a warranted attitude of that kind towards it.[11] It must be something on the basis of which someone could (and appropriately would) come to hold the

[9] I am indebted to Peter Graham for this point.

[10] D'Arms and Jacobson argue that this poses a problem for response-dependent or, as they call them, "neo-sentimentalist," accounts of various evaluative and normative notions, since it shows that, say, the funny can't be understood in terms of amusement's making sense or being warranted by just *any* reasons. There is a distinction between an emotion or attitude's being "the right way to feel" and it's "getting [the relevant value] right." For an excellent discussion of how what they call "fitting-attitude" (or "FA") analyses can deal with the problem of distinguishing reasons of the right from reasons of the wrong kind, see Rabinowicz and Rønnow-Rasmussen (2004). (See also Olson 2004.) I am indebted to Julian Darwall for discussion of this general issue and to Joe Mendola for a question that helped me to see that Strawson's point is an instance of it.

[11] Rabinowicz and Rønnow-Rasmussen put essentially the same point by saying that reasons of the right kind also appear in the content of the attitude for which they are reasons: the attitude is toward something "on account of" these reasons (Rabinowicz and Rønnow-Rasmussen 2004: 414).

attitude as a conclusion of a process of considering (deliberating about) *whether* to do so. In considering whether to believe some proposition *p*, for example, it is simply impossible to conclude one's deliberation in a belief that *p* by reflecting on the desirable consequences of believing *p*. That is a reason of the right kind for *desiring* to believe that *p*, but not for believing that *p*.[12] The *desirable* concerns norms and reasons that are specific to desire, and the *credible* concerns norms and reasons that are specific to belief.

Similarly, the *(morally) responsible* and the *culpable* concern norms for the distinctive attitudes and actions that are involved in holding people responsible and blaming them. The desirability – whether moral, social, personal, or otherwise – of holding someone responsible or blaming her, or reasons why that would be desirable, are simply reasons of the wrong kind to warrant doing so in the sense that is relevant to whether she *is* morally responsible or blameworthy. The former concerns reasons and norms of desire (even if from the moral point of view), and what is thus desirable is simply a different question from whether we are justified in holding someone responsible or blaming her in the relevant sense. The latter concerns reasons and norms that are distinctively relevant to these latter attitudes.

Strawson dubbed the distinctive attitudes involved in holding people responsible "reactive attitudes," with prominent examples being indignation, resentment, guilt, blame, and so on. And Strawson himself pointed out what more recent commentators, notably Gary Watson and Jay Wallace, have since also noticed, namely, that reactive attitudes implicitly address *demands*. They involve "an *expectation of*, and *demand* for" certain conduct from one another (1968: 85, emphasis added).[13] To feel a reactive attitude is to feel as though one has a warranted expectation *of* someone. Reactive attitudes, and actions that express them, must therefore presuppose the authority *to* expect and hold one another responsible for compliance with moral obligations (which must then be standards to which we can warrantedly hold each other as members of the moral community). Strawson claimed also that holding one another responsible with reactive attitudes presupposes that those we hold responsible have that standing as well. In holding someone accountable in this way, we "view him as a

As W.D. Falk pointed out, a favoring that is relevant to value is "by way of true comprehension of what [the object] is like" (Falk 1986: 117). See also Hieronymi (2005).

[12] More precisely, it entails that reasons of the right kind for desiring to believe the proposition exist.

[13] Gary Watson stresses this in Watson (1987: 263, 264). Note also, R. Jay Wallace: "there is an essential connection between the reactive attitudes and a distinctive form of evaluation . . . that I refer to as holding a person to an expectation (or demand)" (Wallace 1994: 19). See also Bennett (1980) and Scanlon (1998: 272–290).

member of the moral community; only as one who has offended against its demands" (1968: 93). In these ways, reactive attitudes can mediate *mutual* accountability.

It follows on Strawson's analysis that culpability and moral responsibility are second-personal phenomena in my sense. They implicitly involve the address of authoritative claims and demands and, therefore, of second-personal reasons. Moral responsibility is responsibility *to* – in Strawson's view (and mine), the moral community. It concerns what the moral community can warrantedly expect and demand of each other. When we hold one another responsible, we express these demands and presuppose the authority to do so. So if Strawson is right, as I think he is, then responsibility *to* is conceptually related to the idea of authoritative demands and, therefore, to practical authority and second-personal reasons – that is, to reasons for acting that are thought to consist in or to derive from authoritative demands.

But the conceptual relations also seem to run in the opposite direction. If one person has practical authority with respect to another, then this would seem to mean, not just that the latter has a reason of whatever priority or weight – whether overriding, silencing, exclusionary, preemptive, or whatever – for acting as the former directs, but also that the latter has some responsibility *to* the former for doing so, that the latter is, in some way or other, answerable to the former. This point can be illustrated by altering our earlier thought experiment to imagine someone, call him now B, who accepts a mandatory norm requiring him always to do what someone in a certain position tells him to do. Suppose that A is now in that position. B will then accept that he must do what A tells him to do. We can imagine that B thereby accepts a reason for complying with A's directives of whatever weight or priority. B might think that the reason always overrides, silences, or preempts any potentially conflicting reasons. But B could still deny, consistently with all of that, that he is in any way responsible or answerable to A (or, indeed, to anyone). Were he to do so, he would seem also to be questioning A's authority over him. "Just because I always have overriding or preemptive reason to do what you say doesn't make me answerable to you or give you authority over me," he might consistently say. A cannot have authority with respect to B, it seems, unless B is in some way answerable to A.

We might put this point by saying that practical authority is not just a relation in the logical sense; it is a standing in a relationship.[14] If A has

[14] I have been helped here by discussion with Jules Coleman.

authority with respect to B, then certain things follow about how A and B may and must relate to one another. If A has the authority to demand that B stay off A's feet, then not only is it the case that B has a reason of whatever weight or priority for doing so on the occasion of such a directive. B is also answerable to A for doing so.

This point is illustrated further by early modern theological voluntarist moral theories, like those of Pufendorf and Locke. The fundamental premise of such theories is that God has superior authority over his creatures. It is absolutely central to the voluntarist picture, moreover, that, because God has authority over us, not only must we do what God says, but we are also accountable to Him for doing so. Unless we were responsible to God for compliance, any sanction God might attach to violating His commands would amount to coercion by threat. Of course, it might be within God's authority so to threaten us, but voluntarists like Pufendorf thought it critical to distinguish between even such justified threats and God's authority to hold us accountable with sanctions. For us genuinely to accept God's authority, Pufendorf thought, we must see ourselves as responsible to God for doing as He directs.[15] (As we shall see, Raz also distinguishes between direction by justified threats and by authoritative directives.)

I take it, then, that there is a strong *prima facie* case for thinking that the four second-personal notions I mentioned at the outset – practical authority (to claim or demand), valid (authoritative) claim or demand, responsibility *to*, and second-personal reason for acting – are interdefinable in something like the following fashion:

- *Practical authority*: someone has practical authority with respect to another if, and only if, the latter has a second-personal reason to comply with the former's valid claims and demands and is responsible to the former for so doing.
- *Responsibility to*: someone is responsible to another if, and only if, the latter has the authority to make some valid claim or demand of the former that the former is thereby given a second-personal reason to comply with.
- *Valid claim or demand*: a valid claim or demand is one that is within the authority of someone having practical authority with respect to another to make of the latter and that the latter thereby has a second-personal

[15] For a discussion, see Darwall (2003).

reason to comply with and some responsibility to the former for so doing.

– *Second-personal reason*: a second-personal reason is one consisting in or deriving from some valid claim or demand of someone having practical authority with respect to the agent and with which the agent is thereby accountable for complying.

Presently, we shall consider the challenge that Raz's *normal justification thesis* poses to my claim that these concepts are irreducibly second-personal. First, however, I want briefly to summarize the ways in which, as I see it, the moral categories that I mentioned at the beginning all involve these four interdefinable notions. Perhaps the clearest case is that of a moral *right*. Feinberg put the point best when he said that "it is claiming that gives rights their special moral significance" (Feinberg 1980: 155). Without rights, others might still accept norms that require treating us in whatever ways we have a right to be treated, but we could not claim this as our right. We would have no guaranteed standing in relating to one another, no authority to claim or demand anything of each other, no place "to stand," as Feinberg says, "look others in the eye," and make claims on one another (1980: 151).

We have already seen how claims of culpability and *moral responsibility* are second-personal. Holding someone responsible and blaming her involves relating to her in a way that presupposes an authority to make demands of her and that she thereby has a reason to comply with these demands. But if this is right, and if *moral obligation* is conceptually connected to moral responsibility – that is, if violations of (all-things-considered) moral obligations are blameworthy lacking adequate excuse – then it follows that moral obligation is a second-personal concept also. What we are morally obligated to do is what members of the moral community have the authority to hold us to.[16] Of course, wrong-making features of action will include facts that are not themselves second-personal, such as that stepping on someone's foot causes avoidable pain, suffering, and inconvenience. But the fact that an action violates a(n all-things-considered) obligation, and so is morally wrong, is an additional reason, a second-personal reason, for not performing it, since it includes the fact that those to whom we are morally responsible have the authority to demand that we not so act.

[16] Depending on what we take the reference of "moral community" to be, this may go farther than what is guaranteed by the concept of moral obligation (viz. that moral obligations are what those to whom we are morally responsible have the authority to demand that we do). According to theological voluntarists, we are morally responsible, not to other moral subjects, but to God.

Membership in the moral community is thus not just being subject to moral demands, but also having the standing to hold one another (and ourselves) responsible for complying with them. I believe this to be a significant aspect of the *dignity of persons*, as was illustrated in our earlier thought experiment of an individual who is committed to forbear acting in various ways that, as it happens, persons claim an authority to demand he not act, but who also recognizes no such authority. Such an individual fails to have respect for persons in some clear sense. It follows that both the dignity of persons and respect for this dignity are irreducibly second-personal (Darwall 2004). To be a person is, as Rawls put it, "to be a self-originating sourc[e] of valid claims" (Rawls 1980: 546). Or, in Kant's words in *The Metaphysics of Morals*, a person's dignity is that "by which he exacts respect [that is, as Kant also says, "demands" it] for himself from all other rational beings" (Kant 1996: 434–435).

Finally, I take the concept of *moral agent* or *person* to be a second-personal notion itself. Locke makes the same point when he says that "person" is a "forensic term" (Locke 1975: 346).[17] To be a person is to be apt for moral accountability, a being to whom second-personal reasons can intelligibly be addressed. But what capacities does this involve? This is the same question that arises in Strawson's "Freedom and Resentment" of how to draw the line between beings whom we appropriately regard from an "objective" perspective as objects of self-protective coercive measures that cannot count as genuinely holding them responsible, however justified these might be, on the one hand, and those who are warranted objects of reactive attitudes and eligible to participate fully in mutually accountable human relations, on the other. Implicit in Strawson's analysis is the following guiding thought. We can only intelligibly hold responsible those we regard as capable of holding themselves responsible – that is, people who are able to take a second-person standpoint on themselves, acknowledge the validity of moral demands and the authority of the moral community, and, in effect, address the demands to themselves through self-reactive attitudes such as guilt. In a word, to be a person, and so apt for accountability, is to have *second-personal competence.*

The emergent conception of the *moral community* is one of *mutually accountable* moral agents or persons, where the second-personal competence necessary for being intelligibly held morally responsible, and so a moral

[17] Note also Kant's remark that "personality" is a feature of human beings considered as "rational and at the same time responsible" (Kant 1999: 26).

subject, is also sufficient for the standing or second-personal authority to hold others and oneself morally accountable.

I claim, again, that the four interdefinable notions of practical authority, valid claim or demand, responsibility *to*, and second-personal reason are all irreducibly second-personal. If this is so, then, to the extent that the moral categories I have just mentioned involve these notions, it will follow that they all have an irreducibly second-personal aspect also. In my view, this is a fact of great importance for moral theory. It means that no set of propositions that do not already involve the interdefinable second-personal notions I have identified can possibly entail any proposition of moral right, responsibility, obligation, and so on. To paraphrase a slogan of Bernard Williams: Second-personal authority out, second-personal authority in (Williams 1985: 181).[18] Of course, it may still be true that, for example, we are morally obligated to maximize overall utility, but this cannot possibly follow simply from the fact that the world would be better if we did. There must be some showing that this is something we reasonably demand of one another.

But what makes it the case that someone has practical authority of any kind (as I contend, for example, that beings with second-personal competence have authority as equal members of the moral community)? And what makes it the case that any claim or demand from someone to another is valid, one that that person has the authority to make on the other? If it is possible to justify practical authority fully in terms of reasons that are not themselves second-personal, then perhaps the notions I have identified are not *irreducibly* second-personal. Maybe their apparently second-personal character is a superficial aspect that can be explained away or otherwise accounted for at some more fundamental level.

This is the challenge that is posed by Raz's *normal justification thesis* which Raz formulates as follows:

> the normal way to establish that a person has authority over another person involves showing that the alleged subject is likely better to comply with reasons which apply to him (other than the alleged authoritative directives) if he accepts the directives of the alleged authority as authoritatively binding and tries to follow them, rather than by trying to follow the reasons which apply to him directly. (Raz 1986: 53)[19]

[18] Williams' slogan was "Obligation out, obligation in." One way of putting the thesis that moral obligation must be understood in terms of second-personal reasons is to say that the formulation in the text is not just a paraphrase of Williams' slogan, but that the point it formulates is the genus of which that formulated by Williams' slogan is a species.

[19] We should note that Raz says here that this is the "normal way" to establish authority, not that it is a necessary, or even a sufficient condition. Since the normal justification thesis poses a critical

Now the reasons that already apply to an "alleged subject" independently of the second-personal reasons putatively generated by some *specific* alleged authority may themselves be partly second-personal, since they may be conceptually related to claims and demands of some other authority. This will turn out to be important if reasons of moral obligation are themselves second-personal in the way I have claimed. Of course, if the normal justification thesis is correct, then it may be possible to establish every authority, including whatever authority we have as equal members of the moral community, by reference to independently existing reasons. So it may be true that whatever standing we have to hold one another answerable for moral demands, like any other practical authority, can be accounted for by virtue of its being the case that we would do better, were we to accept this authority, at complying with reasons that apply to us independently of this authority. If, however, we can account for all practical authority by the normal justification thesis, then it would seem to follow that practical authority and the other notions that are conceptually related to it, although second-personal on their face, are not irreducibly second-personal.

Meeting the standards of the normal justification thesis is not, however, sufficient to establish practical authority. There are cases where one person might very well do better to follow someone else's directives where it seems clear that the latter has no claim whatsoever on the former's will and actions and consequently no practical authority with respect to him. And cases where an "alleged subject" would do better in complying with independent reasons where genuine authority *does* seem to be involved all also seem to involve some assumed background accountability relation that gives the authority's directives standing as second-personal reasons. In these cases, it is the latter that establishes the directives' authority, not the former.

It is worth pointing out that much of what Raz says about practical authority in *The Morality of Freedom* aside from the *normal justification thesis* seems well attuned to practical authority's second-personal character. First, Raz notes that authority of this kind is different, not only from power and coercive threats, but also from *justified* power and coercion. One does not exercise authority over "people afflicted with dangerous diseases," Raz notes, "if [one] knock[s] them out and locks them up to

challenge to my irreducibility claims only if it is taken as providing a sufficient condition, that is how I propose to understand it.

protect the public" even if one "is justified in doing so" (Raz 1986: 25). Such a justified use of coercion would miss, Raz says, an essential element of any exercise of authority purporting to give the person over whom it is exercised a distinctive reason to comply, namely, "an appeal for compliance" and "an invocation of the duty to obey" (1986: 25–26). This seems exactly right. Any such appeal would be an instance of what I am calling second-personal address. It would be an appeal *to* the alleged subjects to recognize the alleged authority and comply therefore with directives that are authorized by it. Moreover, someone can credibly make such an appeal only if he can expect his alleged subject to accept that the subject has some duty or obligation to follow his directives. Without such a duty or obligation in place, which an alleged authority cannot of course create by his own directives, no genuine authority exists.

Second, Raz makes an important distinction between the kind of authority that can give one new reasons for *belief*, including beliefs about what there is reason to do, on the one hand, and genuinely "practical authority" (as he also calls it), which can give one reasons for *acting* that one did not previously have, on the other. Raz rightly rejects a "recognitional conception" of practical authority according to which an authority gives agents no new reasons for acting, just new reasons to believe what reasons for acting they already have. Applying the "recognitional conception" to authority *überhaupt* gives rise to what Raz calls the "no difference thesis": "the view that authority does not change people's reasons for acting" (Raz 1986: 30). Raz points out that one way of seeing that the recognitional conception and no difference thesis cannot be correct is to reflect on the role that practical authority can play in solving coordination problems. There are cases where it is important for everyone to coordinate on one of two options that, so far as antecedently applicable reasons go, are equally choiceworthy. It's fine if everyone drives on the right, or on the left, but everyone had better coordinate on one side or the other. "A wise man," Raz notes, "can tell me which options belong" to a set of optimal choices, "but he cannot tell me which option to choose before it is known what others will do" (Raz 1986: 30). This is, of course, correct. Raz rightly distinguishes between *practical* authority and the kind of authority that a trusted advisor can have in directing us to independently choiceworthy options. There is, as Hobbes famously noted, a distinction between "counsel" and "law" or "command" (Hobbes 1651: XIV.1). Genuine practical authority can give those who are subject to it new reasons for acting by addressing valid claims or demands to those subjects. As I would put it, the relevant reasons are second-personal reasons; their validity depends on the alleged authority's actually having the authority he presupposes when he addresses the demand (or "appeal") for compliance.

Nonetheless, one might still think that what grounds practical authority and so makes it the case that someone can give reasons of this distinctive, second-personal kind are further reasons that are not themselves second-personal. This brings us back to the *normal justification thesis*. The basic idea, again, is that someone earns practical authority with respect to another person if the latter would do better in complying with already applicable reasons were she to accept the former's directives "as authoritatively binding and tr[y] to act on them" than she would if she did not and tried to act on her own assessment of reasons. There is, however, a problem we face right at the outset in interpreting the normal justification thesis. What is it to accept someone's "directives as authoritatively binding"?

If we understand such acceptance to be accepting a directive as a valid demand in the second-personal sense I have been pointing to, then the alleged subject's own normative thought must then be interpreted in second-personal terms. In particular, we must suppose that she not only takes herself to have a reason of whatever weight or priority (exclusionary or preemptive, say), but that she also sees herself as *responsible* for compliance – that is, as answerable to the alleged authority. We must suppose that she, at least, takes it that the fact that she is thus responsible is in itself a reason for her to comply of this distinctively second-personal kind. But if this is so, then a version of Strawson's "wrong kind of reason" problem will arise from her perspective. Just as the fact that there might be desirable effects of treating people as responsible and their actions as culpable is a reason "of the wrong sort" for practices of holding people responsible "as we understand them," so also will the fact that an alleged subject would do better in complying with independently applicable reasons seem to her to be a reason of the wrong kind to think that she really is responsible for complying with some (alleged) authority's directives and therefore that his putative practical authority is genuine.

If this is right, then the beneficial effects of the subject's acceptance of an alleged authority may themselves be hostage to the subject's not also accepting the normal justification thesis herself, since the putative authority she accepts may then be susceptible, from her perspective at least, to, as Mill might put it, "the dissolving force of [the] analysis" that the normal justification thesis purports to provide.[20] Were she to think that the only legitimacy the "alleged authority" can claim is that she would do better if she were to accept it, then this may tend to undermine her acceptance of it, and so its beneficial effects.

It seems more accurate to Raz's idea, however, to suppose that by accepting an alleged authority's "directives as authoritatively binding," Raz means nothing essentially second-personal, but simply that the alleged subject takes the authority's directives as preemptive reasons – that is, reasons that are "not to be added to all other relevant reasons when assessing what to do," but that "exclude and take the place of [at least] some of them" (Raz 1986: 46). Thus A acquires practical authority with respect to B if B would do better in actually complying with independently applicable reasons if B were to treat A's directives as preemptive reasons in this sense.

It is the preemptive character of the reasons that practical authority purports to create, according to Raz's analysis, that enables him to distinguish between genuinely practical authority and the kind of (epistemic) authority that a trusted advisor might have – that is, to make Hobbes' distinction between command and counsel. The only claim an advisor makes as such is on an advisee's beliefs about independently existing reasons and about what actions these reasons support, not on her will. "This is what I think you have good reason to do," an advisor might say, and add, "but I'm not for a moment telling or even asking you to do it," without canceling his advice or anything the advice implied. The improvements to the alleged subject's reason compliance that matter for the normal justification thesis are those that come, not from her being convinced by the alleged authority that there is sufficient independently existing reason to do as he suggests, but from her taking his instructions as *directives* that create *preemptive* reasons.[21]

20 The reference is to Mill in a different context: "But moral associations which are wholly of artificial creation, when intellectual culture goes on, yield by degrees to the dissolving force of analysis: and if the feeling of duty, when associated with utility, would appear equally arbitrary; if there were no leading department of our nature, no powerful class of sentiments, with which that association would harmonize, which would make us feel it congenial, and incline us not only to foster it in others (for which we have abundant interested motives), but also to cherish it in ourselves – if there were not, in short, a natural basis of sentiment for utilitarian morality, it might well happen that this association also, even after it had been implanted by education, might be analyzed away" (Mill 1968: chapter III, §9).

21 Raz does not consider what might be necessary for us actually to take (whether to judge or in some less reflective way regard) someone's directives as giving rise to preemptive reasons. In my view, however, there is a problem here that is similar to the problem we set aside before of how it is possible to regard someone as having genuine authority if one holds the normal justification thesis. For, as I see it, the normal way of taking someone's directives to provide preemptive reasons is to

Now I take it that when Raz says that it is sufficient to establish that A has practical authority with respect to B if it can be shown that B would do better in complying with independently applicable reasons were B to accept A's directives as creating preemptive reasons, he means this to entail also that under such conditions A's directives actually do create such preemptive reasons. It is important to see, however, that these two theses can be distinguished. In fact, all three of the following theses are different:

(I) If B would do better in complying with independently existing reasons were B to treat A's directives as preemptive reasons, then B has sufficient reason so to treat A's directives.
(II) If B would do better in complying with independently existing reasons were B to treat A's directives as preemptive reasons, then A's directives actually are such preemptive reasons for B.
(III) If B would do better in complying with independently existing reasons were B to treat A's directives as preemptive reasons, then A has authority with respect to B. (Normal justification thesis.)

It seems obvious that one could accept (I) without accepting (II) and accept both (I) and (II) without accepting (III). Indeed, one could accept (I) and (II) without accepting the normal justification thesis even if one thought that A's having authority with respect to B entails that A's directives are preemptive reasons.

For our purposes, however, we can simply put aside any reservations we might have about (I) and (II) and simply stipulate that both are true.[22] Our question will still remain, namely, whether the satisfaction of the conditions of the normal justification thesis establishes, not just that the directives of an alleged authority should be taken as preemptive reasons or even that they are preemptive reasons in fact, but the alleged authority is genuine.[23]

take it that he has practical authority in the second-personal sense I have been pointing to, namely, that one has an obligation to comply with his directives and is responsible to him for doing so. In other words, normally one must have authority to be able to give someone preemptive reasons by issuing a directive, and someone must normally regard one as having authority over them to take themselves be given preemptive reason to comply with one's directives. I propose to set this problem aside also.

22 For the record, however, I might say that (II) seems to me almost certainly false. As I see it, the kinds of case where preemptive reasons are most plausibly in play are those that depend on the existence of (second-personal) practical authority.

23 Of course, Raz might hold that A's having authority over B is no more and no less than that A's directives to B give B preemptive reasons. I consider this possibility below.

There seem to be clear cases, however, some that Raz himself considers, where it is hard to see how the normal justification thesis could possibly hold. Raz asks us to imagine that "John is an expert on Chinese Cooking" and that if one wants nothing but "to prepare the best Chinese meal [one] can [one] should just follow John's instructions" (1986: 64). Let us stipulate also that one has no reason to do anything other than prepare the best Chinese meal and therefore, following from our acceptance of (II) above, that John's instructions provide preemptive reasons. The question remains, does John thereby acquire any practical authority over one? It is hard to see how he does. Of course, one would be foolish not to follow his instructions, but if one didn't it is difficult to see why John would have any standing to complain or otherwise hold one to account. Raz says that those with practical authority "have the right to replace people's own judgment on the merits of the case." But what *right* could John have in such a case? Or recall Raz's remark that, unlike merely justified coercion, genuine practical authority involves "an appeal for compliance" and "an invocation of the duty to obey" (1986: 25–26). How, in such a case, could John warrantedly expect that one would have any obligation to follow his instructions, however foolish one might be not to do so? It follows from our stipulations that John's instructions are not mere advice; they provide preemptive reasons. But it is hard to see how that gives John any right to our compliance with his directives or us any obligation to comply with them.

Raz's position about cases of this kind is somewhat equivocal. He grants that we would not ordinarily think that John would have any authority "over" one even if one's Chinese cooking would "prosper" by following his instructions, but points out that one can accept the normal justification thesis and still resist that John has such authority because one might think one would enjoy self-directed Chinese cooking more or have other goals. No doubt, but we can simply stipulate that one has no reason to do anything other than prepare the best Chinese meal, and it still doesn't seem to be the case that John has genuine practical authority as the normal justification thesis requires (1986: 64–65).

However, what if the reasons with which one would better comply themselves concern moral obligations? In such a case, an alleged authority would more plausibly appeal to an obligation to do as he directs. If the only way we can adequately comply with our moral obligations is to treat an alleged authority's directives as preemptive reasons, then there seems to be a sense in which it is plausible to suppose that we would be under an obligation so to treat them. Even so, it wouldn't follow from this that the alleged authority himself thereby acquires any authority (beyond any he might have had already) to hold others to moral demands. After all, treating some appropriately programmed computer's "directives" as preemptive reasons *might* be no less effective, but neither the computer nor the programmer would thereby acquire any special practical authority by virtue of that.

Even if we could extend the scope of authority to an effective moral director by applying the normal justification thesis in such a case, this would still give us no reason to conclude that the second-personal appearances of practical authority can ultimately be explained away entirely by the normal justification thesis. The reason is that moral obligations provide second-personal reasons themselves. Moral obligations are what is warrantedly demanded of us, what we can warrantedly be held to. In the kind of case we are imagining, it is, at best, as if the alleged authority functions as a kind of representative who acquires any special authority he comes to have by virtue of the general authority to hold morally responsible. So even if the normal justification thesis tracks genuine practical authority in a case of this kind, it does so thanks to there being an assumed second-personal authority to hold people to moral demands in the background.

But suppose we attempt to explain the authority to hold people to moral demands itself by the normal justification thesis. If we try to do so based on improvements that would come in our compliance with reasons of other kinds then our moral philosophy will "rest on a mistake," in Prichard's famous dictum (Prichard 2002). Reasons of other sorts are reasons of the wrong kind for distinctively moral authority. But what if we say that moral authority derives from improvements that accepting it would make in our compliance with moral obligations themselves? How then are we to specify our moral obligations? If Mill and I are right, there is no way adequately to characterize what it is to be morally obligatory that does not already involve the authority to hold morally responsible. So we can't explain moral authority itself by the normal justification thesis by claiming that we will do better in complying with moral obligations if we accept that authority, since nothing will count as a moral obligation unless there is already such a thing as the authority to hold morally responsible. I need not assume, of course, that it is impossible to designate moral obligations extensionally in non-second-personal terms, for example, with some list like: acts of kind A in circumstances of kind $C_1$, of kind B in circumstances of kind $C_2$, and so on. The point will nonetheless remain that the mere fact that we will do better in performing acts on the list is impotent by itself to explain the authority to hold morally responsible, since an act's being morally obligatory, and so on the list, is not itself independent of the authority to hold morally responsible and make demands of one another.

Suppose, however, that Raz were to eschew talk of obligation in this sense "all the way down," and simply take the position that all he really means by a duty of obedience is that there are preemptive reasons for following an alleged authority's directives. Similarly, he might hold that the latter is all that it is for someone to have practical authority in the sense in which he has in mind. If we interpret the normal justification thesis as applying to practical authority defined in this way, it seems much more plausible. But it should be clear that practical authority so defined is not a thesis that entails anything about any *right* to obedience or about any *obligation* to obey, at least as we ordinarily understand rights and obligations. So understood, the normal justification thesis is simply a thesis about preemptive reasons. But if that is so, then it is not even relevant to the question of whether second-personal authority, demands, reasons, and responsibility, in the sense that I have delimited, can ultimately be accounted for in terms of considerations that are not themselves second-personal.[24]

My conclusion is that the normal justification thesis poses no serious challenge to my claim that the four notions I have identified constitute a circle of interdefinable, irreducibly second-personal concepts. If we interpret the thesis as concerning practical authority, understood in second-personal terms, then it is either implausible or, in cases where it seems not to be, it borrows plausibility from the implicitly second-personal character of the reasons on which the alleged authority's directives are based (as when she directs us to comply with our moral obligations). And if we interpret the thesis otherwise, it just becomes a thesis about preemptive reasons for acting and so has no direct relevance to the possibility of grounding or otherwise explaining second-personal authority in non-second-personal terms.

Of course, even if the concepts of practical authority, valid demand, second-personal reason, and responsibility *to* I am pointing to are irreducibly second-personal in the ways I am claiming, that doesn't entail that any of these concepts are instantiated – that is, that there are any second-personal reasons, is any second-personal authority, and so on. So we

[24] And it may also be the case, as I mentioned above, that preemptive reasons themselves normally plausibly exist only when there has been a directive of a certain kind with genuine (second-personal) practical authority.

might regard a position like Raz's as a kind of skepticism about practical authority of the kind I am pointing to and as offering a "reforming definition" in the style of Stevenson or Brandt in terms of preemptive reasons. I cannot, of course, establish here that the unreformed second-personal ideas I have described are anything other than what Kant calls "figment[s] of the mind."[25] However, if what I have said here is correct, it will follow that if these ideas are mere figments, then so are the ideas of moral right, responsibility, and obligation and, indeed, the very concept of moral agent or person itself.

[25] At the end of chapter II of the *Groundwork* (Kant 1785), Kant points out that his arguments that autonomy of the will, the unqualified goodness of the good will, and the CI are mutually entailing has derived from an analysis of our moral concepts, and that nothing yet follows from this about whether any of these are actually realized or valid. That, he says, requires a "critique" of practical reason, to which Kant turns in the *Groundwork* III and, of course, *The Critique of Practical Reason* (Kant 1996). I attempt to vindicate these ideas in Darwall (2006).

CHAPTER 8

# *Promises, reasons, and normative powers**

*Gary Watson*

## I PROMISES AND NORMATIVE POWERS

Making a promise makes a normative difference. What difference does it make and how does it make it?[1] I regard promissory obligations as upshots of the exercise of "normative powers," powers to create or rescind practical requirements at will.[2] Specifically, as Joseph Raz says, "To promise is . . . to communicate an intention to undertake by the very act of communication an obligation to perform a certain action."[3] (Raz calls obligations created in this way "voluntary obligations.") In this manner, you establish a new normative relationship with others by, among other things, transferring authority to others to hold you to a particular performance.[4] The result is a voluntary restriction of the range of actions you would otherwise be entitled to perform.

* I indebted to many readers and audiences for helpful comments on and discussion of various versions of this chapter. I owe special thanks to William Bracken, Don Hubin, Olli Koistinen, Niko Kolodny, Olli Lagerspetz, Coleen Macnamara, Christopher McMahan, Glen Pettigrove, Andy Reath, Geoff Sayre-McCord, Neal Tognazzini, Jay Wallace, and Susan Wolf. David Sobel and Steven Wall have been especially helpful. In writing this essay, I have benefited from research support from the Department of Philosophy and the College of Humanities, Arts, and Social Sciences of the University of California at Riverside.

1 Whether that difference is necessarily a *moral* difference is something I explore below.

2 Promissory powers are of course just one type of normative power, which Raz defines generically and provisionally as "the power to effect a normative change." See Raz (1990): 99. Raz's final formulation is more complex in ways that needn't detain us here. For a more recent advocacy of a normative powers view, see Owens (2006).

3 Raz (1977): 218. (Since lying promises are possible, we must allow for "communicating an intention" one does not have.) See also Raz (1986): 173, Raz (1972).

4 Raz asserts a general conceptual tie between authority and normative powers: "A person has authority to the extent that he has power to affect norms", Raz (1972): 96. The linkage of promising with norms of authority is familiar. Cf. also H.L.A. Hart: the promisee comes to have a "temporary authority or sovereignty in relation to some specific matter over the other's will." See Hart (1955), as reprinted in *Contemporary Political Philosophy*, ed. Robert Goodin and Philip Pettit (Oxford: Blackwell, 2006): 323.

This transaction affects what you have reason to do. Some of the reasons that promising creates are "content-independent," as Raz puts it; they depend in part on how they came to be, rather than on the independent desirability of the performance in question. (This is characteristic of all reasons of authority.) Your reason to return the book to me by Friday, for example, is primarily that you "engaged" with me to return it by then, quite apart from the quite different consideration that I might be in need of the book then (a reason you might well have to return the book to someone to whom you don't owe its return).

The conception of promising as an exercise of normative powers is not an account of its normative basis but a specification of what it *is*. Nevertheless, this conception constrains the shape of the relevant normative explanations. For example, if the normative power view is correct, as it seems to me to be, promising gives rise to obligations because it is the undertaking of a commitment to another, not because (as some would have it) the communication of one's intentions creates expectations in the promisee.[5] In my view, expectations enter the picture in a different way. No doubt, the gravity of promise-keeping is affected by the extent to which others come to rely on our word. Furthermore, the importance of being able to rely on one another – of establishing reliable mutual expectations – is, I would argue, part of the account of the grounds of the authority to bind ourselves in this way. I'll return to the question of grounds below.

### *The Structure and Content of Promissory Transactions*

Our promissory transactions create special relationships with one another. These transactions involve distinct elements. Promissory acts might or might not give rise to promissory obligations. When they successfully do so, we can say that a complete promissory transaction has transpired. A promissory act can occur without a promissory obligation if there is no (complete) "uptake," to use Judith Thomson's useful term.[6] Uptake requires both reception and acceptance of the promissory proposal. You haven't "received" the promise if you didn't hear me, for example, or didn't understand what I said. Reception means understanding the utterance as what it is: as the communication of an intention to undertake an

[5] For a sophisticated account of the expectation view, see Scanlon (1998). See also "Promises and Contracts," in Scanlon (2003). All subsequent references to Scanlon in the text are to the former work.

[6] Thomson (1990). All references in the text hereafter are to this work.

obligation of a certain sort. But you can receive a promise without accepting what it proposes.

With Thomson and others,[7] I assume here that a successful promise (a complete promissory transaction) requires acceptance. (What acceptance amounts to is a complicated question.) Without acceptance, there is no deal. A promissory transaction entitles the promisee to demand performance from the promiser. As Thomson insightfully observes, however, once received, the promissory act or proposal already makes a normative difference, whether or not it is accepted; it alters "the world in such a way that uptake [i.e. acceptance] by the promisee makes the promisee have a claim." What the promiser makes normatively possible by a promissory act is that the recipient acquires a claim against the promiser by accepting the proposal (Thomson 1990: 302). To accept the promise is to accept the claim. Hence, a promissory transaction involves exercises of normative powers by both parties to the transaction.

## II SKEPTICISM ABOUT NORMATIVE POWERS

Social life turns on such transactions as these and on the exercise of a vast variety of other normative powers as well. And yet the idea that normative relations can be direct products of (the communication of) volition is somewhat bewildering. Hume declared the process by which a "new obligation arises from [one's] will" to be "one of the most mysterious and incomprehensible operations that can possibly be imagined."[8] He likened these "operations" to "*transubstantiation*, or *holy orders*, where a certain form of words, along with a certain intention, changes entirely the nature of that external object, and even of a human creature" (Hume 1978: 1740 524). Unlike the "priestly inventions" of "holy orders," however, Hume found the mumbo jumbo of promising to be profoundly salutary, so much so that he took promissory obligation to be one of the three "fundamental laws of nature . . . on the strict observance of [which] . . . the peace and security of human society entirely depend."[9]

[7] The need for uptake is widely endorsed, though what it involves is disputed. See Reid (1788): essay V, chapter VI; Melden (1977); Fried (1981); von Wright (1983); Gilbert (2000). For doubts about an acceptance condition, see Downie (1985) and Atiyah (1981).

[8] Hume (1978): 524.

[9] Hume (1978): 526. This is of course the basis of Hume's defense of the validity of the norm that promises are to be kept. Does Hume think this constitutes a defense of the existence of the relevant powers, or rather (in contrast to the religious case) does he think it is only a defense of the immense utility of the *fiction* that such powers exist? I leave this interpretive question open. When I refer to

Hume's puzzles are partly due to the particulars of his moral theory. But even those who question Hume's meta-ethics have found it easy to work themselves into a state of perplexity about this phenomenon. How can one simply, at will, create a reason for oneself or another to act? It is as though promising were tantamount to this: "I hereby give myself a reason to go to Minsk" or "I hereby give you a reason to count on my going to Minsk." If we suppose that the power to obligate oneself is simply inherent in the will, then there would seem to be no normative limits to the obligations we could create. Nothing would stop me from giving myself reasons to do anything, however pointless or pernicious. This seems to speak against the coherence of normative powers.

Here's the heart of the puzzle. To be real, reasons must constrain and guide the will[10] (insofar as we are rational); otherwise there is no normative reality to which the will must answer. If it were sufficient for having a reason to x merely to decide that one has a reason to x, then having or not having that reason would be no constraint at all. A real reason contrasts with mere caprice. To be sure, promising is not just a matter of legislating *in foro interno*. Promising is a partnership, as we've seen. Promissory reasons involve communicating your promissory intentions to another, with the right uptake. If there is a puzzle about volitional reasons, however, it is hard to see how adding further wills to the transaction could help.[11]

### *Reasons and Moral Requirements*

The foregoing diagnosis is hasty in two ways, though. First, it is not true that simply deciding to go to Minsk makes no normative difference by itself. As John Broome has reminded us, we must not confuse being under a normative requirement to *x* with having a reason to *x*.[12] By intending to go to Minsk, you will be under the norm to take what you believe to be the necessary steps to getting there, and to adjust your intentions accordingly. It doesn't follow that your intention gives you the least reason to do any of this, for you can satisfy the requirement by changing your ends,

Humean skepticism below, I mean skepticism arising from the doubts that Hume articulates. I am neither assuming nor denying here that Hume himself was a skeptic on this matter.

10 This thought comes from Raz (1986). "We cannot create reasons just by intending to do so and expressing that intention in action. Reasons precede the will" (1986: 84).

11 The activity of obligating oneself at will has seemed to some to have a suspicious "bootstrapping" quality. For the classical statement of worries about bootstrapping reasons from intentions, see Bratman (1987). Fried discusses the "bootstrap quality" of promissory obligation in particular in Fried (1978): 11–12. I return to the issue of bootstrapping later on.

12 See, among other papers, Broome (2004). See also Scanlon (2004).

which perhaps you ought to do instead. You have a reason either to do what it takes to get to Minsk or to give up your intention.[13] So Hume seems right to suggest that willing cannot itself be an ultimate source of reasons to act as willed, but he would be wrong to say that willing is normatively impotent. You can, by your will, place yourself under a kind of normative requirement that does not itself depend on your will.

Suppose you had good reason to go to Minsk and equally good reason to go to Pinsk. You settle on Minsk. Having done so, it rationally behooves you to follow through or to change your mind. Decisions are defeasibly reason-creating, and here the reason has not been defeated by lack of a reason to do what is intended. Thus, if you don't change your mind, you now have reason to board the train to Minsk rather than the one to Pinsk (assuming the train is the feasible mode of travel). In this way you have voluntarily reconfigured your deliberative circumstances. There is nothing mysterious in this.[14]

A second way in which the skeptical challenge was hasty is that promissory reasons contrast with decision- or intention-based reasons in not being rescindable at will. So it is not true that, on the normative power conception, promissory reasons fail to be real reasons because they couldn't constrain or guide the will. Such reasons originate in the will, on that conception, but their persistence is not at the discretion of the promiser. For (unlike mere intention), it is precisely that discretion that is relinquished in the promissory transaction. Promising puts one under a normative requirement both to *x* and not to change one's mind about *x*ing unless authorized to do so by the promisee. The requirement binds the will to another. Thus, "I have a reason to go to Minsk because I have given myself a reason to go to Minsk," seems to be a bogus answer to the question, "What reason do I have to go to Minsk?" But "I have a reason to go to Minsk because I have committed myself to you to go to Minsk" seems *prima facie* justificatory.

The interpersonal or second-personal nature of promising figures into the answer to skepticism after all; it deflects the worry that arises about intentions, that the practical commitments could not be real rational

[13] Cf. Gilbert: "Suppose I decide to do A at some later time, and then at that later time I do not feel like doing A. Suppose I do not rescind my decision. Then, all else being equal, reason requires that I do A" (Gilbert 2000: 52). I take this to mean: reason requires that (I rescind my decision or do A).

[14] Neal Tognazzini has suggested to me that what bothers skeptics about promises is that, unlike decisions, their very point is to constrain practical reason. Perhaps many simple episodic decisions are not made in order to alter one's normative situation. But, as Bratman and others have argued, decisions for "planning creatures" like us very often aim to determine what will count as deliberatively relevant (what to "treat as a reason").

constraints because they would be rescindable at will. This reply to skepticism doesn't go to the heart of the matter, however, since we still want an account of how reasons or obligations can arise from the wills of the consenting parties in the first place.

### *The variety and pervasiveness of normative powers*

Here it is important to bear in mind the great variety of normative powers. For instance, in addition to promising, there are:

| | |
|---|---|
| *Gifts* | When I give you a book, for instance, I voluntarily transfer to you my entitlement to use the book, relinquishing certain claims. My handing you the book gives rise to new reasons which typically have binding force. |
| *Permissions* | I permit you (or refuse to permit you) to keep your bike in my garage, to sit on my lap, to read my diary, or to teach my children. |
| *Orders* | I order you to leave my house or to clean up your room. I assign you a three-page essay on Hume's account of promising. My exercising the relevant authority can voluntarily change various normative relations. |

What all normative powers have in common is that their successful exercise puts certain parties under norms of practical reason in one way or another. Whether, beyond this, there is an illuminating characterization that unifies this variety, I will not venture to say. Some of the powers on this list (which is of course no more than a sample) depend on our particular positions in social and legal practices, but others, as I argue below, come with an authority that is integral to our basic moral status. All are embedded in contexts of dense social understandings.

Since promissory powers are only some among many types of volitional power, it is very curious that promising has been the main target of skepticism. If promising involves magic, then moral (or normative) transubstantiation appears to be rampant.

## III CONSTRAINTS ON NORMATIVE EXPLANATIONS OF PROMISSORY OBLIGATIONS

The pervasiveness of volitional powers shows how deep and wide skepticism would cut. To dispel the appearance of magic, it would seem, we must provide some sort of grounding for promissory (and related normative) powers. And yet on the normative power conception, that project seems either impossible or unnecessary. Having answered the question how promising obligates – namely by voluntary undertaking – there would seem to be no room for any further normative inquiry (apart from questions of casuistry). It is hard not to sympathize with Thomson's observation that

> There is nothing deeper that either needs to be or can be said about how word-givings generally and promisings in particular generate claims. Their moral force lies in their generating claims; and the fact that they do generate claims is explained by the fact that issuing an invitation is offering to bind oneself, so that when the invitation is accepted, the offer is accepted, and one therefore *is* bound. (Thomson 1990: 303)

Promising binds simply because one's offer has been accepted. That's what offering and accepting *are*. "[T]he relations between promising and obligations are internal," as John Searle puts it. "By definition a promise is an act of undertaking an obligation."[15] The definitional thesis would seem to leave no room for a normative explanation of promissory requirements.

I don't think we can rest content with this definitional stop, however. The target of skepticism is not the definition but the reality of the definiendum. The challenge is to understand, among other things, how promissory powers accord with our understanding of practical reason and with rational and moral agency in general. It is no accident that promising and the like are bound up with human interests in deep ways. How does the power to enter promissory transactions figure in our account of what matters in human life? Why is fidelity a central virtue? Some kind of normative story is called for here.

Consider again the authority of parents (or adults generally) over children. Parental authority is (by definition, if you like) the power, within limits, to control the lives of children, including the authority to use force in certain circumstances. It wouldn't do simply to say, "That's what parental authority *is*, among other things: the power to lay down rules, to issue commands and prohibitions to and regarding the children. Once you know what such authority is, there is no further question about the legitimacy of the rules that issue from such authority." This would be unsatisfactory, not only because there are natural skeptical reactions to the existence of this authority, but because we want to understand how we have it and why its possession and the social relations that it enables have

[15] Searle (2001): 197.

the importance we give them. The questions about promissory power are similar. A demystifying account of promissory (and related normative) powers would have to provide a constructive answer to these questions.

### *Two constraints on normative accounts of promising*

Any satisfactory explanation, I would argue, must meet two constraints. The first one is suggested by Joseph Raz. The will can create reasons, he thinks, "only when there is a non-will-based reason why it should."[16] We seek a rationale of the form, "The communication of promissory intentions gives rise to morally valid requirements because . . .," where the considerations that we cite in our general story will not themselves be the product of normative powers. Otherwise we will have relocated the mystery to a higher level.

Consider the familiar attempt to explain why the type of authority involved in promissory (and other normative) performances is legitimate by invoking the beneficial coordinational effects of "social practices." This is an example of a kind of two-stage theory that would meet Raz's constraint.[17] The appeal to these benefits satisfies this constraint because the value of coordination itself is not dependent on the will. Moreover, it would accommodate the evident connections of promising with human interests in a straightforward way.

However, the evident shortcomings of this appeal as it stands reveal the need for a second constraint. For plainly the emphasis on the benefits of these practices is itself perfectly consistent with skepticism about volitional reasons. Humean skeptics eagerly underscore these commonplaces in their explanation of why the *abracadabra* of promising is so crucial to social life. The belief in normative powers, they think, is a necessary and wholesome illusion. Thus, a *second constraint* on a constructive response to skepticism is that the account of what matters must give grounds to think that the belief in normative powers is not only useful or otherwise desirable but true.[18] An explanation that meets these constraints would be an

[16] Raz (1986): 84.

[17] Raz does not himself accept this specific view. He plausibly says that normative powers "can only be justified if the creation of such special relationships between people is held to be valuable" (Raz 1977: 228). The sort of value Raz has in mind is not only instrumental. It includes the value of establishing and standing in promissory relationships.

[18] In general, many versions of two-tier consequentialism tend to be consistent with skepticism about the practical reasons they are meant to explain. That's their chief drawback. (I discuss these matters

explanation that articulated reasons why individuals have the authority to decide to some extent what normative requirements they are subject to.

Another influential two-stage account is given by John Rawls, who tries to derive a principle of fidelity from a principle regarding participation in fair and beneficial practice.[19] This theory might well meet the two constraints, but critics have rightly recoiled from the thesis that the wrongness of promise-breaking consists in its unfairness.[20] In my view, we should also question the claim that the existence of "a number of persons engag[ing] in a mutually advantageous cooperative venture according to certain rules" is normatively or conceptually required for such promissory transactions to transpire.[21]

Scanlon has put forward an alternative two-stage account. This version is worth emphasizing here precisely because it tries to do without both Rawls'-style social practices and normative powers.[22] Scanlon's aim is to capture promissory obligations by various general principles concerning the creation of expectations in others, principles that are defensible in contractualist terms – that is, principles that no one who is seeking a common basis for living together could reasonably reject.[23]

In my view, the attempt to bypass normative powers by appealing to the creation of expectations will not work. If others come to rely on or to expect your performance as a consequence of your promising, their expectations or reliance standardly depends on their belief that by promising you have thereby obligated yourself to them to perform as promised. In that case, the creation of expectations or reliance is explained by the belief in an antecedent obligation and cannot explain that belief.[24] The expectations are parasitic on the (belief in) normative powers.

in Watson (1998). This problem is an instance of what Darwall calls the "wrong kind of reason" problem. See Darwall (2006), and chapter 7 in this volume.

19 Rawls (1971): 342–350.

20 The worry about fairness was articulated by Melden (1977) and more recently by Scanlon (1998). A corollary, I think, is that fairness views leave out, in Darwall's terms, the second-personal feature of promissory obligation (Darwall 2006). For a partial defense of the social practice view, in the form of a "hybrid theory," see Kolodny and Wallace (2003). For a discussion of the hybrid theory, see Tognazzini (2007).

21 Rawls (1971). Scanlon has forcefully challenged this claim in his work on promising. Raz (1972) is also skeptical about the appeal to practices.

22 The relation of Scanlon's account to the normative power conception is subtle. See Scanlon (1998): 306–309 and (for the contrast with Raz) 403, n. 2.

23 For a very helpful discussions of Scanlon's expectation account, see Kolodny and Wallace (2003); Pratt (2003); Gilbert (2004); Owens (2006); Tognazzini (2007).

24 Here I follow Kolodny and Wallace (2003) and also Pratt (2003). Scanlon is well aware of the worry about circularity and proposes an ingenious solution – see Scanlon (1998): 306–309. For further discussion, see Tognazzini (2007).

We shouldn't misconstrue, then, the undeniable importance of the fact that promising plays a crucial function in coordinating behavior by stabilizing and underwriting expectations. For the expectations in question are expectations that people will (for the most part) act as they have obligated themselves to do; they do not ground those obligations. Expectation views raise a problem of circularity because they put things the wrong way around.

A more attractive contractualist account of promising would, in my view, incorporate rather than bypass promissory powers. We should think of contractualism, of the kind Scanlon has articulated, as identifying not only requirements and prohibitions, but powers. The idea is that, in virtue of various interests and values, no one could reasonably reject a principle that conferred the power to bind one's will in this way. I would stress (with Raz) that the source of this authorization is not only the value of assurance to the promisee (the value of being assured), but also the value of being in a position to bind oneself by making assurances. As I'll explain below, this value is not merely instrumental but integral to our conception of our moral standing. The significance of expectations, coordination, the value of assurance, as well as the interest in forging mutual commitments, would be registered in the standpoint of reasonable rejection. In this way, promise-making and promise-keeping turn out to answer to deep human needs, just as we understand them to do.[25]

Specific non-promissory normative powers are grounded in the same way. For example, no one could reasonably reject principles that established roles whose occupants (say, teachers, or parents) have certain powers to issue authoritative orders, thereby putting others under certain requirements, or reasonably reject principles that provide for ownership and transfer rights to certain goods. Or so it can be plausibly argued.

The contractualist approach just sketched seems to accommodate normative powers rather nicely. Moreover, it does so in a way that satisfies the second constraint we identified earlier. In contrast to second-level consequentialist accounts, contractualism of this kind gives us reason to affirm not only the desirability of belief in promissory (and other) powers, but their existence. For according to contractualism, the possession of these powers is authorized by principles that no one could reasonably reject as a basis for living together. It follows that our belief in their existence is not only

[25] Unsurprisingly, contract law has the same rationale: "to enable individuals to give effect to their wishes to create structures of legal rights and duties, and so to change, in certain ways, their legal position" (Hart 1968: 10).

fortunate but true. It is not just useful to believe or pretend that it is so; by communicating to you my intentions to that effect, I really do make it true that I am obligated to you to tend your garden while you are away. There is a question, though, whether this version of the contractualist account properly satisfies the first constraint. I turn to this question now.

## IV NORMATIVE POWERS AND MORAL STANDING

I suggested before that the values at stake in the possession of normative powers are not entirely instrumental; some are integral to how we think of our moral standing. This point reveals the impossibility of grounding normative powers in general in contractualist theory. Here's what I have in mind.

To (successfully) exercise promissory power is to authorize others to hold you to demands to which you would not otherwise be subject. This power presupposes a general freedom to affect by your consent what others may claim of you.[26] This power of self-determination is crucial to how we understand our status as moral agents. To acknowledge this status is to recognize a moral title to limit the ways in which we may interfere with others' agency, a title to a sphere in which we each have a decisive say-so regarding how others are to treat us.[27] That title is itself a normative power (or bundle of powers). We are under a moral requirement not to do certain things without others' authorization. That I can't limit your freedom in certain ways without your consent goes with the idea that I *can*, normally, limit your freedom *with* your consent. By consent, we expand or delimit our shared normative boundaries. Promising is just one of the ways we exercise our say-so. In other words, promissory power is inherent in the kind of moral standing that we have in mind when we speak of ourselves as autonomous beings, a standing to determine what others may permissibly do.

This means that promissory obligations cannot be comprehended independently of a grasp of ourselves as standing in general moral relations. We should not imagine that normative powers could give rise, *de novo*, to claims among people who otherwise conceived themselves as

[26] The following reasoning is closely related to the argument in Hart (1955). Something similar is also argued in Melden (1977).

[27] This status is often associated with a concept of dignity or a kind of inviolable value. Darwall (2006) explicitly connects dignity with what he calls second-personal authority.

unencumbered by moral commitments.[28] Promissory transactions presuppose a moral standing of the parties that is independent of that transaction.[29] This is an alternative formulation of Raz's first constraint.

Now this kind of moral standing is foundational to Scanlon-style contractualism, according to which the value of "mutual recognition" "underlies our reasons to do what morality requires" (Scanlon 1998: 162). This value is precisely what is realized when we stand ready jointly to authorize the norms of our lives together. What matters most, from the moral point of view, is the attribution of the normative powers that such authorizing presumes.

Accordingly, the contractualist defense of promissory powers we sketched above depends on a notion of normative powers that is not itself derivable from any reflections upon what we could accept as a basis for sharing the world as free and equal rational beings. For this standard is just an expression of the value of mutual recognition, of our acknowledgment that the permissibility of our treatment of one another depends upon our standing to authorize that treatment. Mutual recognition involves, in other words, the acknowledgment of one another's normative powers. It follows that contractualism must presume rather than explain this possibility.[30]

Does this show that any contractualist explanation of promissory powers, such as the one sketched above, must run afoul of Raz's first constraint on normative accounts mentioned before? I think not. The first constraint requires that the values or principles invoked to explain normative powers not be themselves products of the exercise of normative powers. Although contractualism takes for granted the value (or principle) of mutual recognition, of our standing as self-determining beings, it does not hold that this value is itself a creation of the will, a product of normative powers. Given this recognition, contractualist reasoning shows[31] that no one could reasonably reject a principle that permitted us to exercise our powers in a promissory manner. In this limited way, it can

[28] Endorsing a point he attributes to Reid, Darwall writes: "It would be impossible . . . for us to make agreements, promises, and contracts, unless we already took ourselves to be accountable to one another and accorded each other the second-personal authority to undertake these distinctive obligations" (Darwall 2006: 198).

[29] As Ollie Lagerspetz puts it, in a commentary on an earlier draft of this essay, "promises are not a special case that requires an explanation separate from a general understanding of the moral life." For help in articulating the ideas in this section, I am much indebted to Lagerspetz's comments.

[30] This is not meant as a criticism of contractualism as such but only of certain explanatory ambitions that some contractualists might harbor.

[31] Or so I've conjectured. The case would have to be more closely argued.

explain why the communication of certain intentions gives rise to genuine obligations to one another. As for mutual recognition itself, that requires a different story, a story I am not now in a position to tell.

## V AUTONOMY ABOUT PROMISING

Recall the objection that if the normative power conception were correct, then, absurdly, one might, at will, give rise to reasons to do all manner of sinister or silly things. Here I attend to the worry about the sinister, leaving the silly for another occasion.[32] Obviously, this worry is linked to the topic we have just explored, the felt need for a normative account of promissory powers. For, among other things, we would expect such an account to indicate plausible constraints on promissory transactions. Even the limited story told by contractualism is somewhat helpful here. By reference to the generic concerns that define the standpoint of reasonable rejection, one general restriction on promissory power suggests itself at once: Any principle that authorized us to create obligations that violate principles that no one could reasonably reject could itself be reasonably rejected. To put the issue more generally, promissory powers aren't autonomous. They are checked by the moral standing of others, since those powers are grounded in the general normative authority in which that standing consists. Call this the "constrained normative power view."

However, some philosophers regard this attempt to situate promissory obligation in a general account of practical reason as misguided. Consider John Searle's claim (cited earlier) that the "relations between promising and obligations are internal."[33] Promises "are by definition creations of obligations," Searle adds; "and obligations are by definition reasons for action" (2001: 193). In his view, the pressure to look beyond promising itself to a larger story comes from an overly moralized view of the phenomenon. It is a mistake, Searle argues,

[32] The following example illustrates the issue about the silly. Suppose neither A nor B has any interest whatever in traveling to Minsk, and that this is mutual knowledge. It appears that on the normative power view, A can nonetheless incur an obligation to B to make this journey by B's acceptance of A's proposal to do so. The pointlessness of all this needn't prevent them from willing them. The worry is that A would now be bound to B to do something that matters to neither. It certainly would be silly to take any of this seriously. Indeed, it is hard to find this exchange intelligible as anything but a game. What are these people doing? Since normative powers are rationalized by mutual interests that A and B know not to be at stake in this case, it is no wonder that the exchange doesn't give rise to any real commitments.

[33] Searle (2001): 197. Page citations to Searle in the text are to this work.

> to suppose that if you promise to do something evil there is no obligation at all to keep the promise . . . [T]his is obviously wrong. The correct way to describe such cases is to say that you do indeed have an obligation to keep the promise but it is overridden by the evil nature of the promised act. This point can be proved by the method of agreement and difference: there is a difference between the person who has promised to do the act and the person who has not. The person who has made the promise has a reason that the person who has not made the promise does not have. (2001: 194)

*Is* this the correct way to describe such cases? Suppose that, in the course of carrying out a terrorist scheme, I promise you that I will kill the school children while you disable the telecommunication system. Keeping the promise is of course *morally* wrong, but, on Searle's view, the terrorist "has a reason that the person who has not made the promise does not have" (2001: 194). The idea must be that the reason to kill the children is simply swamped ("overridden") by moral considerations.

Call this the Autonomy Thesis. It holds that promissory obligations and their corresponding reasons and entitlements are unconstrained in their origin or existence by any other requirements or prohibitions of practical reason. According to the Autonomy Thesis, (1) "promises are by definition creations of obligations" and (2) "obligations are by definition reasons for action" (Searle 2001: 194). It follows that if we promise to do something iniquitous, as Searle thinks is possible, we thereby acquire reasons to act accordingly.

The Autonomy Thesis leaves it open whether the reasons and obligations necessarily created by promises are moral reasons and obligations. Searle thinks not. Let's assume that, according to this thesis, the obligations and reasons that are "by definition" created in promising need not be moral. If promissory obligations and reasons were inherently moral, the Autonomy Thesis would imply, absurdly, that I could make my actions less pernicious just by promising so to act. For then morality would have at least something to say in their favor. The non-moralized version of the thesis is not saddled with this absurdity. The Autonomy Thesis could then be combined with contractualism or any other account of the *moral* force of promissory obligations and reasons. What this thesis opposes is the idea that these obligations and reasons must answer to general practical norms. Instead, they are to be seen as arising from bare volitional commitment.

The non-moralized version seems to me equally incredible. The idea that in virtue of my terrorist undertaking, I now have *any* kind of reason (however massively "outweighed") to kill the children seems crazy. For then we could transform any otherwise insane project into something with some reason on its side.[34] Similarly, it is hard to credit the idea that my terrorist partner has acquired a legitimate claim – moral or not – to my performing as promised. For I have no standing to give anyone this authority.

The Autonomy Thesis is committed to a substantive and I think false normative position: that we have the power to make valid promissory commitments to anything whatever. I deny this. We should think of promissory transactions as defeasible, with moral requirements being among the defeating conditions. In the remaining sections, I shall speak in favor of this constrained normative power view. A full defense is much more than I can undertake here. My more limited purpose is to show at least that a normative power view need not be wedded to the Autonomy Thesis.

## VI SOME CONSTRAINTS ON PROMISSORY POWERS

Recall the distinction made earlier between promissory proposals and complete promissory transactions. When we speak of making a promise, we sometimes have in mind the promissory act itself, abstracted from the acceptance condition, and sometimes the complete promissory transaction. Undoubtedly, there are immoral promissory proposals. But on that construal of "making a promise," part (1) of the Autonomy Thesis,

(1) Promises are by definition creations of obligations

is false. The question is whether all that is required for a valid promissory transaction is the acceptance of the promissory proposal. Eventually I shall question part (2) of the Autonomy Thesis as well, namely,

(2) Obligations are by definition reasons for action

For now, I will concentrate on (1). I shall argue that even when the condition is met, and a transaction has transpired, normative constraints can invalidate the undertaking.

A natural initial response to the terrorist example is to reject my entitlement to promise such horrible things. The thought here is that my promissory proposal cannot have its intended normative effect unless I am entitled to make and keep the promise. Here again the analogy with

[34] This is just an extension of Bratman's original point about bootstrapping.

gift-giving is illuminating. In promising, we relinquish what we "own" in an important sense, and we can't give what we don't own.[35] Prior to promising, I am free to engage in any number of optional performances. By promising, I transfer my ownership of some alternatives, my entitlement to act within a certain range of options, thereby giving that power to others. Killing children does not lie within the range of options over which I have rightful control. Therefore I can no more transfer say-so with respect to that alternative than I can authorize you to take possession of a car I don't own. I lack the title to these things.

Suppose we both mistakenly think that I own a particular Porsche. I hand over the keys, saying "Happy Birthday; it's yours." Or I say "You're hired" to a hopeful job candidate, who happily accepts, though I have no authority to make appointments. Nonetheless, I haven't hired him or given you the car. The same goes for promising to hire him or to give you the Porsche. I lack the normative power to entitle you in these ways.[36] Just so, the norms forbidding me to murder render it impossible for me to give you a rightful claim to my doing so.

This conclusion is confirmed by other examples of normative powers in the same genus as that of promising, such as permitting or consenting. Out of self-hatred, you consent to be tortured by me. That gives me no title to treat you in that way, it seems to me. For I don't think it is in your power to transfer that right.[37]

[35] See Hart (1955): 323: "Rights are typically conceived of as *possessed* or *owned* or *belonging* to individuals . . . forming a kind of moral property of individuals to which they are as individuals entitled." Gilbert connects owing with owning in Gilbert (2006): 241.

[36] Of course, we might mutually understand the proposal to be that I will first acquire the car, thereby becoming entitled to give it to you. In that case, I might remain under an obligation to acquire the car. It seems to me a tricky matter to exhibit clearly the logical form of a commitment with this sort of structure (such as promising to hire you once I am boss). I am indebted to Neal Tognazzini for this possible interpretation of the example.

[37] Perhaps this is controversial. Some may insist that it would be wrong for me to brutalize you, despite your having, by your consent, entitled me to do so. We must distinguish the question of whether I am wrong to treat you this way from the question of whether I am wronging *you*. You may give me an entitlement that it would be wrong for me to exercise. (Thanks to Coleen Macnamara for pressing this point in conversation.) On the interpretation under consideration, your free consent does have normative effects, namely, that in wrongly torturing you I would not be wronging you. Since it seems to me that I would still be wronging you in these cases, I prefer the initial interpretation. The relation between being wronged and having a legitimate complaint against the wrongdoer is admittedly complicated. There is something obviously infelicitous in your lodging a moral complaint against me for treating you in a way to which you have freely consented. I don't think this complication counts against my preferred interpretation. In a rather different way, cheaters do not lose their right not to be cheated even though they cannot felicitously complain against those who cheat them. In both this and the consent cases, there is a legitimate complaint, based on the wrong to the victims, but the victims are not in a position to lodge it. Others may legitimately make it on their behalves.

Searle's case for the freedom of promissory obligations from moral constraint trades on the observation that "there is a difference between the person who has promised to do the act and the person who has not." The constrained normative power view need not deny that invalid promissory transactions make normative differences, only that they make the kind of difference that the autonomy theorist asserts. In the case in which I "promised" to give you a certain car that (unbeknownst to you) wasn't mine to give, you probably have cause for complaint. However what can be held against me is not that I didn't "give" you the car, but that I made a false or careless promissory proposal. If your expectations were thereby frustrated, the wrongdoing is magnified. However, my promissory proposal does not make it the case that I have an obligation to give you the car, or that you are entitled to demand this from me. Nor do I now have a reason to give you the car. (Perhaps I have an obligation to give you a comparable car or to compensate you if you were harmed by reliance on my word.)

Promissory transactions can change the normative scene in a variety of ways even when they fail to give rise to obligations or reasons to act as promised. In the terrorist case, your complicity severely limits your standing to complain. Perhaps you would be right to complain that I didn't warn you that I was backing down, assuming there was time, thereby unnecessarily leaving you in the lurch, causing you to be harmed in certain ways. My promissory proposal makes the difference that in virtue of changing my mind, I have let you down. In that case, I might bear some responsibility for your particular plight. But the legitimacy of these complaints does not entail that I ever had an obligation or reason to do as promised.[38] As Richard Kraut observes, we should distinguish the question whether promisers have some reason to do as promised from the question whether they are answerable in one way or another to the promisees.[39]

To change the example, suppose that we rob a bank and agree to split the money at an appointed time. If I take all the money and run, surely I've compounded my wrongs by cheating you in this way.[40] But are you entitled to this money in virtue of our agreement? Neither of us is, since the money belongs to the bank. Just the same, our agreement has made

[38] The following seem to me contradictory: R had no right to accept P's promissory proposal to R to do x. R has a right to complain that P did not do x as P promised R he would do.

[39] Kraut (2007): 216, n. 13. Kraut also opposes the Autonomy Thesis. He offers a teleological approach, according to which you have reason to keep a promise only if doing so "does some good." I came across Kraut's discussion too late in the preparation of this essay to take it into account.

[40] Thanks to David Sobel and Steven Wall for this example.

a normative difference. I'm now a cheat as well as a thief. Even if you have no claim to any part of the money, my failure to stick to the agreement marks my treachery, something I may not be able to say about you. Similarly, in the terrorist example, my failure to maintain my end of the bargain might exhibit irresolution or cowardice, rather than a moral change of heart. Unfaithfulness is something that distinguishes me from you in this context. It is possible to act shamefully (or shamelessly) in my relations to you without wronging anyone.

Now in thinking about constraints on normative powers, we should not be misled by the gravity of the wrong involved in the terrorist example. This example is indeed dialectically limited insofar as it invites the suspicion that the invalidity of the transaction depends upon its monstrousness. This suspicion would be friendly to the Autonomy Thesis, for its advocates can maintain that there is a residual obligation and corresponding reason to keep the promise which is simply outweighed by the gross immorality of what is promised.

To test this hypothesis, imagine instead that my promise is to steal 2 dollars from my office mate's wallet in order to provide you with cash for an espresso. The promised action is hardly a great crime, but that doesn't affect the claim that there is no obligation incurred, nor any entitlement of the promisee to demand my performance. Our promissory partnership is illicit, quite independently of the degree of moral gravity of what acting as proposed.

Indeed, examples of minor immoral agreements are in a way *more* forceful against certain versions of the Autonomy Thesis than heinous promises are. According to that thesis, some obligation and corresponding reasons are inherent in any promissory transaction. If we assume that this inherent reason has normative force independently of moral considerations, the Autonomy Thesis predicts that the strength of the case for keeping the promise would be in inverse proportion to the seriousness of the proposed wrong.[41] A point would have to come, it seems, at which the immorality is so minor that I should indeed keep my promise, given its inherent normative force. Examples of promised moral misdemeanors falsify that prediction.[42]

[41] As David Sobel and Steven Wall pointed out to me, the Autonomy Theorist who denies that promissory obligations/reasons are *moral* obligations/reasons *and* also holds that moral reasons always trump non-moral reasons wouldn't be committed to this prediction.

[42] It is important to see that the case against the Autonomy Thesis does not depend on the claim that moral considerations always override or silence reasons of other kinds. For as we've seen, certain versions of that thesis can accept the claim. Furthermore, consider someone who thinks that the

## VII CAN IMMORAL PROMISES BE VALID?

I have been arguing that the Autonomy Thesis is not true of consenting in general and that there is no reason to think that it is true of promising in particular. Promissory powers are constrained by moral considerations. And yet not all immoral promises[43] are simply "stillborn," in Judith Thomson's apt phrase. In contrast to both the terrorist and the petty theft cases, my pledge of a large sum of money to support the local Musical Society's orchestra looks to be valid even when keeping this pledge would entail seriously neglecting my children's need for food and clothing. Here, too, I am promising to do something that I morally ought not to do, but initially it seems right to say that those to whom I have wrongly made the pledge have a claim to payment and would be wronged if I reneged.

### *Thomson's principle*

The difference here is readily explained by a principle proposed by Thomson:

> if a word-giver [e.g. promiser] would have to act impermissibly to make his or her word-given proposition true, then he or she does all the same give a claim – *unless the word-receiver [e.g. promisee] is at fault for accepting the word-giver's word.*[44]

Thomson doesn't venture an account of the conditions in which we can innocently accept promissory commitments which it would be wrong for the promisee to keep, but her suggestion highlights an important difference in the relation between the promiser and the promisee in the two kinds of case we have considered. In contrast to the terrorist, the Musical Society is faultless in accepting my pledge.

terrorist cause is sufficiently important to give the parties to this transaction authority for this undertaking. That is a substantive normative position that, if true, would ground the authority in norms of a different sort. But the Autonomy Thesis asserts that no such normative grounding is necessary, that promissory authority rests on nothing more than the possession of an intact will. That is what I am claiming we should reject.

43 I mean by an "immoral promise" a promise it is morally wrong to make because it proposes something it would be morally wrong for me to do in the circumstances. Some promissory acts are wrong independently of the wrongness of acting as proposed: For example, you've threatened to kill my mother if I promise her that I will mow her lawn. (I am grateful to Don Hubin for prompting me to clarify this distinction and for supplying this kind of example.)

44 Thomson (1990): 315 (my emphasis).

Let's gloss the language of "faulty acceptance" in terms of "entitlement to accept," as follows:

*E*: A promissory transaction gives rise to a valid claim to performance on the part of the promisee against the promiser if and only if the promisee is entitled to accept the promissory proposal.[45]

*E* doesn't supply a criterion of valid acceptance, but the following seems plausible as a *necessary* condition.

*P*: A promisee is entitled to accept a proposal only if the proposed course of action is in itself morally permissible.

*E* and *P* define some of the limits of our normative powers to establish promissory relations. Promisees and promisers are partners in promissory transactions. When the promissory proposal is morally impermissible in itself, they are partners in crime (or misdemeanors). In these cases, the accomplice has no standing to accept this proposal and therefore no valid commitment *to him* has been established. He therefore lacks authority to make claims to my performance.

In contrast, on plausible moral assumptions, there are typically ways of supporting orchestras without violating other claims. In these cases, the promisee accepts my pledge innocently and therefore acquires standing to hold me responsible for my failure to deliver on my word and for its foreseeable consequences. It won't do to dismiss the complaints of innocent promisees by pointing to the fact that the promisers had no morally acceptable way to enact their commitments. It is the burden of promisers to see to it that they are in a position permissibly to carry out their proposals.

## *Obligations and reasons*

The crucial difference between the Terrorist and the Musical Society example is that in the latter the promissory transaction has generated an obligation and corresponding claim. But I deny that this obligation entails

[45] This gloss is in one respect weaker than Thomson's own formulation, since recipients might be at fault for accepting proposals they are entitled to accept. I might be entitled to accept a proposal it would be ungenerous or short-sighted or self-deprecating to accept. Note also that it might be morally objectionable for you to do something you promise to do even though what you propose to do wouldn't violate anyone's valid claims. Suppose you bequeath your vast estate, to which no one else is entitled, to some unworthy cause. The recipient of the promise might be in one way at fault for accepting the commitment, but nonetheless he wrongs no one in doing so. The unfortunate promissory transaction seems valid in this kind of case.

that I have a reason to hand over my children's savings or even a reason to do what I am obligated to do. If (2) (obligations are by definition reasons for action) is understood to have this implication, we should reject that thesis as well. It is probably true that obligations imply reasons of some kind, but they do not imply reasons to fulfill the obligation.

This follows from the possibility of obligations we are unable, now or ever, to fulfill, in conjunction with a plausible assumption about reasons for action. Suppose I pledge a sum of money that I don't have and can't get. I am utterly bankrupt, with no prospect of discharging my obligation. The plausible assumption about reasons is that nothing can speak in favor of my doing what I can't do. Hence, my obligation cannot in this case be a reason to pay the Musical Society the money (as I am obligated to do).[46] Accordingly, it is not true that I ought – here and now – to pay the Musical Society. An ought-judgment is a verdict about what is to be done. What could it mean to say that I ought to pay the Society, when that judgment could not be the conclusion of sound practical reasoning and a basis for a corresponding intention? Just the same, I remain under an obligation to the Society to pay what I've pledged.

The same distinction applies when I cannot *permissibly* fulfill my obligation. Where promisees accept my pledge innocently, they acquire standing to hold me responsible for my failure to deliver on my word and for its foreseeable consequences. But it doesn't follow that they are entitled to my children's savings.[47] I have an obligation to the Society that I cannot rightfully discharge. The Society has a valid complaint and a claim, namely, that I haven't paid them as promised and that I owe them what I've pledged. Nevertheless, it has no claim, in particular, to the embezzled funds.

I conclude that when the promissory proposal is something it is impermissible for the promiser to enact, but one that the recipient can rightly accept, an obligation has been generated but not an unconditional ought or reason to carry out the promise.[48] It is not the case that I ought or have reason to pay the pledge in the circumstances, since I cannot permissibly do so. But the obligation is still relevant to what I ought to do, for it imposes a requirement to act as promised or somehow to make

[46] What I say about obligation doesn't challenge the doctrine that "ought" implies "can," which, suitably interpreted, I take to be true.

[47] Nor am I obligated to deplete the children's trust fund. 'I am obligated to *x*' creates an "opaque context." If I am obligated to pay the Society $1,000 today, and the only way I can do so is to raid the children's trust fund, it doesn't follow that I am obligated to do that.

[48] So this will be a complete or successful promissory transaction as characterized in the first section.

amends. I have a reason to act as promised or to compensate or to seek release. When acting as promised is neither possible nor permissible, no reason to carry it out follows. The promiser is doomed to act badly if the promisee is not obligated to release him. He cannot now avoid wronging someone.

To summarize, when promissory transactions generate obligations to someone to x, they make a normative difference. But they do not necessarily make this difference by giving rise to reasons (in particular) to x. That depends on whether one can possibly or permissibly x. If not, one will only have reasons to do something else instead.

### *Wrongfully accepting permissible proposals*

Is the necessary condition asserted in P sufficient for the promisee to be entitled to accept a promissory proposal, as $P'$ would have it?

$P'$: A promisee is entitled to accept a proposal if and only if the proposed course of action is in itself morally permissible.

No. That $P'$ is false is shown by examples of desperate and coerced promises.[49] Suppose you are stranded in the desert and the only way you can get me to transport you to safety is to promise to sign over the deed to your house when we get back to civilization. You are entitled to do what you propose, let us suppose, but it seems to me that I haven't incurred a right to your signing over the house. For I am not entitled to exploit you in this way. You have a claim to my help that is not conditional on this promissory commitment.

The bearing of this point upon our social and economic world, with its deep inequalities and pervasive exploitation, is difficult to make precise. It would be too strong to say that whenever anyone makes a promise on terms that are unreasonable for the promisee to exact, there is no valid commitment to act as promised. If I have room in my car and am going in your direction anyway, I ought not to charge you anything at all for the ride. Even so, if we agree to a payment of, say, $100, it seems you are bound to pay. One reason for this is that in general we want the freedom to make binding commitments to sub-optimal proposals. There is a

[49] Some coerced promises are valid because the promisee has a right to exact the promise. If a judge has the right to impose a punishment on me, then it might be within her discretion to suspend the punishment on certain conditions, including, for example, that I promise to enter a rehabilitation program. In the ordinary sense, I am forced to accept this promise (on pain of going to jail). (I came across this example in my reading, but I can't remember where. My apologies to its author.)

distinction between whether you ought to accept a promissory proposal and whether you are entitled to do so. Up to a certain point, a greedy or mean-spirited deal is still a deal. But only up to a point. Unfortunately, I am unable to say anything more helpful than this.

## VIII BOOTSTRAPPING AGAIN?

This treatment of innocent acceptance cases defuses a worry about bootstrapping that would otherwise haunt even the constrained normative power view. I objected to the Autonomy Thesis that it would allow us to vitiate the immorality or irrationality of acting in a certain way simply by promising to do so. Unless we reject (2) (as Searle seems to interpret it), the constrained view is open to a similar objection. If what I really want to do is to support the orchestra, then on the assumption that the Musical Society is entitled to accept my pledge, it looks as though I can make what I want to do more reasonable merely by pledging. I would thereby incur an obligation and therewith a reason that now competes with the reasons I have to care for my children. Indeed, in a close call, couldn't my undertaking to act in this way tip the balance in favor of what I want to do? On these assumptions, the case for my donating to the Musical Society becomes stronger just by my willing it to be so. This challenge is deflected, however, by rejecting the principle that one has a reason to do something whenever one has an obligation to do it.

It is possible, though, for you to use your normative powers to create decisive reasons to override prior reasons to comply with your unwanted obligations. Suppose you ought to finish your work – indeed, are obligated to meet a looming deadline. When your friend calls to ask for a ride home, you ought to decline. But you welcome the distraction and so promise to help him. You now have a sufficient reason to stop working, to set aside your pressing business. Is this problematic bootstrapping or a mysterious normative transubstantiation?

If there is a puzzle in this vicinity, it is not a puzzle about normative powers, in particular, but about all ways of deliberately altering the configuration and relative weight of one's reasons. As before, suppose you are looking for reasons to neglect your work. You start a fire in the neighboring woods. Consequently, you have an urgent reason to leave the study, namely to put out the fire. As in the previous example, you voluntarily make it the case that you ought to do something other than finish your work. It makes no significant difference whether you manage to do this by starting a fire or by entering into a promissory transaction. In either case, your ruse is futile.

You are back where you started; what you are obligated to do remains undone by your own doing. You won't thereby have justified or even excused your conduct, as you confusedly supposed you might do. You've merely created a situation in which you can't act well or reasonably, even in acting on the best reasons now available. There is no magic or bootstrapping here, just sleight of hand.

## IX CONCLUSION

In contrast to the Autonomy Thesis, the "constrained normative power" view, as I've called it, holds that the power to create promissory obligations and reasons is circumscribed by other normative requirements, including the moral claims of others. The preceding discussion has gestured at some of these, but clearly it is only preliminary to a more systematic framework. I venture into the exceedingly complex casuistry of promissory and other claim rights not with the hope of providing a detailed substantive account, but with the more theoretical aim of disassociating the normative power conception from the idea that promissory obligations are autonomous, wholly internal to the interpersonal transaction of proposal and acceptance. Promissory powers belong to our general standing as moral agents, and it is only to be expected that our authority to make and accept promissory commitments is checked by the claims and interests of those concerned.

CHAPTER 9

# *Regret and irrational action**

*Justin D'Arms and Daniel Jacobson*

Regret, like guilt and fear, seems in a fundamental respect different from such emotions as amusement and disgust. Whereas amusement presents itself as a response to some *sui generis* form of value, the funny, regret seems to concern something with which we're already deeply concerned, quite independently of our tendencies to regret. What we regret, paradigmatically, are our bad choices or actions: Our *mistakes*, in a word. That is not to say that we can only regret mistakes, or only acts we take to be mistaken; but this is clearly the standard case. In the sense of regret on which we will focus here, it involves reproaching oneself for a decision, and it functions to motivate the agent to try to undo the action if possible and to act differently next time.[1] Though it makes sense to *lament* an unlucky outcome or a poor set of options, if one decided well then *regret* would be inapt (though not impossible) to feel. Regret seems to be about something even a rational but disaffected alien, who was immune to regret, would care about: roughly, making bad decisions. By contrast, such an alien would have no interest, except perhaps anthropological interest, in the funny or the disgusting. Call this concern for mistakes the intentional aspect of regret.

* We wish to thank Mark Jenkins, Jim Joyce, Owen King, and Tim Schroeder, as well as audiences at the Princeton University Center for Human Values, the OSU/Maribor/Rijeka Dubrovnik Conference 2006, Arizona State University, University of British Columbia, and the University of California, San Diego for helpful discussion on these issues. We are especially grateful to David Sobel and Steven Wall for their insightful comments on an earlier draft. Our work on this essay was generously supported by a Collaborative Grant from the National Endowment for the Humanities (NEH). Any views, findings, conclusions, or recommendations expressed in this publication do not necessarily reflect those of the NEH.

[1] These claims about regret can be taken as stipulative, for present purposes, designed to pick out the natural kind of psychological state that we will be referring to as "regret." We do not mean to claim that one must have any particular thought in order to feel regret – not even the thought (much less the belief) that one has made a mistake. Contrary to cognitivist theories of emotion, we hold that sentiments such as regret have intentional content and conditions of correctness (or fittingness) without being essentially constituted, even in part, by any particular judgment or propositional attitude. For an argument against cognitivism, see D'Arms and Jacobson (2003).

Regret factors into human decision-making in another way, however, which would be of no importance to an agent immune to the sentiment. Like amusement and disgust, regret is an intrinsically valenced state: it is painful. Moreover, the pain of prospective regret must be taken into account in decision-making whenever it is predictable. Considered hedonically, in this manner, regret counts against the outcomes in which it can be expected to occur. The prospect of painful regret counts as a reason to avoid such outcomes, just as the pleasure of amusement promised by a good comedy counts as a reason for you to see it. Thus regret has two aspects: hedonic and intentional. As a kind of pain, it constitutes a reason to act; and as an intentional state concerned essentially with choice, it figures as a sensitivity to such practical reasons. Regret seems peculiarly reflexive, in that it can contribute hedonically to the very question it purports to answer.[2]

In this essay we propose to illustrate the phenomenon of regret's reflexivity, and to examine its contribution to questions of practical rationality, partly by considering a well-known puzzle case for decision theory: the so-called Allais paradox. Although the literature on this case often deploys considerations about regret, we think it misconstrues the primary significance of the sentiment in practical reasoning. We hope that this essay will advance that discussion; but our primary use for the Allais puzzle is to motivate some novel suggestions about how regret, and especially the concept of the *regrettable* – that to which regret is a fitting response – bear on practical rationality.[3] Briefly, regret concerns one of the central threads in the concept of practical rationality: the question of what reasoning to use in deciding how to act. Yet regret's counsels on this score conflict intractably with certain formal principles of rational consistency, we claim, thereby creating a tension between good practical reasoning and a standard conception of rational action.

## I ASYMMETRIC REGRET AND BOOTSTRAPPING

Regret contributes hedonically to questions of what to do. When an outcome can be expected to induce regret, this counts, *qua* pain, as a reason

[2] The unique nature of regret's reflexivity can be seen by comparison to guilt, which also characteristically concerns one's own actions and choices. But while guilt is about wrongdoing, at least in part, the aversive prospect of feeling guilt counts as a *non-moral* reason not to do wrong. So one's prospective feelings of guilt, considered hedonically, do not bear on guilt's concern.

[3] On the notion of fitting emotions, see D'Arms and Jacobson (2000a, 2000b, 2006).

not to bring about that outcome. But it is open to question whether such a reason can ever suffice to *swing the balance of considerations*; that is, whether it can make the crucial difference, which changes the proper conclusion of some practical deliberation from one choice to another. Since regret is about mistakes, perhaps it can't swing the balance. Were regret fitting only when directed at actions that are mistakes anyway, then it could not help make an act or choice mistaken, but merely pile on an additional reason: that the choice would predictably lead to this regret. Moreover, were prospective regret able to swing the balance of considerations, it would be self-justifying, in that it would be rational to regret an act only because you will in fact regret it. Such bootstrapping can seem suspect. Nevertheless, we contend that regret can in fact swing the balance of considerations and thereby successfully bootstrap. The fact that some action will predictably lead to regret can contribute decisively to the rationality of regretting it.

Consider the thought that regret cannot swing the balance because you can only expect to regret decisions you already consider mistaken.[4] Of course, should things go badly you will be dismayed, but if regret concerns bad decisions (mistakes) rather than bad outcomes (misfortunes), then a good choice that goes awry doesn't merit regret but something like disappointment. Although we claim that regret concerns mistake rather than misfortune, we nevertheless hold that you can sometimes reliably anticipate regretting an action despite *not* thinking it mistaken. For instance, there are familiar scenarios where it's predictable that whatever you do, you will feel some regret. Major decisions, such as whether to buy a house, are often like this: a forced choice between (what is commonly known as) buyer's remorse and (what we might term) renter's regret. If you decide to buy, you will likely discover problems with the house, or with paying for it, that cause you to regret the purchase; but forgo buying it and you will just as likely reproach yourself for missing the opportunity. Moreover, we think psychologically astute and self-aware people know this and can recognize some such cases in advance. Then they will reliably anticipate regretting whichever decision they make. Not all of these foreseeable regrets would be rational, because not every action open to you can be mistaken; but they can be anticipated nevertheless. Hence the idea that you can only anticipate regretting a choice you already think mistaken is false.

[4] Compare Weber (1998): 108–109, who argues in this manner against the possibility that "decision-making regret," which is approximately our notion of regret in general, can swing the balance.

Notice however that in the case of the forced choice between buyer's remorse and renter's regret, as we've developed it, the anticipated regrets are *symmetrical*, in that one can anticipate equal regret whichever choice one makes. Hence, this prospective regret cannot yet swing the balance; it cannot settle whether or not to buy the house, since one's expected regret weighs equally against both decisions. In order for prospective regret to swing the balance of reasons, one must anticipate feeling it *asymmetrically*: that is, one must anticipate more regret (or greater likelihood of it) about one option than the other. We think it plausible that in some circumstances one can anticipate such asymmetric regret. This can be true, for instance, when one faces a "once in a lifetime" chance – what we will refer to as a *singular opportunity* – which would be inconvenient or expensive, or has some similarly mundane but important reasons opposing it. This is just one example. In the following section, we will argue that certain famous puzzle cases, such as the Allais paradox, provide another instance of predictably asymmetric regret. But for now we want to keep the discussion realistic and non-technical, and it will help our argument about the Allais case for us to have another, more life-like example of the same phenomenon.

Imagine having a chance to spend a week assisting your friend, a marine biologist, collect lizard specimens near the beautiful and exotic Sea of Cortez, at the cost of sacrificing a week of work during an especially busy and important period of your regular life. Suppose that at the point of decision you find the choice a very close call. (Adjust the temptation as needed for this supposition.) It seems that something like the following thought might legitimately aid your decision. If I take the trip I will be harried for a week or two after I get back, but this ordeal will pass and leave no lasting mark on my life; whereas if I don't take the trip, I will always regret passing up a unique experience. Notice that you need not already think that it would be a mistake to forgo the trip, in order to be confident that you would feel asymmetric regret: more regret over passing it up than over going. In this case it seems likely that any regret over going will last only as long as the hectic aftermath, but bouts of regret over staying home may last a lifetime – albeit not continuously. If this decision is really such a close call, it seems that the prospect of regret over forgoing a singular opportunity might suffice to swing the balance of reasons, making it better to take the trip, all things considered. Since we think life-like cases with this general structure are quite familiar, we conclude that it's not just psychologically possible but common for anticipated regret to swing the balance.

At this point, a second objection emerges. In such cases, were it not for asymmetric future regret, it wouldn't be a mistake not to go; so any regret you anticipate feeling will (it seems) be unfitting. The objection holds that an "irrational" – that is, unfitting – emotional response to one's choice cannot make that choice rational or irrational (Weber 1998: 108–109; Williams 1973a: 101 *et seq.*). We reject this line of argument. The most obvious problem with this objection is that unfitting emotions still hurt. Although pain and pleasure are not the only things that matter in outcomes, surely they are among the things that matter. Yet if the painfulness of regret is granted to be a bad feature of it, then there seems no way to deny the possibility that the hedonic aspect of regret can swing the balance. Moreover, once this is granted, the regret you anticipate will be fitting, because its predictable occurrence makes it a mistake to choose the outcome that includes it. In other words, the regret bootstraps.

Admittedly, this result can seem strange. The regret you are predicting purports to be about the choice between actions X and Y; specifically, it seems to involve thinking that you should have chosen Y rather than X. Yet we have stipulated that, aside from the expectation of regret, you had at least as good reason to choose X. Choosing X would not be mistaken, and might even be correct, were it not for the prospect of regret. Could you somehow inoculate yourself against these regrets, you might have more reason to choose X. But people typically cannot inoculate themselves against regret with the thought that, so long as one doesn't feel it, it won't be fitting. The tendency to feel predictable asymmetric regret in various circumstances is not just an individual idiosyncrasy that impedes rational choice, but a pervasive feature of our emotional lives. While a more ideally rational creature might not have to contend with such responses, practical rationality in a human context requires taking them into account and coping with them judiciously in light of our aims – which include the avoidance of pain.

Regret teaches those who are prone to it what policies to adopt, and it provides a painful disincentive for failing to heed these policies. Someone might think regret pointless because an agent can discover his errors, and learn from them, without the unnecessary pain of regret; indeed, some philosophers have argued that regret is always "unreasonable" on these grounds (Bittner 1992). But we consider this suggestion deeply misguided. In our view, many emotions are fitting in certain circumstances due to contingent, and even unfortunate, facts about human nature, including our cognitive and motivational deficiencies.

We began with this example of asymmetric regret because it is relatively straightforward, but the most interesting and important cases concern regret's characteristic motivation of policy change. Suppose that certain "fast and frugal" heuristics for decision-making serve humans well, on the whole (Gigerenzer and Todd 1999). We hypothesize that humans are innately primed to learn certain heuristics and internalize them as policies, and to inculcate and police them with regret. The function of such heuristics dictates that they should be designed for common cases and sensitive to systematic human tendencies; hence, they will very likely deviate from the policies of choice recommended by a purely formal theory for rational agents as such. The tension between good policies for humans as we actually are, and policies that would work better were we differently constituted, creates the appearance of paradox surrounding such puzzle cases as the Allais paradox. Moreover, we think this tension helps explain why the extant responses to those puzzles – both those given by defenders of decision theory and its antagonists – have been inadequate.

## 2 THE ALLAIS PUZZLE AND THE ARGUMENT FROM REGRET

Consider what is commonly known in decision theory as the Allais paradox or puzzle. Here a set of preferences very attractive to common sense conflicts with an axiom of orthodox decision theory that also claims deep intuitive appeal. In the Allais scenario, subjects are asked to choose between two options in two different lotteries: they must choose between A and B, and between C and D, with outcomes and probabilities given in table 1.

The point of this incentive structure is straightforward. The choice between A and B is a choice between a certain payoff in A (of $1,000,000), and a very likely payoff in B with higher expected value but a small chance (0.01) of getting nothing.[5] Those who choose A over B, forgoing the choice with higher expected payoff in order to ensure themselves $1,000,000, presumably do so in order to avoid the risk of disaster in outcome B(p). What is distinctive about the case is that neither

[5] It proves important to distinguish the formal properties of the Allais puzzle from certain non-formal variables that affect people's preferences between the lotteries. Specifically, the amounts of the payoffs (here $1,000,000 and $5,000,000) can vary, so long as the formal structure – the symmetry between the two lotteries, and the choice between higher probability of payoff (in A and C) vs higher expected payoff (in B and D) – remains constant.

Table 1. *The Allais Scenario*

| Outcome of lottery | p | q | r |
|---|---|---|---|
| Probability of outcome | 0.01 | 0.10 | 0.89 |
| A | $1,000,000 | $1,000,000 | $1,000,000 |
| B | $0 | $5,000,000 | $1,000,000 |
| C | $1,000,000 | $1,000,000 | $0 |
| D | $0 | $5,000,000 | $0 |

risk aversion, nor the diminishing marginal utility of money, suffices to explain this preference (Weber 1998: 97–98). If by "risk aversion" we mean the willingness to sacrifice some expected value in order to reduce the probability of a bad outcome, then a strong aversion to risk would equally favor C over D. After all, in that choice too there is precisely the same small (0.01) chance of getting nothing in outcome p vs a moderate (0.10) chance of an equally larger payoff in outcome q. The only difference between the two choices is that in both A and B you get paid in the most likely (0.89) outcome r, whereas in both C and D you get nothing.

Hence, although people surely differ in their willingness to gamble on a higher expected payoff vs a higher likelihood of getting paid, these differences in risk aversion are symmetrical between the two lotteries (A vs B, and C vs D). Since decision theory is neutral as to how risk-averse one should be, it favors neither the prudent nor the aggressive strategy for choosing between a higher likelihood of payoff vs a higher expected payoff. It merely insists upon consistency in risk aversion. Specifically, since both pairs of lotteries have identical outcomes in r, the axiom Leonard Savage calls the *sure-thing principle* says that this outcome should be ignored in choosing between the pairs of lotteries (Savage 1972). But if we ignore the r column, then it seems patently irrational to have different preferences in these two now identical choice situations. Rationality requires preferring either {A and C} or {B and D}. Moreover, the sure-thing principle looks compelling when considered in the abstract: Surely any preference between two choices ought to be based on respects in which they differ, not respects in which they are the same. Yet many people are inclined to choose A over B and D over C, and to regard these choices as rational even after computing the expected payoffs.[6] This

[6] It should be noted that, although the payoff matrix specifies dollar amounts, what subjects are presumed to be comparing are the utilities derived from those dollar amounts.

combination of choices, known as the *Allais preferences* after the puzzle's author, Maurice Allais, finds a difference between the two cases where orthodox decision theory seems to imply that none exists.

The appeal of the problematic Allais preferences is obvious and straightforward, notwithstanding their irrationality by the lights of orthodox decision theory.[7] Those who regard Allais preferences as rational argue that it makes sense to deviate from a strategy of maximizing one's expected payoff in order to secure a certain payoff, but it does not make sense to forgo the maximizing strategy merely in order to increase a small chance of winning. In short, they value a *certain payoff* as such, and they are willing to pay for this certainty.[8] But the sure-thing principle instructs an agent, in deciding between two options, to ignore all those outcomes where there is no difference between the choices; doing so makes the choice between lotteries A and B identical to that between C and D. Since the sure-thing principle effaces just the relevant difference between the two sets of lotteries – that A but not C offers a certain payoff – it obscures the attraction of the Allais preferences for A and D. Indeed, the sure-thing principle impugns the rationality of those preferences by representing them as strictly inconsistent. Yet many people not only have these preferences but retain and endorse them, notwithstanding the principle.

These commonplace but far from universal intuitions favoring the Allais preferences should not be overstated. We suspect that everyone's preferences are sensitive to the amount of the payoffs, and perhaps to the probabilities, in ways that elude any purely formal theory. Reduce the amount of the certain payoff gradually and, we predict, eventually everyone will gamble on the bigger payoff; increase the amount and they will eventually become risk-averse. The difference between people is less *that* they do so than *when* they do: people poorer than we are will likely prefer C to D, while richer people will prefer B to A. The point is that the Allais preferences only appeal to common sense in some intermediate sweet spot, where the smaller payoff is large enough for you to care about, but not so large as to induce you simply to maximize your changes of getting paid. However, while the attractiveness of the Allais preferences should not be overstated, neither should the underlying phenomenon – that we

[7] Although almost all extant axiomatizations of decision theory adopt some version of the sure-thing principle, there is at least one attempt in the literature to do without it (Machina 1982).

[8] It would be nice to be able to say that choice A promises a "sure thing": specifically, $1,000,000. Unfortunately, Savage coined the term "sure-thing principle" to refer to a very different aspect of the same problem, which is much less perspicuously referred to by that name. So we will refer to such vernacular "sure things" as certain payoffs, instead.

value the certainty of a payoff as such – be underestimated. Even people immune to the problematic preferences in the Allais case will often find a complementary choice more compelling, in that they are willing to pay for the certainty of threat elimination. We will return to this point later and illustrate it with another famous example, concerning Russian roulette.

Several arguments have been put forward in response to the apparent conflict between the Allais preferences and decision theory. Some philosophers bite the bullet, either by insisting on the rationality of these preferences on the basis of intuition, or by standing by their theory and the plausibility of the sure-thing principle, and insisting that preferences inconsistent with it must be irrational. But the most interesting argument, and the one most relevant for our purposes, is what we'll call the *argument from regret.* According to this argument, decision theory can accommodate the rationality of Allais preferences by appealing to the subjects' expectation that, should they choose B and get the bad outcome p, they will bitterly regret having passed up the certainty of a substantial payoff. The pain of this regret needs to be included in the payoff matrix along with the zero dollar value of the outcome. Hence the true outcome of B(p), calculated in terms of utility rather than money, is less than zero. Outcome p does not just involve getting no money, the subjects reason; it also involves living with the fact that by choosing B they gave up a guaranteed $1,000,000 payoff and, when they got unlucky with outcome p, they ended up with nothing. The argument from regret attempts to vindicate the Allais preferences without making any direct appeal to certainty, so as to reconcile these intuitively appealing choices with decision theory. Many versions of this argument have been offered. In fact, according to John Broome (1991: 98):

> All the rationalizations of Allais's preferences point out a good or bad feeling you may experience. This feeling, they claim, can rationally be taken into account, as well as the money prizes, in determining your preferences.[9]

What would this argument have to show, in order to have reconciled common sense with decision theory? Note first that the argument must make an additional, often tacit claim: that one will not feel such regret

[9] Broome (1991) and Weber (1998) cite versions of the argument from Kenneth Arrow, Daniel Bell, and Richard Jeffrey. Since the argument from regret considers only its hedonic aspect, it does not matter precisely what feelings it appeals to, only how painful or pleasurable and when they will reliably be felt.

(or another negative feeling) with anything like the same intensity, should one choose lottery D over C, and then receive no payoff. Weber (1998) makes this point incisively, while noting that decision theorists have been insufficiently attentive to the relevant possibilities.[10] Nevertheless, we are inclined to think that the concern with regret in B(p) is ultimately the right focus: these are the most plausible and predictable feelings that might be significant enough to make a difference to the rationality of a choice involving large sums of money. Moreover, we're inclined to think that although all the predictable feelings must be counted, it's plausible to expect regret (and other bad feelings) to be asymmetric between the two lotteries. B(p) is the most painful of the losing outcomes; in particular, it is predictably worse than D(p).

Furthermore, though, a successful reconciliation must be sufficiently robust to vindicate the Allais preferences for a significant proportion of the people who actually have them. It would not suffice to adduce an idiosyncratic character – call him Maurice – who can be predicted to have so much more pain in the unlucky outcome B(p) than in other losing outcomes as to swing the balance for him. While that would rationalize *his* Allais preferences, the task of reconciling the Allais preferences with decision theory has to justify them more broadly than just for some hypothetical character with eccentric emotional dispositions. These constraints reveal two basic problems with the argument from regret, which takes a hedonic approach to vindicating the Allais preferences – notwithstanding Broome's claim that *all* extant rationalizations of them do so. First, the argument is committed to specific claims about the size and likelihood of regret that will not generally (if ever) be plausible. Second, the argument must hold that the Allais preferences would be irrational, *were it not for the prospect of regret*; otherwise the argument from regret would be otiose. This precludes applying a similar strategy in related cases concerning the value of certain payoffs and singular opportunities.

Let's start with the first point, about the specific claims required by the argument from regret. For its hedonic reconciliation of Allais preferences with decision theory to work, the anticipated regrets must be bad enough to outweigh the extra value of the greater expected payoff. That value depends on how one configures the payoff matrix, of course, and we've argued that material (non-formal) considerations are very much relevant

[10] Although we accept Weber's mathematical argument against arguments from regret, we reject both his strategy of differentiating between different kinds of regret and his discounting of those regrets that would be unfitting.

to the question of what to prefer. In the version we're using here, that value is \$400,000. So the argument from regret must claim that Allais preferences are rational because the regret one can reliably expect to have in the unlucky outcome B(p) would be so painful that it's worth forgoing \$400,000 worth of expected payoff in order to avoid a 0.01 chance of getting it. Further, it must claim that this trade-off justifies the Allais preferences robustly. But we doubt that there are many people like Maurice, who prefer to reduce their expected payoff by \$400,000 in order to avoid risking a one in a hundred chance of the admittedly severe regret one can expect in B(p). This attempt at reconciliation relies on the implausible claim that many people will find the predictable but unlikely regret of B(p) painful enough to justify paying the steep price of insurance against it. We wonder if anyone would defend this thesis except as an ad hoc effort to reconcile his theory with common sense.

The second problem with the argument from regret is that it applies too narrowly to make sense of various other intuitions, which have the same basis as the Allais preferences. Imagine that the Allais puzzle came with an offer of inoculation against regret over your choice (or suppose you're choosing for another person, double-blind). We expect many people attracted to the Allais preferences will think that the preferences are still rational in this revised version. These people favor the Allais preferences not just to avoid regret, but because they think it would be a *mistake* to forgo the certain payoff; that is, they think that regret would be fitting, even though they won't feel it due to the inoculation. In short, it would be regrettable to fail to consider the certain payoff offered by A as a reason to choose it – a reason not present in C. The attraction of A is less the protection it affords against regret in B(p) than its *guarantee* of a million dollars. Since the argument from regret leaves these people's preferences incompatible with decision theory, the would-be reconciler still must deem irrational a wide range of commonsense judgments. The argument from regret makes little progress if it only serves to justify a few people's Allais preferences, in just one version of the problem.

Moreover, the argument from regret keeps the sure-thing principle sharply at odds with some commonplace and, we think, even more compelling intuitions about the value of certainty. Consider this analogous case. Suppose you were forced to play Russian roulette with two bullets in a six-chamber revolver. Loss means death. Would you pay more to remove those two bullets, leaving you certain to avoid losing the game, than you would pay to go from four bullets to three? (In either case, payment is excused if you die.) The sure-thing principle implies that you should actually be willing to pay *exactly the same amount* to go from four to three bullets as you would to remove the last two bullets from the gun.[11] Yet most people, including ourselves, would pay more money to remove two bullets and certainly avoid the risk of death in this game – a preference inconsistent with the sure-thing principle. Moreover, the appeal of this preference obviously involves certainty: removing all the bullets from the gun guarantees survival, whereas going from four to three bullets merely increases its probability. (Since the increase in probability is equal between scenarios, as in the Allais case, risk aversion cannot justify the commonsense preferences.) Clearly this preference cannot be vindicated by appeal to the argument from regret, however, since the dead have no regrets – or so we assume.

The argument from regret goes to heroic lengths to vindicate the Allais preferences without allowing the certainty afforded only by A to play any role in justifying them. In our view it ultimately fails because this obscures the real attraction of the Allais preferences, which justifies them if they can be robustly justified. We do not deny that anticipated regrets could justify *some* possible Allais preferences (as in the case of Maurice), nor do we deny that regret plays a significant role in *explaining* why people have these preferences (as we will illustrate in the following section). But we think the argument from regret misunderstands regret's real significance to these cases and, more broadly, to practical rationality.

## 3 CERTAINTY, SINGULARITY, AND THE REGRETTABLE

Although we've argued that the prospect of future regret, considered hedonically, can in principle swing the balance of reasons, we have now shown that it does not do so systematically enough to provide a robust defense of the Allais preferences. Because our discussion until this point has focused on regret's hedonic aspect, however, we have significantly understated the relevance of regret to human practical reasoning. Another aspect of regret can vindicate (certain) Allais preferences and analogous intuitions more robustly, by displaying the normative grounds for according special significance to the certainty of certain payoffs, as such.

Earlier we glossed the intentional aspect of regret as presenting some action or choice to the agent as a mistake. Now we must explicate this suggestion further. In our view, the intentional content of a sentiment is

[11] Gibbard (1990): 15–16 explains why the principle requires this; he credits David Lewis for the original argument.

determined in large part by its motivational role (D'Arms and Jacobson 2006). So the sense of "mistake" that regret concerns can be further specified by investigating how the emotion typically motivates. The obvious role of regret seems to be self-reproach: regret serves to chastise the agent over some choice or decision. By focusing the agent's attention on a specific act and the reasons not to have done it, regret punishes failures to see what should have been done. For instance, many of us make it a policy not to insult others gratuitously. Yet most of us have inadvertently committed such insults – either acting out of anger or, more embarrassingly, simply failing to see what was insulting about a comment until the offense registered – and we have regretted these mistakes.

A central function of this regret is surely forward-looking, in that people are disposed to feel it because of its instrumental benefits. Regret over such *faux pas* motivates looking harder, and its forced reflection on the circumstances of acting may suggest changes in policy. Most simply, it urges one to think twice before speaking so freely – especially after a few glasses of wine. More profoundly, reflections on the circumstances surrounding the regretted insult may lead you to realize that when you feel resentment toward someone, you should be especially wary of such "inadvertent" insults. Even when there is no way to articulate a better policy, regrets can make us better at following policies we already accept. Dwelling painfully on an inadvertent insult can make us better at noticing in the future when we are at risk of giving offense, by training our social sensitivity so as to make salient various cues that resist codification. In a slogan, then, regret's central role is to *inculcate policies*: to introduce them, internalize them through punishment, and train us in their deployment.

In light of this, we think it plausible to say that regret is *about* errors of policy: actions that issued either from a bad policy or the failure to follow good one.[12] Hence regret is not fitting unless one has made such an error. This explains why regret seems misguided in cases where one followed a good policy and got unlucky, despite the human tendency to fall into a "bad outcome, therefore bad decision" fallacy: those are *not* cases on the basis of which one should resolve to act differently next time. Because regret involves self-reproach, though, not every policy error will merit it; sometimes the failure to follow a good policy isn't

[12] We intend "policy" to be understood very broadly, however, so as to include not only explicitly articulated rules for decision but also internalized habits, and even patterns of attention, which partly constitute an agent's ways of deciding what to do.

your fault, perhaps because you couldn't have known better. The errors of policy that count as regrettable – that is, fitting to regret – include only those errors you could and should have known were mistakes. Hereafter our gloss of regret in terms of mistakes should be understood to include these qualifications. Of course, just what counts as regrettable will be contentious. We do not mean to imply that it will always be clear which acts are mistaken, let alone which mistakes merit the self-reproach of regret. Disagreement over whether an action was regrettable can focus on either of these points.

Despite this inevitable disagreement, certain human commonalities dispose most people to regret certain sorts of action, and to find them, on reflection, regrettable. In particular, we want to broach the suggestion that regret inculcates a policy which we'll call *bird in hand* (BIH), after the homily, "A bird in the hand is worth two in the bush." According to BIH, the certainty of a certain payoff provides an additional reason to secure the bird (a valuable outcome) that is in hand (can be had with certainty). This policy is not simple risk aversion or the specious wisdom of hindsight. Although people have some tendency to regret any decision that turns out badly, this response is much more pervasive and intense when the choice involves acting contrary to BIH, whether by ignoring or overriding it. Like many folk adages, BIH offers insight into the heuristics of decision-making that people actually use and reflectively accept. Indeed, we suspect that humans are innately prepared to learn BIH, and to frame decisions in its terms. This deeply ingrained disposition explains the pervasiveness of intuitions about the potential for regret over forgoing a certain payoff. And such systematic human commonalities in our tendencies to regret reveal the policies that it serves to inculcate. We find this conclusion plausible about regret over passing up both birds in hand and singular opportunities. When faced with the choice between a certain payoff and an uncertain but larger one, people are prone to anticipate regret were they to get unlucky. In anticipating regret, you do not just dread pain; you foresee feeling like you've made a mistake. The regret you anticipate will present your action or decision as regrettable, an object of fitting regret (whether veridically or not). Regret thus teaches us to value the certainty of a prospective good.

Even if we are right that humans are prepared to learn BIH, and that regret inculcates and reinforces this policy, it is a further question whether BIH serves as a good policy of choice for normal humans in ordinary circumstances. In considering this question, the first thing to note is that the acceptance utility of a policy differs from its compliance utility. The best policy actually to comply with may not be the best policy to try to inculcate; indeed, it certainly will not be, since the policy with highest compliance utility is very simple: maximize utility. But the advice to maximize utility is nearly worthless, since it can hardly ever be followed. Even the policy of maximizing *expected* utility improves matters only slightly, as both consequentialists and decision theorists routinely grant. As James Joyce puts the point: "No sensible person should ever propose expected utility maximization as a *decision procedure*, nor should he suggest that rational agents must have the maximization of utility as their *goal*" (1999: 80; emphasis in original). The question of what policies to try to adopt, then, is a question about what devices of deliberation will do best for those who utilize them. Answers to that question must rely on some view about what it is for a policy to do well. Decision theory has an answer to that question: good policies will be ones that help the agent realize utility, and the best set of policies for an agent are presumably those that realize as much of that agent's utility as possible. This suggestion is highly contentious in various ways; however, its most controversial aspects are not relevant to our discussion, so we grant this assumption for purposes of argument.

The question of what policies of choice to adopt is partly an empirical question. And it is also an empirical question to what extent the answer will be the same, or similar, for different people. The acceptance value of policies depends on various considerations, including not only one's values and the circumstances one is likely to confront, but also one's cognitive limitations, the costs of deliberation and of getting more information, and facts about one's motivational propensities and weaknesses. It may well be that differences between individuals, in these respects, make a difference to what policies they do well to adopt. Nevertheless, it would be surprising were there no such thing as good advice for human agents in general. Though policies tailored to our individual idiosyncrasies might have even higher acceptance utility, such policies will be difficult to identify and implement, whereas general human policies such as BIH are subject to collective investigation and social reinforcement. We shall now suggest reasons to think that BIH is a good policy for most people, and that this both explains the widespread attraction of the Allais and Russian roulette preferences, and also justifies those preferences at least for some ordinary people (not just Maurice).

Our argument for this claim relies on features of normal humans that would not have to be shared by any rational agent as such. (Indeed, we can grant that some human outliers exist, though we suspect there won't be too many.[13]) Specifically, humans have a common tendency to undervalue what they already have and to overvalue what they lack.[14] Recall that BIH does not counsel greater risk aversion *per se*, but context-sensitive *inconsistent risk aversion* (which is precisely why it conflicts with the axioms of decision theory). If there are powerful temptations to inconsistent risk aversion in the opposite direction, however – that is, to discount the value of what one possesses – then BIH will be *ecologically rational*. As Gigerenzer and Todd explain, "A heuristic is ecologically rational to the degree that it is adapted to the structure of an environment" (1999: 13). We suggest that BIH is a good policy for humans, in typical human environments, because it serves as a check against these tendencies. When we remind ourselves, in deliberation, that the certain payoff afforded by one of our options is a consideration in its favor, this helps direct us toward a better pattern of action than we would pursue had we not adopted BIH. But if BIH figures as a good human policy of choice, then our failure to take the certainty of a payoff as a reason would be the object of fitting regret. It would be regrettable because we would have failed to use a good policy in deliberation.

Accepting BIH as a policy involves treating the certainty of a good result as an extra reason, over and above the intrinsic value of the outcome, when deliberating over what to do. But this does not mean that a certain good is always preferable to any amount of good that is uncertain. A bird in hand is not worth three in the bush, even figuratively speaking. But the heuristic says nothing about what counts as a bird – that is, a good thing – or even about when some good is sufficiently in hand. People intuitively frame some choices as offering certainty, and some risks are so small that we treat them as negligible. One might say, oxymoronically, that they are "certain enough" for BIH to apply. If BIH is indeed a good policy for humans, that is because we are pretty good both at framing our choices in ways that treat things as birds and as in hand, when we do well to weigh the certainty of the good as an extra reason, and also at recognizing cases where that additional reason is not weighty enough and we should instead take the risk.

[13] Moreover, we suspect that their idiosyncrasies will be more situational than global. Thus they might profit by deviating from BIH in their occupation as commodities trader or hobby as gambler, despite accepting BIH in much of their practical reasoning outside these specialized areas where the risks and stakes are peculiarly well specified.

[14] Countervailing evidence might be found in the endowment effect characterized by Kahneman, Knetsch, and Thaler (1999); but their data derive from an artificial experimental situation whose relevance to the ecological rationality of BIH can be doubted. This issue, though fascinating and important, is far too complex to be treated adequately here, except to note that all heuristics have costs, which can be (and often are) exploited by clever con men and brilliant economists alike.

Hence, there is no way of saying just how much weight BIH assigns to certainty, because this cannot be specified precisely or in a context-independent way. BIH itself does not answer this question for us. Despite the inherent vagueness of this policy, however, it conflicts intractably with the sure-thing principle, which entails that the certainty of a certain payoff is *no reason at all*, since only expected utility gives one reason to act. At least, they conflict if the sure-thing principle is intended to provide guidance to agents about how to choose. But one might question whether it is. "The expected utility hypothesis," Joyce writes, "is a theory of 'right-making characteristics' rather than a guide to rational deliberation" (1999: 80). Perhaps defenders of decision theory should allow that policies such as BIH are good ones to live by, then, and encourage us human agents to heed the lessons of our dispositions to regret and internalize policies of choice that will dispose us, *inter alia*, to have the Allais preferences. The decisions we make using BIH will thereby be incorrect, in that they will be contrary to the decision theoretic criterion of rational action; yet the decision theorist might encourage people to use these policies nevertheless, in light of standing human infirmities. We consider this suggestion further in the conclusion.

It's worth noting, however, that this is not the standard view of decision theorists. Although they take the maximization of expected utility as the criterion of rational action, they also take the axioms of their theory to describe more specific, local recommendations that can be applied at the level of individual preferences. The demand that one's preferences be capable of representation as a utility function imposes constraints such as the transitivity of preferences and the sure-thing principle, which are explicitly required to figure in practical reasoning. As Joyce (1999: 80), who is admirably clear about the normative significance of decision theory, writes:

> These local constraints are what should guide a person in her evaluation of prospects. She ought to use them, as Savage puts it, "to police [her] decisions for consistency and, where possible, to make complicated decisions depend on simpler ones." Thus, the direct obligation that the theory imposes is not that of maximizing expected utility, but that of conforming one's preferences to the axioms.[15]

According to this view, we ought to police our preferences in ways contrary to the recommendations of BIH. In the Allais case, we should use the sure-thing principle to discipline our preferences between lotteries, which means we cannot treat the certainty of payoff in A as a reason for preferring it to B.

[15] A minor typographical error in Joyce ("is" for "it") has been corrected in this quotation. The embedded quotation is from Savage (1972): 20.

But whether this is good advice to agents depends, as always, on its acceptance utility: on the costs and benefits of the relevant police work. We suspect that trying to police all one's preferences by the sure-thing principle would be misguided, most obviously because it is enormously difficult to do. The principle is typically introduced with very simple cases. For instance, Savage's original example has it that if you would buy a piece of property if the Democrat wins, and you would also buy it if the Republican wins, then uncertainty over the results of the election should not affect your decision (Savage 1972: 21). This application of the principle seems obvious. But the fact that in the Allais lotteries the preference combination of A and D violates the sure-thing principle is much less obvious, and its application to the Russian roulette case requires an ingenious reconstruction of the problem. In short, people could spend a lot of time and effort trying to police their preferences with the sure-thing principle but still perform poorly at it.

Perhaps the injunction to police one's preferences with the sure-thing principle should be understood to include some sort of clause to this effect: Do so only when you think you can see how, and when it seems worth the time. Then the question becomes how often people will be right about these things and, more specifically, to what extent they will be right on occasions where this advice conflicts with the BIH heuristic. This policy will be an improvement over unrestricted BIH only if the gains it provides when deployed correctly outweigh the losses incurred when deployed in error. We doubt that this will generally be the case.

Where does this argument leave us with respect to the Allais puzzle? Suppose one grants that BIH is a good policy for most humans to adopt, as we've argued. The Allais case is designed specifically to bring BIH into conflict with the sure-thing principle, according to which it is irrational to treat the certainty of the payoff in A as any reason at all. Hence, every attempt to make the Allais preferences consistent with orthodox decision theory uses an argument from regret to supplement the outcomes, as Broome notes. But we've contended that such arguments cannot provide a robust justification of them.[16] They work only for eccentrics like our imagined Maurice, and they don't apply to analogous, even more

[16] Broome (1991): 95–100 introduces the possibility of attempting to individuate outcomes by justifiers, which in the Allais case would mean treating certainty as a justifier. Broome eschews this strategy for justifying the Allais preferences, however, presumably on the grounds he refers to as: "Where does it stop?" Since we don't think this strategy works nearly as well in justifying certainty (where he doesn't use it) as it does in justifying equality (where he does), we'll leave it to others to pursue this possibility.

compelling cases where there can be no predictable regrets. According to BIH, though, the certainty of the payoff in A should be treated as a (*pro tanto*) reason to prefer it to B: a reason not present in the choice between lotteries C and D. But if so then this suffices to show that human agents should not in fact "police our preferences" with the sure-thing principle; more specifically, we should not do so when it conflicts with BIH, as in the Allais case.

Does this argument vindicate the Allais preferences? Not exactly. The conclusion that we humans do well to take certainty as a reason suffices to belie the sure-thing principle as a procedure for practical reasoning. Since we have not made any claims about how weighty a reason this is, however, BIH does not imply anything about how much money (or utility) the certainty of this payoff is worth. We take this to be a feature of our view rather than a bug, because we don't think that the formal aspects of the Allais puzzle dictate any specific answer. We think that reflection on these cases, and on the Russian roulette case as well, shows that the attraction of the Allais preferences cannot be captured with the resources available to formal theory – even when it is allowed to consider prospective regrets in the description of its outcomes.

## 4 CONCLUSION

The forgoing reflections suggest that there is a deep tension between some very plausible claims about rationality and irrationality in action. On one hand, in the usual sense of the term, to call an action irrational is to criticize the reasoning that led to it. Hence, irrational actions are not merely those that fail to exhibit perfect rationality; they are actions that fall far enough below that standard to merit reproach, especially self-reproach, and specifically regret. Indeed, the question of whether an action is far enough below the standard to count as irrational often seems to be precisely the question of whether to reproach oneself for it, or instead to regard the rational imperfection as understandable given one's human limitations. If an action merits regret – which is to say, if it is regrettable in our sense – then it is, paradigmatically, irrational. These seem to us platitudes about the ordinary notion of irrationality in action, which connect it to standards of good practical reasoning.

On the other hand, it is also plausible that actions satisfying the formal demands of consistency – for instance, consistency among the agent's ends, and between his ends, beliefs, and actions or intentions – are paradigmatically rational.[17] While the details of these demands are questions for philosophical theory, the general idea that rationality is a matter of consistency in thought and action seems similarly platitudinous. Moreover, decision theoretic attempts to characterize the specific formal conditions that are constitutive of rationality, such as the requirement of transitive preferences and even the sure-thing principle, have considerable intuitive appeal in their own right.

These plausible suggestions conflict, however. If we are right that certain violations of BIH are regrettable, then the platitudes of practical reasoning show that such actions are irrational. But the Allais puzzle and its cognates show that rationality as consistency – specifically, consistency of risk aversion – can demand just such actions. Surely, though, if an action is rational then it is not irrational: that is a platitude about rationality if anything is. Thus there is a tension between the formal conception of rationality as consistency, and an intuitive (and useful) sense of irrationality as bad practical reasoning which merits the self-reproach of regret.

We do not put this conclusion forward as refuting decision theory, however, for several reasons. First, if we are right that the concept of rationality in action is conflicted in this way, decision theory may yet capture one of its central strands. Second, decision theory can be interpreted as merely a criterion of rational action, which is neutral on the topic of practical reasoning: that is, it remains agnostic about the empirical question of what policies it is best for humans to adopt in decision-making. This approach would seek to resolve the tension by denying that the sense of rationality with which decision theory is concerned has any implications for issues about how best to engage in practical reasoning. While an analogous strategy has been deployed by some consequentialists attempting to make their theory compatible with deeply held and critically endorsed convictions about morality, it comes at a steep cost. If decision theoretic rationality divorces itself from practical reasoning, it becomes less clear what is the point of the theory, and what is the force of its notion of irrationality in action. We suspect that these costs explain why Joyce and Savage put forward the "local" axioms, such as the sure-thing principle, as policies meant to guide agents in their decision-making.

[17] Some philosophers will qualify this claim by saying that formal consistency alone is not sufficient for rationality; the agent's ends must also be substantively rational. Since we are not here considering actions taken in service of putatively irrational ends, nothing hangs on whether this qualification is needed.

Finally, it is open to us to insist that the formal conception of rationality dictates canons of good reasoning as well as a criterion of rational action. This would be to place the following constraint on regrettable action: an action cannot merit regret if the reasoning behind it respects the formal canons of rationality in action. But what *ensures* that the self-reproach of regret cannot be fitting over actions taken by following these canons? Even if our arguments for the normative significance of certainty (in the context of certain payoffs) and singularity (with respect to singular opportunities) do not convince the reader, we take ourselves to have shown at least that the burden is on our opponents to argue that human agents – with their standing imperfections and systematic tendencies to error – are best served by adopting the canons of a formal theory as their policies of decision-making. This is at most only contingently true. And here we have argued, using some standard puzzle cases as well as more life-like scenarios, that there are ample reasons to doubt this conclusion.

CHAPTER 10

# *Mackie's motivational argument**

*Philip Clark*

Mackie doubted anything objective could have the motivational properties of a value (Mackie 1977). And in thinking we are morally required to act in a certain way, he said, we attribute objective value to the action. Since nothing has objective value, these moral judgments are all false. As to whether Mackie proved his error theory, opinions vary. But there is broad agreement on one issue. A litany of examples, ranging from amoralism to depression to downright evil, has everyone convinced that Mackie vastly overstated the motivational implications of moral judgment.

Mackie did go overboard. But did he have to? I think not. Even on the most modest motivational assumptions, Mackie can make objective value look queer and morality look like a sham. I begin with a sketch.

## THE ARGUMENT

(1) If there were such a thing as objective value, recognizing it would be recognizing a reason for action
(2) If there were such a thing as objective value, recognizing it would be recognizing a property that is there independently of one's desires
(3) The recognition of any reason for action has a special connection with the will
(4) The recognition of a property that is there independently of one's desires cannot have that connection with the will

* I thank Joe Boyle, Danielle Bromwich, Terence Cuneo, Steven Wall, Luke Gelinas, Tom Hurka, Jonathan Peterson, Arthur Ripstein, David Sobel, Wayne Sumner, Sergio Tenenbaum, and an anonymous referee for Cambridge University Press.

So,

(5) There can be no such thing as objective value[1]
(6) To think one is morally required to act in a certain way is to attribute objective value to actions of that sort

So,

(7) The thought that one is under a moral requirement is always false

Mackie first goes after objective value. Then he takes aim at moral judgments. Let us take these two stages in order.

For Mackie, to say a thing is objectively good is to say, first, that it is something one has categorical (i.e. desire-independent) reason to pursue, and, second, that the reason is there independently of one's recognizing it. These conditions correspond to what Mackie sees as the shortcomings of naturalism and non-cognitivism, respectively. Naturalism, he says, satisfies the second condition, since claims involving natural properties are true or false independently of our believing them, but fails the first, since natural properties are reason-giving only contingently upon the agent's desires. Non-cognitivism, by contrast, satisfies the first condition, since our evaluative attitudes toward persons and actions are often categorical, but fails the second, since it acknowledges nothing beyond the evaluative judgment itself, in virtue of which the judge could be correct or mistaken. Mackie's assumption that objective goodness would have to be a "property out in the world" serves to remind us that the first condition alone does not secure objectivity.

Mackie thinks objective value, so understood, is a queer property. To see a thing as objectively good is to see it as something one has reason to pursue. But any recognition that something is "to be pursued" has a special connection with the will. Recognizing reasons is unlike recognizing other properties in being "intrinsically motivating."

Now Mackie sees no problem where hypothetical reasons are concerned. A hypothetical reason is one whose existence depends on the presence in the agent of a desire that would be served by doing the action. Thus truthfulness may be "to be pursued" because one has a desire that will be served by being truthful. The recognition of this hypothetical "oughtness" or "to-be-doneness," like any other perception of a reason,

[1] Arguably, what follows from (1) through (4) is just that there is no such thing as recognizing objective value. As will transpire, though, nothing hangs on the appeal to knowledge as opposed to belief.

will have the special connection with the will. But hypothetical to-be-pursuedness is a subjective kind of value. It is objective value that Mackie finds problematic.

To be objectively good is to be something one has categorical reason to pursue. A categorical reason is one that is "not conditional upon any present desire of the agent to whose satisfaction the recommended action would contribute as a means" (1977: 29). So the recognition that a thing is objectively good must be both a reason judgment, with the special connection to the will, and the recognition of a property that is there in the world independently of one's desires. Mackie does wonder how the thought of a property that is there regardless of one's desires could have the motivational consequences of a reason judgment. Why wouldn't the motivation depend, as it does with any ordinary belief, on further facts – in particular, facts about the agent's desires? How could the recognition of an objective property have the motivational implications of the recognition of a value?

Seeing no solution, Mackie concludes that nothing is objectively good. He then uses this conclusion to raise a skeptical problem about morality. The link is Mackie's claim that to think one is under a moral requirement to act in a certain way is to attribute objective goodness to actions of that sort. Thus to think one is morally required to be honest, or generous, or fair, is to regard it as true independently of one's thinking it that one has categorical reason to act in these ways. In thinking one is morally required to act, then, one attributes to the action a property that nothing could possibly have.

## SO WHAT IF AMORALISM IS POSSIBLE?

The second stage, specifically premise (6), commits Mackie to the idea that moral judgments inherit the special connection to the will that he attributes to reason judgments. This is because, for Mackie, moral judgments *are* reason judgments. They are judgments of objective value, and judgments of objective value just are judgments that something is categorically to-be-pursued in the sense that one has a desire-independent reason to pursue it. One can challenge Mackie here by raising the possibility of an amoralist, that is, someone who knows how she must act if she is to act morally, but who takes a "So what?" attitude toward morality. If amoralism is possible, premise (6) is false. This ruins the argument for (7), which is the error theory in its canonical form.

Philosophers divide on whether amoralism is possible. But I think this controversy is beside the point. Even if amoralism is possible, the argument against objective value may succeed. For while the possibility of amoralism affects premise (6), it does not touch the first stage. The first stage does rely on a motivational assumption, but it is an assumption about reason judgments, not about moral judgments. The amoralist makes moral judgments, but her "So what?" attitude signals a failure to make the corresponding reason judgments. The thought behind premise (3) is that moving beyond the "So what?" attitude is moving beyond indifference, or motivational neutrality, to a state in which you see the action as bearing on something you care about. This does not mean amoralism is impossible. It just means that if the amoralist gets over her "So what?" attitude her will must be engaged.

But now how do we get to an error theory about morals, if not through premise (6)?

One suggestion is that we don't. One might think the possibility of amoralism would insulate morality from Mackie's argument (Foot 1978; Brink 1986; Copp 1995: 35). On this view, given that moral judgments are not judgments of objective value, the queerness of objective value is contained. If there are no objective values, this won't mean that morality is fraudulent or false or some kind of myth.

But others sense that all is not well. There are two main concerns. One is an appeal to phenomenology. We experience moral requirements as having a kind of inescapable authority.[2] We take morality to be authoritative in the sense that whatever morality requires of us is what we have reason, perhaps even most reason, to do. And we take morality to be inescapable in the sense that whatever it requires, it requires regardless of whether the action serves one's desires or furthers one's interests. Taken together, these doctrines imply that if an action is morally required, then the agent has reason to do it regardless of whether it serves her desires or furthers her interests (Joyce 2001: 42, 77). Which is to say that if morality tells us to pursue something then that thing is objectively good in Mackie's sense. So if there are no objective values, morality cannot be all it seems.

The other worry is that the very point of moral discourse is threatened. Sometimes when things turn out not to be what they seemed, the point of talking about those things survives. Take motion (Joyce 2001: 95–98). It seems absolute; either a thing is moving or it isn't, period. But physics now

[2] See Brink (1997): 255–264.

says motion is relative. This blow to the appearances does not threaten the point of talking about motion, however. We go on saying of things that they are moving, and rightly so. But not all cases are like this. Compare talk of witches. If it turns out that no one has any supernatural powers, then the point of talking about witches is lost. Instead of going on talking about witches, we have to admit that nothing answers to the concept. The second worry, then, is that moral discourse resembles talk of witches more than it resembles talk of motion (Joyce 2001: 96). If there are no objective values, this is more than just a blow to the way morality seems. It actually undermines the point of talking about moral requirements.

Now we can see why it seems so telling to bring up the amoralist. As the second worry suggests, morality's commitment to objective value goes deeper than mere phenomenology. The analogy with motion misses something. This makes the analogy with witches look good. But the suggestion that moral judgments are like witch judgments puts objective value into the content of moral judgments. Part of what it is to think someone is a witch is to think she can do magic. That is why one cannot go on thinking there are witches after discovering that no one can do magic. If this is our model of morality's commitment to objective value, then we wind up saying that part of what it is to think of an action that you are morally required to do it is to think that you have a categorical reason to do it. And that rules out the possibility of amoralism.

But there is a better account of the threat to morality. Morality does need objective value more than motion needs absoluteness. But the threat is not that moral judgments are all false. It is that morality itself, considered as a way of thinking about reasons, can't be true. This is an error theory, but not an error theory of moral belief. The error is in the moral way of thinking about reasons, not in judgments about what morality requires. What we really need to worry about is an error theory of the moral outlook.

To see what an error theory of the moral outlook is, and how it differs from an error theory of moral belief, consider the following scenario. Suppose that amoralism is possible. The amoralist has beliefs, even correct ones, about what morality requires. But she takes a skeptical stance toward morality nonetheless. She understands that moral requirements are inescapable, that whatever morality requires it requires regardless of her interests and desires. But she doesn't see morality as authoritative. She rejects the idea that whatever morality requires, one thereby has reason to do it. Herein lies her "So what?" attitude.

But if it is possible to reject that idea then it is also possible to accept it. I'll call *moral* anyone who, like the amoralist, understands what morality requires and that its requirements are inescapable but, unlike the amoralist, accepts the authority of morality. A moral person so understood is going to have to believe in objective values. An error theory of the moral outlook says the moral person's view of things is false, because there are no objective values. By hypothesis, however, the amoralist and the moral agent both understand what morality requires. So this is not an error theory of beliefs about what morality requires. It is an error theory of the moral way of thinking about reasons.

How, though, could one accept an error theory of the moral outlook and still speak of a correct understanding of what morality requires? In virtue of what would moral beliefs be true? The answer is that there are truths about how moral thinking goes (Foot 2001: 12). Part of the moral way of thinking about reasons, for instance, is that considerations of fairness are categorical reasons, that truth-telling is objectively to-be-pursued, that people's wills are to-be-respected, that it is on the whole objectively bad to harm others, and so on. The amoralist understands as well as anyone else that this is how the moral view goes. It just isn't his view. So his understanding of what morality requires consists in a grasp of how moral thinking goes. This is the correct understanding that he shares with the moral agent.

In this respect the amoralist is like someone who understands a theory but does not accept it. Imagine a Christian biology graduate student taking questions in an oral defense of his thesis. He is asked to describe the evolution of the butterfly wing. In fact he doesn't believe the butterfly wing evolved. He believes butterflies were created a few thousand years ago, complete with wings as we know them. He is also a talented young biologist, and delivers a description the evolution of the butterfly wing that surpasses anything his teachers could muster. He even offers a novel hypothesis that is later confirmed. For him, though, this is all just an exercise, like working out the implications of the assumption that time travel is possible. He doesn't accept the evolutionary theory any more than he accepts the possibility of time travel. He knows how the theory goes, and can even extend it to new cases, but does not accept what it says. Likewise, the amoralist understands the moral way of thinking about reasons, but thinks differently himself.[3]

[3] It may seem there can be no truths about the moral way of thinking, given that people disagree about what morality says. But a theory can admit of different interpretations, compatibly with there being plenty of truths about what the theory says. Quantum mechanics is one example. Moral disagreement, as I see it, is disagreement in the interpretation of one theory of reasons, and morality just is that theory.

This account of the content of moral judgments has implications for the metaphysics of morality. We routinely distinguish moralities, by which we mean the moral codes of different groups or individuals, from morality, by which we mean something else. But it isn't clear what sort of thing morality is supposed to be. Usually an author's language will suggest one of two possibilities. Morality may be construed as a collection of entities like oughts, moral facts, or moral properties, or it may be construed as a system of rules or laws. On the present view, morality is neither. Rather, it shares a metaphysical category with such things as views, theories, doctrines, and ideologies. If we picture it as a collection of oughts, moral facts, or moral properties, our talk of morality looks metaphysically extravagant. The entities in question appear *sui generis*, and seem superfluous to any useful explanation (Harman 1977: 3–10). But construed my way, our talk of morality adds no new type of thing to our ontology. Views and theories were there already. The claim that morality is real is no more problematic, metaphysically speaking, than the claim that the Big Bang theory is real. But when it comes to views, ideologies, and the like, there is another question we can ask. We can ask whether they are true. This is where we depart from the conception of morality as a system of rules. Rules are not views. A rule banning black-soled shoes in the gym, for instance, is not ripe for assessment as true or false, accurate or inaccurate. If morality is an idea, by contrast, then there is a question of the truth of morality itself.

Now we can see how, even if amoralism is possible, Mackie's argument threatens morality. Earlier we noted two ways in which morality might be committed to the existence of objective values. One was phenomenological; moral requirements feel inescapably authoritative. The other was that moral judgments commit us to objective values in the way that witch judgments commit us to supernatural powers. But now we have a third way to understand how morality is committed to objective values; if there are no objective values then morality itself, considered as way of thinking about reasons, is false. This allows us to explain how Mackie's argument would undermine the point of moral discourse, without bringing objective value into the content of moral judgments.

Moral judgments, on this view, are not reason judgments.[4] They are judgments about how the moral way of thinking about reasons goes. If part of the moral view of reasons is that considerations of fairness are

[4] Thus we reject premise (6) of the sketch.

categorical reasons, then it is simply true that morality requires fairness. But this leaves it open whether considerations of fairness are categorical reasons. If they are not, then the moral view of reasons is false. Because it does not treat moral beliefs as reason beliefs, this proposal is neutral on the possibility of amoralism. The amoralist's understanding of what morality requires may be correct, even if (as she believes) morality is a false ideology. So we avoid putting objective value into the content of moral belief. But we can still see how Mackie's argument strikes at the heart of morality. The threat is not that moral beliefs are false, but rather that morality itself is a false way of thinking about reasons. This explains how Mackie's argument would undermine the point of moral discourse. The point of thinking about what a theory says is certainly called into question when the theory is found to be false. So while the point of talking about motion is not much affected by the discovery that motion is relative, the point of discussing the moral view of reasons is seriously affected by the news that morality is a false view of reasons. So even if amoralism is possible, the first stage of Mackie's argument spells trouble for morality.

## STAGE ONE

As we have seen, however, the first stage is a motivational argument. It uses the idea that the recognition of a value entails a disposition of the will. Mackie's puzzle is how the recognition of anything objective could carry that entailment. To appreciate the difficulty, one must see through a number of tempting replies. For instance, one might reply that there is no special problem about objective value, beyond some very general worries about normativity. Or one might say Mackie assumes an implausibly strong form of internalism about reason judgments. Or one might say the puzzle disappears if we construe value on the model of a secondary quality. In the space that remains, I argue that we cannot rest with these answers.

## WHY PICK ON OBJECTIVE VALUE?

Is the problem really specific to objective value? The intuition that reason judgments engage the will applies, it seems, to reason judgments generally. Surely we need an account of how the thought that a thing is subjectively to-be-pursued gets its grip on the will. And this question becomes even more pressing when we notice that people can be mistaken in their judgments of what they want. Why think there is any special difficulty about judgments of objective value?

The reason there is no particular puzzle about judgments of subjective value, Mackie can say, is that these judgments have an automatic relevance to the task of deliberation. When we reason about what to do we try to bring our behavior in line with what we care about. We aim, in other words, for a certain sort of fit between our actions and our subjective motivational set (Williams 1981).[5] But judgments of subjective value are themselves about the relation between one's desires and different actions one could do. To think an action is subjectively good is, roughly, to think it stands in the privileged relation of fit to one's desires. Thus judgments of subjective value automatically engage the aim that drives practical reasoning. Insofar as one deliberates, one will have the goal that these judgments need in order to motivate. This explains the special connection between judgments of subjective value and the will. Note that the explanation is no less apt in cases where one is mistaken about what is in one's subjective motivational set. Even if I am wrong about what I want, the aim of fitting my behavior to my desires will explain why I am moved by my judgments about which actions fit my desires.

But objective value judgments are by definition *not* about how actions are related to one's desires. The straightforward explanation we gave above will not work for them. There appears to be nothing about their subject matter that gives them any automatic relevance to the task of practical reasoning. So why aren't they just as neutral, motivationally speaking, as any old factual judgment?

## QUEERNESS ON A SHOESTRING

It might seem, though, that to get this puzzle airborne one would need to exaggerate the motivational force of value judgments. Mackie sometimes writes as if seeing something as "to-be-pursued" would have to entail actually pursuing it. But in view of phenomena like weakness of will and depression, it seems clear that value judgments carry no such guarantee. One might agree, then, that objective values with that kind of power would be queer properties, while denying that objective values must have that kind of power.

[5] For a different picture of the aim of deliberation, see Clark (2007).

But in fact there is no need to exaggerate. To see this, consider the case of belief-desire pairs.[6] Belief-desire pairs are intrinsically motivating if anything is, and yet they carry nothing like a guarantee of action. Moreover, it would be puzzling how a belief alone – a belief with no desires in its content – could be like a belief-desire pair in its motivational implications. Ordinary factual beliefs are not like this. The belief that there is a cat in the next room, for instance, lacks the motivational spin of a belief-desire pair. It might incline you to enter the room or to avoid entering it, depending on your desires. But a belief-desire pair, say the belief that Chutney is in the next room together with a desire to pet him, is not motivationally neutral. This sort of mental state entails a disposition of the will if anything does. On the other hand, any number of things can prevent it from issuing in action. Maybe you remember only too late that you wanted to pet Chutney before leaving for work, or you recall the vet's warning not to touch the cat right after the surgery, or you are too tired or sad to feel like moving, though you would pet him if he came within range, or you fall asleep, or get distracted by a phone call.

For Mackie's purposes it would be enough if value judgments were comparable to belief-desire pairs in what they entail about choice. But the logical connection between belief-desire pairs and choice is highly attenuated. One cannot refute the argument from queerness, therefore, by pointing out that the logical connection between value judgment and choice is similarly attenuated. One must go farther, and deny that value judgments have entailments comparable to those of belief-desire pairs. Indeed one might hold that Mackie's argument can run on fumes. Perhaps any degree of motivational bias would be enough. As Garner says, "the difference between a compulsion and a nudge may be only quantitative" (1990: 144). What matters is not the strength of the nudge, but that some nudge is entailed.

## DID INTERNALISM DIE OF BOREDOM?

The question now is whether value judgments are like belief-desire pairs in terms of what they entail about how the agent will choose. More specifically, we want to know whether thinking something is objectively good carries this sort of motivational bias. There are strong reasons for thinking it would have to. There are also popular reasons for thinking it

[6] For my purposes, we can say an agent has a belief-desire pair just in case, for some $\phi$ and $\psi$, she wants to $\psi$ and believes she can $\psi$ by $\phi$-ing.

does not. In this section I first consider what Mackie can say in support of the motivational premise he needs. Then I explain why the popular counterexamples don't work.

The thesis in question is undoubtedly a form of internalism. But let us be clear on what sort of internalism this is. Since, for Mackie, thinking something is objectively good is thinking one has categorical reason to pursue it, we are looking at internalism about reason judgments. Moral judgments, as I argued earlier, are another matter. The specter of the amoralist is a challenge to internalism about moral judgments. But since the amoralist, with her "So what?" attitude, does not see morality as giving her reasons, the possibility of amoralism does not affect Mackie's internalism about value judgments.

To see why Mackie would accept internalism in this form, consider the connection between reason judgments and the "So what?" question. As we've seen, Mackie's argument threatens to generate an error theory even if amoralism is possible. The threat is to the moral person's way of thinking about reasons. The amoralist might grant that there are "moral reasons," in the sense that there are truths about what morality requires. But there is a sort of reason judgment that she does not make, namely the sort that would cure her of her "So what?" attitude, thereby converting her to the moral person's way of thinking. Mackie's worry is that the moral way of thinking can't be true, because of its commitment to categorical reasons. This tells us something about the notion of reason judgment that figures in the argument from queerness. A reason judgment is what is missing insofar as one says "So what?" It is what puts one beyond the "So what?" attitude (Joyce 2001: 41).

But think of what it takes to put someone beyond the "So what?" attitude. Suppose your friend has no plan to return the book he has borrowed from the library. You try pointing out that it is overdue. You suggest that someone else might want it. You warn that he may have to pay a fine, lose his privileges, have his registration blocked. He just shrugs and says "So?" What would it take to get him over this bout of "So what?" and into a reason judgment? Mackie's thought, I suggest, is that it would require connecting the action up with something the agent cares about. Nothing you can say about the action is going to end the "So what?" attitude unless it connects the action with something that matters to your friend.[7]

[7] The idea is not that if you see a reason to, say, clean the oven you will want to clean the oven. Who could want that? It is that if you see a reason to clean the oven you must see the action as connected with something you care about, like whether your house smells like an oven.

Now suppose you hit on something that works. You point out that he signed a letter of intent that had the library rules in fine print. As it turns out, keeping his word is important to him. The penny drops. He gave his word. This does strike him as a reason. But now if keeping his word is important to him, and he knows he will be keeping his word only if he returns the book, then he is in a state that is like a belief-desire pair in terms of what it entails for choice. Indeed it is tempting to say he actually has a belief-desire pair at this point. But there is no need to insist on the word "desire." What matters is that the reason judgment entails a comparable disposition of the will. There is no guarantee that he will return the book, of course, or even that he will decide to, but no such guarantee attaches to belief-desire pairs either. If this is right, Mackie gets the internalism he needs.

There are many who, like myself, find the internalism obvious. Once we see reason judgments as terminators of the "So what?" attitude, the game is over for us. But others argue that the internalism is false. Some cite sloth and depression as conditions that can completely decouple one's will from one's reason judgments. Here is an example from Michael Smith:

> As we saw earlier, Michael Stocker observes that various emotional and physical factors – "spiritual or physical tiredness," "accidie," "weakness of body," "illness," "general apathy or despair," "inability to concentrate," "a feeling of uselessness or futility," and so on; "depressions," as he generically terms them – can sap our desire to do what we value doing . . . The depressive may thus know full well that the rational thing for her do to is, for example, to get up and get on with her life: to go to work, to visit a friend, to read a book, to cook a meal, or whatever. But the effect of her depression may be precisely to remove any desire at all that she has to do any of these things. Having no desire to get up and get on with her life, she may therefore simply do nothing – or, at any rate, nothing intentionally. (1994: 135)

Take someone who thinks she has a reason to get dressed and drive across town. Her friend Miles is in the hospital. She does not say "So what?" to this. Friends, she believes, visit their friends in hospital. And she "values" being a friend to Miles. But according to Smith, it does not follow that she wants to get dressed and drive across town, or that she wants to visit Miles, or even that she wants to be a friend to Miles. For she may be suffering from sloth, or depression, or the like. And these conditions can "sap our desire to do what we value doing."

Valuing, Smith says, does not entail wanting. But does this claim bear on Mackie's internalism about reason judgments?

Note first that if it is to have any bearing at all, valuing has to be understood in a particular way. It must be understood as placing the agent beyond the "So what?" attitude. Otherwise, depression's ability to sap our "values" tells us nothing about the reason judgments that figure in Mackie's argument. Suppose, for example, that you have the Monday blues. Your partner points out that a productive member of society would be getting out of bed and going to work. To see this as a reason to get up is precisely not to respond with an asocial shrug and a "What's that to me?" If we construe valuing in such a way that it is possible to value being a productive member of society while sticking to this "So what?" stance, then valuing will not entail reason judgment. In that case Smith's separation of valuing and wanting is plausible, but Mackie will be happy to agree. His point is about reason judgments.

So now let's construe valuing as a state that puts one beyond the "So what?" stance. Here I think we will find that there is a limit to what depression can do, short of eliminating the valuing altogether. It can't remove all the sap. For now a person who values being a productive member of society is someone to whom this matters. If it didn't matter to him, if he didn't care, his attitude would be "So what?" Indeed this is why accidie is so exasperating. If it were all the same to you what sort of friend you were to poor Miles, you might be quite happy to linger at home in your pajamas. But given that you value being a true friend, being productive, coming through for your children, and so on, you are beyond indifference. It can't be all the same to you.

This is enough to make objective value look queer. How could the recognition of an objective feature of a thing necessarily put one beyond indifference? With other objective properties, there is no such entailment. One just registers a feature of the world, which one may care about or not. Why should a mere difference in subject matter bring such a difference in logical consequence? Why would this one region of the world be different from all the rest? This is what motivational skepticism is all about. No one can blame Mackie for seeing a puzzle here.

Let us pause and review the argument as reworked by me. It is still an argument for an error theory, but not for an error theory of moral belief. The new conclusion is that the moral view of reasons can't be true, because the moral view is that fairness, altruism, equality, and so on are objectively good. The threat is that morality itself, viewed as an ideology or theory about reasons, is false. We must therefore turn our attention to the first stage. Because they are reason judgments, judgments of objective value must place the agent beyond the "So what?" attitude. But it is puzzling how a judgment with no desires in its content could carry that entailment. Thus the idea of something that is both objective and a value looks incoherent. Apparently, the moral person's view of things cannot be correct. For the moral person is the one who not only understands the moral ideology but accepts it, thereby transcending the "So what?" stance.

This argument is remarkably restrained in its motivational assumptions. As we've seen, it is neutral on the possibility of amoralism. If amoralism is possible, this undermines the case for an error theory of moral belief, but an error theory of the moral outlook still looms. So there is no assumption that moral judgments have any special connection with the will. Moreover, while there is an assumption that reason judgments have a special connection with the will, the assumed connection is highly attenuated, coheres with the familiar effects of listlessness and depression, and is otherwise very hard to deny. Whatever flaws this argument may have, excessive internalism is not one of them.

It may seem unfair, though, to insist on a conception of reason judgments as putting the agent beyond the "So what?" attitude. There are other conceptions of reason judgment. A person can realize she has a "reason of etiquette" to answer an invitation in the third person, while viewing the rules of polite society as a complete charade. This sort of reason judgment need not put one beyond the "So what?" attitude. But it may still be a categorical judgment, for one may understand that the rules make no exceptions for the case where the action does not happen to serve one's interests or desires. As long as this sort of categorical reason judgment can be true, why does it matter if the other sort is always false?

The answer is that if the other sort of categorical reason judgment is always false, then the world cannot be as the moral person sees it. To be moral is to make the sort of reason judgment that takes you beyond the "So what?" stance in regard to things like fairness, truthfulness, altruism, and equality. If the moral way of thinking about those things is false, we get an error theory of the moral outlook.

Still, it may seem that the modest form of internalism that I say drives Mackie's argument is too weak to make for any real puzzle, because it amounts to no more than the claim that reason judgments engage the will insofar as one is rational. To say *that* is not to say that reason judgments necessarily engage the will. Perhaps one will admit that if there were categorical judgments the making of which entailed that one actually cared about the object of the judgment, that would be odd and in need of some explanation. But surely our watered-down version of internalism does not commit us to that.

What I am suggesting, though, is that our watered-down version still does commit us to that. Mackie's thought, as I understand it, is not that if you are beyond saying "So what?" to considerations of fairness, say, then fairness will matter to you if you are rational (Korsgaard 1986; Smith 1994: 92–129). It is that if you are beyond saying "So what?" then fairness actually does matter to you. If it didn't, your attitude would be "So what?" And then you would await some further argument to get you beyond this stance. The examples people use to sever the connection between reason judgment and the will do not refute this form of internalism.

But perhaps there is some sleight of hand here. Expressions like "matters to" and "cares about" have a distinctly evaluative tone. One could scarcely be said to care about something if one saw absolutely no good in it. This might seem to trivialize Mackie's internalism. If the very idea of caring has evaluation packed into it, then the claim that value judgment entails caring might seem to lose its interest. But this is a flat mistake. It may be that caring about something entails thinking it is good. But Mackie is asking about the entailment in the opposite direction. He is saying that thinking something is objectively good, since it is in part thinking one has reason to pursue the thing, must entail caring about something connected with the object of the pursuit. His question is how a judgment whose truth conditions were objective in his sense could entail that. This question cannot be answered by pointing out that caring entails a thought of good.

Alternatively, suspicion may fall on the "So what?" attitude itself. Those who reject Mackie's internalism are free to offer up their own understandings of that stance. For instance, they might say the "So what?" attitude consists in the lack of a thought together with a lack of concern.[8] Thus the "So what?" stance toward fairness would be the absence of a thought that fairness is a reason together with a failure to care about fairness. If this is right then the dispute is really about how these two elements of the "So what?" attitude are related. Those who reject Mackie's internalism think you can have the thought and lack the caring, whereas Mackie denies this. Clearly it would beg the question for Mackie simply to assert his view of the matter.

But Mackie does not simply assert his view. His point is that thinking of something as a reason entails being beyond the "So what?" attitude

[8] I am grateful to the anonymous referee who brought this up.

toward it. And his opponent agrees with that. On the proposed analysis, the "So what?" attitude consists in two absences. Unless both the caring and the thought are absent, one is beyond the "So what?" attitude. This means the thought alone entails that one is beyond the "So what?" attitude. Now how, Mackie wants to know, can one be beyond "So what?" without being beyond indifference? This is a fair question. There is no begging going on.

At this point one might just grant that the sort of reason judgment I have in mind really does entail a disposition of the will, and turn one's attention to the task of explaining how it could have that feature given that there are no desires in its truth conditions. This might seem easy enough. Perhaps the problem is just that Mackie assumes a certain view of what it takes for a thought to motivate. Perhaps he is assuming that beliefs can only motivate as parts of belief-desire pairs. Then there would be a puzzle about how the mere recognition of an objective feature of the world could guarantee the presence in the agent of the desire required for the belief to motivate. But surely the claim that beliefs can only motivate as parts of belief-desire pairs is open to question. One way around Mackie, then, is to assert that reason judgments can motivate by themselves, i.e. not as parts of belief-desire pairs.

But this is not a way around Mackie. The rejection of the so-called Humean Theory of Motivation cannot be an answer to Mackie's challenge, because it is the occasion of Mackie's challenge. As he points out, the argument from queerness fixes a leak in Hume's famous argument that reason can never be an "influencing motive of the will." Mackie takes Hume to have argued that values cannot be objects of knowledge, since knowledge is motivationally inert whereas value judgments are not. As it stands, this argument is open to an objection:

> Someone might object that Hume has argued unfairly from the lack of influencing power (not contingent on desires) in ordinary objects and ordinary reasoning, and might maintain that values differ from natural objects precisely in their power, when known, automatically to influence the will. (1977: 40)

That is, one can ask Hume how he knows that *all* knowledge lacks influencing power of its own, unless he has already decided that value judgments are not knowledge. Perhaps value knowledge is special in this regard.

Mackie then offers the argument from queerness as a reply on Hume's behalf. Hume should say, says Mackie, that this response is committed to values being very odd properties, odd because it is puzzling where they come by their special power to motivate.

Understood this way, there is an extremely valuable point at the heart of the argument from queerness. It is a point against those who posit beliefs that motivate by themselves, beliefs whose influencing power is "not contingent upon desires," as Mackie puts it. The point is simply that it is hard to see why a mere difference in the subject matter of a belief would make a difference in the way the belief motivates. If what we are doing with our evaluative beliefs is just another case of registering the way things are, then why does their motivating us not depend, in the same way as any other, on background desires about how things are? That is what Mackie wants explained.

Nor does it help to say, with Smith and Korsgaard, that value judgments are about reasons and reason judgments motivate on pain of irrationality. As we've seen, the internalism that needs explaining is stronger than that.[9] What follows from the fact that you see certain considerations as reasons for you to act is not just that those considerations will matter to you if you are rational, but that they actually do matter to you. Otherwise your attitude would be "So what?"

## THE SECONDARY-QUALITY ANALOGY

Almost none of the extant replies to Mackie is even designed to explain what he wants explained. One that is, however, starts from the idea that value is in certain respects like color. When it comes to registering the way things are, there are cases and cases. Sometimes the question at hand is one that can be understood without bringing in the idea of any sort of subjective response. Thus we can understand the question "Is water an element?" without bringing in the idea of how water looks or smells or feels. But we can't understand the question "Is benzine red?" without understanding it as a question about the appearance of benzine. We have to bring in the idea of a subjective response, specifically the idea of a thing's looking red to someone. If Mackie were assuming that the question "Is it good?" must be of the former kind, i.e. intelligible apart from the notion of any subjective response, then we might accuse him of stacking the deck against objective value. Surely colors are objective in their way. Why won't it do to say values are objective in that way (McDowell 1985)?

[9] Similar remarks apply to the idea that something like Davidson's Principle of Charity can resolve Mackie's puzzle (Wedgwood 2004: 408). It may be that to count as an agent at all one must, in general, care about the things one sees as reasons. But that doesn't explain why, in order to count as seeing something as a reason, one must care about that thing.

But Mackie does not assume objective value would have to be intelligible independently of the notion of a subjective response. He assumes the opposite. The idea of value, for Mackie, is the idea of a thing's being to-be-pursued. For a thing to be objectively good is for it to be true, independently of one's believing it and independently of one's desires, that it is to-be-pursued. There is no understanding this idea apart from the notion of a subjective response, namely pursuit. If this is what we mean by "secondary quality," then in his motivational argument Mackie presupposes that objective value is a secondary quality.

This may seem to open the door to an explanation of the thing Mackie wants explained. Perhaps we can understand objective value on the model of an objectivist view of secondary qualities, in which something like caring, desire, or pursuit takes the part of, say, a visual experience of red. Gloss redness as the property of being "such as to look red." A thing can be such as to look red even if there are observers to whom it never looks red, and even if there is no one to whom it always looks red. Moreover, a thing can look red to an observer without being such as to look red, in the relevant sense. Thus on this view redness meets Mackie's two criteria of objectivity. The color of a thing is what it is regardless of how the thing looks to me. And the property is there independently of my thinking it is; I can be mistaken as to whether an object is such as to look red. The property is relational, but relational between the objects and color perceivers as a group, not between the objects and any individual.

The suggestion, then, is that objective goodness could be the property of being such as to be wanted, where again that property would be there regardless of my particular desires, and regardless of my judgments about what is such as to elicit desire. Here too the property would be relational, but relational between the objects and desirers as a group, not between the objects and any individual.

This looks like a way of reconciling the objectivity of a property with the motivational implications of recognizing that something has the property. For the definition of objective value now makes reference to a desiderative response. On closer inspection, however, this move does not solve the motivational problem. For on the objectivist view of color, I can know that something is a certain color without its looking that color to me. I put on my rose colored glasses, and now my milk looks pink to me. On the objectivist view of secondary qualities the milk is still white because it is still such as to look white, in the relevant sense. Moreover, I can know it is white, despite its looking pink to me, because I can know it is such as to look white. If we model objective value on this view of color, we will have to grant that it is possible to know something is objectively good without wanting it. For this will be strictly analogous to knowing something is white, despite its not looking white to you. The secondary-quality analogy therefore fails to explain how the recognition of a property that is there independently of one's desires and judgments can have the motivational implications of a reason judgment. Consequently it does not meet Mackie's challenge (Blackburn 1997: 171). Value judgment, he will say, carries an entailment that has no parallel in color judgment. But if ordinary factual beliefs can only motivate as parts of belief-desire pairs, then why should value beliefs be any different? What is so special about the property of objective value that it effects this sea change in the nature of the motivational explanation?

## CONCLUSION

Mackie did overstate the power of moral judgment. He was cavalier in dismissing the possibility of amoralism, and his exuberant caricature of what objective values would have to be like does overlook phenomena like listlessness and depression. He got carried away. But these excesses are incidental. The motivational argument from queerness raises a serious skeptical problem about morality,[10] and it does so on very modest assumptions about what objective values would have to be like.

[10] I think Mackie's puzzle can be solved, but the solution requires a specific understanding of the practical syllogism and its role in deliberation (Clark 2001; 2007).

CHAPTER 11

# *The truth in Ecumenical Expressivism**

*Michael Ridge*

Early expressivists, such as A.J. Ayer, argued that normative sentences are not truth-apt, and many found this striking claim implausible. After all, ordinary speakers are perfectly happy to ascribe truth and falsity to normative assertions. It is hard to believe that competent speakers could be so wrong about the meanings of their own language, particularly as these meanings are fixed by the conventions implicit in their own linguistic behavior. Later expressivists therefore tried to arrange a marriage between expressivism and the truth-aptness of normative discourse. Like many arranged marriages, this has not been an entirely happy one. In particular, the marriage has seemed to depend on so-called deflationist theories of truth, and these may well turn out to provide at best a shaky foundation for any marriage. Before advising the parties to file for divorce, though, we should first see whether expressivism itself has not been misunderstood. I argue that the marriage of expressivism to the truth-aptness of normative discourse can indeed be saved, though only in the context of a version of expressivism I call "Ecumenical Expressivism."

## I EXPRESSIVISM AND DEFLATIONIST TRUTH: HOSTAGES TO FORTUNE

A guiding idea behind expressivism is that the meaning of normative predicates should be understood in terms of the way in which they are conventionally used to express pro-attitudes. This idea finds its most natural home in a broadly Lockean philosophy of language. Locke famously argued that the meanings of words in natural languages should

* Many thanks to Matthew Chrisman, Jeff Ketland, and an anonymous referee for useful comments. Thanks also to the participants and organizers of the conference on Practical Reason and Moral Motivation held in Helsinki in December 2005, at which I also got very useful feedback on this material.

be understood in terms of how they are used to express states of mind (see Locke 1975). Locke himself focused on the ways in which language allows us to express ideas. However, there is no reason in principle to restrict the Lockean approach to ideas as opposed to other states of mind, including non-cognitive states. A useful foil is found in the Sellarsian tradition. Lockeans explain the meanings of words and sentences in terms of the states of mind they are conventionally used to express. Very roughly, Sellarsians take the opposite approach, and explain the contents of our states of mind in terms of commitments to affirm or deny corresponding sentences (see, e.g., Brandom 1994).

The Lockean approach has in modern times been considerably refined. The classic work of philosophers like H.P. Grice is also germane here (see Grice 1968). Grice helpfully distinguishes speaker meaning from sentence meaning, a distinction which is perhaps best introduced through examples. I might use the sentence "Well, that donut was delicious" ironically to mean that the donut in question was disgusting. While I mean that the donut was disgusting, my sentence nonetheless literally means that it was delicious. Indeed, it is only because of the sentence's literal meaning that I am able to use it ironically to convey the opposite. Speaker meaning depends on the particular intentions of a given speaker, whereas sentence meaning depends in the first instance on background conventions. For a modern and extensively worked out rendition of a broadly Lockean approach (see Davies 2003).

Within this broadly Lockean framework, the expressivist argues (very roughly) that normative sentences conventionally function primarily to express suitable desire-like states of mind.[1] This is in contrast with ordinary factual assertions which, on the Lockean account, conventionally function to express beliefs about what the world is like rather than desire-like states. Here it is important to emphasize the distinction between expressing a desire and reporting that one has it. I can report that I approve of the Mets simply by asserting that I do – for example, by saying, "I approve of the Mets." In doing so I directly express my *belief* that I approve of the Mets, thereby reporting my approval of them. By contrast, I can directly express my approval of the Mets with a suitable interjection – for example, by saying, "Hooray for the Mets!" In both cases I indicate my approval of the Mets, but in the former case I do this by expressing a belief about my approval of them.

[1] I provide a more detailed discussion of exactly how we should define expressivism in section II below.

Early expressivists like A.J. Ayer took the analogy with interjections seriously. They argued that because normative sentences express (and do not report) attitudes, and moreover do not report anything, that they are simply not apt for truth or falsity. Although ordinary folks do without hesitation use the language of truth and falsity in normative contexts, this is all a mistake, or so Ayer argued. This is a lot to swallow, and Ayer's own argument relied on an extremely controversial and implausible verificationist theory of meaning. Moreover, many critics of these early forms of expressivism have quite reasonably found it incredible that ordinary speakers could be so deeply confused about their own everyday discourse.

Later expressivists have tried to preserve the core insights of expressivism while accommodating the idea that normative sentences might, after all, be truth-apt. Simon Blackburn is perhaps the most famous exponent of this approach (see Blackburn 1984, 1993, 1998). Blackburn's idea is to "earn the right" to the realist-sounding things ordinary folks say within an expressivist framework. Blackburn calls his approach "quasi-realism" to mark the fact that it allows us to mimic realist discourse within what is, at some level of abstraction, an anti-realist position. Allan Gibbard takes a similar approach, and sometimes characterizes himself as a sort of quasi-realist (Gibbard 2003: 181).

In his early attempts to marry expressivism to the truth-aptness of normative discourse, Blackburn flirted with a coherence theory of truth, albeit a non-reductionist one (Blackburn 1984: 256–257). However, coherence theories seem to make unintelligible the very idea that the best development of our current stock of beliefs, as informed by future experiences, could be false. Since this idea does seem intelligible, it would be unfortunate if the only form of truth with which expressivism could find domestic bliss was coherentist truth. Blackburn has more recently moved to what I shall call a deflationist conception of truth.[2] More accurately, Blackburn wavers between holding that deflationism is all there is to say about truth and the view that deflationism is at any rate all there is to truth about moral (and, more generally, I suspect, normative) claims.

The basic inspiration for deflationist accounts of truth stems in part from the deep problems facing more robust theories of truth, perhaps

[2] Blackburn and Gibbard instead refer to this view of truth as "minimalist," but other philosophers (most notably Crispin Wright and those influenced by his work; see Wright 1992) use "minimalism" and its cognates to refer to a slightly more robust view of truth. Since "deflationism" and its cognates is, by contrast, pretty unequivocally used to denote a very slender notion of truth, I prefer that terminology.

most notably, so-called "correspondence theories." In light of the apparently grave difficulties facing more robust conceptions of truth (a summary of which would go well beyond the scope of this essay), the deflationist begins with the hypothesis that saying (or thinking) p is true is really no different from saying (or thinking) that p. Deflationism is suggested by some of Wittgenstein's remarks, though Wittgenstein himself would probably not have found it useful to develop a philosophical theory of truth. For an early defense of deflationism as a philosophical theory, we should instead turn to F.P. Ramsey (see Ramsey 1978). More recently, the idea has been developed in some detail by Paul Horwich. Horwich maintains that there is nothing more to understanding the truth predicate than there is to understanding the equivalence schema, "It is true that p if and only if p" (Horwich 1990: 7). This schema is similar to the one found in the important work of Alfred Tarski on truth in formal languages, though Tarski's schema ranges over sentences rather than propositions. Tarski calls his own schema the "T schema" (see Tarski 1958).

It is easy to see how deflationism might seem like a powerful tool for quasi-realists like Blackburn and Gibbard. For suppose there really is nothing more to saying that it is true that charity is good than there is to saying that charity is good. This suggests that the expressivist can indeed allow that normative utterances are truth-apt. The point will simply be that in saying that it is true that charity is good one is expressing one's attitude in favor of charity in just the same way that one does when one says that charity is good.

However, deflationism is itself hardly a platitude. For a start, some technical results suggest that contemporary forms of deflationism are incompatible with Godel's incompleteness results. The worry was developed independently by Jeff Ketland and Stewart Shapiro (see Ketland 1998 and Shapiro 1998).[3] The details of these results would, unfortunately, take us too far afield here. Suffice it to say that it is not at all obvious how deflationism can avoid the force of this critique.

A second, and less technical, worry about deflationism is that, on at least some construals, it seems to require understanding of all instances of the T-schema in order to count as grasping the concept of truth (see Gupta 2005a). If this really does follow from deflationism, it would indeed be worrying. For instances of the T-schema can range over all sorts of exotic concepts, ranging from the concept of a quark to the concept of a snail.

[3] For further clarification, see the discussion at www.homepages.ed.ac.uk/jketland/corrigendum.html.

Clearly, a speaker does not have to have mastery of all possible concepts over which the truth predicate can range (that is, all possible concepts!) in order to grasp the concept of truth. For an interesting deflationist reply to this objection, see Hill (2002); Gupta replies to Hill in Gupta (2005b). Again, this is not the place to delve into the interesting details of this debate.

A third worry about deflationism is that it is incompatible with the platitude that a sentence's meaning plus the relevant worldly fact(s) suffice to fix the sentence's truth-value. This worry is developed in co-authored work by Dorit Bar-On, Clair Horisk, and William G. Lycan (see Bar-On, Horisk, and Lycan 2005a, 2005b). More precisely, the worry is that if (as many of its defenders claim), deflationism is incompatible with the appeal to truth-conditions in the theory of meaning, then deflationism cannot be squared with this apparent platitude about how truth-values are fixed. In fact, deflationists may actually be able to avoid this commitment, but this too is not obvious. Again, I cannot delve into the interesting details of the debate (though Bar-On, Horisk, and Lycan do in their Postscript).

Perhaps each of these three worries (as well as others I have not mentioned here) about deflationism can be dealt with adequately. Indeed, in spite of these worries, I remain cautiously optimistic about the tenability of deflationism. However, it would be a shame if the fortunes of expressivism were so closely tied to the fortunes of deflationism. After all, the motivations for expressivism are not particularly closely tied to debates in the philosophy of mathematics that drive the Ketland/Shapiro objection to deflationism. It would therefore be disappointing for those sympathetic to expressivism if the tenability of expressivism turned out to rely, in the end, on such seemingly philosophically distant considerations. We should see whether we can insulate expressivism from the debate over deflationism while still arranging a suitable marriage between expressivism and the truth-aptness of normative discourse. In the rest of this essay, I try to do just this. If successful, the account provided here provides expressivists with insurance against the refutation of deflationism. First, though, I must introduce the version of expressivism I want to defend: "Ecumenical Expressivism."[4]

## II INTRODUCING ECUMENICAL EXPRESSIVISM

So far, I have deliberately left my characterization of expressivism vague. In this section, I want to suggest a slightly unorthodox way of

[4] I have developed this view in more detail in Ridge (2006a) and Ridge (forthcoming).

understanding the debate between expressivists and cognitivists. This new framework turns out to provide a new strategy for saving the apparently fragile marriage of expressivism to the truth-aptness of normative discourse; I develop this strategy in sections III and IV.

Much of the debate between cognitivists and expressivists stems from the rather Janus-faced character of normative judgment.[5] In some respects, normative judgments seem like ordinary beliefs. We call them "beliefs," as when we say things like, "Britney believes that she ought to spend more time at the tanning salon." Most pertinently for present purposes, we do not hesitate to classify them as true or false. In other respects, normative judgments seem more like desires. Normative judgement is practical; it reliably guides action. Changes in normative view reliably track changes in motivation. We tend to question the sincerity of someone who claims that she really ought to do something but shows no signs whatsoever of being motivated to do it, feel bad about not doing it, etc. Failure to act on one's all-things-considered normative judgement is irrational.[6] This contrasts with acting contrary to what one believes is required by merely conventional norms like those of etiquette.

These competing characteristics of normative judgments have led to the formation of two diametrically opposed philosophical camps – the cognitivists and the expressivists. Cognitivism is traditionally defined as the doctrine that normative sentences express beliefs rather than desires. Expressivism, by contrast, is traditionally defined as the doctrine that normative sentences express desires rather than beliefs.[7] Casting the debate in these terms unfortunately masks the following logical space:

*The Ecumenical View*: Normative sentences express *both* beliefs and desires.

On the traditional way of carving up the meta-ethical territory, the Ecumenical View seems to imply that neither expressivism or cognitivism is correct. In that case, one of the central meta-ethical debates of

[5] In the next few paragraphs, I draw heavily on Ridge (forthcoming).

[6] This is not uncontroversial, but this is not the place to discuss the controversy. For a contrasting view, see Arpaly (2000).

[7] For example, David Brink characterizes the expressivist as holding the view that, "moral judgments must express the appraiser's non-cognitive attitudes, *rather than her beliefs*" (Brink 1997: 9, emphasis added) while "cognitivists interpret moral judgments as expressing cognitive attitudes, such as belief, *rather than non-cognitive attitudes*, such as desire" (Brink 1997: 5, emphasis added). Frank Jackson and Philip Pettit characterize expressivism as holding that moral utterances express desires rather than beliefs (Jackson and Pettit 1998). Although these views are often formulated as views about moral judgment in particular, it is clear that they are very often taken to be plausible views about normative judgment more generally.

the past century has been a tempest in a teapot. This might be a welcome conclusion to those weary of apparently interminable debates about those doctrines. However, the issues at stake in that debate remain live ones even if the Ecumenical View is correct. We can usefully redraw the terms of that debate within an ecumenical framework as follows:

*Cognitivism:* For any normative sentence M, M is conventionally used to express a belief such that M is true if and only if the belief is true.

*Expressivism:* For any normative sentence M, M is not conventionally used to express a belief such that M is true if and only if the belief is true.

The distinction is exclusive but not exhaustive. There is logical space for hybrid views according to which some but not all normative sentences express beliefs which provide their truth-conditions.[8] For present purposes I put such views to one side. Also, expressivism as characterized here does not include the positive thesis that normative sentences function to express pro-attitudes. I have not included this in my definition of expressivism simply because I want to emphasize the ecumenical idea that this thesis can be common ground between expressivists and cognitivists. For it should be clear enough that, characterized in these terms, there can be both cognitivist and expressivist versions of the Ecumenical View. The Ecumenical Cognitivist and the Ecumenical Expressivist agree that normative sentences express both beliefs and desires. They disagree about the connection between the truth of the belief expressed and the truth of the sentence.

Here there is a divide between expressivists like Ayer and more quasi-realist expressivists like Blackburn and Gibbard. The former will claim that normative sentences are not truth-apt and so trivially do not inherit the truth-conditions of any belief they express. Quasi-realists, though, want to insist that normative sentences *are* truth-apt. The difficult question then becomes how to maintain that normative sentences conventionally function to express beliefs, are truth-apt (*contra* Ayer) and yet do not automatically inherit the truth-conditions of the belief they express as ordinary assertions seem to do. Before we can usefully explore this question, though, we must first develop Ecumenical Expressivism in a little more detail.

[8] Paul Edwards and David Wiggins have defended such views. See especially Edwards (1955).

On the version of Ecumenical Expressivism I favor, normative sentences express:

(1) A suitable state of approval of actions insofar as they would garner the approval of a certain sort of prescriber.

And

(2) A belief which makes suitable anaphoric reference back to that prescriber.

A prescriber is someone who is disposed to offer various prescriptions, where prescriptions include commands, advice, suggestions, and the like; it is in effect a generalization of the more familiar idea of an Ideal Advisor conception of normativity. The basic idea is best illustrated through examples. Suppose I am a utilitarian. In that case, my claim that charity is right expresses my perfectly general attitude of approval to actions insofar as they would garner the approval of a certain sort of prescriber, which in this case is one who approves of actions just insofar as they promote happiness. My claim *also* expresses a belief the content of which is fixed via anaphoric reference back to that sort of prescriber (the one which figures in the content of the attitude I expressed). In this case, the belief is that such a prescriber would be disposed to insist on giving to charity.

The example of a utilitarian is purely illustrative. The account here is compatible with most speakers only having at best an inchoate conception of the sort of prescriber of whom they approve. Most ordinary speakers do not have worked-out normative theories, and our meta-normative theory must accommodate this. Fortunately one's approval of an even inchoately conceived sort of prescriber can be expressed, and one can have some idea of at least some of her properties. I could be sure that the sort of prescriber of whom I approve would condemn torture but approve of charity – e.g. without having a fixed conception of her overall nature (whether she is a utilitarian, a Kantian, or something else altogether).

Elsewhere, I have argued that Ecumenical Expressivism so understood offers the expressivist new resources with which to deal with the notorious "Frege–Geach" puzzle, the possibility and irrationality of akrasia, and the otherwise vexing challenge to provide an expressivist account of the distinction between what Michael Smith has called certitude, robustness, and importance.[9] I also argue that the Ideal Prescriber element of the account also helps provide a plausible account of pluralism about

[9] See Ridge (2006a) and Ridge (forthcoming).

reasons and incommensurability as well as a plausible account of the distinction between supererogation and deontic necessity (e.g. moral duty).[10] However, I do not have space to rehearse these arguments here, but must simply lay the view out so as to show how it might help with truth-aptness.

## III

As we saw in section I, existing attempts to marry expressivism to truth-aptness depend on a deflationist understanding of truth. In section I, I have explained how reliance on a deflationist theory of truth gives hostages to fortune. It is worth seeing whether Ecumenical Expressivism offers a more promising path to marital bliss for expressivism and truth-aptness for normative discourse. In section IV, I argue that it does. The key idea is to remain neutral on the correct (non-deflationist) theory of truth, but instead give a novel account of how the truth-bearers for normative sentences are fixed. It turns out that Ecumenical Expressivism provides some handy tools with which to do this. First, however, we need to back up and get a better picture of the logical space the proposed theory will occupy, which is the main topic of the present section. This is actually a rather delicate matter. In order to hone in on the logical space I have in mind, we first must consider just what implications expressivism has for certain assumptions implicit in our everyday discourse. I begin by laying out some of the relevant assumptions.

Ordinary folks happily characterize both normative judgments and descriptive judgments as beliefs. We are just as happy to say that Dorothy believes that she is not in Kansas any more as we are to say that she believes that she ought to follow the yellow brick road. Moreover, we do this without any suggestion that "belief" might be ambiguous, picking out one state of mind in normative contexts and another, rather different, state of mind in descriptive contexts. More controversially, ordinary folks seem to take "belief" to denote a psychological natural kind with certain characteristic features.[11] According to common sense, beliefs represent the world as being a certain way, have a propositional content which can be

[10] In Ridge (forthcoming) and in a draft of a book I am writing on this topic.

[11] Here I am skirting around an enormous literature in the philosophy of mind, where there is a big debate between so-called "theory theorists" and "simulation theorists" (and other views as well). The text commits me to a kind of theory theory, albeit one which is compatible with the use of simulation in the relevant sense to decide whether someone else has the relevant theoretically understood state of mind. For discussion of alternative views, see Carruthers (1996).

true or false, can be based on evidence and perception, and stand in logical relations to one another. These and other folk platitudes about beliefs fix a sort of folk theory which ordinary people implicitly think fixes a natural kind which will figure in a mature theory of human psychology. Ordinary folks do not, after all, have much inclination to eliminative materialism, and they presumably think that psychology studies the ways in which we form and revise our beliefs. This is not to say that the folk theory of beliefs is set in stone. Ordinary folks realize that empirical research can surprise us, and therefore should be prepared to revise elements of their theory of beliefs in light of what the best science (and, for that matter, the best philosophy) tells us. However, the idea that some successor to our ordinary notion of belief will figure as a natural kind in a mature theory of human psychology does seem to be part of our common sense perspective. Adequately defending this ambitious thesis would, of course, be a tall order, but here I am just laying out what I take to be some plausible assumptions to see where they lead. Finally, given a Lockean philosophy of language, ordinary practice seems to assume that the truth of an assertion is a direct function of the truth of the propositional content of the belief the assertion is conventionally used (in the context) to express. On this view, truth is in the first instance ascribed to propositions. The truth of a belief is then fixed by the truth of its propositional content. The truth of an assertion is, in turn, fixed by the truth of the belief it is conventionally used (in the context at hand) to express (and hence, of course, by the propositional content of that belief).[12]

Expressivism, whether ecumenical or non-ecumenical, seems inconsistent with this common sense perspective. For on any plausible version of expressivism, the real natural kind picked out by "belief" in a mature theory of human psychology will not map neatly on to our ordinary uses of "belief." Understood as a natural kind, beliefs are states which function to represent the world; they have what is typically referred to as a "mind to world direction of fit." I am here glossing this direction of fit in terms of the biological function of belief, though this is controversial.[13] Beliefs have other features (such as playing certain roles in inference, say) which distinguish them from other sorts of representational states (such

[12] A special story must be told here about so-called "conventional implicatures." I lack the space to explore that difficult terrain here. For a useful discussion, see Davies (2005): 147–160.

[13] For a survey of different ways of cashing out the "direction of fit" metaphor, see Humberstone (1992).

as perceptual states), but we need not get into these further details to see the problem.

On a standard (non-ecumenical) version of expressivism, so-called "normative beliefs" are simply not beliefs in this natural kind sense at all. They are instead pro-attitudes, the function of which is to prompt the agent to act in ways which bring about their content rather than to register the way the world is anyway. Ecumenical Expressivism holds that so-called "normative beliefs" are actually belief/pro-attitude pairs in the natural kind sense of "belief." Expressivism therefore seems to upset our ordinary conception of ourselves. We think that our use of "belief" is causally regulated by a single unified natural kind which has some and perhaps all of the features our common sense theory of beliefs as representational states of a certain sort associates with belief. Given expressivism, though, our use of "belief" is causally regulated not only by beliefs in this strict natural kind sense. Our use of "belief" is also causally regulated by either pro-attitudes of a certain sort (Non-Ecumenical Expressivism) or by certain sorts of belief/pro-attitude pairs (Ecumenical Expressivism).

This basic point is familiar enough. On a quasi-realist version of expressivism, we should be happy to continue talking about normative beliefs even though normative beliefs are actually (at least partially) constituted by pro-attitudes while descriptive beliefs are not. Indeed, this idea has already been made explicit in the work of Non-Ecumenical Expressivists. Allan Gibbard, for example, distinguishes what he calls "prosaic beliefs" from "plan-laden beliefs," and argues that normative beliefs are plan-laden while descriptive beliefs are prosaic (Gibbard 2003: 221). Presumably, he would be happy to allow that our ordinary uses of "belief" are causally regulated by the disjunction of these two sorts of belief. Simon Blackburn makes a similar point (Blackburn 1998: 79); Neil Sinclair explores a similar distinction (Sinclair 2006).

Ecumenical Expressivism might seem to hold an advantage here, insofar as Ecumenical Expressivism does at least allow that our normative utterances express beliefs in a strict sense of "belief" as well as pro-attitudes. However, the Ecumenical Expressivist also insists that the sentence uttered is not semantically guaranteed to be true just in case the belief expressed is true. This is meant to pick up on the idea that the point of normative discourse is to discuss how to live rather than to discuss how the world is. This, in turn, is meant to pick up on the idea that the relevant notion of agreement in these contexts is something like Charles Stevenson's notion of "agreement in attitude" or Gibbard's notion of "agreement in plan."[14] At least in the natural kind sense of "belief" as a robustly representational state, Ecumenical Expressivism allows that I can admit that the belief expressed by your sentence is true but without semantic confusion deny the truth of what you have said. For example, my utilitarian friend may say that charity is right and thereby express a belief whose content is (roughly) that a utilitarian saint would approve of charity. I might agree that such a saint would approve of charity, and hence agree that the content of the descriptive belief expressed is true, but deny that charity is right – and hence deny that "charity is right" is true. Given Ecumenical Expressivism, I can deny this without semantic confusion simply by refusing to approve in the relevant way of a utilitarian saint and instead approving of a sort of prescriber who (by my lights, anyway) would not insist on charity.

So Ecumenical Expressivism (like Non-Ecumenical Expressivism) still seems to imply that part of our implicit pre-theoretical understanding of ourselves is flawed. For we pre-theoretically might have supposed that assertions, whether normative or descriptive, express beliefs *qua* representational natural kinds, and that the assertion is true just in case the belief expressed is true. Ecumenical Expressivism severs this connection between the truth of the belief (*qua* representational natural kind) and the truth of the assertion. So in spite of being closer to common sense than Non-Ecumenical Expressivism in allowing that normative utterances do express beliefs *qua* representational natural kinds, Ecumenical Expressivism does imply that our understanding of ourselves is in an important way mistaken.

At this point, someone unsympathetic to expressivism might say, "so much the worse for Ecumenical Expressivism, for we surely are not this badly mistaken about ourselves." This, however, would be far too glib. Consider an analogy. For centuries, and even to this very day, most ordinary folks have endorsed a dualist understanding of the mind that infects their understanding of beliefs and desires. A powerful battery of philosophical objections and empirical evidence strongly suggests that this self-understanding is simply false, and it would be far too glib to suggest that we simply could not be so badly mistaken about ourselves. If the arguments against dualism are powerful enough, then it is the dualist self-understanding which must give way, and not the anti-dualist views in the philosophy of mind. The same sort of point can be made on behalf of expressivism. If the arguments in favor of Ecumenical Expressivism are

[14] See Stevenson (1944) and Gibbard (2003).

powerful enough, then it is our understanding of ourselves, and not Ecumenical Expressivism, which must give way. Furthermore, given the quasi-realist account of how it would be incredibly useful for us to treat our normative commitments as beliefs, it would not be surprising if we developed an assertoric discourse in which to express those commitments. This, in turn, might make it easy to see how we could fall into the trap of assuming that normative and descriptive assertions all function to express beliefs in precisely the same sense even if they did not in fact do so.

Indeed, in a perverse way, the fact that expressivism entails that one part of our self-understanding is mistaken is actually a dialectical advantage. For quasi-realists have often been accused by their critics of being victims of their own success. The worry is that insofar as their project succeeds, the quasi-realist can accommodate *everything* a realist would say. In that case, though, the very distinction between realism and quasi-realism vanishes and their own view is best understood as a form of realism.[15] The line of argument pursued here suggests that this objection misses its mark. Expressivism upturns some of the ways in which we otherwise might pre-theoretically understand ourselves, and therefore does not leave everything as it was before. The distinction between expressivism and cognitivism therefore remains a robust one.

It seems that our understanding of how truth ascriptions work breaks down in the case of normative discourse. For that understanding assumes that declarative sentences express beliefs in a univocal sense across both normative and descriptive contexts, and that a given sentence is true just in case the belief expressed is true. Ecumenical Expressivism suggests that this understanding of ourselves is false. So should we conclude that the real lesson of Ecumenical Expressivism is that normative discourse is not truth-apt after all? Perhaps A.J. Ayer was not so far off as contemporary expressivists like to think. However, we must not jump to hasty conclusions. Before throwing out the truth-apt baby with the cognitivist bath water, we should pause to consider other cases in which our common sense theory in some area of discourse has turned out to be defective in some way.

Two examples are worth briefly canvassing and contrasting here – the history of "jade" and "witch." As in the case of "belief," ordinary folks made various assumptions about the reference of "jade" and "witch." Before modern chemistry demonstrated the falsity of this assumption,

[15] See Wright (1985) and Harcourt (2005). For a reply to Harcourt, see Ridge (2006b).

ordinary folks may well have assumed that "jade" picked out a genuine natural kind. This is speculative; it is hard to say with any confidence whether ordinary folks thought about jade in this way, but for present purposes we can just assume for the sake of argument that this was so. The philosophical lesson I want to draw here does not depend on the historical accuracy of this claim. It turns out that jade is not a natural kind. Our use of "jade" is actually causally regulated by two distinct natural kinds – jadeite and nephrite. From the point of view of mineralogy, these two stones represent distinct kinds, in spite of the superficial similarity. This mineralogical discovery could have led us to decide that there is no jade, but instead we just accepted that jade is actually not a natural kind. In this case, we let the underlying nature of the stuff which causally regulates our use of the term determine its reference, rather than our theoretical assumptions about the nature of that stuff.

The case of "witch" is rather different. Witches presumably were taken to represent a sort of supernatural kind. Being a witch was associated with various supernatural powers, relations with the devil, and so on. It turned out, of course, that there are no women with these supernatural powers, relations with the devil, and so on. Just as with the case of jade, there turned out to be a divergence between what causally regulated our use of the term "witch" and the folk theories people had about the underlying nature (supernature?) of witches. Unlike the case of jade, though, in the case of "witch" the fact that no entities answered well enough to our theories about the nature of witches led to the conclusion that there are no witches. In this case, the theory took precedence over the nature of the stuff which casually regulated our use of the term, as opposed to vice versa. This was not inevitable or necessary. We could have concluded that our theory of witches was radically wrong, but continued to hold that there are witches. The idea would be that the nature of witches is fixed by what causally regulates our use of "witch," and here we could have held that witches are simply a certain sub-set of women with no supernatural powers or relations with the devil, but who had certain features which for various sociological reasons made them vulnerable to accusations of supernatural mischief.

Someone might insist that this different treatment of "jade" and "witch" is just arbitrary, and in certain respects it is. For all language is conventional and in that sense somewhat arbitrary. However, what is arbitrary is that we use a particular word ("witch" rather than "smitch") to have a certain meaning. What need not be arbitrary is whether we have a word with that particular meaning in the first place. The point is that the point of our discourse about jade in ordinary life was not held hostage to whether jade was really a natural kind. Jade continues to be an attractive gemstone, and the superficial features by which we pick out jade and which causally regulate our use of "jade" continue to have an obvious point and utility quite apart from whether jade is in fact a natural kind. For the jeweler's purposes, the distinction between jadeite and nephrite has little or no importance. So it made sense to continue to use "jade" to pick out the disjunction of jadeite and nephrite.[16] By contrast, the whole point of discourse about witches really was driven by theory. Apart from an interest in picking out women with certain supernatural powers and connections with the devil, it is not clear what function witch discourse would fulfill. So it also made some sense, upon learning that there are no women with the relevant supernatural powers, etc., to conclude that there are no witches, rather than conclude that witches are a certain sociologically defined sub-set of women. So our different treatment of these cases was in a deeper sense not arbitrary after all.

We are now in a position to return to expressivism and truth. Ecumenical Expressivism entails that at least some of the stuff that causally regulates our use of "belief" is rather different from our folk theory of the nature of beliefs. In particular, Ecumenical Expressivism entails that our use of "belief" to refer to normative judgments is in tension with our underlying folk theory as a unified and non-disjunctive kind which is constant across normative and descriptive contexts. So at some level of abstraction, the problem that arises here is a bit like the problem that arose with "jade" and "witch." In which case, we can ask whether we should treat "belief" more like "jade" or more like "witch."

In fact, things are slightly more complicated than this. For in the case of "jade" and "witch" there was simply no real natural kind which could plausibly be taken to be the referent of the term. Jadeite and nephrite are presumably natural kinds, but neither has any more plausible claim to be the referent of "jade" than the other, so "plumping" for one as the referent really would be arbitrary. Such an arbitrary decision would be fine, of course, but we are trying to see whether there are any non-arbitrary decisions we can make in the case of our discourse about beliefs. The contrast is that it is quite plausible (though still controversial) that there really is a natural kind which answers to many of our folk platitudes about beliefs. Eliminative materialists and certain other theorists will deny

[16] See Putnam (1975): 241–242.

this, but though I lack the space to argue for this here I do not think they have made a good case for their radical claims. Beliefs may be rather different in many ways from our folk conception, but it at least seems to me to be an open question whether the states that partially (normative discourse to one side now) regulate our use of "belief" do not indeed form a natural kind whose distinctive and theoretically germane features include having certain representational features, having propositional content, and so on.

The upshot is that, upon being convinced of Ecumenical Expressivism, we have more choices worthy of consideration with respect to "belief" than we did in the case of "jade" and "witch." First, of course, we could just conclude that there are no beliefs in much the same way that we concluded that there are no witches. I take it, the ingenuity of eliminative materialist's defenders notwithstanding, that this is not a very plausible view and in any event not at all well motivated by Ecumenical Expressivism.

Second, and much more interestingly, we could conclude that the reference of "belief" is unequivocally fixed by the natural kind which figures in a mature theory of human psychology and which best fits with our folk theory of the nature of beliefs. Given Ecumenical Expressivism, this would entail that we could no longer literally speak of normative beliefs. For beliefs will now simply be the representational states which only partially constitute a so-called normative belief, and a hybrid of a belief and a pro-attitude is not, on this construal, itself a belief. This option would be unlike both the case of "jade" and "witch" and would be more like the case of a theoretical term which does refer to a natural kind but where some of our folk assumptions about the kind, most notably that there are normative beliefs, end up being rejected outright. A better analogy might be "motion," since motion presumably is a concept which figures in a mature account of physics. However, given relativity theory, motion must be understood in terms of relativistic understandings of space and time, whereas our ordinary concept of motion (and least prior to relativity theory) arguably relied on an absolute theory of space and time.

An obvious cost of this first linguistic approach is that we must give up talk of normative belief. Such talk might still be quite useful insofar as we think the analogies between so-called normative beliefs and descriptive beliefs are important, though. So-called normative judgments do, after all, figure in rational inferences, stand in logical relations to one another, and so on if the quasi-realist project succeeds independently on these other fronts, and I have argued elsewhere that it does.[17] This very naturally suggests a third option, which is closer to the case of "jade" though still importantly different. We could simply allow that "belief" is ambiguous between referring to the relevant natural kind and referring to the stuff which causally regulates our use of "belief" in ordinary discourse. By contrast, in the case of "jade" we took it univocally to refer to the stuff which causally regulates our use of the term, simply because there was no kind we could non-arbitrarily choose to be the referent of the term. On this third approach, "belief" has a strict and theoretically defined sense and a much broader sense which is fixed by what causally regulates our use of the term. In the strict sense, which is fixed by what a mature theory of human psychology tells us, "belief" refers to a natural kind with certain distinctive features. In this sense of "belief" there are no normative beliefs. However, in a wider sense of "belief," the meaning of which is fixed by the stuff which actually causally regulates our use of "belief," beliefs do not represent a natural kind. In this broader sense a combination of a belief in the strict natural kind sense and a suitable pro-attitude is itself a belief; not so in the strict natural kind sense of "belief." In this broader sense of "belief" there are normative beliefs, but they are constituted by beliefs (in the strict sense of "belief") and pro-attitudes.

In my view, this third option is the most plausible, although this is itself a normative question about how our linguistic conventions should evolve in the (no doubt vanishingly unlikely!) event that we should all agree that Ecumenical Expressivism is true. This question is of philosophical interest quite apart from any fantasies of universal expressivism and large-scale linguistic reform, though. For the mere fact that we could preserve most of our ordinary practices in normative discourse without any major costs by such a shift suggests that our current discourse, while not entirely without defect, is not so far off the mark either. That, in itself, is a happy conclusion for those with quasi-realist ambitions.

Why, though, is this third option the most sensible one? Here the point is that there is a good reason that we have come to treat our normative judgments as beliefs. Normative judgments figure in rational inferences, we think we can give good and bad reasons for them, and it is important to us to reach agreement (in attitude) with one another about them or else explain to our satisfaction why those with whom we disagree have a flawed perspective. These standard quasi-realist points of commonality

[17] See Ridge (forthcoming).

between normative judgments and beliefs in the strict natural kind sense suggest that it would make a great deal of sense to hold onto a word which refers to the broader set of beliefs in the strict sense as well as normative beliefs (which are, of course, hybrid states on the theory on offer). We do not have to use "belief" for this purpose, of course, though I think that as long as we are careful not to equivocate, this would be fine. The main point is to retain a place in our conceptual economy for this broader category; we need not use "belief" to refer to it. We could instead use "belief" to refer only to the relevant natural kind and stipulate that some predicate, "judgment," say, refers to the broader class of descriptive beliefs and so-called normative beliefs. To avoid confusion in what follows, though, I shall simply use "natural-kind-belief" and "causal-regulation-belief" to disambiguate my uses of "belief" throughout.

Fully defending the choice of this third option would require a lot more argument than I will be able to present here. I must instead offer a very large promissory note, albeit one I try to make good elsewhere.[18] Suppose, though, that we agree that this is the right way for expressivists to go. The key question to ask now is how, within this framework, we should accommodate the truth-aptness of normative discourse.

## IV TRUTH REGAINED

According to Ecumenical Expressivism, my judgment that X is required is constituted in part by my belief (in the natural kind sense) that a certain sort of prescriber would insist on X. This naturally suggests that by my lights "X is required" is true just in case X would be insisted upon by the relevant sort of prescriber. So perhaps my remarks about the truth of other people's sayings and thinkings should itself be understood in expressivist terms, in the following way. You say that charity is required, and I agree, though I have no idea whether you endorse the same overall normative outlook as me. In judging that your view is true, I simply believe that it is true that the relevant sort of prescriber would insist on charity. This leaves it open whether we do in fact approve of the same sort of prescriber. You might approve of a utilitarian saint and I might approve of a Kantian saint even though we both agree that charity is required. So we cannot assume that our agreement is best understood in terms of agreement in belief in the natural kind sense of "belief." Instead, our agreement will be a sort of agreement in attitude, a concept most famously discussed by Charles

[18] In forthcoming work.

Stevenson (see Stevenson 1944), or perhaps instead what Allan Gibbard calls "agreement in plan" (see Gibbard 2003), or perhaps some further notion of agreement in conative states that is different from both of these. Given our respective pro-attitude/belief pair, we both are committed to favoring a way of living which involves charity when it is possible, anyway. In this sense, we agree in that we both take charity to be the thing to do. The appeal to agreement and disagreement in attitude (or in plan, to follow Gibbard), however, is a familiar move for the expressivist to make.[19] In itself this introduces no new difficulties for Ecumenical Expressivism.

The basic idea here is make use of our account of how claims and judgments about truth fix a particular truth *bearer* to explain the truth-aptness of normative discourse. This is in contrast to the deflationist approach discussed in section I, which instead relies on a particular account of truth itself. The account developed here is compatible with any of the main theories of truth discussed in the literature – deflationist, correspondence, identity, coherence – insert your favorite theory here. The key theoretical moves to make are ones which take us from a truth-claim to a suitable truth-bearer – a suitable proposition, in this case. We can then understand the claim that the relevant proposition is true in whatever way the best theory of truth indicates. Ecumenical Expressivism in this way does not give hostages to fortune. How, though, do we generalize this account?

The basic idea is that to say someone's belief (in the broad sense) that p is true is to say that there is a proposition q which (at least partly) constitutes what we might characterize as the *correct* way to believe that p, and q is true. Crucially, though, "correct" in this formulation is itself an expressivistic notion and not a disguised reference to truth in any way. The same approach works for normative utterances as well as beliefs, just cast in terms of the belief they would express with that utterance *if* they accept the judgment in the right way. What counts as "the right way" is given by one's normative outlook – by the sort of prescriber of whom one approves. So, in particular, claims in which "p is true" are used should be understood as follows. Take any sentence "p" in which locutions of the form "q is true" are used. On the proposed account, an utterance of "p" expresses two states of mind:

(1) A suitable pro-attitude to a certain sort of prescriber
(2) The natural kind belief that r, where r is what you get when you take "p" and replace all uses of "q is true" with "there is a proposition s, a

[19] See also Gibbard (2003): 268–287; Gibbard distinguishes his own account of disagreement in *plan* from Stevenson's account of disagreement in *attitude*.

natural kind belief in which would (at least partly) constitute the causal regulation belief that q for anybody who endorses *that* sort of prescriber (anaphoric reference back to the content of the pro-attitude in (1) here), and s is true."

Notice that this approach makes central use of the idea that normative judgments are partially constituted by beliefs in a strict sense – natural kind beliefs. That means the approach is unavailable to Non-Ecumenical Expressivists like Blackburn and Gibbard. So if the approach works, it provides an additional reason (beyond those I have explored elsewhere) to favor Ecumenical Expressivism over its Non-Ecumenical rivals.

The general schema for truth-ascriptions given above is a mouthful, but the basic idea is actually not all that complex. Suppose I say that what the Pope believes about charity is true. I thereby express my general pro-attitude to a certain sort of prescriber and the belief that, given one's endorsement of that sort of prescriber as fixed, there are certain propositions one would need to natural kind believe in order to count as having the same causal regulation beliefs as the Pope about charity, and those propositions are true. To make the example more concrete, suppose I am a utilitarian. In that case, my utterance expresses my approval of a utilitarian saint and my belief that to accept the Pope's belief about charity *while approving of that sort of prescriber (which here just is a utilitarian saint)* would involve believing certain propositions, and those propositions are true. So if I learned that the Pope thinks charity is required, then if I continue to think that his views are true this is because (given my normative outlook) I shall believe that the proposition one would need to believe in order to count as believing that charity is required while approving of a utilitarian saint is true. For me, this will be the proposition that charity would be insisted on by a utilitarian saint, though for the Pope the relevant proposition may be different – for him, the relevant proposition might be that charity would be insisted on by God. The fact that the Pope does not approve of the same sort of prescriber as me does not prevent me from judging that his views on charity are correct. I shall so judge, though, not because I think his beliefs about the sort of prescriber of whom he approves are true. Rather, insofar as I am a self-conscious utilitarian, I shall judge that his beliefs are true insofar as the beliefs one would have to hold in order to agree with the Pope about charity while approving of a utilitarian saint are true. Once again, my agreement with the Pope will be agreement in attitude rather than agreement in belief, but that is a standard expressivist move. The fact that you can agree with the Pope's views on charity while not endorsing the same sort of prescriber as him is, in my view, a virtue of the account. For intuitively we can agree with someone's verdict in a particular case while disagreeing with the background normative theory on which his judgment in the particular case is based. Kantians and utilitarians can agree that lying is generally wrong.

It should be clear enough how this account allows me to admit that the natural kind belief expressed by someone's normative utterance is true without allowing that the sentence he uttered is true. Suppose I know you are a Kantian and you say that charity is required. You thereby express a natural kind belief, the content of which is given by the proposition that a Kantian saint would approve of charity. I could therefore without inconsistency allow that the natural kind belief you expressed in saying charity is required is true without admitting that what you said is true. For by my lights, the approval of a utilitarian saint provides the truth-conditions for your sentence, not the approval of a Kantian saint.

It might sound odd to say that I could allow that the belief you expressed is true but also insist that what you said is not true. Here the distinction between natural kind beliefs and causal regulation beliefs does some real work, though. For it is only the natural kind belief expressed by your utterance that I can consistently allow is true while denying the truth of what you have said. For to endorse the truth of the causal regulation belief you have expressed is really just to endorse your claim that charity is required (or whatever) is true. I cannot, of course, do that and at the same time consistently deny that it is true that charity is required. For to do that would be to simultaneously express the beliefs that the relevant sort of prescriber would and would not insist on charity.

It should also be emphasized that the account on offer, if it works at all, generalizes nicely across normative and descriptive contexts. I have so far explained how the account works in normative contexts simply because that is the hard case. In the cases in which truth is ascribed to purely descriptive judgments, the expression of approval of a certain sort of prescriber in order to fix on the relevant proposition is a sort of idle wheel, doing no essential work, but also causing no problems. For trivially, the belief which (at least partially) constitutes your belief that grass is green if you endorse the same sort of prescriber as me will still just be the plain old natural kind belief that grass is green. For in the case of ordinary descriptive beliefs, one's belief is not constituted at all by one's approval of a prescriber in the first place. So the nature of the belief remains constant across all possible normative outlooks. It might seem odd that we must keep the special machinery developed for normative contexts in place even in contexts of purely descriptive discourse, where that machinery is clearly an idle wheel. However, this overlooks the point that discourse about truth is often very useful in contexts in which someone tells us that something is true without our yet knowing whether the relevant something is normative or descriptive. We therefore need an account of truth-ascriptions that can work in such "topic-neutral" cases.

Another worry one might have about the account developed here is that it makes claims about truth normative, though not because truth itself is normative (we are here neutral on the nature of truth itself). Instead, normativity enters the scene to help pick out the relevant truth-bearer(s) – the relevant proposition to which truth is ascribed. This may seem weird, but in fact I think it is actually an advantage of Ecumenical Expressivism as developed here. For the proposal on offer provides us with a useful resource with which to deflect an otherwise powerful objection to the plausible Humean idea that you can never derive an "ought" from an "is." The objection, pressed by Mark Nelson (Nelson 1995), is roughly as follows (the example is my own, not Nelson's). That the Pope believes that charity is good is, even on an expressivist account, a matter of descriptive fact – a fact about the Pope's psychology. However, it can also seem plausible to suppose that the fact that the Pope's beliefs about charity are true (if it is a fact) is also a purely descriptive fact. Certainly, the fact that his beliefs about charity are true does not in itself entail any normative conclusions, and indeed is logically consistent with nihilism. Also, the truth-fact can hold in worlds in which the Pope has no normative beliefs but still has beliefs about charity. However, these two facts provide the basis for a valid argument that charity is good:

(1) The Pope believes that charity is good.
(2) All the Pope's beliefs about charity are true.

So,

(3) Charity is good.

Here we apparently can derive a normative conclusion from what seemed like purely descriptive/factual premises, so Hume's claim about not being able to logically derive an "ought" from an "is" breaks down. It should be clear enough where this argument goes wrong on the account of truth-attributions proposed here. Claims about truth *are*, it turns out, normative in an important sense, and not purely factual. For such claims express a speaker's pro-attitude to a suitable prescriber, and this pro-attitude constitutes the speaker's conception of how one ought to live. Indeed, it is only by understanding judgments of truth in this way that we can preserve what we might call the topic-neutrality of truth judgments – their ability to range freely over normative and non-normative contexts alike. So the proposed counterexample to Hume's dictum does not hold on the account offered here, which provides a further (indirect) argument in favor of it, at least insofar as we find Hume's dictum itself plausible.

So far I have focused on what we should say about attributions of truth to what other people say or think, but there is a further question. For we can ascribe truth directly to propositions. Here, though, we simply need to make clear whether "proposition" is being used in a strict and philosophical sense or in a sense in which its meaning is somehow fixed by whatever causally regulates our use of the term. In the former case, all propositions in the strict and philosophical sense are descriptive and we understand ascriptions of truth to those in whatever way the best theory of truth holds – deflationist truth, correspondence truth, coherentist truth – whatever the best theory tells us. If, however, we leave open that some of the propositions in question are normative then, given expressivism, we must understand "proposition" in a much more deflationist way. Just as we must allow for strict and looser senses of "belief" we must do the same for "propositions."

Here, though, we do not need to posit two different kinds of entities as we did in the case of "belief" (natural kind beliefs and natural kind/pro-attitude pairs). Here the idea is that from the point of view of metaphysics alone there are only the descriptive propositions; there is no metaphysical need to posit an independent realm of normative propositions. That way lies Moorean non-naturalism. Instead, the point is that to take a descriptive proposition to also constitute a normative proposition is to take up a certain attitude – to decide to live in a certain way, to be disposed to urge others to live in that way (when being fully honest and candid, anyway), and so on. In particular, to claim that a proposition p in the broad sense of "proposition" is true is to express one's approval of a certain sort of prescriber and one's belief that the strict-sense proposition one would need to believe in order to count as believing that p while at the same time approving of that sort of prescriber is true. So, for example, if I say that the proposition that charity is required is true, I express my approval of a certain sort of prescriber as well as my belief that the (strict-sense) proposition one would need to believe in order to count as believing that charity is required while at the same time approving of such a prescriber is itself true. So the account on offer can be extended easily enough to ascriptions of truth to propositions as well as beliefs and sentences.

## V CONCLUSION

I have argued that existing attempts to marry expressivism to the truth-aptness of normative discourse give hostages to fortune by relying so heavily on deflationist theories of truth (section I). I have argued, however, that we can avoid giving such hostages to fortune by embracing what I have called Ecumenical Expressivism (developed in section II). Ecumenical Expressivism gives us the resources with which to construct a suitable account of truth-attributions in the broadest "topic-neutral" sense (sections III and IV). An important advantage of this account is that it does not depend on any particular view of how we should understand truth in the most fundamental sense – truth as it should be understood with respect to purely descriptive discourse. In order to make this move we must be willing to broaden our conception of key psychological and semantic predicates, most notably "belief" and "proposition." In addition to being ecumenical in our expressivism, we should also be ecumenical in our construal of predicates like "belief" and "proposition." This is not a trivial move, but insofar as Ecumenical Expressivism is otherwise plausible, we thereby have good reason to take these further ecumenical turns.

CHAPTER 12

# *Voluntarist reasons and the sources of normativity**

*Ruth Chang*

*In virtue of what* does a consideration provide a practical reason? Suppose the fact that an experience is painful provides you with a reason to avoid it. In virtue of what does the fact that it's painful have the normativity of a reason – where, in other words, does its normativity come from? As some philosophers put the question, what is the *source* of a reason's normativity?

This question should be distinguished from two others. One is: Which sorts of consideration ultimately provide practical reasons? That is, are practical reasons given by one's desires, by evaluative facts about what one desires, or by some hybrid of the two?[1] This question concerns which considerations are the ultimate bearers of practical normativity. The question of source, by contrast, concerns *that in virtue of which* the considerations that ultimately bear normativity – whichever they are – do so. Another question is: What is the nature of normativity? That is, is normativity an irreducibly distinct justificatory force, a motivational force, or a volitional force? This question concerns normativity's essential features. The question of source, by contrast, concerns *that in virtue of which* something has normative force, whatever the nature of this force.

The questions of the source, bearers, and nature of normativity are logically distinct but naturally related. If normativity is an irreducibly distinct justificatory force, then it is natural to think, as Plato did, that its ultimate bearers are irreducibly normative facts and that its source is an irreducible normative reality. If normativity is a motivational force, then

* For very helpful discussion of earlier drafts of this essay, thanks go to Kit Fine, Shelly Kagan, Frances Kamm, Jeff McMahan, Tristram McPherson, Derek Parfit, Peter Railton, and Larry Temkin. This essay is a precursor to a longer, closely related one – still in draft form – which has been presented to numerous audiences. Many people helped me with that longer essay, and their generous suggestions, comments, and criticisms have no doubt influenced the presentation of ideas in the present chapter. I am indebted to them.

[1] Desire-based and value-based views are the main ways in which philosophers have attempted to systematize the ultimate bearers of practical normativity. For a state-of-the-art discussion of these two views, see Derek Parfit (forthcoming). I explore a hybrid view in Chang (2004c).

one might conclude, as Hume did, that its ultimate bearers are desires and that normativity derives from a relation involving our desires. And if normativity is some kind of volitional force, perhaps Kant was right: normativity has its source in the will, and the ultimate bearers of normativity are facts about the consistency of willing actions. But none of this clustering of views is forced upon us.

The question of source is sometimes obscured because it gets folded into questions of the nature and ultimate bearers of normativity – hence my concern to distinguish those questions. But it also gets obscured because, for many philosophers, the question of source is illegitimate, or if legitimate, has only a degenerate answer. Such "normative externalists," as I will call them, think there is, strictly speaking, *nothing* in virtue of which a consideration is reason-providing – there are just the irreducibly normative facts that such-and-such considerations provide reasons.[2] Nevertheless, such externalists must allow that there is a sense in which the "source" of normativity is found in irreducibly normative facts. It is in this sense that the fact that an experience is painful provides a reason to avoid it in virtue of the irreducibly normative fact that being painful provides a reason to do so. Normative externalists, then, can be said to locate the source of normativity in a realm of external, irreducibly normative facts.

Normative internalists, by contrast, locate the source of normativity in mental states internal to us, and in particular, in desires and dispositions to which we are for the most part passively related.[3] A consideration has the practical normativity of a reason in virtue of its serving or furthering our procedurally constrained desires or dispositions. So, for example, being painful provides a reason to avoid it in virtue of one's fully informed desire to avoid pain. The desires that provide the source of normativity might be ones we must have in order to be rational or indeed to be agents at all, but they are not themselves states of agential activity.

Finally, normative voluntarists locate the source of normativity in us, but not in our passive states. Rather, normativity has its source in something we *do*, and, in particular, in our active attitudes of willing or

[2] Normative externalists include Clarke (1706), Ross (1930), Prichard (1968), Nagel (1970), Moore (1971a), Scanlon (1998), Raz (1999), Dancy (2000), Shafer-Landau (2003), Wallace (2006), Wedgwood (2007), Parfit (forthcoming) among others.

[3] Normative internalists include Hume (1978), Williams (1981), Falk (1986), Railton (1989, 2003), Smith (1994, 1999), Brandt (1996), Broome (1997), Velleman (2000), and, arguably, Rawls (1971).

reflective endorsement.[4] By willing something, that is, by actively engaging our volition, we can give a consideration the normativity of a reason. So, for example, if we will a law or principle according to which we avoid pain, the fact that an experience is painful can thereby be action-guiding. According to normative voluntarists, the source of practical normativity is to be found neither in irreducibly normative facts nor in non-cognitive states towards which we are passive. Normativity is rather borne of activity of the will.

Of these three main approaches to the source of normativity, I think it is fair to say that voluntarism is the runt of the litter. It strikes many philosophers as too bizarre to be taken seriously. How can we magically endow a consideration with the normativity of a reason simply through an act of will? Can we really turn a consideration into a reason – giving it action- or attitude-guiding force – simply by willing something? But some philosophers, most notably contemporary neo-Kantians such as Christine Korsgaard, have offered ingenious arguments in defense of our having such normative powers.[5] And voluntarism has an impressive pedigree reaching back to Hobbes, Locke, Pufendorf, and Kant, among others. Thus, the starkest divide in approaches to normative source is arguably between those who think we can create normativity and those who think that normativity is somehow given to us.

In this essay, I try to make sense of this divide by suggesting a form of voluntarism that straddles it. It seems to me that Hobbes, Locke, Kant, and their progeny offer us an important insight about normativity that we should not ignore. This is the thought that we *can* confer normativity or value on things. At the same time, externalists and internalists are right to be suspicious of the claim that all normativity derives from the will. Surely some normativity is given to us and not created by us.

Voluntarism is most plausible, I suggest, if we understand the normativity we create as hierarchically related to the normativity we do not create. Thus "hierarchical voluntarism" rejects an assumption that normative externalists, internalists, and standard voluntarists all share,

[4] Since the distinction between "passive" and "active" mental states is notoriously problematic, the line between internalists and voluntarists may not be a sharp one. For paradigmatic examples of voluntarism, see Hobbes (1651), Pufendorf (1672), Kant (1785), and Korsgaard (1996b). Korsgaard has done the most to raise the question of normative source to contemporary philosophical consciousness, though sometimes even her discussion of source is folded in with other issues about normativity, such as its nature.

[5] See Korsgaard (1996b).

namely, that practical normativity has an univocal source. According to this assumption, *all* practical reasons have their normative source in irreducibly normative facts, or in the agent's desires, or in her will. While standard forms of voluntarism maintain that all practical (or moral) reasons have their normative source in the agent's will, hierarchical voluntarism maintains that voluntarist reasons – reasons whose normative source is an act of will – depend on there being *non-voluntarist* reasons – reasons whose normative source is not an act of will. More specifically, it holds that an agent cannot have a voluntarist reason unless her non-voluntarist reasons have "run out." If this is right, then the answer to the question, "In virtue of what is a consideration reason-providing?," is not univocal; sometimes a consideration is normative in virtue of an act of will and sometimes not. In this way, practical reason is marked by a deep duality in its source.[6] This duality suggests a fundamental difference between practical and theoretical reason, but I won't be pursuing that issue here.

My case for hierarchical voluntarism centers on two puzzles about human rationality and agency. The first might be glossed as follows: How can we have *most* reason to do something when our reasons have in some sense "run out"? Sometimes it seems that our reasons fail to determine what we should do, and yet further deliberation determines that we have most reason to choose one alternative over the others. How can this be? The second puzzle begins with the thought that we *make*, through an act of agency, our ideal rational selves – you make yourself into someone who has most reason to spend weekends at wild parties, and I make myself into someone who has most reason to spend weekends quietly reading books at home. But how can we *make* ourselves into agents with these distinctive ideal rational selves if we are rationally required to follow our reasons? I will have more to say about these puzzles in due course, but for now it's worth noting that they are largely assumed to be unrelated. Those interested in the first tend to focus on questions about the "incommensurability" or "incomparability" of reasons or values. Those interested in the second tend to focus on how an agent

[6] Sidgwick (1907) famously thought that practical reason is marked by a duality, but his was a duality in the *kinds* of reasons or values relevant to action. He thought that reasons of individual prudence were wholly incomparable with reasons of impartial beneficence – that there was no way to put them together by a normative relation such as "stronger than." (I suggest some reasons to think that there isn't this duality in Chang [2004a].) But Sidgwick was a monist about the source of normativity since he located normativity in irreducibly normative facts about value or "points of view." See Sidgwick (1907), book III, chapter 14, book IV, chapter 6.

can be "self-governing" or the "author of her own life." What I want to suggest is that the puzzles are linked by a common, attractive solution found in hierarchical voluntarism.

Any defense of voluntarism must confront what is commonly taken to be its fatal flaw. The putatively fatal objection, raised by Clark against Hobbes, and more recently, by Gerald Cohen against Korsgaard, goes something like this: IF the source of the normativity of our reasons is in our willing something, then practical reasons become objectionably arbitrary. The Mafioso, for example, can in principle will the violent deaths of his enemies and thereby create reasons for himself to bring about those deaths. But he has no such reasons. Therefore voluntarism is false. Part of the task here will be to clarify how this objection should be understood. As we will see, while standard forms of voluntarism fall prey to this objection, hierarchical voluntarism does not.

I end the essay with some speculative remarks about how hierarchical voluntarism fares better than its standard relatives in separating views about the source of normativity from views about its nature. As we will see, standard forms of voluntarism are held hostage to two of the three main conceptions of normativity, while hierarchical voluntarism is arguably plausible no matter which conception of normativity is correct. In this way, hierarchical voluntarism can provide the will a secure place in understanding the source of normativity, however normativity itself is to be understood.

## I

A voluntarist reason is one whose normativity derives from an agent's act of will. But which act of will? The simplest form of voluntarist reason is one an agent might have by willing – or as I shall say, "taking" – a consideration to be a reason. Suppose you take the dulcimer tones of the harp as a reason to play the harp. By taking the dulcimer tones to be a reason, you can – under suitable conditions – make this consideration a reason for you to play. You can create a new voluntarist reason to play the harp through an act of will. The bearer of normativity is, we are supposing, the fact that the tones of the harp are pleasant. That fact gives you a reason to play in virtue of your taking it to be a reason – in virtue of your act of will. I am going to take this simple form of voluntarist reason as my working model. The view I want to explore, then, is that under suitable conditions, by taking something to be a reason you can thereby endow that thing with the normativity of a reason. Why should we believe that we have such normative powers?

Sometimes the reasons in a choice situation fail to determine what one should do. It might turn out, for example, that some reasons favor pursuing a career as a lawyer while others favor pursuing a career as a scuba diving instructor, and there is no all-things-considered conclusion about which career one has most reason to pursue. I shall say that in such cases one's reasons have "run out." Still, one must make a choice. In some such cases, when one chooses – say, to become a lawyer – it seems that one has *most reason* to choose it. How can this be?

To understand the puzzle, we need to start with the idea of reasons "running out." Sometimes the reasons for choice *determine* what you should do. In this case your reasons deliver the conclusion that you have *most* reason to choose one alternative over the others. You have most reason to choose x over y if the reasons for x outweigh, trump, silence, exclude, cancel, bracket, or are more stringent than the reasons for y. Your choice of x is rationally determined.

Sometimes, however, the reasons for choice *underdetermine* what you should do. This can happen in one of two ways. Your reasons might deliver the conclusion not that you have most reason to choose one alternative but that you have *sufficient* reason to choose any of two or more alternatives. You might have sufficient reason to choose x or y if the reasons for x are equally as weighty as those for y, or if they are "on a par," or, perhaps, if they are incomparable.[7] In this case, although the choice of either is justified, your reasons don't determine *which* you should choose. You have multiple rationally eligible options but no reason to choose one over the others. Whichever you choose, your choice, though justified, is rationally underdetermined. As some philosophers say, all you can do is "pick" rather than "choose."[8] When you pick, you justifiably choose on the basis of reasons, but your reasons do not determine your choice.

A more radical way your reasons might underdetermine what you should do is by failing to deliver the conclusion that you have most *or* sufficient reason to choose either alternative. When your reasons fail to deliver any justified choice whatsoever, we might say that they *break down*. When your reasons break down, there is no justified choice to be had; whichever alternative you choose, your choice will be beyond the scope of practical reason. Some philosophers think that reasons never

[7] For a description of the distinction between equality, parity, and incomparability, see Chang (1997) and (2002). I believe that one's non-voluntarist reasons must be "on a par" in order for voluntarist reasons to have a role in practical reason. But that is another story.

[8] See Ullmann-Margalit and Morgenbesser (1977).

break down. Those who think they do tend to think they do when the alternatives are incomparable. Indeed, some incomparabilists define incomparability as the failure of practical reason to deliver any justified choice among the alternatives. In any case, if reasons break down, all you can do is "plump" for no reason rather than justifiably pick or choose on the basis of reasons.

To summarize. There are two ways your choice can be justified: when you have most reason to choose that alternative or when you have sufficient reason to choose it among others. But there is only one way a choice can be rationally determined: when you have most reason to choose that alternative. When your choice is not rationally determined – that is, when you have sufficient reasons to choose among several alternatives or when your choice is beyond the reach of practical reason – your reasons *run out*. Reasons run out when they fail to deliver a univocal answer to the question, "What should I do?" When reasons run out, it seems that all one can do is pick or plump for no reason.

Some philosophers deny that reasons ever run out; all choice is rationally determined.[9] For the purposes of this essay, I am going to assume that reasons do run out, and that the cases in which they do range from the most mundane – what dessert to eat, what to wear, how to answer social invitations – to the most profound – how and where to live, which career to pursue, whether to have children, with whom to make a life, and so on. If this is right, underdetermination by reasons is a wide and deep phenomenon. If the assumption about the scope and significance of cases in which reasons run out is mistaken, then the scope and significance of voluntarist reasons will have to be adjusted accordingly. Insofar as there are cases in which reasons run out, however, there is room for voluntarist reasons, or so I will now try to show.

## 2

Suppose that you are faced with a choice between a career as a philosopher and one as a trapeze artist. You have investigated each career from every angle, vividly imagined yourself writing philosophy articles and swinging

[9] Some philosophers who deny that reasons ever run out suggest that they appear to do so only because they are underspecified or not fully articulated. See Taylor (1985); Richardson (1994); Millgram (1997); and Helm (2001: esp. chapter 6). Insofar as some of these authors go on to suggest that one way of further specifying or articulating these reasons is through an act of will, their views are congenial to the spirit of the view presented here.

under the big top, carefully considered and re-considered the reasons for and against each career, thought long and hard about how the reasons for and against each relate, sought advice from people whose judgment you respect, and so on. Suppose that, as a result of careful and thorough investigation, you come to believe that, all things considered, the reasons for and against each career have run out.

What should you do? It seems it would be a mistake for you simply to pick or plump for one career. Even if you have sufficient reason to choose either career and the choice of either would be justified, it seems odd to think that you might simply pick between them as you might between cans of soup. And if the choice between careers is beyond the scope of practical reason, plumping for a career for no reason also seems a mistake. Rather, it seems what you should do – and what many seemingly perfectly rational agents *do* do – is to continue to deliberate in the hopes of coming to a conclusion about which one has most reason to choose. Indeed, it seems perfectly possible that further deliberation might lead to a rationally determined choice.

But now we have a problem. If, as it seems, one's reasons have run out, how can it be appropriate to continue to deliberate about which alternative to choose in the belief that further deliberation might determine which one has most reason to choose? If one has sufficient reason to choose either career, then one does not have most reason to choose either. One should simply pick one, and further deliberation would be irrational. And if the choice between the careers is beyond the scope of practical reason, then again further deliberation would be pointless. One should simply plump for one career for no reason.

As stated, the problem has a ready solution. Although we can grant that reasons sometimes run out, perhaps we can never *know* that they have in any particular case. So it is always appropriate, other things equal, for an agent who believes that her reasons have run out to revisit her reasoning to make sure that they have. Thus when you continue to deliberate about the two careers, you are, as it were, checking your sums. Maybe you failed to give one of the reasons its proper weight or overlooked a detail that might turn out to be important to your decision. In this way, it can be appropriate to deliberate further when you believe that your reasons have run out. Further deliberation, as a corrective measure, can lead to a rationally determined choice.

But we can reformulate the problem in a way that sidesteps this epistemic maneuver. Although we may never be in a position to *know*, in some strong sense of "know," that our reasons have run out in any particular case, we can, however, be *practically certain* that they have. If you are practically certain that p, it is irrational for you to act on the assumption that not p. It would be irrational, for instance, to revisit your deliberation about whether p. If, for example, you are practically certain that you turned off the lights, it is irrational for you to check to see whether you did. Practical certainty might be understood as knowledge that is relativized to a practical context.[10] What it takes to know that you turned off the lights might be very different from what it takes to know that you turned off the gas oven. Practical deliberation is often like this; we reach a point in deliberation at which it would be practically irrational to second-guess ourselves.

Now suppose that after careful and thorough investigation of your reasons you are practically certain that the reasons for and against the philosophy and circus careers have run out. You conclude with practical certainty that they fail to determine that you have most reason to choose one of the careers. We might say that you know, for practical purposes, that the reasons have run out. Nonetheless, it seems that it could be perfectly appropriate to continue to deliberate about which career you should choose. How can this be? On the one hand, it is practically irrational to revisit the matter. On the other, it can be appropriate to continue to deliberate about which to choose.

Our first puzzle, then, is this. How can it be appropriate to continue to deliberate about which alternative to choose when one is practically certain that one's reasons have run out?

The puzzle can be deepened. Suppose you have a choice between chicken pot pie and roasted squab *au jus* for dinner. After careful and thorough deliberation about your reasons – fill in the details as you like – you are practically certain that your reasons have run out. Unlike in the careers case, however, in this case it seems perfectly appropriate to pick or plump for one of the dinners. Indeed, further deliberation might be irrational. But how can picking or plumping be appropriate in the dinners case but not in the careers case? By hypothesis, the structure of the reasons in each case is the same – you are practically certain that the reasons have run out. Given that reasons run out in a wide variety of cases, how is it that in some cases it can be appropriate to pick or plump while in other cases it is not?

Our puzzle, then, has two aspects. First, how can it be rational to continue to deliberate in the belief that this deliberation may lead to a

[10] For a view of knowledge that contextualizes it to the agent's practical interests, see Stanley (2005).

rationally determined choice when one is practically certain that one's reasons have run out? Second, sometimes when one is practically certain that the reasons have run out, it can be appropriate to pick or to plump, but other times it is not. What could explain the difference between such cases given that in both one is practically certain that the reasons have run out?

It might be suggested that when a decision, such as one between careers, is important, it is appropriate to continue to deliberate in the hopes of arriving at a justified choice. Decisions about important matters should not be a matter of picking or plumping. And since a decision between careers is important and one between dinners is not, this explains why it is appropriate to pick or plump in the one case but not in the other.

This suggestion, however, falls short of what is needed. Granting that a decision between careers is typically important, why should this make it appropriate to continue to deliberate if, by hypothesis, one is practically certain that one's reasons have run out? How can the importance of the decision be relevant to the structure of the reasons there are for deciding between two alternatives?[11] And given that the structure of reasons in both the careers and dinners cases is the same, how can the importance or lack of importance of the decision – presumably irrelevant in both cases – explain why picking or plumping can be an appropriate response in the one case but not in the other? That would be like trying to explain why it is appropriate to pick or plump between dinners but not careers by pointing out that one is wearing red shoes.

## 3

So how is our puzzle to be explained? To keep things simple, let's focus for now on its first aspect. How can it be appropriate to continue to deliberate and to believe that further deliberation might lead to the conclusion that one has most reason to choose one alternative over the other when one is practically certain that one's reasons have run out?[12]

[11] Even if the importance of the decision could be made to be relevant to the reasons for and against each alternative, this factor should then be reflected in the structure of the reasons which, by hypothesis, have with practical certainty run out.

[12] It should not be thought that the appropriateness is a matter of instrumental rationality. The appropriateness of continuing to deliberate is not like the rationality of some cases of self-deception or wishful thinking in which being in the state is good in some way. It is, to borrow a distinction made by Derek Parfit, object-given, not state-given. See Parfit (forthcoming).

Two thoughts appear to be in tension. On the one hand, one's reasons have run out, and therefore one doesn't have most reason to choose one alternative over the other. On the other hand, further deliberation might lead to the conclusion that one has most reason to choose one alternative over the other. How could both these thoughts be correct?

The most promising strategy for pursuing a solution to our puzzle, I believe, is to allow that deliberation about what to do can have two distinct stages. At one stage of deliberation, one might be practically certain that one's reasons have run out. Reasons underdetermine which alternative one should choose. But there might be a second stage at which further "deliberation" of a different kind can lead to a rationally determined choice. If this is right, the key to a solution is to determine what these two stages might be.

With this idea in mind, an immediate suggestion might be that the distinction between two stages of deliberation is given by the distinction between comparative and non-comparative justification of choice. Perhaps at one stage of deliberation we determine whether we have most reason to choose an alternative because it is the *best* of all the others, while at a second stage we determine whether we have most reason to choose it because of its intrinsic or deontic – i.e. non-comparative – features. So perhaps in the careers case you are practically certain that neither career is better than the other and thus practically certain that your comparative reasons have run out. You are practically certain that you don't have most reason to choose one career over another because it is better than all the rest. But at the second stage of deliberation you can consider the non-comparative reasons for choosing one of the careers. Perhaps pursuing the philosophy career would display the virtue of nobility and joining the circus would fulfill a promise you made. In this case, further deliberation about one's non-comparative reasons could lead one to a rationally determined choice.

But this misunderstands the puzzle. When you deliberate about the reasons for and against the two careers at the first stage, you do not artificially restrict your deliberation only to that concerning your comparative reasons. If you promised your mother long ago that one day you would run away and join the circus, that is one of the reasons you take into account in the first stage of your deliberation. Your deliberation includes both comparative and non-comparative reasons, and your conclusion is that these reasons have run out. The puzzle is how we can be practically certain that both our comparative and non-comparative reasons have run out and at the same time appropriately continue to deliberate with the belief that this further deliberation might tell us what we have most reason to choose.

A more promising view is suggested by remarks of Joseph Raz.[13] Raz suggests that when reasons run out, the *will* plays a role in determining what to do. Suppose, to borrow one of Raz's examples, you are trying to decide between a banana and a pear for dessert. The banana has got a lot of potassium, which is good for your heart, and the pear has got a lot of vitamin C, which is good for your immune system, but there is no all-things-considered truth about which you have most reason to choose. Your reasons have run out. (Raz assumes that a rational deliberator can know this.) Raz thinks that you can then *will* to have the banana, which, in the normal course of events, *causes* you to choose the banana. So you choose the banana.

There are two possibilities here.[14] Your willing the banana might make it true that you have most reason to choose the banana or it might not. If it doesn't, Raz's view does not help us to solve our puzzle, for we need to explain how it can be true that you have most reason to choose an alternative when your reasons have run out. Raz's view would simply give a causal explanation of how one comes to choose an alternative when reasons have run out.

Could willing an alternative explain how one could have most reason to choose that alternative? It is hard to see how it could. To think that it could would involve double-counting one's reasons. When you conclude that the reasons for and against the banana and pear run out, you have already "counted" the reason in favor of the banana, namely that the banana is full of potassium and good for your heart. At the first stage of deliberation, then, the fact that the banana is full of potassium and good for your heart does not give you most reason to choose it. At the second stage of deliberation, after you will to have the banana, the very same reason that failed to give you most reason to choose the banana at the first stage gives you most reason to choose it in the second. But this is just to count the reason for choosing the banana twice. Why shouldn't the reason in favor of the pear similarly be counted twice?

[13] See Raz (1997, 1999: chapters 4–5).

[14] I find it difficult to know which alternative best represents Raz's intended view. Raz says that the choice of the banana is "rational," but it was also rational before one willed it because one has sufficient reason to choose the banana or the pear. There may be an ambiguity here in "rational"; a choice can be "rational" in the strong sense of being rationally determined – that is, being what one has most reason to choose – but it can also be "rational" in the weak sense of there being sufficient reason to choose it among other alternatives. Our concern is to explain how a choice can be rational in the strong sense when one is practically certain that one's reasons have run out.

We could try modifying the view to avoid this problem by suggesting that willing an alternative adds normative weight or significance to the reasons that support the alternative one wills. Return to our careers case. When you are practically certain that your reasons have run out, by willing to join the circus, you can give the reasons in favor of the circus career extra normative force. The extra force of these reasons can then give you most reason to choose that career.

The trouble with this suggestion, however, is that it entails that one always has greater reason to choose an alternative after one wills it than before one wills it, and this isn't always the case. Suppose you have a choice between two evils – say, betraying a friend and causing a stranger to suffer physical pain. After careful investigation, you are practically certain that your reasons have run out. Suppose now that you *will* that the stranger suffer. It doesn't follow that you thereby have greater reason to cause his suffering than you had before your act of will. It might be that because you now will his suffering, you have less reason to choose this alternative than you did before you willed it. Willing the suffering of others may make the suffering of others a worse alternative than it was before one willed it. Whether one has more reason to choose an alternative after one wills it is a substantive matter that should not be built into an account of practical deliberation.

Although this last suggestion fails to explain our puzzle, it goes some way towards what I believe is its correct solution. It gives a role to the will in the second stage of deliberation and, more importantly, recognizes that the will can be a source of normativity. Our puzzle, however, requires us to explain how further *deliberation* is appropriate, and it is unclear how willing an alternative can be a form of deliberation. As I now want to suggest, the proper role of the will in the second stage of deliberation is not to will an alternative but to will a reason that supports an alternative. This willing creates normativity by creating new reasons whose normativity derives from the very act of will. And as we will see, creating reasons through an act of will is part of a deliberative process of making oneself into the distinctive rational agent that one is.

## 4

From our discussion so far, we can extract two general principles for our puzzle's solution. First, in thinking about what to do, there may be different stages of deliberation. If, at one stage, one is practically certain that one's reasons have run out, there may nevertheless be another stage in which further deliberation yields a rationally determined choice. Second, this further stage of deliberation is one in which the will has some role to play. Our questions then are how to understand these two stages and what the role of the will at the second stage might be. Voluntarist and non-voluntarist reasons, I believe, provide an attractive way of answering these questions.

Our non-voluntarist reasons are the reasons we ordinarily take ourselves to have – reasons whose normativity derives either from normative reality or from our desires, but not from our own act of will. They typically include facts about the alternatives, about ourselves, and about the relation between the alternatives and ourselves. So, for example, your non-voluntarist reasons to choose the philosophy career might include the fact that philosophy is a noble pursuit, that you have a strong desire to better understand a particular philosophical problem, that you are especially suited to abstract thinking, that you would enjoy teaching Plato to undergraduates, and so on. Since these are the reasons given to us and not given by us, we might call them our *given* reasons. Our voluntarist reasons, by contrast, are the reasons we create for ourselves by taking a consideration to be a reason when our given reasons have run out. Thus when your given reasons for choosing one of the careers run out, you can take a consideration in favor of one of the careers as normative for you, thereby creating a new, voluntarist reason to choose that career.

I suggest that given reasons have a role in the first stage of deliberation, and when they run out, voluntarist reasons have a role in the second. Our given reasons are the only reasons we have at the first stage of deliberation, and when they run out, there can be no rationally determined choice on the basis of those reasons. But it does not follow that a rationally determined choice is precluded. There is a second stage of deliberation in which we can create new voluntarist reasons which, in conjunction with our given reasons, may deliver an alternative we have most reason to choose. In this way, it can be appropriate to continue to deliberate to a rationally determined choice when we are practically certain that our reasons have run out.

To see how the proposal might work, return to the careers case. Suppose, for simplicity, that there are only two given reasons relevant to the choice between them. In favor of the philosophy career is the intellectual satisfaction you would get from a life of contemplating deep philosophical questions. In favor of the career as a trapeze artist is the thrill you would get from nightly daredevil stunts under the big top. Suppose that after careful and thorough investigation of these reasons, you are practically certain that they fail to deliver an all-things-considered truth about what you have most reason to do. Your given reasons have run out.

At this stage in your deliberations it can be appropriate for you to take a consideration as a reason in favor of one of the careers, thereby giving yourself a new, voluntarist reason to choose that career. You might, for instance, take your cousin's whim that you join the circus, or the secret delight you would get from wearing sequins, or the financial gain that would accrue to the manufacturers of trapeze rope in Korea as a reason to choose the circus career. Although your cousin's whim, your secret delight, and the manufacturers' pecuniary gain are not, by hypothesis, relevant to your choice between the careers, when your given reasons have run out you can, through an act of will, make them reasons that are relevant to your choice.[15] You can take any consideration that counts in favor of an alternative, even if irrelevant to the choice, as a reason for you to choose that alternative. In this way you can create a voluntarist reason you didn't have before that might then give you most reason to choose the circus career.[16]

You might instead take the thrill of performing stunts under the big top as a reason to choose the circus career. In this case the voluntarist reason you create shares its content with a given reason you already have. This might seem strange. How can a single consideration – the thrill of performing under the big top – provide you with both a given and a voluntarist reason? Doesn't this amount to double-counting your reasons? There is double-counting of reasons only if reasons are individuated by their contents alone, but it is unclear why reasons should be individuated in this way. Why shouldn't a single consideration have normativity with two different sources and thus provide two distinct reasons? Consider an

[15] Some philosophers think that in any given choice situation, *every* consideration that counts in favor of the alternative is a reason relevant to a choice involving that alternative. So, for example, the fact that ordering steak for dinner in New York will help, in a Rube Goldberg-like way, a child in Argentina with her homework is a reason, albeit a "small reason," to order it. I have offered some considerations against this view in Chang (2004b). But if the view is correct, then the two cases described below ultimately describe a single kind of case. If every consideration that counts in favor of the alternatives is already a given reason at the first stage of deliberation, then the role of the will should be understood instead as creating new, voluntarist reasons that share content with one's given reasons.

[16] It might be objected that if one's voluntarist reasons must always be reasons which antecedently to any act of will count in favor of choosing an alternative, the source of their normativity is not truly the will but in whatever it is in virtue of which the reason counts in favor. This is to conflate the content of the reason with the status of being a reason. While a given content cannot count as a reason *as a conceptual matter* unless that content counts in favor of the action, it does not follow that the source of the normativity of that reason cannot be the will.

analogy with physical force. A single object – say, an apple – can exert two distinct physical forces on another object, one gravitational and the other electromagnetic. The forces are distinct because the "sources" of those forces are distinct. Similarly, a single consideration – the thrill you would get – can provide two distinct reasons in virtue of two distinct sources of normativity. It might be a fact of normative reality, for instance, that you have a reason to pursue what thrills you, and it might also be the case that by taking your thrill as a reason, you can endow it with the normativity that derives from your will. Just as an apple can exert two distinct forces on an object, a consideration can provide two distinct reasons for action. The considerations that provide the contents of your given reasons may also provide the contents of your voluntarist reasons.[17] So sometimes what we take to be a reason is a consideration that already provides a relevant given reason and sometimes not.

This view about the possible contents of one's voluntarist reasons fits nicely with the phenomenology of choice in the cases of interest. Sometimes when we are practically certain that our reasons have run out, further deliberation takes the form of *agonizing* over the considerations that provide the contents of our reasons. When you are practically certain that your reasons for the philosophy and circus careers have run out, you may nevertheless find yourself agonizing over the intellectual satisfaction you would get from the philosophy career and the thrill you would get from the circus one. Agonizing over these considerations – otherwise inexplicably irrational – can be understood as deliberating over whether and which such considerations to create as new, voluntarist reasons for yourself. Other times, further deliberation takes a different form – we focus on factors that count in favor of an alternative but aren't by our own lights relevant to the choice. For example, your cousin's whim that you join the circus is, by hypothesis, irrelevant to your choice between the two

[17] Although, I believe, reasons should not be individuated by their contents, there is a variant of the view presented here that could avoid relying on this claim. Instead of creating new, distinct voluntarist reasons, perhaps an act of will can transform given reasons into reasons *part* of whose normativity is a creation of the will and *part* of whose normativity is given. It might do this by endowing one's given reasons with special normative weight so that we have the "same" reason but with added normativity that derives from the will.

Note that this variant does not run afoul of the difficulty raised for the modified version of Raz's view. That view had the implication that by willing an alternative, one thereby had more reason to choose it than one had before one willed it. Willing more weight or significance for a particular given reason does not have this implication because it allows that even though one creates greater weight for a particular reason, the reasons overall to choose the alternative after willing may remain unchanged or even be weaker due to organic unities and the like. It correctly leaves the normative relations among reasons a substantive matter.

careers. But you might nevertheless take her whim as reason-providing for you and thus make it a voluntarist reason to choose the circus career.

It might be wondered how deciding whether to take a consideration as normative for oneself can be a form of deliberation. Unlike the sheer willing of an alternative, willing a consideration to be a reason is part of the process of making oneself into a distinctive normative agent, that is, creating one's own "rational identity." I will have more to say about this below, but for now we can note that if the creation of voluntarist reasons is a part of rational self-governance, we have a tidy explanation not only of the first but also of the second aspect of our puzzle.

Recall that in some cases when we are practically certain that our reasons have run out, it seems appropriate to pick or plump, while in other cases further deliberation seems to be in order. Typically, it seems appropriate to pick or plump between dinners but not between careers. If creating reasons for oneself is making oneself into a distinctive normative agent, then the difference between the dinners and careers cases can be explained by the role such choices play in one's rational identity. "Who you are," rationally speaking, typically involves which career you pursue but not which dinner you eat. Choices between dinners are not usually occasions on which one "makes" oneself into the distinctive rational agent one is. But they might be. A world-class chef might create reasons for herself to choose one dinner over another when her given reasons have run out. But since most of us have normative identities that are not bound up with what we have for dinner, it seems appropriate to pick or plump between dinners. Careers are a different matter. Your rational identity may very much be a matter of the career you pursue. If it is, then when your given reasons to choose between careers have run out, you have an opportunity to make yourself into the kind of agent for whom there are stronger reasons to fly under the big top than to sit at home contemplating the nature of reasons.

At the heart of our puzzle is a common assumption about practical deliberation. Deliberation is a matter of discovering, recognizing, investigating, appreciating, and engaging with the reasons there are. If one is practically certain that one's reasons have run out, then deliberation seems to have finished its job. How could further deliberation yield the result that one has most reason to choose one of the alternatives? Once we allow that deliberation may also involve the *creation* of reasons – and as we shall see, forming our ideal rational selves – the puzzle disappears. While it can be true at the first stage of deliberation that one's given reasons have run out, one can create new, voluntarist reasons at a second stage that may then lead to a rationally determined choice. In this way, voluntarist reasons explain how we can have most reason to choose an alternative when our (given) reasons have run out.

## 5

There is a second puzzle to which voluntarist reasons seem to provide a tidy solution. How can rational agents both be fully responsive to reasons and at the same time exercise control over who they are, rationally speaking? Each of us has the power to make ourselves into a person with a distinctive *rational identity*, as someone who, for example, has stronger reasons to become a scuba diving instructor rather than a lawyer, or to spend her leisure time fly fishing rather than listening to opera. But if being rational is responding appropriately to our reasons, it is not clear how *we* can get enough distance from our reasons to be able to make ourselves into one kind of distinctive rational agent rather than another. The "we" of agency seems to disappear; there is only the rational agent's responsiveness to her reasons but no active *making* of oneself into one kind of rational being rather than another.

To understand this puzzle we need first to understand the notion of a rational identity. Your rational identity is your ideal rational self. It is a function (perhaps a simple conjunction) of the reasons that determine what you have most reason to do in actual and hypothetical choice situations. Consider the whole range of possible choice situations you and I might face. What you have most reason to do in those situations is different from what I have most reason to do. We have distinctive rational identities. This set of rationally determining reasons can be described in a rough-and-ready way by general roles rational agents can play – tinker, tailor, soldier, spy – and general attributes they can possess – extrovert, fun-loving, people-oriented, party-going. Your rational identity, in short, is who you would distinctively be were you perfectly rational. It is the rationally angelic you.

Your rational identity need not be how you conceive of yourself. You might think of yourself as shy and retiring, but if you have most reason to choose bungee jumping and karaoke over book-reading and museum-going, your rational identity will not match your self-conception. In this way your rational identity differs from what Christine Korsgaard calls your "practical identity." For Korsgaard, a practical identity is a "description under which you value yourself, a description under which you find your life to be worth living and your actions to be worth undertaking – it is how you see yourself."[18] A rational identity, by contrast, is not a self-conception but rather a description of your normatively ideal self – a loosely unified way of understanding the reasons that justify doing what you have most reason to do.

Nor is your rational identity your personality or character. You might be a self-aggrandizing, malevolent egomaniac and thus lie, cheat, and steal for your own advantage. But since, presumably, you don't have most reason to lie, cheat, and steal, the reasons you have to perform these actions are no part of your rational identity. Moreover, the reasons you might mistakenly think you have – even to do what you in fact have most reason to do – are no part of your rational identity. Your rational identity is constituted by the reasons you objectively have that rationally determine what you should do. In this way, your rational identity is not given by what Michael Bratman calls your "self-governing policies." A self-governing policy is "a policy of treating a desire as providing a justifying end in motivationally effective practical reasoning" – in short, a policy of treating certain considerations as reasons.[19] You might have a self-governing policy of treating your desire to take advantage of others as a justifying reason to lie, cheat, and steal. But if you don't objectively have such a reason, this desire – and the self-governing policy that underwrites it – are no part of your rational identity. Your rational identity is the ideally rationally agent within, not the rational agent you subjectively take yourself to be.

Most philosophers concerned with explaining "self-governance" and being "the author of one's own life" focus on how we make ourselves into creatures with the foibles and peculiar irrationalities or personality that we each actually have.[20] But the sort of self-governance of interest here is not a matter of how we make ourselves into the actual, rationally flawed creatures that we are, but of how we make ourselves into creatures – however flawed – with certain *ideal rational identities.* Through self-governance, I make it true that I have most reason to spend my Saturdays collecting stamps and you make it true that you have most reason to spend your

[18] Korsgaard (1996b): 101. Korsgaard argues that our "local and contingent practical identities" derive their normativity from our "human identity" – the practical identity we cannot but help have as self-conscious, reflective agents. Our practical identities in turn determine our reasons. According to Korsgaard, we have the reasons we do because of our practical identities. The view of voluntarist reasons developed here is close to the reverse. Our rational identity is something we create through taking considerations to be reasons. We have the rational identity we do because of our voluntarist reasons. Our reasons determine our rational identity, not the other way around.

[19] Bratman (2007): 40 and part I generally. See also Bratman (1999).

[20] See, e.g., Bratman (2007).

Saturdays playing the harp. We are authors not only of our actual lives but also of our ideal rational lives – of the best we can be, rationally speaking. The governing of our ideal rational selves is arguably the central – and most exalted – exercise of rational agency.

But, granting that each of us has a rational identity, why should we think that we "make" those identities? Perhaps our rational identities just happen to us – we come born with them, or they are shaped by our environment. On such a view, the reasons that rationally determine what we should do always come to us unbidden; perhaps they are a causal function of the desires and dispositions with which we are born and the environment in which we act. There is no genuine agency involved in crafting one's rational identity; instead we sit back and relax – our ideal rational selves, like our toenails, grow without any agency on our part. Indeed, perhaps agency itself is nothing more than the "proper [causally specified] functioning of thoughts, beliefs, emotions, and desires" – there is no "you" or "me" apart from the complex causal–functional operation and structure of our various mental states.[21]

This line of thought may, in the end, be correct as part of a reductive account of agency, just as sub-atomic physics may, in the end, provide the ultimate explanation of everything. What is true at this deep level of theorizing is something about which we should probably keep an open mind.[22] But at the level of "shallow" philosophical theorizing about rational identity, such views ride roughshod over the pre-theoretical conviction that there is such a thing as agency, and that agency is somehow involved in our best rational selves being what they are. At this level of theorizing, it is hard to believe that everything I have most reason to do – pursue a life of quiet contemplation on philosophical issues – and everything you have most reason to do – pursue a frenetic life of family, social relationships, and political activism – is just passively given to us,

[21] Railton (2003): 200. See also Velleman (2000).

[22] The challenge to reductionists is to provide an account that gives us something recognizably like activity of the will. It will not be sufficient to provide a naturalistic explanation that simply corresponds to or subvenes genuine activity of the will. Nor will it be sufficient to succeed in reducing something that is not recognizably genuine agential activity. My own view is that these two constraints don't leave enough room for the requisite reduction to succeed and that "proper functioning" will be an irreducibly normative matter. It is perhaps worth noting that most naturalists about agency or the will find themselves having to appeal to something that seems itself or through the role it plays suspiciously non-natural, such as "identification," "wholeheartedness," "satisfaction," "endorsement," "adopting a self-governing policy," "treating as a reason," and so on, for the will to do the work it does. In any case, what I say here does not turn on whether agency can be naturalistically reduced.

with no agency on our part. Of course the desires we are born with and the environment in which we live play large roles in determining the reasons we have and thus what we have most reason to do. But there is nevertheless some sense in which *we*, apart from the bubbling cauldron of our properly functioning beliefs, desires, and the like, can exercise genuine agency in "making" ourselves into agents with one rational identity rather than another. We need to explain this sense.

## 6

The problem arises in trying to find a sense in which we can "make" our own rational identities that is compatible with our being fully responsive to our reasons. To see the difficulty, consider three ways you can be fully responsive to your reasons.

Your reasons might give you most reason to choose one alternative; they might give you sufficient reason to choose either of several alternatives; or they might break down, putting your choice beyond the scope of practical reason.

If your reasons break down, then by hypothesis you can only plump for no reason. Plumping for no reason does not involve the sort of agency that goes into making one's own rational identity. This is because making yourself into an agent who has most reason to do one thing rather than another is a practically rational activity and thus within the scope of practical reason.[23]

If your reasons determine that you have *most* reason to choose a particular alternative, then being fully responsive to your reasons requires that you to choose that alternative. How can you then make your own rational identity if, to be rational, you must follow your reasons and do what you have most reason to do? It seems that any "making" of your rational identity in this case would simply be a matter of doing what is rationally required of you. It seems that you don't have enough distance from your reasons in such cases to make yourself into an agent with one set of rationally determining reasons rather than another.

Suppose instead that your reasons give you *sufficient* reason to choose either of two alternatives. Are you now in a position to make your own rational identity? While you are not rationally required to choose one

[23] Existentialists, and non-existentialists who make room for "existential commitment," think that when reasons break down, one can existentially plump for an alternative for no reason. But they do not think that by doing so, one is creating one's *rational* identity. See Sartre (1994); cf. Gibbard (1990): 166–168.

alternative over the others, it is not clear how, by picking, you can make yourself into an agent who has most reason to do one thing rather than another. Merely picking what you have sufficient reason to choose does not give you most reason to choose it. By picking, you don't make it true that you have most reason to choose one thing rather than another and thus don't "make" your rational identity.

Of course by picking what you have sufficient reason to choose, you can change what you *subsequently* have most reason to choose. When you have sufficient reason to choose either x or y, you can justifiably pick either. Suppose you pick y. Your choice of y is justified even though you don't have most reason to choose it. Now suppose you are faced with a choice between y and x-minus, only slightly less choiceworthy than x. Again you have sufficient reason to choose y or x-minus. But given that you have previously chosen y, you now, arguably, have most reason to choose y over x-minus – if you had sufficient reason to choose x-minus given your previous choice of y, you could be money-pumped.[24] By picking, then, it seems you can change what you subsequently have most reason to do. And by changing what you subsequently have most reason to do, you change the reasons that comprise your rational identity. Perhaps by picking y you have "made" yourself into the sort of agent who has most reason to y instead of x-minus.

The fact that by picking an alternative you change what you subsequently have most reason to do does not, however, by itself show that you have exercised the sort of agency involved in making yourself an agent with a distinctive rational identity. You can do many things that change what you subsequently have most reason to do – you can have a child, tell a lie, or run round the neighborhood in your underwear. But if you have most reason to do these things, or if doing these things is beyond the reach of practical reason, then even though doing these things changes what you subsequently have most reason to do, you haven't exercised the relevant sort of agency. What you subsequently have most reason to do is grounded not in your will but in something beyond your will. Similarly, if you pick one thing over another, that may change your subsequent reasons. But you don't exercise the relevant sort of agency – you don't make it the case that you have most reason to do one thing rather than another when what you have most subsequent reason to do is grounded in the rational equivalent of a coin flip.

[24] See also Chang (2005).

So the challenge is to explain how doing what one has sufficient reason to do can involve the sort of agency exercised in making one's own rational identity.

Voluntarist reasons provide an attractive answer to this challenge. When you have sufficient reason to do either of two things, you have sufficient *given* reasons, and instead of picking between those alternatives, you can create for yourself a voluntarist reason that may then give you all things considered most reason to choose one alternative over the other.[25] If, for example, your given reasons for the philosophy and circus careers run out, you might take the challenge of understanding a difficult philosophical problem as normative for yourself, thereby giving yourself a voluntarist reason to choose the philosophical career. This voluntarist reason, in conjunction with your given reasons, may now give you most reason to choose that career.[26] In this way, you can make yourself into an agent who has most reason to choose the philosophy career by creating for yourself reasons that rationally determine that choice. In short, you make your own rational identity by creating for yourself some of the reasons which determine it.

Our given reasons leave us what we might call *a space of rational freedom*. This is the freedom to choose one alternative over the others on the basis of reasons, without acting contrary to our all-things-considered given reasons. We might think of our given reasons as drawing a line in the sand around our agency. We can do or feel whatever we like, but we can't go past *here*. Beyond this boundary, we are free to create voluntarist reasons that may give us most reason to choose one alternative over the others.[27]

The sense in which we "make" our rational identities, then, is the sense in which, when our given reasons have run out, we create for ourselves reasons that make it true that we have most reason to choose one alternative over another. We can be fully responsive to our reasons – always doing what we have all-things-considered most or sufficient reason

[25] This is not to say that whenever you have sufficient reason to do either of two things, you can always either pick an alternative or create a voluntarist reason in favor of one. As I've already suggested, I believe there is a specific way in which one has sufficient given reasons that gives rise to the possibility of voluntarist reasons. This is when alternatives are "on a par."

[26] Of course, your voluntarist reasons don't guarantee delivery of a rationally determined choice. If both your given and voluntarist reasons run out, then you can only pick or plump for no reason.

[27] A full story of voluntarist reasons will include an account of further constraints on the creation of such reasons. Sometimes the creation of such reasons is constrained by considerations deriving from the coherence and unity of agency. Rational requirements might be another constraint on the creation of voluntarist reasons. I cannot explore these issues here.

to do and plumping when our reasons break down – and nevertheless make ourselves into agents with distinctive rational identities. We are slaves to some reasons and masters of others.

Imagine two worlds, one with me and the other with my Dopplegänger. Suppose we start out having the same given reasons. And yet I have most reason to spend my free time train-spotting while my Dopplegänger has most reason to spend her free time collecting stamps. It is plausible that our given reasons don't determine how we should spend our leisure time – our hobbies and personal projects are within the space of rational freedom in which we can make ourselves into an agent with one kind of rational identity over another. While I take the sighting of a rare steam train to be normative for me, my Dopplegänger might take the sighting of a rare stamp as normative for her. The same goes for weightier choices. My financially bereft Doppelgänger and I might each find that we have sufficient reason either to keep our only child or to give him up to a loving, wealthy family who will give him a wonderful life neither of us can provide. I might take the importance I attach to my child as a voluntarist reason to keep him.[28] My Dopplegänger may instead take the wonderful life in store for her child as a voluntarist reason to give him away.

When given reasons run out, it is through *taking* considerations to be reasons that we make our rational identities. If, when your reasons run out, you tend to take only considerations that make essential reference to you as normative for you, your ideal rational self might be self-involved. If you take only considerations that make no such reference, perhaps your rational identity is self-effacing. If you tend to take the features of chocolate as reason-providing, your ideal rational self might be a chocoholic. And if, as many philosophers have argued, we often have sufficient given reasons to choose either a partial act or an impartial one, we craft our rational identities as "partialist" or "impartialist" by the reasons we create for ourselves in such cases. If this is right, some of the most intractable ethical problems may have no universally rationally determinate solution; rather they belong in the space of rational freedom enjoyed by each rational agent.[29]

[28] Indeed, I might find myself unable to do anything other than take our relationship as a reason not to give him up. In this way, hierarchical voluntarist reasons may provide a general framework for understanding Frankfurt's "volitional necessities." Cf. Frankfurt (1988); and, relatedly, Williams (1995).

[29] This view of voluntarist reasons and rational identity, I believe, also has applications to groups and, in particular, to institutions such as the judiciary and other government-like organizations which can create voluntarist reasons when their given reasons run out. See Chang (2009).

In short, we make our rational identities by giving ourselves voluntarist reasons. This crafting of our distinctive rational identities is, in a way, what life is all about. And voluntarist reasons are, I believe, at the heart of our doing so.[30]

## 7

Creating for ourselves voluntarist reasons is a fundamental exercise of our normative power. Unlike existential plumping, it is a rational power – one creates a reason that may give one most reason to choose a particular alternative, thereby making one's own distinctive rational identity. And, unlike picking, it is a power to change what we have most reason to do in the very choice situation and beyond. It is by the creation of voluntarist reasons that we have a solution to our two puzzles: we can sometimes have most reason to do something when our reasons have run out, and we can be fully responsive to our reasons and yet nevertheless make ourselves into distinctive ideal rational selves.

But can agents really *create* normativity? At issue here is not the ersatz "normative power" involved in, say, making a promise to meet someone for lunch. There is quite plausibly a normative principle according to which, very roughly, if you successfully communicate to me your willingness to meet me for lunch, you now have a reason to meet me for lunch. By willing to meet me for lunch, it seems that you have given yourself a reason to do so. But this is not the sort of willing involved in a genuine

[30] Other philosophers have held views which I take – perhaps in some cases with a dose of wishful thinking – to be broadly sympathetic to aspects of the view presented here. Some related ideas and discussions include Korsgaard's notion of a practical identity from which one's reasons are derived (Korsgaard 1996b: 100–128); Margaret Urban Walker's thought that "narrative understandings of the moral construction of lives" help to explain the responsibilities we have to those with whom we stand in some relation (Urban Walker 1998: 107–129, 109); Jennifer Whiting's claim that we make our metaphysical identities through what we care about (Whiting 1986); Peter Railton's account of agential activity needed to stop a regress in reasons (Railton 2003); Michael Bratman's appeal to self-governing policies in explaining self-governance (Bratman 2007); Raz's view of the role of the will among "incommensurables" (Raz 1997); Thomas Nagel's discussion of "reasons of autonomy" (Nagel 1986: chapter 9); David Velleman's exploration of the "freedom" we have to do something by intending to do it such that the intention causes its own fulfillment (Velleman 2000: 200–220, 213–215); Robert Nozick's claim that "the (precise) weights to be assigned to reasons is 'up to us'" (Nozick 1981: 294–316); and Samuel Scheffler's claim that some values involve our "seeing" things as valuable in order for them to have that value (Scheffler 2001: chapters 6–7). For many of these philosophers, appeal to voluntarist reasons will be uncongenial, but only because they believe they need not make such an appeal to make the claims they want to make. I am unsure whether this is so, and am even less sure if we are to take seriously the two puzzles discussed in this essay. In any case, some philosophers offer what I take to be clearly competing views about the domain I claim is covered by voluntarist reasons. The most interesting, to my mind, is Sartre (1946).

normative power. In willing to meet me for lunch, you simply satisfy the antecedent of a principle that holds when such-and-such conditions are satisfied, one has a reason to do so-and-so. The source of the normativity of this principle may be an irreducible normative reality. If so, your willing to meet me for lunch does not create normativity; rather, the normativity is already given by the source of the normativity of the principle whose antecedent condition you have satisfied through an act of will.[31]

Many philosophers reject the idea that we can create normativity because they think that if the normativity of our reasons derives from our wills, then reasons may be objectionably arbitrary. This was Samuel Clarke's attack against Hobbes' voluntarism and, more recently, Gerald Cohen's objection to Korsgaard's.[32] As Cohen points out, if reasons are voluntarist, then a Mafioso can will himself a reason to murder his rival. But it seems clear that the Mafioso has no such reason.[33]

This objection, usually taken to be fatal, is directed against voluntarist reasons *per se*. But it is unclear how the objection finds its intended mark. Consider the following toy scenario. Suppose the universe is fundamentally chaotic and that the *only* practical reasons there are concern how to tie one's shoelaces – whether to use the single-loop or the double-loop method. All other actions and attitudes not concerned with the tying of shoelaces are a matter of plumping and beyond the reach of reason. Suppose that your given reasons for tying your shoelaces in either of these methods have run out – you either have sufficient reasons to tie in either method or how you should tie is, like everything else, beyond the reach of practical reason. By taking the efficiency of the single-loop method as a reason, you can thereby create a voluntarist reason for yourself to tie in the single-loop method. You now have a voluntarist reason to tie in the single-loop method which, in conjunction with whatever given reasons you have for tying in that method, might give you most reason to tie in that

[31] Cf. Scanlon (1998: chapter 7).

[32] It is also Jane Eyre's objection to Mr. Rochester's declaration that he has passed a law unto himself to improve his character. Jane says, "The human and fallible should not arrogate a power with which the divine and perfect alone can be safely intrusted." Rochester: "What power?" Jane: "That of saying of any strange, unsanctioned line of action, – 'Let it be right.'" Charlotte Bronte (1847: chapter 14).

See Clarke (1706) and Cohen (1996): 167–188. The objection, to put it another way, is that standard voluntarist views like Korsgaard's really amount to what Korsgaard calls "heroic existentialism." See Korsgaard's epilogue (1997: 215–254).

[33] See Cohen (1996): 183–4. Kantians attempt to block this objection by putting constraints on rational willing so that all rational willing turns out to be moral willing, but such constraints are notoriously problematic.

method. You might instead take the beautiful symmetry of the double-loop method as a reason to tie in the double-loop method, perhaps thereby giving yourself most reason to tie in that method. Or you might take and then "untake" these considerations as reasons if you change your mind about them.

The voluntarist reasons you create are arbitrary in the sense that there are no reasons for you to have created those rather than others. But the fact that you could have, so far as your reasons go, created a reason to tie in the double-loop method rather than in the single-loop method does not, it seems to me, make the reasons you create to tie in the single-loop method *objectionably* arbitrary. To be *objectionably* arbitrary the reasons you create should be ones that lead to substantively objectionable conclusions about what you have all-things-considered most or sufficient reasons to do. We intuitively think that you have most or at least sufficient reasons not to harm people for pecuniary gain. If you could, like the Mafioso, just will yourself a reason to shoot the kneecaps off your rivals that would justify your doing so, the reason you create would be objectionably arbitrary. But the reasons you create to tie your shoelaces one way rather than another don't seem like this. If voluntarist reasons were objectionably arbitrary *per se*, they should be objectionably arbitrary even when what is at stake is only how your shoe laces get tied.

I suggest that those who think that voluntarist reasons are objectionably arbitrary do not object to voluntarist reasons *per se* but rather to the objectionable conclusions about what we are all-things-considered justified in doing that voluntarist reasons might entail. This is indeed a problem for the standard forms of voluntarism that derive from Kant and Hobbes. If voluntarist reasons are the only sorts of practical reasons there are, then we can in principle create reasons that justify our doing things that we aren't justified in doing.

If voluntarism is understood in the hierarchical form suggested here, however, the voluntarist reasons we give ourselves will not be objectionably arbitrary. This is because the hierarchical relation between one's given and voluntarist reasons guarantees that we can never create a voluntarist reason that goes against our all-things-considered given reasons. You can't create a voluntarist reason unless your non-voluntarist reasons have run out. So, for example, the Mafioso can't create a reason to harm his rival since his given reasons require him not to do so. Thus he can't give himself a reason that justifies his doing so. We can create voluntarist reasons only in the space of rational freedom afforded by our given reasons. While our hierarchical voluntarist reasons are arbitrary in the sense that we have no reasons to have one set rather than another, this arbitrariness does not lead to any substantive objection concerning what we are justified in doing. In this way, hierarchical voluntarism avoids what is widely considered the most fundamental problem with voluntarism.

## 8

There is another way in which hierarchical voluntarism steals a march on voluntarism in its standard forms. Here is a sketch of what I have in mind.

Three fundamentally different conceptions of the nature of normativity loosely underwrite the arguments among externalists, internalists, and voluntarists about the source of normativity. If normativity is an irreducibly distinct justificatory force, then its source is very plausibly in irreducibly normative facts. If instead it is a kind of motivating force, then where else to find its foundations but in desires and other motivational states of the agent such as the will? And if it is volitional force, then normativity plausibly has its source in the will or perhaps in other motivational states.

Standard forms of voluntarism depend for their plausibility on understanding normativity as something other than an irreducibly distinct justificatory force. For how can we, by a mere act of will, create such force? As some voluntarists have argued, normativity must be a volitional or motivational force since it is hard to see how an irreducibly justificatory force could "get a grip" on agents.[34] If normativity turns out to be an irreducible justificatory force, standard forms of voluntarism are in trouble.

Hierarchical voluntarism, by contrast, is not held hostage to the debate about normativity's nature. Suppose practical normativity is an irreducible justificatory force. While it is hard to believe that mere willing can create this force, it is not so hard – at any rate, less hard – to believe that willing *under the condition that one's all-things-considered given reasons have run out* can create this force. A rough analogy might help. Suppose you are given a blank piece of paper and some watercolors, and are told to create a beautiful forest scene. You will likely fail (if your artistic skills are like mine), painting lopsided trees with badly-proportioned features. If instead you are given the outline of a forest scene drawn by a master and are asked to color in the lines, you may well produce a beautiful forest scene. In this way, a constrained normative power may be more powerful than an unconstrained one. Coupled with the thought that one's willing

[34] See, e.g., Korsgaard (1997). For a good reply to this objection, see Parfit (forthcoming).

under the requisite conditions constitutes one's rational identity, it becomes all the more plausible that the reasons that are part of one's rational identity could in principle have an irreducible justificatoriness about them.

If, on the other hand, normativity is a kind of motivational or volitional force, then the voluntarist reasons one creates will naturally bear motivational or volitional force. If the reasons that constitute your best rational self are made by you, they naturally bear motivating force. And since they are the product of your will, they naturally bear volitional force. In this way, hierarchical voluntarism can in principle straddle all three conceptions of the nature of practical normativity. If hierarchical voluntarism is right, then whatever the nature of normativity turns out to be, there is a place for the will in understanding its source.

My aim here has been to sketch the beginnings of what seems to me the most plausible view of voluntarist reasons by showing how such reasons can solve two puzzles about rational action and agency. If the arguments here are right, such voluntarist reasons – hierarchically related to non-voluntarist reasons – are able to capture the main insight of voluntarism – that we can confer normativity or value on things – without falling prey to its main difficulty. They put the will in its proper place.

# *Bibliography*


Adler, J. (2002) *Belief's Own Ethics*. Cambridge, MA: MIT Press.

Aristotle (2000) *Nichomachean Ethics*, trans. R. Crisp. Cambridge: Cambridge University Press.

Armour-Garb, B. and Beall, J.C., eds. (2005) *Deflationary Truth*. Chicago: Open Court Press.

Arpaly, N. (2000) "On Acting Rationally Against One's Best Judgment," *Ethics*, **110**, April: 488–513.

Atiyah, P.S. (1981) *Promises, Morals and Law*. Oxford: Oxford University Press.

Austin, J.L. (1961) "Ifs and Cans," in *Philosophical Papers*. Oxford: Oxford University Press.

Baier, K. (1966) "Moral Obligation," *American Philosophical Quarterly*, **3**: 210–226.

Bargh, J.A. and Chartrand, T.L. (1999) "The Unbearable Automaticity of Being," *American Psychologist*, **54**: 462–479.

Bar-On, D., Horisk, C., and Lycan, W.G. (2005a) "Deflationism, Meaning and Truth-Conditions," in B. Armour-Garb and J.C. Beall, eds., *Deflationary Truth*. Chicago: Open Court Press: 321–343.

(2005b) "Postscript to 'Deflationism, Meaning, and Truth-Conditions'," in B. Armour-Garb and J.C. Beall, eds., *Deflationary Truth*. Chicago: Open Court Press.

Baron-Cohen, S. (1995) *Mindblindness: An Essay on Autism and Theory of Mind*. Cambridge, MA: MIT Press.

*et al.* (1999) "Value Judgments: Testing the Somatic-Marker Hypothesis Using False Physiological Feedback," *Personality and Social Psychology Bulletin*, **25**: 1021–1032.

Baumann., P. and Betzler, M., eds. (2004) *Practical Conflicts: New Philosophical Essays*. Cambridge: Cambridge University Press.

Baumeister, R.F. (1997) *Evil: Inside Human Violence and Cruelty*. New York: W.H. Freeman: 209–210.

Bennett, J. (1980) "Accountability," in Z. Van. Stratten, ed., *Philosophical Subjects*. Oxford: Clarendon Press.

Binkley, R. (1965) "A Theory of Practical Reason," *The Philosophical Review*, **74**: 423–448.

Bittner, R. (1992) "Is it Reasonable to Regret Things One Did?," *The Journal of Philosophy*, **89**: 262–273.

Blackburn, S. (1984) *Spreading The Word*. Oxford: Oxford University Press.

(1993) *Essays in Quasi-Realism*. Oxford: Oxford University Press.

(1997) "How to Be an Ethical Anti-Realist," in S. Darwall, A. Gibbard, and P. Railton, eds., *Moral Discourse and Practice*. Oxford: Oxford University Press: 167–178.

(1998) *Ruling Passions*. Oxford: Oxford University Press.

Boethius (1902) *The Consolation of Philosophy*, trans. Cooper W.V. London: J.M. Dent.

Bond, E.J. (1983) *Reason and Value*. Cambridge: Cambridge University Press.

Brandom, R. (1994) *Making It Explicit*. Cambridge, MA: Harvard University Press.

Brandt, R. (1979) *A Theory of the Good and the Right*. Oxford: Oxford University Press.

(1996) *Facts, Values, and Morality*. Cambridge: Cambridge University Press.

Bratman, M.E. (1981) "Intention and Means-End Reasoning," *The Philosophical Review*, **90**: 252–265.

(1987) *Intention, Plans, and Practical Reason*. Cambridge, MA: Harvard University Press; reissued by CSLI Publications, 1999.

(1999) *Faces of Intention*. New York: Cambridge University Press.

(2001) "Taking Plans Seriously," in E. Millgram, ed., *Varieties of Practical Reasoning*. Cambridge, MA: MIT Press.

(2007) *Structures of Agency: Essays*. New York: Oxford University Press.

"Intention, Belief, Practical, Theoretical." Forthcoming in S. Robertson, ed., *Spheres of Reason*. Oxford: Oxford University Press.

Brink, D. (1986) "Externalist Moral Realism," in *The Spindel Conference: The Southern Journal of Philosophy*, supplementary volume, **24**: 23–41.

(1997) "Kantian Rationalism: Inescapability, Authority and Supremacy," in G. Cullity and B. Gaut, eds., *Ethics and Practical Reason*. Oxford: Clarendon Press: 255–291.

Bronte, C. (1847) *Jane Eyre*. London: Penguin.

Broome, J. (1991) *Weighing Goods*. Oxford: Basil Blackwell.

(1997) "Reasons and Motivation," *Aristotelian Society Supplement*, **71**: 131–146.

(1999) "Normative Requirements," *Ratio*, **12**: 398–419.

(2004) "Reasons," in R.J. Wallace, P. Pettit, S. Scheffler, and M. Smith, eds., *Reason and Value: Themes from the Moral Philosophy of Joseph Raz*. Oxford: Oxford University Press: 28–55.

(2005) "Have we Reason to do as Rationality Requires?—A Comment on Raz," *The Journal of Ethics and Social Philosophy*, Symposium I, www.jesp.org.

(2007) "Wide or Narrow Scope?," *Mind*, **116**: 359–370.

(2008) "The Unity of Reasoning," unpublished manuscript. Forthcoming in S. Robertson, ed., *Spheres of Reason*. Oxford: Oxford University Press.

Browning, C. (1992) *Ordinary Men: Reserve Police Battalion 101 and the Final Solution in Poland*. New York: HarperCollins.

Campbell, R. and Hunter, B., eds. (2000) *Moral Epistemology Naturalized: Canadian Journal of Philosophy*, supplementary volume, 26, Alberta: University of Calgary Press.

Carruthers, P. (1996) "Simulation and Self-Knowledge: A Defence of Theory-Theory," in P. Carruthers and P.K. Smith, eds., *Theories of Theories of Mind*. Cambridge: Cambridge University Press: 22–38.

Chang, R. (1997) "Introduction," in R. Chang, ed., *Incommensurability, Incomparability, and Practical Reason*. Cambridge, MA: Harvard University Press: 1–34.

(2002) "The Possibility of Parity," *Ethics*, **112**: 659–688.

(2004a) "All Things Considered," *Philosophical Perspectives*, **18**: 1–22.

(2004b) "Putting Together Morality and Well-Being," in P. Baumann and M. Betzler, eds., *Practical Conflicts: New Philosophical Essays*. Cambridge: Cambridge University Press: 118–158.

(2004c) "Can Desires Provide Reasons for Action?," in R.J. Wallace, P. Pettit, S. Scheffler, and M. Smith, eds., *Reason and Value: Themes from the Moral Philosophy of Joseph Raz*. Oxford: Oxford University Press.

(2005) "Parity, Interval Value, and Choice," *Ethics*, **114**: 331–350.

(2009) "Some Reflections on the Reasonable and the Rational in Conflict Resolution," *Aristotelian Society*, supplementary volume.

Clark, M.S. and Fiske, S.T., eds. (1982) *Affect and Cognition*. San Diego: Academic Press.

Clark, P. (2001) "The Action as Conclusion," *Canadian Journal of Philosophy*, **31**, 481–506.

(2007) "How Reason Can Be Practical: A Reply to Hume," *Poznan Studies in the Philosophy of the Sciences and the Humanities, 94: Moral Psychology*, Sergio. Tenenbaum, ed. Amsterdam: Rodopi: 213–230.

Clarke, S. (1706) "Discourse Concerning the Unchangeable Obligations of Natural Religion, and the Truth and Certainty of the Christian Revelation", in D.D. Raphael, ed., *British Moralists 1650–1800*. Indianapolis, IN: Hackett: 191–225.

Cohen, G. (1996) "Reason, Humanity, and the Moral Law," in C. Korsgaard, *The Sources of Normativity*. Cambridge, Cambridge University Press: 167–188.

Copp, D. (1995) *Morality, Normativity, and Society*. Oxford: Oxford University Press.

(2001) "Realist-Expressivism: A Neglected Option for Moral Realism," *Social Philosophy and Policy*, **18**: 1–43.

Csikszentmihalyi, M. (1990) *Flow: The Psychology of Optimal Experience*. New York: Harper & Row.

D'Arms, J. and Jacobson, D. (2000a) "The Moralistic Fallacy: On the 'Appropriateness' of Emotions," *Philosophy and Phenomenological Research*, **61**: 65–90.

(2000b) "Sentiment and Value," *Ethics*, **110**: 722–748.

(2003) "The Significance of Recalcitrant Emotions (or, Anti-Quasi-judgmentalism)," reprinted in Anthony Hatzimoysis, ed., *Philosophy and the Emotions*. Cambridge: Cambridge University Press.

(2006) "Anthropocentric Constraints on Human Value," *Oxford Studies in Metaethics*, **1**: 99–126.

Damasio, A. (1994) *Descartes' Error*. New York: Putnam.

Dancy, J. (2000) *Practical Reality*. Oxford: Oxford University Press.

(2004) "Enticing Reasons," in R.J. Wallace, P. Pettit, S. Scheffler, and M. Smith., eds., *Reason and Value: Themes from the Moral Philosophy of Joseph Raz*. Oxford: Oxford University Press.

Darwall, S. (1983) *Impartial Reason*. Ithaca, NY: Cornell University Press.

(1986) "Agent-Centered Restrictions From the Inside Out," *Philosophical Studies*, **50**: 291–319.

(2002) *Welfare and Rational Care*. Princeton, NJ: Princeton University Press.

(2003) "Autonomy in Modern Natural Law," in L. Krasnoff and N. Brender, eds., *New Essays on the History of Autonomy*. Cambridge: Cambridge University Press.

(2004) "Respect and the Second-Person Standpoint," *Proceedings and Addresses of the American Philosophical Association*, **78**: 43–59.

(2006) *The Second-Person Standpoint: Morality, Respect, and Accountability*. Cambridge, MA: Harvard University Press.

Davidson, D. (1963) "Actions, Reasons and Causes," reprinted in *Essays on Actions and Events*. Oxford: Oxford University Press, 1980: 3–20.

(1970a) "Mental Events," reprinted in *Essays on Actions and Events*. Oxford: Oxford University Press, 1980: 207–229.

(1970b) "How is Weakness of the Will Possible?," in J. Feinberg, ed., *Moral Concepts*. Oxford: Oxford University Press, reprinted in *Essays on Actions and Events*. Oxford: Oxford University Press, 1980: 21–43.

(1971a) "Agency," reprinted in *Essays on Actions and Events*. Oxford: Oxford University Press, 1980: 43–46.

(1971b) "Psychology as Philosophy," reprinted in *Essays on Actions and Events*. Oxford: Oxford University Press, 1980: 229–245.

(1973) "Freedom to Act," reprinted in *Essays on Actions and Events*. Oxford: Oxford University Press, 1980: 63–83.

(1976) "Hempel on Explaining Action," reprinted in *Essays on Actions and Events*. Oxford: Oxford University Press, 1980: 261–277.

(1978) "Intending," reprinted in *Essays on Actions and Events*, 2nd edn. Oxford: Oxford University Press, 1980: 83–102.

Davies, W. (2003) *Meaning, Expression and Thought*. Cambridge: Cambridge University Press.

(2005) *Nondescriptive Meaning and Reference*. Oxford: Oxford University Press.

Davis, W. (1984) "A Causal Theory of Intending," *American Philosophical Quarterly*, **21**: 43–54.

Dijksterhuis, A. *et al.* (2006) "On Making the Right Choice: The Deliberation-without-Attention Effect," *Science*, **311**: 1005–1007.

Downie, R.S. (1985) "Three Concepts of Promising," *Philosophical Quarterly*, **35**: 259–271.

Edgington, D. (1995) "On Conditionals," *Mind*, **104**: 235–329.

Edwards, P. (1955) *The Logic of Moral Discourse*. New York: Free Press.

Enoch, D. (2006) "Agency, Schmagency," *The Philosophical Review*, **115**: 169–198.

Falk, W.D. (1986) "Fact, Value, and Nonnatural Predication," in W.D. Falk and K. Baier, eds., *Ought, Reasons, and Morality: The Collected Papers of W.D. Falk*. Ithaca, NY: Cornell University Press.

Feinberg, J. (1980) "The Nature and Value of Rights," in *Rights, Justice, and the Bounds of Liberty*. Princeton, NJ: Princeton University Press.

Fiske, A.P. (1991) *Structures of Social Life: The Four Elementary Forms of Human Relationships*. New York: Free Press.

Foot, P. (1978) "Morality as a System of Hypothetical Imperatives," reprinted in *Virtues and Vices*. Berkeley: California University Press: 157–173.

(2001). *Natural Goodness*. Oxford: Clarendon Press.

Frankfurt, H. (1988) *The Importance of What We Care About*. Cambridge: Cambridge University Press.

Fried, Charles. (1978) *Right and Wrong*. Cambridge, MA: Harvard University Press.

(1981) *Contract and Promise*. Cambridge, MA: Harvard University Press.

Garner, R. (1990) "On the Genuine Queerness of Moral Properties and Facts," *Australasian Journal of Philosophy*, **68**: 137–146.

Gibbard, A. (1990) *Wise Choices, Apt Feelings*. Cambridge, MA: Harvard University Press.

(2003) *Wise Choices, Apt Feelings*. Cambridge, MA: Harvard University Press.

Gigerenzer, G. and Todd., P. (1999) "Fast and Frugal Heuristics: The Adaptive Toolbox," in *Simple Heuristics That Make Us Smart*. New York: Oxford University Press.

Gilbert, M. (2000) *Sociality and Responsibility*. Lanham, MD: Rowman & Littlefield.

(2004) "Scanlon on Promissory Obligation: The Problem of Promisees' Rights," *The Journal of Philosophy*, **101**: 83–109.

(2006) *A Theory of Political Obligation*. New York: Oxford University Press.

Goleman, D. (1995) *Emotional Intelligence*. New York: Bantam.

(2006) *Social Intelligence*. New York: Bantam.

Greenspan, P. (1975) "Conditional Oughts and Hypothetical Imperatives," *The Journal of Philosophy*, **72**: 259–276.

Grice, H.P. (1968) "Utterer's Meaning, Sentence Meaning, and Word Meaning," *Foundations of Language*, **4**: 225–242.

(1971) "Intention and Uncertainty," *Proceedings of the British Academy*, **57**: 263–279.

(1974–5) "Method in Philosophical Psychology (From the Banal to the Bizarre)," (Presidential Address), *Proceedings and Addresses of the American Philosophical Association*: 23–53.

Gupta, A. (2005a) "A Critique of Deflationism," in B. Armour-Garb and J.C. Beall, eds., *Deflationary Truth*. Chicago: Open Court Press: 199–226.

(2005b) "Postscript to 'A Critique of Deflationism'," in B. Armour-Garb and J.C. Beall, eds., *Deflationary Truth*. Chicago: Open Court Press: 227–233.

Haidt, J. (2001) "The Emotional Dog and Its Rational Tail: A Social Intuitionist Approach to Moral Judgment," *Psychological Review*, **108**: 814–834.

Hampton, J. (1998) *The Authority of Reason*. Cambridge: Cambridge University Press.

Harcourt, E. (2005) "Quasi-Realism and Ethical Appearances," *Mind*, **114**: 249–275.

Hare, R.M. (1971) "Wanting: Some Pitfalls," in R. Binkley, R. Bronaugh, and A. Marras, eds., *Agent, Action, and Reason*. Toronto: University of Toronto Press: 81–97.

(1993) "Could Kant Have Been a Utilitarian?," in *Kant and Critique: New Essays in Honor of W.H. Werkmeister*. Dordrecht: Kluwer Academic.

Harman, G. (1976) "Practical Reasoning," reprinted in *Reasoning, Meaning, and Mind*. Oxford: Oxford University Press, 1999: 46–74.

(1977) *The Nature of Morality*. New York: Oxford University Press.

(1986a) *Change in View*. Cambridge, MA: MIT Press.

(1986b) "Willing and Intending," in R. Grandy and R. Warner, eds., *Philosophical Grounds of Rationality*. Oxford: Oxford University Press: 363–380.

(1995) "Rationality," in D.N. Osherson *et al.*, eds., *Thinking: An Invitation to Cognitive Science*, 3. Cambridge, MA: MIT Press. Reprinted in G. Harman, *Reasoning, Meaning and Mind*. Oxford: Oxford University Press.

Hart, H.L.A. (1955) "Are There Any Natural Rights?," *The Philosophical Review*, **64**: 175–191.

(1968) "Prolegomenon to the Principles of Punishment," in *Punishment and Responsibility*. New York: Oxford University Press.

Hassin, R.R., Uleman, J.S., and Bargh, J.A. (2005) *The New Unconscious*. Oxford: Oxford University Press.

Hauser, M.D., Chomsky, N., and Fitch, W.T. (2002) "The Faculty of Language: What Is It, Who Has It, and How Did It Evolve?," *Science*, **298**: 1569–1579.

Helm, B. (2001) *Emotional Reason*. Cambridge: Cambridge University Press.

Hempel, Carl. (1961) "Rational Action," reprinted in N.S. Care and C. Landesman, eds., *Readings in the Theory of Action*. Bloomington, IN: Indiana University Press, 1968: 285–286.

Hieronymi, P. (2005) "The Wrong Kind of Reason," *The Journal of Philosophy*, **102**: 435–457.

Hill, C. (2002) *Thought and World: An Austere Portrayal of Truth, Reference, and Semantic Correspondence*. Cambridge: Cambridge University Press.

Hobbes, T. (1651) *Leviathas*. New York: Prometheus Books.

Hoffman, M.L. (1982) "Development of Prosocial Motivation: Empathy and Guilt," in N. Eisenberg, ed., *The Development of Prosocial Behavior*. New York: Academic Press.

Horwich, P. (1990) *Truth*. Oxford: Oxford University Press.

Hubin, D. (1999) "What's Special about Humeanism," *Noûs*, **33**: 30–45.

Humberstone, L. (1992) "Direction of Fit," *Mind*, **101**: 59–83.

Hume, D. (1978) *A Treatise of Human Nature*, ed. L.A. Selby-Bigge and P.H. Nidditch. Oxford: Oxford University Press.

Hurley, S. (1989) *Natural Reasons*. Oxford: Oxford University Press.

Hursthouse, R. (1999) *On Virtue Ethics*. Oxford: Oxford University Press.

Jackendoff, R. (2002) *Foundations of Language: Brain, Meaning, Grammar, and Evolution*. Oxford: Oxford University Press.

Jackson, F. and Pargetter, R. (1986) "Oughts, Options, and Actualism," *The Philosophical Review*, **95**: 233–255.

Jackson, F. and Pettit, P. (1998) "A Problem for Expressivists," *Analysis*, **58**(4): 239–251.

Joyce, James M. (1999) *The Foundations of Causal Decision Theory*. Cambridge: Cambridge University Press.

Joyce, R. (2001) *The Myth of Morality*. Cambridge: Cambridge University Press.

Kahneman, D., Knetsch, J.L., and Thaler, R.H. (1999) "Experimental Tests of the Endowment Effect and the Coase Theorem," *The Journal of Political Economy*, **98**: 1325–1348.

Kant, I. (1785) *Groundwork of the Metaphysics of Morals*, trans. H.J. Paton. New York: Harper Torchbooks.

(1966) *Metaphysics of Morals*, trans. M.J. Gregor. Cambridge: Cambridge University Press.

(1987) *The Critique of Judgment*, trans. W.S. Pluhar. Indianapoli, IN: Hackett.

(1996). *Critique of Practical Reason,* in *Practical Philosophy*, trans. and ed. M.J. Gregor. Cambridge: Cambridge University Press.

(1999). *Religion Within the Boundaries of Mere Reason*, eds. A.W. Wood and G.Di. Giovanni. Cambridge: Cambridge University Press.

(2007) *Critique of Pure Reason*, trans. Norman Kemp-Smith. Houndmills: Palgrave.

Kavka, G. (1983) "The Toxin Puzzle," *Analysis*, **43**: 33–36.

Ketland, J. (1998) "Deflationism and Tarski's Paradise," *Mind*, **108**: 69–94.

Kolodny, N. (2005) "Why Be Rational?," *Mind*, **114**: 509–563.

Kolodny, N. and Wallace, R.J. (2003) "Promises and Practices Revisited," *Philosophy and Public Affairs*, **31**: 119–154.

Korsgaard, C. (1986) "Skepticism about Practical Reason," *The Journal of Philosophy*, **83**: 5–25.

(1996a) *Creating the Kingdom of Ends*. Cambridge: Cambridge University Press.

(1996b) *The Sources of Normativity*. Cambridge: Cambridge University Press.

(1997) "The Normativity of Instrumental Reason," in G. Cullity and B. Gaut, eds., *Ethics and Practical Reason*. Oxford: Oxford University Press: 215–254.

(1999) "Self-Constitution in the Ethics of Plato and Kant," *Journal of Ethics*, **3**: 1–29.

Kraut, R. (2007) *What is Good and Why: The Ethics of Well-Being*. Cambridge, MA: Harvard University Press.

Locke, J. (1975) *An Essay Concerning Human Understanding*, ed. P.H. Nidditch. Oxford: Oxford University Press.

Machina, M. (1982) "Expected Utility Analysis Without the Independence Axiom," *Econometrica*, **50**: 277–323.

Mackie, J.L. (1977) *Ethics: Inventing Right and Wrong*. Harmondsworth: Penguin.

McCann, H. (1991) "Settled Objectives and Rational Constraints," *American Philosophical Quarterly*, **28**: 25–36.

McDowell, J. (1979) "Virtue and Reason," *The Monist*, **62**: 331–350.

(1985) "Values and Secondary Qualities," in T. Honderich, ed., *Morality and Objectivity*. London: Routledge & Kegan Paul: 110–129.

McNaughton, D. and Rawlings, P. (1991) "Agent-Relativity and the Doing–Happening Distinction," *Philosophical Studies*, **63**: 167–185.

Melden, A.I. (1977) *Rights and Persons*. Berkeley: California University Press.

Mellor, D.H. (1978) *Foundations: Essays in Philosophy, Logic, Mathematics and Economics*. London: Routledge.

Metcalf, J. and Mischel, W. (1999) "A Hot/Cool System Analysis of the Delay of Gratification," *Psychological Review*, **106**: 3–19.

Mill, J.S. (1998) *Utilitarianism*, ed. Roger Crisp. Oxford: Oxford University Press.

Mitchell, P. (1997) *Introduction to the Theory of Mind: Children, Autism, and Apes*. London: Arnold.

Moore, G.E. (1971) *Morality and Objectivity*. London: Routledge and Kegan Paul: 110–129.

(1993) *Principia Ethica*, ed. T. Baldwin. Cambridge: Cambridge University Press.

Morton, J.M. (in progress) "Practical Reasoning and the Varieties of Agency," PhD thesis, Stanford University.

Murphy, S., Haidt, J., and Bjorklund, F. (forthcoming) "Moral Dumbfounding: When Intuition Finds No Reason," in preparation.

Nagel, T. (1970) *The Possibility of Altruism*. Oxford: Clarendon Press.

(1986) *The View From Nowhere*. New York: Oxford University Press.

Nelson, M. (1995) "Is it Always Fallacious to Derive Values from Facts?," *Argumentation*, **9/4**: 553–562.

Nozick, R. (1981) *Philosophical Explanation*. Belknap Press, Harvard University.

Olson, J. (2004) "Buck-Passing and the Wrong Kind of Reasons," *Philosophical Quarterly*, **54**: 295–300.

Owens, D. (2002) "Epistemic Akrasia," *The Monist*, **85**: 382–383.

(2006) "A Simple Theory of Promising," *The Philosophical Review*, **115**: 51–77.

Parfit, D. (1984) *Reasons and Persons*. Oxford: Clarendon Press.

(1997) "Reason and Motivation," *Aristotelian Society Supplement*, **71**: 99–130.

(2001) "Rationality and Reasons," in D. Egonsson, J. Josefsson, B. Petterson, and T. Rønnow-Rasmussen, eds., *Exploring Practical Philosophy: From Action to Values*. Burlington, VT: Ashgate: 17–39.

(forthcoming) *Climbing the Mountain*. Oxford: Oxford University Press.

Peacocke, C. (1979) *Holistic Explanation: Action, Space, Interpretation*. Oxford: Oxford University Press.

Pettit, P. and Smith, M. (1990) "Backgrounding Desire," *The Philosophical Review*, **99**: 565–592.

Pratt, M. (2003) "Promises and Perlocutions," in M. Matravers, ed., *Scanlon and Contractualism*. London: Frank Cass.

Prichard, D. (2007) "Recent Work on Epistemic Value," *American Philosophical Quarterly*, **44**: 85–110.

Prichard, H.A. (1968) *Moral Obligation and Duty and Interest: Essays and Lectures by H. A. Prichard*, ed. W.D. Ross and J.O. Urmson. Oxford: Oxford University Press.

(2002) "Does Moral Philosophy Rest on a Mistake?," in J. McAdam, ed., *Moral Writings*. Oxford: Oxford University Press.

Pufendorf, S. (1672) *De Jure Naturae et Gentium*. Lund; *On the Law of Nature and Nations*, trans. C.H. Oldfather and W.A. Oldfather. Oxford: Oxford University Press, 1934.

Putnam, H. (1975) "The Meaning of Meaning," in *Mind, Language, and Reality*. Cambridge: Cambridge University Press: 215–271.

Quinn, W. (1991) "Putting Rationality in Its Place," in *Morality and Action*. Cambridge: Cambridge University Press.

Rabinowicz, W. and Rønnow-Rasmussen, T. (2004) "The Strike of the Demon: On Fitting Pro-Attitudes and Value," *Ethics*, **114**: 391–423.

Railton, P. (1989) "Naturalism and Prescriptivity," *Social Philosophy and Policy*, **7**: 151–171.

(2003) *Facts, Values, and Norms: Essays Toward a Morality of Consequence*. Cambridge: Cambridge University Press.

Ramsey, F. (1929) "General Propositions and Causality," reprinted in Ramsey's *Philosophical Papers*, ed. D.H. Mellor. Cambridge: Cambridge University Press.

(1978) "*Facts and Propositions*," in D.H. Mellor, *Foundations: Essays in Philosophy, Logic, Mathematics and Economics*. London: Routledge: 40–57.

Raphael, D.D., ed. (1991) *British Moralists 1650–1800*. Indianapolis, IN: Hackett.

Rawls, J. (1971) *A Theory of Justice*. Cambridge, MA: Harvard University Press.

(1980) "Kantian Constructivism in Moral Theory," *The Journal of Philosophy*, **77**: 515–572.

Raz, J. (1972) "Voluntary Obligations and Normative Powers II," *Proceedings of the Aristotelian Society*, supplementary volume, **46**: 79–101.

(1975)*Practical Reasons and Norms*. Princeton: Princeton University Press.

(1977) "Promises and Obligations," in P.M.S. Hacker and J. Raz, eds., *Law, Morality, and Society: Essays in Honor of H.L.A. Hart*. Oxford: Oxford University Press: 210–228.

(1986) *The Morality of Freedom*. Oxford: Oxford University Press.

(1990) *Practical Reason and Norms*. Princeton, NJ: Princeton University Press.

(1997) "Incommensurability and Agency," in R. Chang, ed., *Incommensurability, Incomparability, and Practical Reason*. Cambridge, MA: Harvard University Press: 110–128.

(1999) *Engaging Reason*. Oxford: Oxford University Press.

(2004) "Personal Practical Conflicts," in P. Baumann and M. Betzler, eds., *Practical Conflicts: New Philosophical Essays*. Cambridge: Cambridge University Press.

(2005) "The Myth of Instrumental Rationality," *Journal of Ethics and Social Philosophy*, www.jesp.org, **1** (1).

(2008) "Reasons: Normative and Explanatory," in C. Sandis, ed., *New Essays on the Explanation of Action*. Basingstoke: Palgrave.

Reid, T. (1788) *Essays on the Active Powers of the Human Mind*. Cambridge, MA: MIT Press.

Richardson, H. (1994) *Practical Reasoning about Final Ends*. Cambridge: Cambridge University Press.

Ridge, M. (2005) "Reasons for Action: Agent-Neutral vs. Agent-Relative," *Stanford Encyclopedia of Philosophy*, http://plato.stanford.edu/entries/reasons-agent.

(2006a) "Ecumenical Expressivism: Finessing Frege," *Ethics*, **116**: 302–336.

(2006b) "Saving the Ethical Appearances," *Mind*, **115**: 630–650.

(forthcoming) "Ecumenical Expressivism: The Best of Both Worlds?," in *Oxford Studies in Metaethics*, 2. Oxford: Oxford University Press.

Rosenthal, D. (1997) "A Theory of Consciousness," in N. Block, O. Flanagan, and G. Guzeldere, eds., *The Nature of Consciousness: Philosophical Debates*. Cambridge, MA: MIT Press: 729–753.

Ross, W.D. (1930) *The Right and the Good*. Oxford: Clarendon Press.

Salovey, P. and Mayer, J.D. (1990) "Emotional Intelligence," *Imagination, Cognition, and Personality*, **9**: 185–211.

Sartre, J.P. (1946) *Existentialism and Human Emotions*. New York: Citadel Press, 1994.

Savage, L.J. (1972) *The Foundations of Statistics*, 2nd edn. New York: Dover.

Scanlon, T.M. (1998) *What We Owe to Each Other*. Cambridge, MA: Harvard University Press.

(2002) "Replies," *Social Theory and Practice*, **28**, April: 337–358.

(2003) *The Difficulty of Tolerance*. Cambridge: Cambridge University Press.

(2004) "Reasons: a Puzzling Duality," in R.J. Wallace, P. Pettit, S. Scheffler, and M. Smith, eds., *Reason and Value: Themes from the Moral Philosophy of Joseph Raz*. Oxford: Oxford University Press: 230–246.

Scheffler, S. (1982) *The Rejection of Consequentialism*. Oxford: Clarendon Press.

(2001) *Boundaries and Allegiances*. Oxford: Oxford University Press.

Schneewind, J. (1998) *The Invention of Autonomy*. New York: Cambridge University Press.

Searle, J. (1983) *Intentionality: An Essay in the Philosophy of Mind*. Cambridge: Cambridge University Press.

(2001) *Rationality in Action*. Cambridge, MA: MIT Press.

Sehon, S. (2005) *Teleological Realism: Mind, Agency, and Explanation*. Cambridge, MA: MIT Press.

Setiya, K. (2005) "Cognitivism about Instrumental Reason: Response to Bratman," comments on Michael Bratman, "Intention, Belief, Practical, Theoretical," conference on Practical Reason, University of Maryland, April.

(2007) "Cognitivism about Instrumental Reason," *Ethics*, **117**: 649–673.

Shafer-Landau, R. (2003) *Moral Realism: A Defense*. New York: Oxford University Press.

Shah, N. (2003) "How Truth Governs Belief," *The Philosophical Review*, **112**: 447–482.

(2006) "A New Argument for Evidentialism," *The Philosophical Quarterly*, **56**: 481–498.

(2008) "How Action Governs Intention," *Philosophers' Imprint*, Ann Arbor, MI: Scholarly Publishing Office, University Library, University of Michigan, http://hdl.handle.net/2027/spo.3521354.0008.005.

Shah, N. and Velleman, J.D. (2005) "Doxastic Deliberation," *The Philosophical Review*, **114**: 497–534.

Shapiro, S. (1998) "Truth and Proof – Through Thick and Thin," *The Journal of Philosophy*, **95**: 493–521.

Shoda, Y., Mischel, W., and Peake, P.K. (1990) "Predicting Adolescent Cognitive and Self-Regulatory Competencies from Preschool Delay of Gratification," *Developmental Psychology*, **26**: 978–986.

Shultz, W., Dayan P., and Montague, R.P. (1997) "A Neural Substrate of Prediction and Reward," *Science*, **275**: 1593–1599.

Sidgwick, H. (1907) *The Method of Ethics*, 7th edn. Indianapolis, IN: Hackett.

Sinclair, N. (2006) "The Moral Belief Problem," *Ratio*, **19**: 249–260.

Skorupski, J. (1999) *Ethical Explorations*. Oxford: Oxford University Press.

Smith, M. (1994) *The Moral Problem*. Oxford: Blackwell.

(1998) "The Possibility of Philosophy of Action," in J. Bransen and S. Cuypers, eds., *Human Action, Deliberation and Causation*. Dordrecht: Kluwer Academic: 17–41.

(1999) "The Definition of Moral," in D. Jamieson, ed., *Singer and His Critics*. Oxford: Blackwell: 38–63.

(2004) "Instrumental Desires, Instrumental Rationality," *Proceedings of the Aristotelian Society, supplementary volume*, **78**: 93–109.

(2006) "Is That All There Is?," *Journal of Ethics*, **10**: 75–106.

Stanley, J. (2005) *Knowledge and Practical Interests*. Oxford: Oxford University Press.

Stevenson, C. (1944) *Ethics and Language*. New Haven: Yale University Press.

Stocker, M. (2004) "Raz on the Intelligibility of Bad Acts," in R.J. Wallace, P. Pettit, S. Scheffler, and M. Smith, eds., *Reason and Value : Themes from the Moral Philosophy of Joseph Raz*. Oxford: Oxford University Press.

Strawson, P.F. (1968) "Freedom and Resentment," in *Studies in the Philosophy of Thought and Action*. London: Oxford University Press.

Stroud, S. (2006) "Epistemic Partiality in Friendship," *Ethics*, **116**: 498–524.

Tarski, A. (1958) "The Concept of Truth in Formalized Languages," in *Logic, Semantics, Metamathematics: Papers from 1923 to 1938*. Oxford: Oxford University Press.

Taylor, C. (1985) *Human Agency and Language: Philosophical Papers I*. Cambridge: Cambridge University Press.

Thoma, S.J. *et al.* (1999) "Does Moral Judgment Development Reduce to Political Attitudes or Verbal Ability?," *Educational Psychology Review*, **11**: 325–341.

Thompson, M. (1995) "The Representation of Life," in R. Hursthouse, G. Lawrence, and W. Quinn, eds., *Virtues and Reasons*. Oxford: Clarendon Press.

Thomson, J.J. (1990) *The Realm of Rights*. Cambridge, MA: Harvard University Press.

Timmerman, J., Skorupski, J., and Robertson, S., eds. (forthcoming) *Spheres of Reason*. Oxford: Oxford University Press.

Tognazzini, N. (2007) "The Hybrid Nature of Promissory Obligation," *Philosophy and Public Affairs*, **35**: 203–232.

Ullmann-Margalit, E. and Morgenbesser, S. (1977) "Picking and Choosing," *Social Research*, **44**: 757–785.

Urban Walker, M. (1998) *Moral Understandings*. New York: Routledge.

Velleman, J.D. (1989) *Practical Reflection*. Princeton, NJ: Princeton University Press.

(2000) *The Possibility of Practical Reason*. Oxford: Oxford University Press.

(2007) "What Good is a Will?," in A. Leist and H. Baumann, eds., *Action in Context*. Berlin and New York: de Gruyter and Mouton.

Von Wright, G.H. (1983) *Practical Reason*. Ithaca, NY: Cornell University Press.

Wallace, R.J. (1994) *Responsibility and the Moral Sentiments*. Cambridge, MA: Harvard University Press.

(2001) "Normativity, Commitment, and Instrumental Reason," *Philosophers' Imprint*, **1** (3).

(2006) *Normativity and the Will: Selected Essays on Moral Psychology and Practical Reason*. Oxford: Oxford University Press.

Watson, G. (1987) "Responsibility and the Limits of Evil: Variations on a Strawsonian Theme," in F.D. Schoeman, ed., *Responsibility, Character, and the Emotions: New Essays in Moral Psychology*. Cambridge: Cambridge University Press.

(1998) "Some Considerations in Favor of Contractualism," in J. Coleman and C. Morris, eds., *Rational Commitment and Social Justice: Essays for Gregory Kavka*. New York: Cambridge University Press: 168–185.

Weber, M. (1998) "The Resilience of the Allais Paradox," *Ethics*, **109**: 94–118.

Wedgwood, R. (2004) "The Metaethicists' Mistake," *Philosophical Perspectives*, **18**: 405–426.

(2007) *The Nature of Normativity*. Oxford: Oxford University Press.

Whiting, J. (1986) "Friends and Future Selves," *The Philosophical Review*, **95**: 547–580.

Wiggins, D. (2001) *Sameness and Substance Renewed*. Cambridge: Cambridge University Press.

Williams, B. (1970) "Deciding to Believe," in *Problems of the Self*. Cambridge: Cambridge University Press: 136–151.

(1973a) "A Critique of Utilitarianism," in J.J.C. Smart and B. Williams, eds., *Utilitarianism: For and Against*. New York: Cambridge University Press.

(1973b) *Problems of the Self*. Cambridge: Cambridge University Press.

(1981) "Internal and External Reasons," in *Moral Luck*. Cambridge: Cambridge University Press.

(1985) *Ethics and the Limits of Philosophy*. Cambridge, MA: Harvard University Press.

(1995) "Moral Incapacity," in *Making Sense of Humanity*. Cambridge: Cambridge University Press.

Wittgenstein, L. (1953) *Philosophical Investigations*. Oxford: Basil Blackwell.

Wright, C. (1985) "Review of Simon Blackburn, 'Spreading the Word'," *Mind*, **94**: 310–319.

(1992) *Truth and Objectivity*. Cambridge, MA: Harvard University Press.

Zajonc, R. (1980) "Feeling and Thinking: Preferences Need No Inference," *American Psychologist*, **35**: 151–175.

# Index